# TAKING BACK POLITICS

## AN INSIDER'S GUIDE TO WINNING

### by Cathy Allen

*TAKING BACK POLITICS:* An Insider's Guide to Winning
A Jalapeño Press Publication/ June 1996

Cover Design by Ted Cabarga, Winning Directions, San Francisco
Book Design by Gaye Anthony
Photos by Kim Zumwalt

Library of Congress Catalog Card Number: 96-96600
ISBN 0-9653112-0-1

Printed in Toronto, Canada

To Jane Brown
who believed in me before I did.


To Becky, Amy, Joey and Hattie
and all the other kids who will have to clean up politics if we don't.

# TABLE OF CONTENTS

# TABLE OF FORMS

# ACKNOWLEDGMENTS

Acknowledgments are like wills: they give you reason to remember the good people who have gotten you where you are, and they force you to understand that no truly outstanding venture is ever accomplished alone.

I became consumed by campaigns and candidates 15 years and more than 250 campaigns ago. Governors and senators, congress members and mayors, state legislators and judges, initiatives and bonds—I have worked for the best. My business, Campaign Connection, was established six years ago under the premise that women, people of color and members of the gay community need to be at the power tables of politics. At that time I authored *Political Campaigning: A New Decade*, a campaign manual that predicted women would begin to run in record numbers. The book correctly assumed that many women and candidates of color would win because the real people of this country were getting tired of politics as usual. They would want people who looked like them, worked like them, raised families like them, and reflected the same values as working America.

Since that time, I have worked on campaigns from Alaska to New England; trained would-be political women and men from Florida to Hawaii; and helped put together special political action committees in 14 states. Every election eve I face my own shortcomings, and live to realize that campaigns offer few guarantees. For every lesson I have learned, there are more exceptions than rules, and more interesting ideas that may work for one campaign, only to be bad news for another.

However, there are some truths worth writing down—which is the purpose of this book. It was only in my own defense that I attempted this first how-to campaign manual written for the completely naive—or the selfless candidate who just wants more clues as to what's going on. In helping hundreds of candidates, it seemed only too logical that there should be a text that could at least give candidates and managers some background and lessons learned from bitter and heartbreaking experiences. This book is that end result.

My goal for the past four years has been to provide a comprehensive look at today's campaigns. To accomplish this task, I turned to the best: more than 100 campaign consultants, candidates, political professionals, journalists and friends—all of whom contributed to the learning revealed in these 376 pages.

The most important truths were learned in four campaigns: Suzanne Little's state senatorial race in Alaska, Tom Nolan's congressional race in California, Jim Street's mayoral race in Washington state, and Betty Patu's city council race in Seattle. Although Campaign Connection has been blessed by winning the vast majority of our races, these campaigns were some we lost.

It is through losing you learn about campaigns. In winning, the temptation is too great to assume that you did everything well. In these races with Suzanne, Tom, Jim and Betty, the lessons actually sank in—forever. Four tremendous candidates: four true friends, four great campaigns—and learning you can't escape.

There have been others. I have been mentored by the best political consultants in the country—Joe Rothstein, John Ashford, Matt Reese and Ralph Murphine. Pollsters Don McDonough of Evans-McDonough, Heidi von Szeliski and Bob Meadow of Decision Research and Celinda Lake of Lake Research have taught me the importance of knowing what you're talking about—instead of shooting from the hip. The gems of fundraising were greatly improved by Madalyn Schenk who taught me about the *feel, felt, found* rule. As fundraising is frequently the area where most candidates need the⬜most help, we have dealt with it extensively—and completely, thanks to Joyce Lindsay, Karen Cooper, Robert Kaplan, Pat Evans and the ever-hustling Jim⬜KainberEvery campaign should have fundraising help as good as these pros.

When it comes to field organization, Sue Tupper, Beth Doglio, Judy Baker and Russell Lafountaine know how to get the job done and I have borrowed generously from their teachings. Although field campaigns are in my genes, I learned a lot more tricks of the trade from Canadians Jim Kirk, Les Campbell, Michael Balagus, Ron Johnson, and Dennis McGann—all of the New Democratic Party. Dawn Laguens, Dean Rindy, Doc Schweitzer, and Michael Shannon are media gurus—masters and mistresses of video punch—whose teachings you will see summed up in the *Paid Media* chapter. And when it comes to local campaigns, no one knows more about targeting, field operations and people than Joel Horn.

Kathleen Schafer, president of Leadership Connection and a talk-radio hostess in her own right, contributed heavily to the *Speeches and Image* chapter. Her pizzazz and presence created a great anchor for the rest of the book. As a child of the feminist movement, I grew up thinking that image was a bunch of male-chauvinist bunk. She changed all that—for me and for countless others who can now speak from their own confidence and appearance.

The truth about voters, message, voter contact and targeting—as well as what works and what doesn't—came from late night arguments, discussions, laughter and tears with my good friend Tony Fazio. One of the true patriarchs of the political business, Tony has seen it all. What he hasn't created, he has "spun" and deserves credit. I'm indebted to all the gang at Winning Directions, Tony's South San Francisco direct mail business. No campaign should be without the Winning Directions team—anchored by Kevin Reilly and the best political graphics guy in the business—Ted Cabarga—to whom I am particularly indebted for the cover of this book.

The book would never have been completed if it hadn't been for the dedicated staff at Campaign Connection. While I tried diligently to complete this book before another election day passed, my general manager Tom Van Bronkhorst ran the show. Pat Strosahl filled in with his usual attention to substance, issues and relevance, which I still refuse to learn. The Campaign Connection team helped me learn—and win—more campaigns than I usually am credited with. That team includes: Gaye Anthony, Irving Kwong, Channapha Khamvongsa, Clark Wilson, Noah Bopp (and the Oberlin College Cole Program who sent him to me) and the indefatigable Jane Brown—who believed in me before I believed I could make a business in politics actually succeed.

Gaye Anthony served as more than editor and director—she is the person responsible for the book getting done. Having worked for two and a half years, and through four revisions, she is the mistress of detail and the champion of consistency. Mary Coltrane helped with the final edits. Marcel Wieder took over the publishing details, adding his patience, political expertise and penchant for the publishing process. His help and friendship, which I hope will last a lifetime, will result in a Canadian version of this same book.

Other friends who contributed generously to the truths of political campaigning collected here include Regina LaBelle, who has had to listen to me write this book for at least four years. Reuven Carlyle, arguably the best wordsmith in the country, helped me perfect the saga of the message. Char and Sam Hunt actually read the book as we were writing it, and they remain my dearest friends. Maura Brueger, Anders Davidson, Dan Tritle, Amy Kurtz, Julie Kline and John and Dianne Lindback are among the best campaign professionals in the business; I learned far more from them, I suspect, than they may ever have learned from me.

And, of course, no acknowledgment would be complete without the hundreds of little and big lessons learned from the candidates who have run that long gauntlet with me. From Pat Thibaudeau to Patty Murray, from Tony Knowles to Steve Cowper, from Jolene Unsoeld to Jennifer Belcher, I have been privileged to work with governors and mayors, senators and congress members, statewide officers and school board members. I have worked with more than 100 winning state legislators and more than that in local elected leaders. If there is one thing I know above all, it's that the more you know about politics, the more you realize how much more there is to learn.

My deepest thanks to Margaret, Joanne, Suzanne, Pat, Jolene, Patty, Terry, Jennifer, Dawn, Jeanne, Marilyn, Lorraine, Rosemary, Judy, Sherry, Sue, Kay, Catherine, Anita, Barbara, Georgia, Diane, Jackie, Connie, Eve, Shirley, Betty, Joyce, Fran, Theda, Georgianna, Mary, Tracy, Darlene, Jean Marie, Susan, Nancy, Paige, Maggi, Faith, Janice, Sylvia, Tina, Georgette, Cynthia, and Helen—all woman of the world who have made a difference for all of us.

And, I can't forget the guys who have made me stray from my mission to elect women (because they are great people despite the fact they are men): Tony, Joe, Bill, Larry, Steve, Norm, Will, Paul, Michael, Ed, Dow, Gary, Ron, Pat, Jim, Hans, Dale, Frank, John, George, Bob, Rick, Tom, Don, Jack, Jeff,

Fred, Gerry, Sam, Russell, Kim, Mike, Dave, and—men who have proven they can care as well as lead.

One last note, though my politics is decidedly—and forever—progressive, Democrat, feminist, and unabashedly knee-jerk liberal, I am grateful for the tolerance and respect a few of those on the "other side" have afforded me over the years. A handful have even taught me new tricks of the trade. Republicans Mike Murphy, Steve Excell and John Giese of Paragon, Inc., Brett Bader of the Madison Group and John Carlson all keep me on my toes so I can see what they will do next.

And, to bring this back to where it started, my special thanks and appreciation to Tim Zenk and Perrin Kaplan who introduced me to Gretchen Sorenson, the Region X Small Business Administration chief. Gretchen had the guts and gumption to go where no other bureaucrat nor banker would go in helping me obtain the financing to get this book started. Because of women like Gretchen, more of us women in business may actually succeed.

As you can see, this book is the result of hundreds of people's efforts: all of us trying to understand how we might better catch the wavelength of a country full of people who don't like what they are getting. Trying to decipher what they want and where they wish to go has filled these pages. Hopefully, it will help those who seek to lead; perhaps it will help them appreciate voters as much as I do. Despite what the rest of us might think, the voters truly do get the last word.

Thank God.

Cathy Allen

June 1996

# TODAY'S POLITICAL CLIMATE

## POLITICS 101

Time was when running for office meant you wore out several pairs of shoes going door-to-door, actually talking to voters. Your campaign was filled with volunteers or you simply didn't run. You spoke from the heart, not from polls. You kept your job—and your family. No one had heard about opposition research, and political consultants hadn't been invented.

And that was just 25 years ago.

How times have changed.

If you are a good citizen who's registered to vote—and you vote in every election—each fall you may be besieged with 30 or more mailed brochures, pestered by a dozen or more phone calls, polls, or campaign calls disguised as polls (called push polls), and met on your doorstep by volunteers canvassing to see what the poor voter thinks about the candidate.

If you vote by mail through absentee ballot programs, you'll get all the above, and then some. If you're a senior, you'll get more than you would ever want to read.

On the other hand, if you're a registered voter who seldom votes, you may get nothing. If you are under 30 years old, you may never get a piece of mail nor a phone call, even though you vote all the time.

These days, if you're the candidate, you hire one full-time person to run your campaign, and a few others to schedule you and help you raise money. Other groups may form an "independent expenditure" around you, informing voters about your candidacy, and by law they allegedly cannot coordinate anything with you. Political action committees (PACs) may dump money into newspaper ads or TV spots, attempting to persuade voters about your candidacy. And the state party may have its own "helpful" strategy, perhaps producing a slate card mailed to voters to encourage them to vote for you.

Campaigns in the '90s require tremendous amounts of energy (and as much good sense and timing) if they are to succeed. Imagine—in less than twelve months, as a candidate you have to hire a complete staff and get it working as a team; determine a full marketing plan and raise enough money to pay for it; and develop a successful press plan designed to make the candidate look good in the face of negative attacks. And just when you start to get the hang of doing things right, it's over. All of your efforts come down to one day: election day, and the number of votes you entice into your corner.

Campaign rules are changing. There's more government intervention in the political process, including citizen initiatives and referendums that seek to define term limits and the costs of campaigns, and dictate who can contribute. In the next few years there will be major changes in how we vote (more vote-by-mail and absentee ballot plans), when we vote (special elections), and who is actually voting (more independent voters, young people and minorities).

The challenge to get your message out among the thousands of other messages being mass-produced is daunting to say the least. A recent poll conducted by the National Woman's Political Caucus of likely people to run for office revealed that only 18 percent of the men and 8 percent of the women would ever consider running for office. The reasons? Unable to get the money, not enough time, no stomach for negative campaigning, and not knowing how to run were among the reasons most often cited. The invasion of personal privacy, the cost of running, the long hours, the family sacrifices that have to be made and the minimal benefits of serving (most elected officials take a pay cut to serve in office) make elected office less palatable and not the high honor it used to be.

Considering what you might do once elected has been replaced with worrying about where the money for the next brochure will come from, or how to get the press to respond to your web page press conference.

Yet few seats go unchallenged. Even though 90 percent of incumbents are re-elected, few elected officials are unopposed. Despite the difficulties, politics and campaigns are a growth industry.

We are painfully close to having the process overtake the passion. Politics is a business, a profession, a high-stakes chess game, and a challenge of details set to an ever-changing strategy. Good leaders still emerge, but only if they are good campaigners who know how to pick a team and are willing to do all the tedious, often insulting tasks to get to the victory circle.

*The question becomes: will we produce a generation of great campaigners well-versed in "spin-speak" and fundraising, or will great leaders emerge despite the process?*

Every election cycle, more than a half million people run for office. In the future, this list will increase, not decrease. Despite the hesitancy of good people to even think about running because of the demeaning nature of campaigns, more people will run.

This book seeks to give you, the would-be candidate, a chance to take back the politics that seem locked behind the doors of political consultants.

To be sure, this business is no longer for amateurs. It is brutal, costly and comes with no guarantees. Whether it be local water boards, city councils, judgeships, state legislatures or the U.S. Congress itself, running for office is not only politics, it's big business. Thousands of people who will never run for office will make their living off politics. The political professional is now found in college career counseling books, the yellow pages and classified ads. Former volunteers, steering committee members, losing candidates and bored public relations professionals are turning to careers in political consulting and its many specialties. Degrees in campaign management are now offered at some colleges and universities.

In the last 20 years, there have been more changes in how we campaign than in the entire century that preceded them. The emergence of computers, research, polling and focus groups, the paying for political tasks that used to be done by volunteers—like phone banks and even going door-to-door— have all made significant changes to the way we campaign for office.

Some would argue— correctly—that the more sophisticated we get, the more fickle the electorate becomes. Just when we think the pollsters, the media consultants and the fundraisers have a foolproof system to produce winners on election day, the voters play their wild cards and baffle the pundits.

For the individual candidate who is thinking about running, the task seems daunting. While it's true that the time is right for change-agent candidates, it's also true that candidates need a more sophisticated image than just as an "outsider" on the ballot. With campaigns becoming increasingly professional and competitive, even the seemingly naive candidate with a newcomer look is likely to be packaged by sophisticated media consultants and a campaign manager who knows what it takes to win.

We are in the midst of a decade of major change; change that could help you—or stop you from being a good candidate right now:

*Term limits:* Limiting the number of terms an elected official can serve will mean a dramatic increase in the number of open seats—the most politically advantageous situation a new candidate can face.

*Redistricting:* With new district lines drawn after the 1990 census came new seats in 1992, and with that came new incumbents who are not yet entrenched and easier to pick off.

*Year of the woman:* Thanks to the scores of new women elected in 1992 at every level of government, it's no longer unusual to see women on the ticket.

*Third party:* People are so disenchanted with politics that new parties, no parties, and counter-parties are springing up all over, with independent voters being the new in-crowd.

*Angry white males:* After having been taken for granted and being bored with the choices, white, straight men who never used to vote have found their way back to the ballot box, making their alleged mainstream message salable again.

*Throw the bums out:* Voters are increasingly more critical of insiders and incumbents, and the press is magnifying this unrest, making some longtime incumbents more vulnerable than in the past.

***New voters:*** Through the "Motor Voter" program, many citizens who typically never register (about 25 percent of the population) are now registering at motor vehicle registration offices. Some of these voters are voting, which is altering candidate strategies.

***Vote by mail:*** Good government crusades and legislation to make voting easier for all has resulted in more ballots being mailed, replacing the need to vote in person on election day. This means that some voters are getting their ballots three and four weeks before election day, necessitating targeted communications to them sooner.

***Campaign finance reform:*** There are many versions: no contributions from political action committees; limits on campaign contributions and spending; public financing; and restrictions on who can contribute. The one constant in all this reform is that campaigns are still costing more, not less.

***Independent expenditures:*** The fine art of supporting candidates, but allegedly not being tied to candidates, is proliferating all over the country. Independent expenditures are usually made by businesses, unions, associations or special interest groups that dump big money into campaigns, but don't work directly with the campaign.

These changes in the political climate are perhaps not as influential on your running as the growing professionalization of politics. Politics is big business. The days of rousting a few of your friends out of the doldrums of their traditional schedule to run a campaign from your garage are dwindling. You will need at least a few of the more than 56 different kinds of consultants identified in *Campaigns & Elections** magazine's Political Pages directory, which lists more than 2,500 different national vendors seeking to help you with your political aspirations.

There is still much that candidates can do for themselves if they start early and have a strong plan that makes sense for their district and positions them best against their opponents.

This campaign manual outlines the essentials of what to do to compete with the best. It gives you clues as to what's going on out there in the world of populist politics—and it will hopefully get you elected without a long list of consultants you probably cannot afford.

For the sake of aiming at a target campaign, this book is written for a candidate running for a state legislative race. For campaigns that are larger, more resources (people, money and time) would be required. For campaigns that are smaller, less would work. In all campaigns, however, your district profile,

---

*Campaigns & Elections, 1511 K St. N.W. #1020, Washington, D.C. 20005-1450, (202) 638-7788.

the formidability of your opposition and your initial name familiarity will give you a good indication of what you will need to mount a campaign to win.

Throughout the book, you'll see:

**Helpful tips**
(watch for the finger-pointing hand);

**Money-saving ideas**
(look for the dollar sign);

**Important things to remember**
(see the string tied around the index finger);

**Disasters in the making**
(find the time bombs);

**Priority items**
(see the star); and

**Great ideas**
(look for the light bulb).

Before you begin, keep in mind that even though all campaigns are different, some common denominators make each campaign similar. Though few generalizations work for everyone, the following basic rules emerge.

- *There is no one perfect way to win a campaign.* Devise your plan based upon good research that makes sense for your district (even if it has to be revised later). It should serve as a foundation for what you do and how you spend your money.

- *There are at least a dozen different ways you could win your campaign: you just have to find one that works for you.* What doesn't work is taking a little of this and a little of that and trying to make all your steering committee members happy.

- *No one thing you do wrong will eliminate you from the campaign.* However, an inability to learn from your mistakes and get back to the plan can stop your campaign short of victory. Don't dwell on the flub-ups. Pick yourself up, get back to your agenda and forge ahead.

➤ There's no one perfect way to run a campaign.
➤ There are a dozen ways to win.
➤ No one thing you do will eliminate you.
➤ Don't try to do everything.
➤ Beware of meetings.
➤ Make good business decisions.
➤ Make sure your chain of command is understood.
➤ Watch out for your friends.
➤ Assume nothing.
➤ Stay informed.
➤ Focus on what's important.
➤ Ask everyone for money.
➤ Never ask a volunteer to do something you wouldn't do yourself.

- *Do not attempt to do everything, for then you will surely do nothing well.* Whatever you do to get your message out, do it best. Too often campaigns start off with the right intentions, but because an opponent decides to buy giant billboards or hot air balloons at carnivals, a good campaign is altered and the budget is drained before the voter contact plan can be completed.

- *Beware of meetings that go nowhere but rehash the same old ideas of what should be done.* Meetings often take up much of the critical first third of a campaign. Candidates, staffers, volunteers and even fundraisers often go to too many meetings and end up getting little real work done. The most productive meetings are held by two people—and they're usually over the phone.

- *Make decisions that reflect good business sense.* Shop around and find the best deals. Just because a vendor has always done the yard signs for most of the political campaigns in your area, don't be afraid to ask someone new. More and more people are getting involved in the business of politics—and the competition should help your budget.

- *Make sure that your chain of command is known to everyone in the campaign.* Have a list of your key people with an understanding of what each person's role is, and post it. Many campaigns falter when an uninformed person makes a decision simply because no one else was around to make it.

- *Watch out for your friends.* In the heat of the campaign, it is seldom your enemies and opponents that defeat you—it is your friends. You generally can predict what your opponents will do, but you never know what your friends will do. Explain the rules regarding who speaks for the campaign.

- *Assume nothing.* Campaigns go from confusion to chaos to crisis. Your job is to get the work done in the midst of this uproar. Check your details. Check your list of things to do. Check on who is responsible for what. Double-check appointments, directions to important meetings and commitments that volunteers make to help. In campaigns, there is no luck you don't make yourself.

- *Stay informed—not only about your own campaign, but about what people are thinking.* Candidates have lost serious ground because they appeared at a forum not knowing about a serious police incident reported in the morning paper.

- *Stay focused on what's important.* Don't get caught in the details. Delegating—especially if you could do it better, faster and cheaper—is hard for any candidate to accept. But, you should stick to what you do best: meeting voters, raising money and being visible.

- *Ask everyone for money.* Train all your close supporters and staff to ask for money. Memorize different ways to ask for money. Solicit money from home, in the car, at work, between meetings, and at events. The process need not be tedious, but it must be persistent.

- *Never ask a volunteer to do something you wouldn't do yourself.* In this world of building grassroots support, volunteers are highly important people, and they're about to be an endangered species. If you don't use them well, you will lose them fast.

These "Golden Rules" can help provide a method to get you through the madness which is today's political campaign.

# DECIDING TO RUN

## ARE YOU READY?

**2**

What makes perfectly sound individuals decide to disrupt their lives, throw caution to the wind, and run for office? It certainly isn't the money, as most legislators make less money in public service than they did prior to getting elected. It isn't because of the great powers afforded you, as every elected official must go through years of climbing the ladder to committee chairmanships—only to find that once you get to the top, there are dozens out to unseat you. It's not the prestige, as you spend most of your time in meetings, cutting budgets or trying to explain to people why you can't help them.

Why would you run for office?

There are as many answers as there are candidates. Unfortunately, most people with the urge to run for public office fail to recognize the difference between running for office and serving in office. The only similarity between running and serving is that both require a candidate and a high tolerance for rubber-chicken luncheons.

Most people think about running for office when a friend or colleague suggests it. However, most of these friends are nowhere to be found by the time you ask them for a contribution to your campaign. Running for office is serious, risky business. You need to base your decision on more than tea leaves, astrology readings and a few friends' advice.

Running should depend on a well thought-out analysis of:

- Your chances of winning.
- The amount of money you can raise.
- The support team you can assemble.
- Your name recognition.
- Your ability to withstand negative attacks.
- Your personal vulnerabilities.
- Your family, job and financial considerations.
- Your hunger for the job.

### Why would you run for office?

- ➤ To give back to the community.
- ➤ To change the way government works.
- ➤ To contribute to needed change.
- ➤ To become more self-fulfilled.
- ➤ To represent real people and give common concerns a real voice.
- ➤ To have a job that pays you to be involved in politics.
- ➤ To work to correct a specific problem.
- ➤ To make a difference.
- ➤ To continue the move towards prominence in your life.

# Who's Running—and Winning?

Women, candidates of color, gay and lesbian candidates, former reporters, entertainers, college students, senior women, former welfare moms, even straight, white men who aren't lawyers; these are all part of the new crop of candidates getting elected.

## How to Beat an Incumbent

**To beat an incumbent:**

➤ Swing district
➤ Early money
➤ Name recognition
➤ Message of change
➤ Eighty percent of budget on voter contact
➤ Right place at right time
➤ Good press relations
➤ Accomplished speaker
➤ Good timing
➤ Campaign professionals
➤ Strong primary
➤ Take the punches
➤ Fight back
➤ Talk about values
➤ Effective databases
➤ Experience
➤ Opposition research

Incumbents are incumbents for good reasons: they have money, and know how to raise it; they've done this job of being a candidate before; they have the computers and databases needed for organization; and they know how to win. It's little wonder that most incumbents running for re-election in this country are returned to office, despite all the talk about throwing the bums out. The simple truth is that voters want to throw generic bums out of office—not the ones who live in their backyard.

But there are more people who run against incumbents each year than there are incumbents. And more challengers are beating incumbents. In the past few election cycles, there have been many similarities among candidates who have beaten incumbents:

- Living in a swing district where neither Democrats nor Republicans always win.
- Raising money early—and having personal money to put into the campaign (at least 15 percent of the budget).
- Having good name recognition.
- Having a message that positioned the difference between the candidate and the incumbent early: a message of change, "one of us," anti-establishment, the outsider and not part of the problem.
- Spending more than 80 percent of the campaign budget on direct voter contact.
- Being in the right place at the right time with the right message, such as women in 1992, Republicans in 1994, independents on the local level, etc.
- Not afraid of the press.
- Being able to speak well—even inspire—and sticking to the message.
- Good timing more than good luck.
- Having newcomers on the campaign, but having it driven by professionals with solid campaign experience.
- Making an unexpectedly strong showing in the primary.
- Having a strategy that kept the candidate in sync with the top of the ticket.

- Being ready and able to take the punches, and fight back when needed.
- Talking more about values than the specifics of issues.
- Having effective databases from the start—with someone who knows how to use and maintain them.
- Having great opposition research and using it.

There are other characteristics that make the recent successful challengers impressive: they had extensive resumés with experience in the private sector—some having as many as five earlier careers. They were people who had some prior experience working with a legislature, city or county council, and many had served on school boards.

This new generation of leaders took the time to put their campaigns together correctly. While many challengers spend most of their time learning how to run for office, more and more candidates are making the decision to run as much as a year and a half before the election day face off, and they know what to do when the campaign heats up.

# Making the Decision

Not everyone should run for office. Are you cut out to take the pressure, the public fishbowl lifestyle, and the constant demands for public service?

Deciding to run is one of the most important decisions you will make in your life. Whether to run, when to run and whom to run against are questions which can paralyze even the most seasoned politico. However, this decision process need not be an aimless, disorganized one that goes on for months. The process does need to be organized, as does the campaign to follow, but it's not so hard, if you can separate the important from the trivial.

We know that women take at least twice as long to decide to run for public office as men do. Women traditionally look for the most perfect moment. If everyone waited for the perfect moment, 95 percent of today's new candidates would never run. The most important criteria can boil down to four factors:

- Do I have what it takes to run and to serve?
- Can I raise the money?
- Will my constituents find me enough like them to elect me?
- Can I beat the other candidates who are likely to run?

Answering these questions requires some work, some research and some honest soul-searching. Let's start with some very basic questions. Write down your answers and share them with trusted mentors, advisors and other political people who have traveled this path in the past.

---

**The "perfect" time to run for office:**

➤ The kids are out of high school.

➤ I'm in the right place in my professional career.

➤ I have enough money saved to be able to afford it.

➤ I have a good campaign manager

➤ I have a dozen fundraisers who will be on my finance committee.

➤ There's an open seat in the race.

**...but it never happens.**

1. Why do you want to run?
2. What have you done for your fellow constituents?
3. What issues can you call your own?
4. What is your message?
5. What office will you run for?
6. Do you have the time to put together a good campaign?

After you have explored the above questions, it's time to go into some of the real nuts and bolts of running for office.

# Financial Considerations

**Personal:** What kind of money can you afford to put into your own campaign? Understand that most first-time candidates contribute 15 percent of the campaign budget from their own bank account.

**High donors:** Do you know 200 people who will give you at least $100 each? Who are they? Where might you find them? Are there candidates whom you have supported in the past who might give you a list of, and an introduction to, their high donors? Where can you get lists of people who traditionally give to every major campaign like yours?

**Organizational help:** Are there coalitions you can build with progressive organizations? Do you have lists of members of politically important groups? What groups will help you raise money?

# People Resources

**Volunteers:** Do you know 20 people who would give at least five hours per week, starting now, to help you run? Have you donated a lot of personal volunteer time to political organizations, so that you might expect some reciprocity in the future?

**Finance committee:** Do you have a dozen acquaintances who have raised money for other candidates or organizations who would be willing to do the same for you? Do you have friends who have organized fundraisers in the past? Can you find party or local activists who would help you organize events?

**Key staff:** Understanding that most first campaigns have few resources for hiring campaign staff, do you have three or four people who are willing to accept key responsibilities in your campaign? Do you have someone to help you with the press? How about a scheduler? What about a treasurer? A field/GOTV (Get Out The Vote) organizer?

**Endorsements:** What elected officials can you get to anchor your steering committee? What community leaders' names will you be able to place on your letterhead? Do you have seniors, key women, leaders of color, business and labor leaders who will give your candidacy credibility?

**The press:** Have you received press coverage in the past? Have you been on radio or TV talking about an important issue? Does the press ever call you for your opinion on local matters? Do you know who in the press will be covering your campaign? Have you made any recent speeches, written an op-ed piece for the newspaper, or been asked to be on a radio talk show?

# Background

**Personal:** Do you have the personality to be a candidate? Can you delegate responsibility? Can you convince others that you are worthy of their trust? Do you have a strong image? Are you willing to sharpen your presence? Can you handle criticism, or praise, without losing control? How much of your private life are you willing to share with the public? Will your family be willing to have a public role in this campaign?

**Experience:** Have you held important positions of authority or responsibility? Have you been appointed to a board or commission? Are you a joiner of many organizations, but not a leader of any? Do you have a college degree? How does your resumé stand up to that of others who have run for this seat?

**Professional:** Can you afford to give up your job for this campaign? Do you have another source of income to help you survive while you campaign? What happens if you lose? Can you get your job back, or get another?

**Closet:** What's in yours? Have you ever been arrested? Have you ever been accused of sexual harassment, been caught drinking while driving, evaded your taxes, been sued for misconduct or failed to pay child support? What kind of employment problems have you had? Have you been fired for cause? Have you fired people who are sure to work against you? Have you been involved in projects that attracted scandal? Have you ever been involved with organizations that received a lot of press for radical actions? Have you been caught in a public lie? Is there anything in your past that could destroy your chances of winning?

More important than what's in your closet, can you stand to have these items mentioned in public without losing control? In so many cases, it's not the perceived problem that defeats a candidate, its how the candidate reacts to the problem.

# Chances of Winning

***Who*** else is in the race? Have you done research on the other candidates who are likely to run? Will these other candidates have more money, name recognition, traditional support from organizations, or volunteers than you? What is your niche among the voters? Where can you expect to win support that these other candidates may not?

***How*** about your constituents? Who traditionally votes in your district? What is the voter profile (Democrat, Republican, "Perotite," conservative, liberal, etc.)? What foothold has the Christian Coalition or other right-wing groups achieved in your district? Are there special-interest groups that control a large segment of the votes? Have there been civil rights issues placed on the ballot through initiatives or referendum? How did they fare?

***What*** else is on the ballot? What other issues or candidates will be on the same ballot as your prospective race? As these may bring out certain classes or numbers of voters, will you be on the majority side of these issues?

# Making the Decision Without Driving Yourself Crazy

All of these questions require your time and careful attention. They do not require two years before making your decision. Most candidates do not handle the process of deciding to run in a way that is based on fact rather than emotion. To make the decision, consider the questions above and then:

***Sit*** down and discuss your answers with trusted friends who know you well. It is important not to delude yourself. You may think you have had a significant impact on your community or an issue, only to learn that others viewed your role as quite minimal.

***Talk*** with elected officials and party leaders about your chances of getting their support. Ask them if you should run. Though most never venture a "yes" or "no" answer, it is important that you have them in the loop, should you decide to run.

***Make*** a realistic assessment of the money you think you can raise or donate to the campaign personally. Then cut it in half and see if you have enough to run a campaign.

***Call*** a volunteer committee meeting for a Saturday afternoon. Tell your friends and supporters they will be needed for three hours to help you decide whether or not you should run. See how many show up. Count how many you have left after three hours, and that will give you an idea of what kind of volunteer help you can depend on in the heat of the campaign.

*Give* yourself a specific amount of time to decide. Many processes drag on for months and months. You don't need that much time, and you risk being seen as someone who can't make up her mind. Meanwhile, other candidates are kicking off their campaigns. The earlier you decide, the more planning and fundraising you can do.

# Are You Ready to Run?

## Part I

Deciding to run for office need not be an aimless, disorganized process that goes on for months. It is, however, one of the most important decisions you will make in your life. How and when to make that decision should be orchestrated as carefully as the campaign itself.

## The Basics

Why do you want to run? _____

What have you done for your fellow constituents? _____

What issues can you call your own? _____

What is your message? _____

What office will you run for? _____

Do you have the time to put together a good campaign? _____

## Baseline Resources:

Money:  Personal savings _____        People:  Volunteers _____

        High donors _____                Finance committee _____

        Organizations _____              Key staff _____

## Do People Know Who You Are?

Speeches _____                Newspaper stories _____

TV or radio _____             Name recognition _____

Op-ed pieces _____            Guest appearances _____

## Positions of Authority/ Leadership

1 _____    4 _____    7 _____

2 _____    5 _____    8 _____

3 _____    6 _____    9 _____

## Key Endorsements You Could Get

1 _____    4 _____    7 _____

2 _____    5 _____    8 _____

3 _____    6 _____    9 _____

# Are You Ready to Run?

## Part II

## Personal Reality Check

Are you convincing?

Do you have an authoritative voice?

Are you in good physical health?

How is your personal appearance?

Can you delegate?

Do you dress like a professional?

Can you sell yourself?

Can you be "just" the candidate?

How is your sense of humor?

Can you get angry without losing control?

Can you handle criticism?

How will your family deal with the campaign?

Can you come back if you lose?

Can your career withstand an election?

Do you handle compliments well?

Can you share your personal and family life with the public?

## What's in Your Closet?

| | | |
|---|---|---|
| Drunk driving | Fired from a job | Questionable financial dealings |
| Lied on résumé | Messy divorce | Mental health treatment |
| Tax evasion | Sexual harassment | Drug use |
| Speeding tickets | Bankruptcy | Public arrogance |
| Poor voting record | Lawsuits | Failure to file tax returns |
| Criminal record | Absenteeism | Health problems |

## The Rest of the Political Landscape

What political options are available to you? _____

Where is your best target constituency? _____

How well do you know your district? _____

Open seat or incumbent? _____

Who else might run, and how will it affect you? _____

When will you make the decision? _____

FORM 1: ARE YOU READY TO RUN?

# OFF AND RUNNING

## GROUNDWORK

Y ou've decided to run. You're excited, but overwhelmed with the number of things that have to be done. You spend most of your time wondering what to do first. In many ways, running a campaign is similar to having a baby: it follows a trimester schedule.

The first third of your campaign, which can range anywhere from five or six weeks to three months, is planning. It is putting together the backbone of the campaign so that you can rely on this foundation for what is to follow. The first thirty days of a campaign are as important as the last thirty days, for if you don't have that sturdy backbone and structure to make the campaign work, then the last thirty days—when you have little time for organization—may be your undoing.

In the second trimester of the campaign, you gather resources: money, services, in-kind contributions, advice, consultants, staff and people. You begin the implementation of your fundraising plan and you gather supporters everywhere you go. During this trimester you get busy gathering the team and supplies that will make the difference in the last thirty days of the campaign.

The final trimester is implementation. Most consultants would tell you otherwise, but you could put the entire strategic plan of your campaign on the front page of *The New York Times*, and it wouldn't make or break your campaign. Strategy—costly, creative, experienced and intuitively right on—means little if you don't have the resources to implement it. Campaigns come down to getting your message to the right people during the last weeks of the campaign. You need to do that in a variety of ways.

The golden rule of all campaigns: Get the right message to the right, targeted people at least three to five times in the last three weeks before voting.

More campaigns are lost by not following the golden rule than by nasty opposition research and last-minute attacks in the closing days of the campaign.

> *Remember:* Right message,
> Right time,
> Right target,
> In the right variety of ways.

> ### The Golden Rule
>
> *Get the right message to the right, targeted people at least three to five times in the last three weeks.*

# *Getting Started on the Right Foot*

So how do you begin a campaign? The first things that traditionally signal the beginning of a campaign are:

- Opening a campaign bank account.
- Getting a post office box and a bulk mail permit from the postmaster.
- Filing candidacy papers along with a letter of intent to run with the appropriate government agencies.

These simple moves usually alert the press and the proper authorities, as well as your potential opponent, that you are a serious candidate, and that your campaign has actually begun. As you set the stage for a good planning effort, it's important to assess where you are so you can focus on what you need in the areas of expertise, resources and other help. A good self-analysis—often painful, but necessary—will help you build a base upon which the rest of the campaign plan can be built.

## Reality Check

### *Candidate vs. Opponent*

Honestly assess your positive points along with your less-than-positive attributes. On the positive side there are the qualities that will make you a good candidate, such as a good sense of humor, the ability to delegate, being a good speaker who can organize her thoughts and answer the tough questions, having a good relationship with the press, being undaunted by asking for money, having the ability to attract volunteers, being a hard worker with a good internal management clock, being physically fit, being a quick study, and having a natural ability to put people at ease. These are attributes that go into making a good candidate.

Negative attributes include having an aversion to raising money, an inability to delegate, a hair-trigger temper, being aloof or abrupt, being unconcerned about your image, easily distracted or having a hard time focusing, being monotone or boring, having trouble listening, being so issue-oriented that you have a tendency to pontificate on points no one else wants to hear about, having alcohol problems, combativeness, being so suspicious that you have a hard time trusting anyone, and being vindictive.

None of these means you are a good candidate nor a bad candidate; rather they give you an indication of what you have working for you in this game of on-the-job candidate training.

**Positive attributes of some candidates:**

- Good sense of humor
- Able to delegate
- Good public speaker
- Can answer tough questions
- Good press relations
- Easily asks for money
- Hard worker
- Physically fit
- Quick study
- Naturally puts people at ease

After you have examined your own candidate qualities, apply the same scrutiny to your opponent:

- Is your opponent perceived as someone who can raise a lot of money—or at least significantly more than you?
- Does he have many high-roller friends whom he can count on for money?
- Does he have high name recognition?
- What is his "claim to fame"?
- Does he have an impressive resumé?
- What is his income level? Is he richer than you?
- Has he ever run for office before?
- Does he have a natural link to any of your constituencies?
- Does he have friends in labor, business or the senior community?
- What is his age?

The first step in assessing your strategy begins with understanding what you have going for you and what you have to watch in positioning yourself against your opponent(s). This review is not simple, easy, nor an exercise in delusion. This is the time to put your personality cards on the table, so that you can be aware of how your attitude, qualities and emotional nature may influence the course of the campaign. It can help your entire campaign— and especially you.

## Constituencies

Once you have a sense of yourself as a candidate—and a sense of your opponent—you should begin the task of seeing how you each stack up in the eyes of the district voters.

- What is the class profile of the district? Is it composed of a socioeconomic level similar to yours?
- What about the geography—do you live in the most populated area where the neighbors know you, or are you a recent transplant whom people may distrust?
- What's the economic base? Are your voters industrial workers, college students with part-time jobs, farmers, or hi-tech computer gurus? Will your background play favorably with these voters, and how will you bridge any gaps?
- What is the makeup of the district's households? Is there a gender gap, with more women than men? Are there significantly more seniors than any other age category?
- What's the voter history? Is there a traditionally high turnout in the district in election years similar to this one?

> **Negative attributes of some candidates:**
>
> ➤ Aversion to raising money
> ➤ Hair-trigger temper
> ➤ Difficulty delegating
> ➤ Being aloof and abrupt
> ➤ Difficulty focusing
> ➤ Monotone voice
> ➤ Difficulty listening
> ➤ Drug or alcohol problems
> ➤ Tendency to pontificate
> ➤ Combativeness
> ➤ Difficulty trusting

District demographics, the actual lay of the land and its history will help you figure out how to respond in ways that will build bridges to targeted voters.

# Core Constituencies

Voters want to know why they should vote for you. They want some proof that you are more like them than your opponent is. And they want evidence that you are not one of the "same old, same old" politicians who will tell them anything just to get elected. They are looking for someone they can trust.

The fact that you are running for office already makes you a tough sell, as voters grow more cynical with each election. To build trust, build your bridges through the demographic pluses you have with your voters. People who belong to certain blocks of voters can make the difference between your winning and losing. To reach them, it's necessary to understand the criteria you share with them.

## Class

Voters tend to seek and vote for people who are similar to themselves. The class criteria refers to socioeconomic class—if you share the same class with a majority of swing voters, then you should use that base to appeal to them. Examples include labor communities, minority populations, low-income and working families.

## Ethnicity

It is really critical, in looking at your district, to appreciate the blocks of voters from minority groups. For example, in districts where there are Filipino-Americans, Korean-Americans, or other large Asian-American constituencies, there is a likelihood of block voting. The word will get out to the district who the favored candidate is. These communities are very necessary to voter-registration and get-out-the-vote drives. In many cases, it is important to remember the ethnic voting blocks when putting together your campaign team. Key members of your team should be visible members of these communities. You also need to keep these groups in mind when developing your message. Your general message must include something with which these ethnic groups can connect.

## Military

Do you have large blocks of military voters in your district? These people can be active-duty personnel stationed in the district, retired veterans, Vietnam vets, or VFW members. They vote in droves. If you share their past, make sure your literature highlights your military background.

## Gender

Gender can help you if you are a woman candidate or hurt you if you're running against one. Women vote for women in higher percentages than men do. "Women's" issues draw women in greater numbers than men to a woman candidate. Such issues include reproductive choice, health care, child care, education, pay equity, the environment, affordable housing and equal rights. And, in many districts throughout the country, you will find that more women are voting than men.

## Generation

We have only to look back to the 1992 presidential election to see the power of generational voting preferences. This criteria can be used very effectively on three levels:

1. A candidate's age can put her in step with a whole core group of the voting population, and it can also contrast dramatically with her opponent's age.
2. Age plays well when contrasting "new ideas" with "old ideas."
3. Age can be used to create a split among those in power and those excluded from the insider's circles.

A call for generation change can come from either young or older candidates—all that is required is a stark difference.

Any discussion on generation must address seniors. We know they are the best voters and often make up the largest single block of voters. Over 55 percent of the perfect voters in this country are seniors, and as such they are critical to your formulation of a winning message.

> **What do you have in common with your voters?**
>
> ➤ Class?
> ➤ Ethnicity?
> ➤ Military?
> ➤ Gender?
> ➤ Generation?

# Special Constituencies

Additional constituencies you should keep in mind are environmentalists, developers, PTSAs, and any kind of special educational group.

All these groups should be considered as you go about the process of developing your message, staffing your campaign, soliciting volunteers, organizing early support, and raising money.

# The District

What does your district look like? Is it rural, urban, suburban, or some or all of these? The physical makeup of the district may play a direct role not only in how you develop your message, but also how you can campaign. Obviously a rural community is a tough one in which to campaign door-to-door. On the other hand, a district filled with apartment complexes is also one which will be hard to penetrate for district literature drops.

Drive around your district. In the early days of the campaign, get a good look at what's there. Are there scores of churches? What about schools? Where are they in relation to the neighborhoods? Are students still bussed from great distances to attend public schools?

What about the transportation services? Do most of your voters ride to work in single-occupancy vehicles, or do a growing number commute by bus, carpool or other alternative transportation? What about bike trails, parks and other amenities? Take an inventory and talk to others about how your voters live, work, play and educate their children.

What about crime? What are the crime statistics for the region, the cities and the communities you will represent? Where are the dangerous areas of the district, and what is being done to curb crime?

Check out the economic pulse of the district. What are the industries that make the area tick? Where do your voters get their paychecks—and what is their median income? What is the economic forecast? Are people being laid off, or are jobs being created? Will the children of your voters be able to live in the area when they graduate from high school and college? What is the average education level of the area now?

All of these considerations give you a chance to scope out the people, read up on the issues and begin the soulful process of understanding what your voters are thinking as they go about their day-to-day tasks of raising kids, going to work, and trying to build a life that is fulfilling. If you know the status of the people in your district, you won't be caught off-guard or be uninformed about local issues that are blowing up as you are campaigning. Remember that what they think is important may not be the same issues your poll told you are important.

Most candidates enter a race and think they are already informed about all the pertinent facts when they declare their candidacy. However, a quick review of (and drive around) the district often gives them a different story.

## Know your district:

➤ Demographics
➤ Transportation
➤ Schools
➤ Neighborhoods
➤ Churches
➤ Parks
➤ Bike trails
➤ Industry
➤ Income levels
➤ Employment
➤ Crime
➤ Education
➤ Important issues

# The Media

As you start organizing your campaign, do a media inventory. Who are the most important media people in your district? Is there more than one dominant newspaper? Are the newspapers' endorsements considered critical to delivering the vote? What about local radio talk shows? Is there one that is the darling of the print media—and who do you know who has connections there? What news shows or TV programs are produced locally that you might be able to infiltrate? What is your access to cable TV or local-access-channel programming?

Seek out local media moguls and find out how they see the district. Get their background and overview. One thing generally shared among the media is that they are almost always willing to meet with new or prospective candidates. Call them, tell them you have decided to run for office and that you would like to sit down and get to know them better. Give them a chance to know you, too. Some political reporters might be reticent to spend an hour and a half chit-chatting, but keep trying to make inroads. Talk to the financial reporter or a beat reporter. Often, if you get off on the right foot with your initial contacts in the press, it will help you have cordial relations over the long haul.

Ask reporters their opinions. Often they will initially respond that they want to stay objective and not venture opinions. However, most reporters are hard-working, honest members of the community and they have developed well-researched thoughtful positions on most issues concerning their own backyards. With a little coaxing you can usually get them to give you the benefits of their hard-work assessment of the community. (Besides, many reporters secretly believe they could do a better job representing the people than most candidates.)

# *Rules and Regulations*

In every state there is a burgeoning bureaucracy known as either the elections office, the public disclosure commission or some other name for the watchdog and enforcement arm of government. This is the office that oversees campaigns. These agencies are traditionally understaffed and overworked, particularly given the plethora of new regulations on how campaigns must be run.

Suffice it to say that overseeing campaigns is a growing business.

With initiatives, legislative reform, public financing, more PACs, new independent expenditures, and a host of characters seeking to change how we campaign, government is put in the unenviable task of monitoring it all—and doing so with fewer resources. As a candidate you will need to understand the process and regulations to which your campaign must adhere.

Regulations dictate that you disclose who is financing your campaign and how you are spending the money, as well as personal information such as a personal financial statement and the nature of your assets. These regulatory agencies create all kinds of forms and review your campaign at certain periods of the campaign cycle. All records are open to public and press inspection. Be aware of what the agencies are looking for and what your opponent could be looking for.

Each campaign regulatory body usually publishes a booklet that explains what you have to do, what forms you need to fill out, what information you must provide and the time by which you must provide it. When you start thinking about running for office, ask them to send you this information. Read it and understand it. (Note: if you want to keep your early indecision quiet, then send someone else to get a copy of the rules, as some states record who is requesting information packets.)

Once you have accepted contributions to your campaign or filed candidacy papers with the appropriate agency, your campaign has officially started. You must keep detailed records of all contributions received and all expenditures made. They are reported to the appropriate state and local agencies at set intervals (usually every 30 days). The forms your campaign will be submitting will require the care of a person with incredible attention to detail and accuracy. This person, usually the campaign treasurer, not only must be someone you trust, he or she must be someone who you know will follow all rules and regulations to the letter. Remember, in a campaign there is only one person whose mistakes can get you thrown in jail—and that person is the one who files these disclosure papers.

Inaccurate or incomplete reports, or the late filing of a report, may not only come back to haunt you, but may cost you votes. The press review these reports regularly, checking on how much candidates have raised. And you can count on your opposition poring over these files, looking for any inconsistency or illegality which they can "leak" to the press. These reports provide a public accounting of how the campaigns stack up against one another. In a political world where much is still undercover until the tallies are in on election night, public disclosure reports accurately reflect what money is coming into your campaign and what money is going out.

In filing these forms, do not give away too much information. Make sure that you comply with the letter of the law without detailing any additional information that your opponent can use. In many cases just naming your consultants and your printer gives your opponent critical clues as to what you are likely to do.

Completing public disclosure forms accurately requires a lot of time and a thorough knowledge of the local—as well as state or federal—rules and regulations. Local agencies all the way up to the FEC (Federal Elections Commission) offer classes to candidates and campaign treasurers. Party organizations as well as individual consultants sometimes offer these classes. This is time well spent for the key money collector on your campaign. It is a must for any novice treasurer.

**Public disclosure:**

➤ Your personal financial status.
➤ Who contributes to your campaign.
➤ What debts the campaign has.
➤ How much money you have raised.
➤ Where expenditures are made.
➤ When money is received.
➤ When money is spent.

# Managing Your Time

Once you decide to run for office, you have a seemingly endless list of things to do. Candidates often think they must inquire about finding the cheapest yard signs in town, write the definitive position papers, scout for the perfect headquarters, order bumper stickers, or interview a plethora of consultants. The truth is that even the best candidate in the world can't do it all, so you need to prioritize your efforts. Some of the things you should do include the following:

## Training

Most candidates have the painful task of learning how to be a candidate while they are juggling the everyday details of the campaign. Take advantage of trainings designed to bring you up to speed on the specifics of being a candidate early in the campaign. These trainings can help you learn how to be an effective candidate now, when you have the time to let this information sink in.

How do you ask for money? How do you make small talk that can be helpful to the campaign, as well as just pass time? How do you remember people's names? How should you look, dress and present yourself? Where do you find volunteers who don't come with the baggage of old campaigns? There are a hundred critical questions a candidate needs to be able to answer if she is ever to sleep. To assist you in this process, you should consider attending one of the many candidate training sessions available. Political parties, *Campaigns & Elections* magazine, individual political training consultants, women's political groups, and business associations all offer various forms of training. Take advantage of them. They will be well worth your time.

## Fundraising

You need to work on developing your high-donor list as soon as possible. Though there are many aspects of a fundraising plan, start with building your best prospects. This list should be a compilation of close friends, colleagues and political people who have been your supporters in the past. Focus on those people who you believe can give you at least $100 each. Every key donor you can pick up early in the race is worth double to you, as they will either contribute again later in the campaign, or bring another high donor to your coffers (usually a spouse or colleague).

Now is also the time to begin acquiring lists. Try to get these on computer disk so that you can easily generate mailing labels. The best lists often come

**Twenty-one ways to be more visible:**

1. Get a message. Know what you intend to do to make this world a better place, then translate that message so that your friends understand it.

2. Know your areas of expertise. Find one or two issues that you can contribute to, and work to make a difference.

3. Package yourself so you look better than ever— then make the time to keep yourself that way.

4. Join organizations that give you a chance to learn, to align with new people, to listen and to lead.

5. Give public testimony on something important to you.

6. Write letters to the editor.

7. Listen to talk radio shows and call in to offer your two cents worth.

8. Write an op-ed piece for the newspaper.

9. Get yourself quoted in the newspaper attending a rally, an event or public hearing.

10. Volunteer to lead a new project, even though you know nothing about the subject. See how people react.

11. Give credit where credit is due; help someone win an award. Create an awards ceremony in your town.

12. Plan to be politically involved. Budget $1,000 a year to give to your favorite candidates.

from political parties and local clubs, teachers, business leaders, community organizations, labor leaders, women's organizations, senior groups, environmentalists, gay/lesbian organizations, and people interested in schools or children's issues.

PACs—the bane of every good government candidate—are still the best and quickest way to get money into a campaign. You should start summarizing the top forty or so PACs in one list and begin to understand their endorsement process, the key players, how much they have to give, and whether you could be an early endorsed candidate.

# Visibility

Get out and meet the political insiders. Take a look at all those organizations that you have belonged to over the years and see if you can count on support from their activist members. Early visibility can come from many activities and involvements. These options should be undertaken with a reasonable degree of restraint, as you do not want to appear to be a chronic complainer or an obvious opportunist.

Also, don't wear yourself out; pace yourself. There are lots of visibility opportunities; select ones where the issues and forums play into your campaign theme.

# Campaign Organization

Scouting for key people for your campaign team can take a week or a year, depending on when you ask the right people the right questions about committing to your campaign. The most effective way to look at "trolling" for a team is to watch the campaign people whom you admire from past campaigns. The earlier you start, the more time you will have to explore your options.

Every campaign needs at least eight key players to make the team functional. In most legislative races, you will only be able to pay for one or two (the campaign manager and perhaps a fundraiser). To augment your other needs, you'll need to scout for volunteers to serve as field organizer, scheduler, press person, volunteer coordinator, mailing coordinator, and phone bank supervisor. Some campaigns have several other key supervisors, such as endorsement chair, finance committee chair (and members of that committee), events committee chair, yard sign coordinator, someone to drive the candidate to events, and get-out-the-vote organizer.

In addition to the paid staff and key volunteer leaders, you will need a dedicated, trustworthy treasurer. Talk with other treasurers first to understand the nature of the job and all the requirements placed on the position. You also will require someone, other than you, who understands the nature of computers and campaigns.

## Technology

Computers, copy machines, fax machines, modems, pagers, phone systems, cellular phones, and access to the Internet—all are part of today's technical campaign revolution. At the start, you should find the person who will be most responsible for your campaign computer needs. Don't make the mistake most campaigns make by buying the hardware and software you think will work, only to find that your computer coordinator thinks the investment is a waste—or at least not what he or she would have preferred.

Basic computer functions include fundraising, scheduling, record-keeping, volunteer management and targeting field operations. Potential computer use evaluations should begin as soon as possible, so that you can purchase the computer system and begin inputting data immediately.

## Consultants and Pollsters

Professional help is important, even if you only contract with a consultant for a few hours to tell you what not to do. Many candidates first try to go it alone, talking with friends, politicos and former candidates. After getting enough conflicting information, or too much information, candidates usually come to the conclusion that a political consultant is needed to get them started. Find out who has a good reputation in your area and ask for a brochure or packet from them. Look at more than one consultant. If your campaign can afford a pollster, also do the same for them. To determine voter preferences on issues, voter perceptions of your candidacy, your opponent's weaknesses or the popularity of other elected officials whom you might like to use to profile your candidacy, nothing beats a having a pollster on board early.

## *Early Positioning and Message Development*

As you start to campaign, you probably will not have a completed poll; you won't have a campaign plan; and you won't have a snappy slogan, much less a campaign message. However, you still need to be able to talk to folks about why you are running. People will want to know about your experience, and they will want to know how you think you can win. If they are political insiders, they will also want to know what your message is.

---

**Twenty-one ways to be more visible:**

13. Start a political account for yourself, putting in $100 every pay period.
14. Get some expertise in the areas where you feel insecure: public speaking, image, voice or issues.
15. Do a reality check. Ask your friends or mentor what might stand in the way of your leading.
16. Learn how to raise money, how to ask people for money. Host a fundraising event.
17. Give yourself a timeline for leadership and plan your ascension.
18. Find out what appointments are open on the local, regional and state levels. Apply for one and lobby for it.
19. Do an assessment of the public offices available in your region, and what open seats there will be. Then position yourself to be in the right place at the right time.
20. Get to know the movers and shakers in your area. Attend events where they will be, and get to be on a first-name basis with them.
21. Adopt the "just take three" theory. Make time to help: (1) someone ahead of you who needs assistance to go further; (2) someone at your level who needs a little push to step forward; and (3) someone whom you can help to find a faster, easier way to the top than you did.

---

You need to have an interim message. This message should be simple and short. It should reflect how you are most like your constituents and most unlike your opponent. And it should go to the heart of how you think you can win.

"I'm running because no one on the council has ever been a daycare owner. Most have never run a business, much less a business with children. With all the regulations we've made, isn't it time that someone who represents the most important resource in this city has a seat at the policy table? My opponent has been talking about change for 10 years, yet we have more problems because we don't put kids first. I intend to campaign on that simple message, 'Kids first.'"

# Signature Gathering

In many states, filing petitions filled with supporters' names is accepted in place of expensive filing fees. In areas where this applies, it is always important to have those names in place early. It signals to the press, as well as political insiders, that you have your act together. It gives you a chance to use the volunteers you have assembled—and it forces you to get volunteers before they are snatched away by other campaigns.

Signature gathering needs to take place everywhere you go, in addition to areas where there are lots of registered voters:

- Shopping malls and grocery stores.
- Local meetings and luncheons you attend.
- Outside schools or daycare centers.
- Local community events, parades, fairs, and festivals.
- Busy downtown pedestrian intersections.
- Outside sporting events.
- Annual meetings of organizations you belong to.

Make sure you understand the rules for signature gathering. Check with your elections office to see if they have special forms which must be used. Gathering the names is a good test of your discipline, your organizational skills and your ability to draw people into the campaign.

# Pre-emption Strategy

More time is wasted in the early days of the campaign trying to talk, browbeat or otherwise coerce other prospective candidates out of the race. There are really only two effective ways of persuading another person not to run.

The first is to have far more money in the bank than your opponent.

The second is to prove you have overwhelming broad-based support.

A great example of the second happened in Montana. A week before filing, a woman candidate in Helena expected two worthy opponents. She took out a full-page ad in the local newspaper listing five hundred supporters from across the district. The ad featured photos of the candidate with her supporters. This was an expensive move that you generally wouldn't see early in a campaign; however, it worked. No one else filed, and she ran unopposed in the primary and did not have a strong opponent in the general.

Other methods used in the name of pre-emptive strategy include talking to your potential opponent, having emissaries talk for you, having special interest groups apply pressure on your behalf, or placing press stories extolling your campaign's strengths. Candidates dream of having few or no opponents. However, trying to talk a candidate out of running is seldom worth the effort put into it. In fact, several candidates report more success in getting an opponent out of the race by urging him to run. It seems that opponents expect you to try to muscle them out of the race, so if you use the reverse strategy and urge them to run, they get hit with the realities of what it takes, plus a strong dose of your self-confidence.

While the reverse psychology has worked for some, it's not nearly as effective as having money in the bank and a massive list of early endorsements.

**To persuade your opponent not to run:**

➤ *Have far more money in the bank.*
➤ *Show overwhelming broad-based support.*

# *Clearing the Decks*

As you get ready to make the change from private citizen to candidate, you need to make sure that your personal life is under control. First, look at yourself and make sure you're up to speed and ready for the task ahead. This is the time to get your yearly physical exam, visit the dentist, and see the eye doctor (be sure to get an extra pair of glasses—select frames and lenses that will work in front of TV lights and on camera). It's good to know that you're in tip-top shape.

Next, look at your family. Convene a family summit. Sit down and talk about what running for office really means for them. Find out if they are ready to accept new responsibilities, such as doing the laundry, cooking meals, taking over household finances, mowing the lawn, gardening, shopping, and generally picking up the slack for you. It is important that your family is as ready for you to run as you are.

This is also the time to get your support system in place. Long-time personal friends will need to be extra supportive. You should be able to turn to these people as a respite from the intensity of the campaign. It is tremendously important to have some friends who have nothing to do with your campaign. You need to be able to go to them and vent about all the stupid things that happen in the campaign. They may be your only touchstone to reality.

Before the campaign gets too crazy, establish a family calendar of known important dates in everyone's life (birthdays, graduations, plays and recitals, baseball games, etc.). In the same vein, place a campaign calendar on the refrigerator that has key campaign dates on it. As important milestones are known, make sure someone on the campaign has the responsibility for getting those dates on the family calendar.

How about your car? One thing we know about campaigns is that Murphy's law reigns supreme. If the candidate's car is going to break down, it will do so at the most inconvenient time—like on the way to a major televised speech. You have to make sure that the things you rely on are in working order. If you even think something may be wrong, take care of it now. The same thing applies to your house. If you have an appliance that is marginal (and crucial to the family's survival, like the microwave, the washing machine or the VCR), now is the time to replace or repair it. The truth is, once the campaign gets into full gear, you are likely to have less money and less time to deal with the little crises that can become big family problems if not taken care of quickly.

# *Conclusion*

A campaign beginning is filled with exuberance. It is often filled with tons of great ideas, "what-ifs" and energy. To get started on the right foot, you need to concentrate on the most important tasks, thus setting the right tone for the rest of the campaign.

The best meeting is the one between two people, and it's usually held over the phone.

Many campaigns waste valuable time putting together scads of meetings. The best meeting is the one between two people, and it's usually held over the phone. Beware of campaigns where all you do is meet to ponder what ought to be done—rather than reporting what has already been accomplished. In this early phase of the campaign you truly need to focus on building a backbone sturdy enough to support a winning campaign.

# THE CAMPAIGN PLAN

## THE FOUNDATION OF YOUR CAMPAIGN

A campaign plan is a written document that contains all the basic strategies that set the course for your campaign. The plan becomes the document that all key campaign people can refer to in order to ensure that their components fit the general strategy of the campaign. The campaign plan is a clear description of what you are doing, when. It outlines what you have, what you need to solicit, and how to prioritize your resources.

## The Importance of a Plan

If you don't have a map laid out to take you through the maze of your campaign, you are likely to stray in any of a hundred directions that your friends, colleagues and armchair advisors recommend—instead of keeping firmly to your goal.

A campaign plan is a living document. It is a process; it helps create consensus among the people who are going to be in your campaign. Succinctly put, the campaign plan outlines the rules of the game. It is also confidential. There should be only one copy, and that should be kept under lock and key. It is really the most strategic document in your campaign. It has been referred to as the nerve center of the campaign, clearly reflecting the candidate's style and themes.

> **A campaign plan:**
>
> ➤ *Assessment of facts*
> ➤ *Positioning*
> ➤ *General strategy*
> ➤ *Message*
> ➤ *Targeting*
> ➤ *Budget*
> ➤ *Timeline*
> ➤ *Conclusion*

Traditionally, the campaign plan is written by the consultant or campaign manager. Often the plan is drafted by the manager but overseen by a consultant who has expertise in the type of campaign being run. It is written when the dynamics of the race are clear. If you know who's going to be in the race, what kind of race it will be (i.e., an open seat, or a challenger race), and who's on your team, then it's time to write the plan.

Normally it is written in the first third of the campaign. If you decide to run in December, you should have your campaign plan written by the end of March. If it is an open seat and there are many players continually emerging, you need to anticipate who could change the plan by entering the race.

The campaign plan can be anywhere from ten to thirty pages in length, depending on how detailed you want it to be. The best plans are short, sweet, and to the point. They settle on the points you want to use to determine the course of your campaign.

A campaign plan includes:

***An assessment of facts:*** Taking a look at the political landscape in which you are choosing to run, understanding and assessing the demographics, as well as the political realities.

***Positioning:*** How you are going to run against your opponent. You need what is called a political wedge, that element that really separates you from your opponent.

***General strategy:*** What you are going to do and when, how your campaign will unfold and how you will use your resources.

***Message:*** Your message, slogan, and theme. This is the critical part of your campaign. It is what you are going to be saying, who you will say it to, and how you will say it.

***Targeting:*** How many votes do you need to win, and how will you get them? Where do these voters live? Targeting is perhaps the most misunderstood campaign technique. However technical it appears to be, it offers you the best strategic help in saving money.

***Budget:*** How much money you are going to need and when you are going to need it. A budget can be as simple as a one-page cash-flow chart that explains all your projected cash outlays and the timing of each.

***Timeline:*** An outline of what you are going to do and when you will do it. This can be in the form of a calendar that attaches a date to every major event and each step of your campaign strategy.

***Conclusion:*** This outlines all the critical areas you must address to win. It examines the foundations of the campaign and the roadblocks to success.

These are the basic parts of a campaign plan. A media plan may be added, outlining when to have press conferences, what the reporting deadlines are, and how to address critical issues. Field plans are occasionally included in the campaign plan. They provide details on doorbelling plans, your yard sign strategy, and information on precinct organization. The plan can also include endorsement strategies.

Although all these things can be included in a campaign plan, the best plans are those that deal directly with key responsibilities of the campaign.

> *A political wedge propels voters to your side and prevents them from slipping back into your opponent's column.*

# Assessment of Facts

Research needs to be done soon after you decide to run for office. You will obviously be taking a look at the political history of your district, determining who has run and won in the past, and how they accomplished it. Hopefully, you will have talked to people who have run earlier campaigns to get the "lay of the land." You also need to have examined the demographics; who lives in the district, where do they live, and how does this information fit into your strategic plan?

Important in your assessment of facts is an analysis of what else is on the ballot. What other races are being run? What issues will appear? How will these things affect your positioning?

## District Voters

You need to survey the voters of your district's political subdivisions. Who are the important players in this campaign whose votes are likely to make a difference in the race? You need to look at seniors, women, absentee voters, union members—anyone who is likely to influence the outcome of your campaign.

## Fundraising Potential

You need to honestly assess your ability to raise money. What is your financial base? How much money was raised for this position in previous years? How much are you likely to raise? How much is your opponent likely to raise? Can you fund all those things necessary to your campaign plan?

## Research and Polling

How much research and polling information is already available to you? Hopefully, you have in hand figures that will give you a good idea of what the voters are thinking. You should look at any polling information that examines voter attitudes during the last year. A campaign is not run in a void. Information is always being updated, and attitudes change. Make sure that you are truly examining the voters' attitudes and not just looking for justification of your own beliefs.

> **The facts:**
> ➤ District voters
> ➤ Fundraising potential
> ➤ Research and polling
> ➤ Open seat or incumbent
> ➤ Election year dynamics
> ➤ Campaign finance reform
> ➤ Being realistic

## Type of Seat

What kind of race are you facing? Are you an incumbent? A challenger? Is it an open seat? Each kind of race is dramatically different.

- *As an incumbent* you should get out early and strong. You need to show a strong established base and proceed from a position of strength.

- *As a challenger* you must start even earlier in order to demonstrate that you are credible and that you can raise money. Your goal is to pre-empt others from entering the race by having the largest bank balance and the most key endorsements.

- *As a candidate for an open seat,* you face more of a free-fall. Often you won't know who, or how many opponents you'll face until the filing deadline. And you won't have a clue of how costly the campaign will be. With an open seat you are likely to be forced to run hard in both the primary and the general elections. This makes for a longer and more strategic race.

## Election Year Dynamics

Critical to your campaign strategy is the kind of campaign backdrop you will be facing. Is it an off-cycle year? Is it a municipal election year? Is it a presidential election year? You need to assess the place in the campaign cycle that your race falls, as it strongly impacts the number and kinds of voters you should target.

## Campaign Finance Reform

Are there are new election laws that will impact your race? Regulation reform continues to make a difference in all levels of campaigns. Right now many states, cities and even the federal government are putting into effect new campaign financing laws that will impact the way candidates can receive money and the types of in-kind contributions candidates may accept. The "bundling" of campaign checks (a special-interest group collects small checks from its members, delivering them to the campaign in a bundle) is now being regulated in some states.

## Being Realistic

Above all, you must be realistic in assessing your campaign strategy. If you are running in a presidential year when a number of other top spots (governor, U.S. Senate, and other state elected officials) are on the ballot, your chances of raising money as a new candidate are likely to be less positive. There is a limit to the political disposable income that contributors have. The more people competing for dollars, the less you can plan on receiving.

This assessment of facts is necessary to get the alignment of your campaign backbone straight. You need to know what you are dealing with in order to make informed decisions about reaching your targeted voters.

# *Positioning*

Exactly as it sounds, positioning is the process of defining yourself and your candidacy in contrast to your opponent. You need to assess your own positive and negative traits as well as those of your opponent. While this is not a report from the opposition research team, it is a good place to start contrasting styles, experience and other qualities that will separate you from your opponent.

In every campaign, you need to develop a "political wedge." This is the issue, message or position that pits swing voters against your opponent—and can bring the momentum to you. If you know that a majority of voters think as you do on a specific issue—and it contrasts with your opponent— that is your political wedge. It propels voters to your side and prevents them from slipping back into your opponent's column.

Examine your positive traits. How do they compare or contrast with your opponent? Are you a good fundraiser and he is not? Are you more experienced in the issues of the day? Are you more of a work horse? Have you recruited a more dedicated volunteer force? If you can answer "yes," then consider all these attributes in your positioning. If you are in a swing Democratic district, and you are running against a Republican, use that to your advantage.

*Positioning makes it easy for your targeted voters to make the decision to vote for you.*

Exploit the differences between you and your opponent. Emphasize his less-than-positive traits. Have a strategy on how to bring them out: how to make voters understand those differences. Lead voters to the natural conclusion that you are one of them and your opponent is not. Keep in mind the press, seniors and any other targeted groups you need to impress. Convince those special constituencies in your district that you are with them and your opponent is not.

Contrast your styles. If you have an open, caring, effusive style, if you are a listener, or if you have a reputation for crusading for the right causes—and your opponent is seen as not outgoing, insensitive to people, elitist or lacking support in more populist groups—then you will want to emphasize these differences.

In short, you want to highlight the best about you and the worst about your opponent.

Positioning does not mean taking a position on critical issues. But positioning should give you the ability to contrast the most controversial issues that come up during the course of the campaign. Positioning makes it easy for your targeted voters to make the decision to vote for you.

# General Strategy

This is the critical summary of what needs to be done in order to win, taking into account the above evaluations and positioning. You need to assess the resources you have at hand and explore how to obtain more. You set up the wedge with your opponent and look for opportunities to maximize the differences between you.

Prioritize. Determine the course the campaign will follow during the coming months. Establish a logical progression, from planning and research, to accumulating resources (both money and volunteers) and finally to implementation.

The general campaign strategy talks very specifically about:

- What the candidate is going to spend time doing.
- The campaign's focus.
- The parameters for what gets done when.

It is a smart and critical analysis of what needs to be done.

The general strategy includes how to secure a very specific number of votes and where to find them. It tells how the campaign will target both primary and general election voters. It outlines a strategy for moving swing voters to your column.

This is a blueprint for the kind of campaign you will run. It may be direct-mail driven, heavy in radio and TV, or it may include a lot of field work. The plan will also include how voter contact will be carried out during the final weeks of the campaign.

General strategy depends on you, your assets and resources, your position in contrast with your opponent(s), and it gives everyone the sense that the campaign has one direction.

# Message

Targeting is the mathematics of a campaign; message is the literature and language of it. Message and strategy go hand in hand. The key strategic question is, "How do we get our message to our targeted voters?" Your message is the one thing you want your voters to remember. It must be simple, direct, easy to remember and compelling enough to make voters sit up and take notice.

Your message is particularly unique to your campaign, and it properly positions you against your opponent. It should be part of anything that you and the rest of your campaign do. Press events, brochures, phone bank scripts, your speeches—all need to contain the same message. It should be specific enough to set you apart from the rest of the pack, yet general enough so you might use it in different ways.

The basic questions to be answered by your message include:

- Why are you running and why should anyone vote for you?
- What makes you different from your opponents?
- What issues concern you? (No more than three.)

In campaigns that are fortunate enough to have a poll, the polling analysis gives you the best clues as to the focus of your message:

- It outlines the important issues of the district.
- It gauges which of your ideas are most acceptable/desirable to the voters.
- It tells you which of your issues/concerns/positions are less acceptable to the public.
- It tests which of your slogan ideas resonates best with the voters you need to reach.

> *Your message should be an attention-getting, substantive slice of your soul, delivered with energy, enthusiasm and conviction. It is uniquely yours and captures your expertise, vision and warmth.*

A poll can also help you frame those messages that go to the heart of your swing voters. For example, the results may show that middle-aged women were among the most undecided, but that they traditionally support a person with your profile. After looking at the crosstabulations of the poll, you might learn that this group is particularly concerned about crime, and they think that education plays a role in limiting crime. Thus you would focus your message to these voters—and your message should address crime and education.

Writing a message can be a long, drawn-out process if you let everyone who touches the campaign review it. Or you can settle on a quicker process by allowing the people who write your campaign plan to suggest a message after reviewing the research.

Your message can start with an issue, a kind of style, a specific position you may take on a controversial issue, a value important to you or a general message of what you intend to do.

# Issues

Big issues such as the economy, transportation, education, and crime are often bases for campaign messages. But issues specific to an area or the times can also be appropriate, such as the environment or health care. While issues often bog a message down by being too specific or long-winded, they provide a candidate the opportunity to strut one's stuff. An issue-based message usually presents a problem along with your personalized, and hopefully tested, solution.

# Vision

Making life better for the future, offering an ideology such as a return to better times, calling for stability, inspiring the right kind of change, offering a new generation of leadership—all are examples of "the vision thing."

# Style

Offering an open approach to government, being accessible 24 hours a day, trustworthiness, and being direct with the voters are all examples of messages which put style center-stage. Often style is the favorite, as it offers candidates an ability to use it with issues, vision and specific positions. In these days of voter distrust, style messages seek to build a more desirable bridge with voters.

# Position

From gun control to pro-choice, from no more taxes to cleaning up our waterways, these position-based messages are popular from local to statewide races. Supporting the Republican-generated "Contract with America" is a recent example of a position-based message.

# Values

Restoring family values, understanding a woman's right to choose reproductive freedom, taking the pledge to stand by our country's flag are all recent values-based messages that have been used with great success.

Your message needs to consider the top of the ticket. If you share the ticket with several members of your party, know what they are saying. If these other candidates sharing your party's limelight are spending lots of money on radio, TV and newspaper ads, you might be able to piggyback your own message on theirs, especially if you can't afford the same level of media exposure.

From the overall message should come one or two paragraphs that will be the core of your message. You will repeat this over and over—thousands of times—during the course of the campaign. It helps to like your message. Make it something that fits your style.

The message is the overview. The theme comes next. It should reflect how you intend to run your campaign, making it a metaphor for how you would run government. The theme takes your message and gives it action. The theme is usually translated to a powerful phrase called a slogan.

Slogans are the words that unite all the parts of your campaign. The slogan is the last thing a candidate says in a speech, going door-to-door, or before he goes to bed at night. It appears on all brochures, on the campaign stationery, and on yard signs and bumper stickers if possible. It's a good idea to place the slogan on your campaign T-shirts as well.

Campaigns fortunate enough to afford a poll often test up to five proposed slogans to see how they are received by the targeted voters. Campaigns should stick to one slogan for the duration of the campaign, though candidates can be forgiven if they change the slogan in the early days of the campaign after seeing the reaction of people along the campaign trail.

Some of the best slogans are not written by consultants, nor managers, nor candidates. They are suggested by campaign workers, or a member of the public after a candidate's speech.

# *Targeting*

Campaigns often suffer from two common predicaments when it comes to targeting. Either they spend way too much time and energy trying to specifically target their swing voters (by extrapolating analyses from other earlier candidate and issue elections), or they spend too little time at that task.

At one extreme you might see, "I'll target Caucasian women over the age of fifty who are homeowners that live in the southern third of the district, but only those in precincts where the environmental initiative did well and where the majority cast ballots against incumbents last year." At the other extreme is, "I'll target voters who vote all the time in the primary; and in the general, I'll concentrate on those who voted three out of the four most recent elections."

Targeting is like taking your first statistics, physics, or geometry class—the first time you get lost, you figure you will never understand it and try to drop out of the class. However, upon completing the course, you realize that there was a very good reason to persevere.

In campaigns the same is true. A little math goes a very long way in helping you win—and at a lower cost. Targeting is a quantitative analysis done to reduce the number of voters you will concentrate on during the campaign.

As you know, not everyone in your district is registered to vote. In many

**Campaign Slogans**

➤ In touch with today's Hartford
➤ Because there's no place like home
➤ Stay with the person who got us here
➤ A fresh voice... a new approach
➤ Don't throw away a good thing
➤ A work horse, not a show horse
➤ A mayor who will build bridges
➤ Protect our city's neighborhoods
➤ Actions speak louder than words
➤ The right person at the right time
➤ The know-how to get things done
➤ Leveling the playing field—for all of us
➤ For real solutions to real problems
➤ Integrity: the art of living honestly
➤ Leadership that makes a difference
➤ Marilyn Samuelson: your neighbor
➤ Because nothing counts like results
➤ The sensible choice for city council
➤ A different kind of Congressperson
➤ Finally, a leader we can be proud of
➤ Guts in government —novel concept
➤ Face the facts: it's time for a change
➤ A solid record of effective leadership
➤ The person to protect Alaska's future
➤ A candidate as independent as you are

areas, fewer than 67 percent of eligible voters are registered. Of the registered voters, fewer than 50 percent actually vote in most state and local elections. (They mostly vote only in presidential elections.)

So, do you want to send your campaign material to every household in the district? Do you even want to send it to all registered voters, when half of them have never voted for someone with a party affiliation like yours? Of course not.

Targeting begins with some simple assumptions and grows to a complex analysis of how many votes you need to win and how you will get them.

## Why Should You Target?

Targeting allows you to spend less money to reach fewer voters who should be easier to persuade. You know from receiving very generic mailings from organizations or individuals that a message can be too broad to connect with you. In your campaign, if you treat everyone with the same message, your voters will have little reason to think you are talking to them specifically—and out goes your message (and brochures) to the recycling bin.

Targeting focuses your time and money on the people most likely to respond to you. And it eliminates the need to be all things to all people. Your goal is to inspire enough people to put you over the top.

## The Voter Universe

Generally, you start with how many people live in the district. Then, how many are registered to vote? From there, how many are projected to vote this year? Determine how many people are running against you, and do some simple analysis.

For example, if there are 150,000 adults who live in your district, and about 100,000 are registered to vote, there are probably 60,000 who vote in presidential year elections in November (with only half that number voting in the primary). Of those 60,000, there are some people who will never vote for you, either because of your party affiliations or something else trackable. There's another segment that, for the same reason, will vote for you regardless of what you do. If these groups total 10,000, then that leaves 40,000 undecided voters. If you combine the voters who live in the same household, that leaves about 30,000 households. To win, you will need 20,001 votes.

# Targeting Pyramid

Total number of people who live in your district:

## 150,000

Number of those who are registered to vote:

## 100,000

Projected turnout in this year's election:

## 60,000

Subtract those voters who you know
will never vote for you, leaving:

## 50,000

Subtract those who surely
will vote for you, leaving:

## 40,000

undecided voters, or

## 30,000

undecided house-
holds to contact;
with 2 people
in the race,
you need

## 20,001

votes.

FORM 2: TARGETING PYRAMID

# Targeting Priorities

In every race, it is important to know who's with you and who's likely to be against you. The quest is not to concentrate on just those voters who have shown a background of support for candidates like you; the quest is to find those voters who display an independent voter style. While lots of voters say they always vote for the person, not the party, more than half of voters usually vote one party preference. However, that remaining 50 percent can be the key to your winning or losing.

Your priority is to know in which category the people expected to cast ballots in your election are likely to be:

- *Traditional supporters:* These voters have shown some history of voting for people like you, usually through party registration. You need to know who they are so you can cross them off your list of people on whom to spend your resources. These voters are important to target on election day (your Get-Out-the-Vote priority) but they don't need to be sent all the expensive, persuasive material. Contrary to popular opinion, these are not your top priority; rather, they are your third-highest priority.

- *Lazy supporters:* These are the voters who, if (big if) they vote, would vote for you. The trouble is, they seldom vote in off-year elections, or in primaries, or in down-ballot races. These are your second-highest priority.

- *Swing voters:* These are voters who vote for Democratic presidents, but Republican governors; they vote for liberal city council members but conservative state legislators. They are your top-priority targeted voters: the ones you will spend the most amount of time and money reaching.

- *"No way" voters:* These people will never vote for you. They have demonstrated a history of not voting for a person with your party or organizational affiliation. These people are important to identify, because you don't want to spend a lot of money trying to convince them, and you don't want to inadvertently coax them into voting on election day. (You hope they stay home.)

- *Not-yet-registered voters:* This is the growing number of people who are not registered to vote, but if they were, would vote for you. Minority groups, college students and economically-depressed area residents are common examples of potential voter groups you might target. However, since the effort to register must also be coupled with an equally strong effort to get these newly-registered voters to actually vote on election day, they become a low priority for most campaigns.

# Targeting Box

| | Perennial Voters | Occasional Voters | Non-Voters |
|---|---|---|---|
| **Support you** | **A**<br>No program | **D**<br>Primary focus of GOTV and Vote by Mail | **G**<br>Consider GOTV (if you need it) |
| **Swing voters** | **B**<br>Primary focus for message communication | **E**<br>Secondary focus for message communication | **H**<br>No program |
| **Support your opponent** | **C**<br>Possible communication, if you need it | **F**<br>No program | **I**<br>No program |

FORM 3: TARGETING BOX

## Targeting Box Explanation

***Perennial voters:*** No Get-Out-the-Vote effort is needed, as these people always vote anyway.

**Box A:** This is the campaign's core base of support. Most campaigns waste resources by trying to communicate with them or applying organization tactics to get them to vote, or both. These voters already support your campaign and are habitual voters. Leave them alone.

**Box B:** This box represents the campaign's number one communications target. These voters will show up to vote, no matter what, so the campaign needs to persuade them to vote for the candidate.

**Box C:** This box is a communications target only as a last resort in campaigns (mostly futile efforts) where there is nowhere else to go to make up the votes. Box G is usually a better target. However, every voter in this group that you can switch to your side is also one less vote for your opponent.

***Occasional voters:*** These people have some voter history, but are not consistent voters. Organization and GOTV are important for this group to be effective.

**Box D:** This group is the primary focus of the GOTV effort. In some cases the entire organizational effort is targeted to effect a higher turnout of Box D voters.

**Box E:** This is a secondary focus of message communication. These voters are more "expensive" votes for the campaign than Box B. Not only must the campaign persuade voters, they must also be motivated to vote.

**Box F:** These voters should be left alone. They support your opponent and are infrequent voters.

***Non-voters:*** These people make up between 15 and 25 percent of the electorate. Non-voters should be considered in the targeting plan only if there is no other way to put together a winning vote. These people rarely, if ever, vote. Go after these people only as a last resort.

# Determining Voter Behavior Trends

Before you get out the computer programs and spreadsheets, let's start with a proper foundation. Your voters have predictable trends in their election-day habits. You need to find out about those trends for at least three good reasons:

1. *The information is available*, and it's fairly inexpensive.
2. *You can visually present it on maps* to give a clear picture of who's important to the campaign, and who's likely to be more of a target for your opponent's efforts.
3. *It gives you a quantitative picture* that is far more dependable than the group intuition of your steering committee.

The trends to uncover first are:

• Average partisan turnout: by choosing several (more than 10) races, you can determine what the core party partisanship is—and thus know if you're in a friendly precinct or not.

- Voter attention span, or percent of energy index: if the voters turn out in large numbers for the top-of-the-ticket races, but fade out by the time they get to state and local races, then you should either concentrate resources on them, if they look persuadable, or cut them off your list of targeted voters.

- Party partisanship drop-off, or efficiency index: if your average party vote in a precinct reveals that the incumbent of the same party is falling below average in specific precincts, then as a challenger you should target those voters who appear reluctant to vote for the incumbent.

- The home of lazy voters: if you find precincts that show a strong support for candidates like you in heavy-turnout years, but a weak turnout in the other three years, this may inspire you to target these voters, particularly if the voter trend of the entire district is usually that of a party other than yours.

# Building Your Voter Files

Voter files are those computer databases that allow you to collect, sort and then produce on mailing labels, walking lists and phone bank cards, the names, addresses and phone numbers of your targeted voters. Once you have completed your initial gathering of past election totals and chosen the right races on which to base your own targeting formula, you can begin to build your voter files.

If you have a poll that tests your background and issues of importance to the district, you could have a reasonable assessment of your base. A base is a solid group of voters very likely to support you. If you have served on the local school board, on several community groups and have been quoted in the newspaper often, you may start out with as many as 15 percent of the voters who think you are their early preferred choice for the open state legislative seat. That's your base.

If you are running against an incumbent from another party, there might be a history of former candidates who have run against him. Average the amount of opposition that the incumbent has had, and that might give you a base.

Although you won't know exactly who those voters are, you will be able to tell through your poll what kind of profile these supporters have. From this base, you need to determine who is likely to support you if they were to hear your message. This is where the quantitative meets the qualitative.

Start with the number of voters who are likely to vote, which you can determine by doing your own research and analysis or by asking your local elections officials. Vendors who sell labels and lists are also good sources of information.

After determining how many votes you need to win, start building the list of groups you can access. List vendors can tell you how many of the people who are likely to vote in your upcoming election are:

- Seniors, or members of other specific age groups.
- Women, and men.
- People with ethnic last names.
- Homeowners rather than renters.
- Residents of certain demographic areas in town.
- Democrats, Republicans or non-partisans.

# Party vs. Precinct Targeting

As part of the targeting analysis, you'll start with one of two major targeting characteristics, depending on whether or not voters in your state are registered by party affiliation. If they are, it makes your targeting easier, and the accuracy of hitting the best voters higher. If they are not, more sophisticated analyses must be done. In such cases, you will look at the voting records of your key voters over several years and many races. You'll be looking for the "average partisan turnout."

Other factors to be considered include votes on particular issues, initiatives, and important local candidates. Be careful when taking special-election data, as there can be many reasons why these voters turned out to vote. For example, special elections on hot issues may not affect everyone in the same way. If the vote was about locating a waste dump in a certain area, turnout was probably very high in that area. Also, special elections bring a smaller turnout, thus skewing the percentages. These reviews are always less accurate than party-identified precinct preferences, but most local and county volunteer experts still target more by these issue elections, in addition to candidate elections, than by party identification.

# Demographic Targeting

The goal of good targeting is to find the best voters to respond to your profile, issues, party, local roots, resumé, etc. The premise is to ready a message that will convince these voters that you are most like them. If you can find these people, then you will need to reach them less often and less dramatically. This is the core reasoning which drives today's campaign targeting.

Instead of painting a broad-brush message to all your likely voters, you can focus a more direct message to subsets of the total number of people likely to vote. In 1992, many women candidates were particularly successful in targeting women voters. Older candidates often target older voters. Some candidates have been able to target people with higher or lower incomes, higher or lower education levels, whether or not they have children in school and a compilation of other factors. The most popular targeting is the targeting of voters from your own party.

Demographic targeting can then be overlaid on geographic targeting, or you can figure out a plan that allows specifically targeted messages to be sent to certain segments of your target, and different messages to others.

# Getting Help to Target

As important as targeting is to all campaigns, it is frightening how few people actually allocate resources or challenge the local experts who tend to do the targeting for the party. Targeting requires:

- Gathering a lot of data.
- Choosing the right races to use in your base formula.
- Doing lots of addition, multiplication and division.
- Careful selection of precincts after the math is done.
- Checking your decisions along the way.
- Ensuring that your target is the best you can do.

While you can do all of the above yourself, why on earth would you want to make these key strategic decisions part of on-the-job training? You certainly didn't learn algebra that way.

Your choices for help include:

1. *The local hometown volunteer expert.* In every community, targeting experts have evolved over the years. Next to securing a local treasurer, these should be the first people you coax into your support column. They know about voter behavior trends and indexes. In some cases, they have evolved past their prime, and may use formulas that are outdated. However, they become a base for your team's efforts.

2. *A computer program* (and a computer guru to work it). More than two dozen programs are on the market (see *Campaigns & Elections* magazine's Political Resources directory) that can help you download a target from general election offices. You usually buy the program (programs range from $1,000 on up), buy the voters list from the city, state, or county, add other factors that are available, and either have your guru or a third-party computer firm put your targeted voters into the program so you can sort them as you want. This home-base data central can save you money, as you can then generate your own labels and lists. However, it can also paralyze your campaign if you don't have someone proficient enough to develop it, use it and fix it if something goes wrong.

3. *Local groups, organizations or political parties.* Often the people with the highest stakes in every election cycle have their own lists—or access to voter files. In many states, the election offices provide updated voter files each year to the Democratic and Republican Parties. If you are in good standing with these folks, you might be able to get your targeted voter files for free, or at a nominal cost. In many cases, these party lists are quite advantageous for you to use, as they also have additional information you can't buy from private vendors, such as data from phone banks and door-to-door canvassing. If you know a list contains identified Democrats, pro-choice voters, people who support a specific initiative, etc., clearly that list may help you target a specific message to them.

4. *Private vendors.* Label and list vendors are cropping up all over the country as technical targeting becomes big business. For some years many states have had only one major vendor selling these voter files, keeping the price fairly steep for most campaigns. However, these vendors are now being challenged by local upstart companies offering to download your target onto a disk and then get you set up to use it. They may require that you house the list with them, but the competition is having a good effect on the market. With private vendors you usually have to figure out all the subjective information regarding what you want your target to reflect, and then they generate the lists from the precinct priorities you give them.

5. *Direct-mail vendors.* In many cities, in Washington, DC and throughout California, there are vendors specializing in direct mail who also will help you with targeting. As direct mail is the best way to target specific populations, targeting and direct-mail messaging go hand in hand. If you know that you have to convince a majority of senior women in the northern precincts that you support their issues, while not alienating younger voters, then direct-mail targeting and mailings usually become your answer. In many cases these direct-mail consultants are very adept at suggesting the targets you have to reach and figuring out what the message to those people should be. They have the computer programs and the capacity to produce mailing labels, affix them to your brochures, sort and bag the brochures by carrier route and deliver them to the post office. While not cheap, this practice is growing, and it keeps your targeting housed with professionals which would most likely ensure the message gets out on time to the right target.

# Using Your Voter Files

One you have settled on a specific number of votes that it takes to win, and determined where you expect to get those votes, you need to ensure that all campaign activities are directed to those voters. To reach them, you:

- Send them your brochures.
- Call them through your phone banks.
- Meet them walking door-to-door.
- Concentrate your yard signs on them.
- Place cable TV ads they will see.
- Place radio spots they will hear.
- Purchase bus signs and billboards for them to see.
- Schedule time to speak or be visible to them.
- Concentrate your budget on them every day.

Once you have built your target and have voter files either in your office or with experts you trust, you begin the process of persuading. If your plan calls for phone banks and/or door-to-door canvassing, you can then improve on those voter files with updated information as you get it.

If a targeted voter tells you that he's voting for you, his name goes on the GOTV list, or perhaps the list for the next fundraising letter. If a targeted voter says he's not voting for you, then he's taken off the list so you don't spend another dime on him. If he remains undecided, you beef up the communication.

Targeting becomes the key to your work plan, which is why your targeting should be completed before you build your budget. How can you determine what you have to spend, and raise, if you do not know how many people you must persuade? No matter how much experience you have had in campaigns, demographics or math, you can follow the basic steps in getting yourself a pertinent target.

# *Budget*

Your budget is the driving force behind all campaign strategy. On a single page of paper you must be able to succinctly match dollars, strategy, timeline and cash flow. No element of your campaign plan is as important as your budget. It tells you how much money you must raise, when, and for what. It gives you the scope of your campaign and tells you what kind of strategy you will use to reach your targeted voters.

There are five general areas in most budgets. The first and most important is voter contact.

# Voter Contact

The most important money you spend during your campaign doesn't go to pay staff or consultants; it's not for opening an office or to pay the telephone bill. It goes to reaching your targeted voters several times with a compelling message. Voter contact can be done in many different ways: TV, direct mail, radio, going door-to-door, phoning, putting up yard signs, or buying billboards and bus signs. Whatever method you choose, the quality of your voter contact will determine the success of your campaign.

The first thing you need to decide is what forms of voter contact you will use. 60 to 70 percent of your budget will go to voter contact, 80 percent if you are challenging an incumbent. The common elements found in this part of your budget are:

- Design fees
- Printing
- Brochures
- Yard signs
- Invitations
- Labels and lists
- Postage
- TV production and placement
- Radio production and placement

- Newspaper ads
- Flyers and posters
- Bus signs
- Billboards
- Bumper stickers
- Balloons
- Buttons
- T-shirts
- Other gizmos

It is important that you understand the costs associated with each of the above items and also the value that each contributes to your campaign.

## *Design Fees*

This is one area of your campaign where you want the best. Invest in professional help in the production of your voter contact material—someone who has done political art before. With the desktop publishing revolution, everyone seems to think they can do their own political brochures. However, a computer, a desktop publishing program and the desire do not make one an expert. Any money you allocate for professional help in this area is well spent. It may cost from $500 to $2,500 for the concept, design and layout of a brochure, but a professional touch significantly increases the likelihood that your targeted voters will read the material.

## *Printing*

There are any number of things to be printed during the course of your campaign, beginning with letterhead, #10 envelopes, remittance envelopes and perhaps business cards. After that there will be fundraising letters, event invitations, brochures, yard signs and thank-you cards. In short, printing costs will be a significant portion of your budget, so it is worth your while to interview several printers and understand all their charges. Costs vary significantly from state to state, city to city, and printer to printer. You may want to do business with a union print shop, which will allow you to have a union "bug" printed on your material. If available to you, it is important that this bug be placed on all your printed material, including letterhead, envelopes and business cards, as well as your brochures.

*The most important money you spend during your campaign goes to reaching your targeted voters several times with a compelling message.*

## Brochures and Flyers

The printing cost of brochures ranges from $0.15 per piece for a simple black-and-white piece that you do from your office to $0.50 or more per piece for a large, multicolored, sophisticated design. Flyers can be done at your local quick-print shop for pennies apiece, and posters done by your local newspaper or printer can cost from $0.30 to more than $1.00 each.

## Yard Signs

The printing cost of yard signs can be as low as $1.00 per placard if done in quantities of more than 2,000. This does not include the lumber needed to assemble them, and keep in mind that two placards are needed for a double-sided sign. When all costs are totaled, you can count on as much as $3.00 per double-sided sign (assembled by volunteers, of course).

## Labels and Lists

After you have figured out your target, you go to a label-and-list vendor to purchase the mailing labels for your brochures. The same lists should be used for your door-to-door campaign and phone banks. These labels and lists can range anywhere from 1 to 4¢ per name. To have the labels affixed to the brochures and the brochures sorted and bundled for bulk mailing will cost 2 to 3¢ per piece.

## Postage

There are a number of different prices that the U.S. Postal Service charges for mail. The cheapest is mail that goes carrier-route sort and is within certain size limits. To be sure you have accurate information, always check with your post office to determine the per-piece rate for your type of mailing. Visit your local bulk-mail post office and meet the people in charge. It will be well worth your time. These individuals can be helpful by providing tips on the cheapest and fastest way to get your mail out. It is also essential to get approval of your direct-mail pieces from the Post Office before you have them printed. Just imagine delivering 30,000 labeled and sorted brochures to the post office only to have them tell you that they don't meet regulations and cannot be mailed!

## Paid Media

The design, production and placement of TV, radio and newspaper ads also is a part of your voter contact budget. Regardless of which medium—or combination of media—budget most of your money here. Determine costs ahead of time and then allocate funds for each step. If TV is part of your plan, it will be your biggest expenditure. However, if you determine that your production costs for TV will be higher than your placement costs, you may want to reconsider its use. Cable TV and special videos also fit in this category. Radio costs significantly less than TV for both production and placement.

## Billboards and Bus Signs

As with most voter contact pieces, there are two costs associated with billboards and bus signs: the design and production of the pieces and then getting the pieces to the voters, in this case rental of the space where they will be displayed. The boards are costly to produce—thousands of dollars to make the signs is not unusual. Placement runs for periods of time, two weeks to a month or more, and can cost up to $5,000 for a large billboard in a critical location for a month.

## T-shirts, Buttons, Balloons and Gizmos

Gizmos should never be more than 1 or 2 percent of your voter contact budget. You must take care to ensure that your money is spent to move voters to you rather than just recognize your name. Buying a button machine (about $200) is often a better investment than paying $.50 or more apiece for hundreds of buttons that are gone all too soon.

## Miscellaneous

There should always be room in your voter contact budget for good ideas. But remember to ask yourself, "Will this move my targeted voters?" Voter contact is the reason you have a budget. It is the mechanism by which you reach your key voters. Your dollars need to be spent on moving voters, not making your supporters happy with gizmos that may be fun and unique but not your best investment.

# Fundraising

As the old saying goes, "It takes money to make money." In fact, it takes lots of money to raise money. You need fundraising tools to attract money to your campaign. These tools include such simple things such as letterhead, postage and envelopes. Make sure that at least 15 percent of your total budget is allotted to fundraising. This amount should never go higher than 20 percent.

## Direct Mail

You will need to pay to print and mail letters asking for contributions and to print remittance envelopes in which to send the money to you. Budget for monthly mailings to your donor list.

## Events

If you have a fundraising event, you will have to pay to print and mail the invitations. There is nothing more frustrating to candidates than putting enormous amounts of time, energy and money into fundraising events. However, you do need to put enough energy and money into these events so that they are done correctly. If you rent a location, pay for the food and drinks, or rent sound equipment to make your function successful, remember all of these cost money.

# Staff and Consultants

Your most important fixed costs are apt to be for your campaign staff and consultants.

## Paid Staff

In many races the only paid staff member is the campaign manager. However, you may determine that it is in your best interest to pay someone to do fundraising full or part time. In a large campaign, you may also hire a media person, a volunteer coordinator or field director and a scheduler. Any one or all of these may be key to your campaign, depending on its size and your resources.

## Consultants

The specialists you should consider to help you run your campaign include a general consultant, a media consultant, a direct-mail consultant, an image consultant, a pollster and a photographer. Any of these will provide an extra tug on your campaign purse strings. With any consultant, clarify how big that tug will be and when you have to pay. Make sure you know exactly what is included in their fees.

# Office and Materials

The other portion of your fixed costs will be rental of your campaign headquarters, telephones, fax machines, copy equipment, utilities, and any other supplies that you may need. Combined with your staff and consultants, these fixed costs should not be more than 15 percent of your total budget.

## Office Space

It's important to get the best deal available. Your cost should be no more than $500 to $1,000 a month. It is well worth suffering the inconveniences of a few rough boards or ugly carpets to save money for your voter contact plan.

## Equipment

When it comes to technological toys (computers, software, telephones, fax machines etc.), free is your best option. What can you provide the campaign? Do staff members have anything to contribute? (Often they have their own computers that they will loan to the campaign.) Can you solicit items from your supporters? However, in your search for free items, make sure you get equipment that can do the job.

# Miscellaneous

Travel, meals and volunteer expenses (pizza and soda for mailing parties, etc.) are some of the other expenses your campaign needs to budget for. Approximately 5 percent of your budget should be dedicated to miscellaneous expenses.

## Travel

Campaigns usually do not pay mileage at the per-mile rate allowed by the federal government. Instead, a campaign typically reimburses the candidate and certain staff members for out-of-pocket expenses such as gas and the cost of lodging.

## Food and Meals

If the campaign can afford it, covering the candidate's cost of attending community dinners or meetings is an appropriate expense. It is a good idea to check local and state campaign regulations for what is a legal expense. In some areas it is illegal to use a campaign check to pay for attendance at another candidate's fundraiser. However, there is an unwritten rule that most candidates will allow other candidates free admission to their events.

## Good Ideas Account

Every campaign has an abundance of great ideas. Unfortunately, most of these ideas cost money. Your goal is to allocate a little bit of your campaign budget to fund the really outstanding concepts. Buying cups so that your volunteers can pass out ice water at the county fair is an example of funding a good idea. Good ideas are usually one-time expenses that are done for a very particular effect. Renting a hot-air balloon for your state convention, sky writing, and flying a banner behind an airplane are examples of things that have been done.

It's important to keep the proper balance among categories in the budget. Continually compare your budget plan to what is actually happening. If at some point the amount spent on voter contact drops to 50 percent, you need to reexamine your spending. If you are running a strong incumbent race, it may not be important. However, if you are in a tight challenger race, you may find it necessary to reduce your fixed costs to keep your voter contact percentage high.

It is helpful to treat your campaign as a small business. You need to be prudent, and you need to be accurate, as it will save you headaches in the long run. If you have budgeted for an expensive campaign and your contributions run behind, you need to continually assess what budget adjustments need to be made. Most campaigns develop both a high-budget plan and a low-budget plan in anticipation of these problems. However, the best plan is a realistic assessment of what you will need to spend and how much you can raise.

# Timeline

A campaign timeline is the easiest part of the campaign plan to write. It involves compiling all key dates and deadlines and placing them on one calendar that extends for the duration of the campaign. The timeline reiterates the voter contact plan milestones, and emphasizes those key dates that involve endorsement announcements. The key dates include, but are not limited to:

- Public disclosure reporting deadlines
- Newspaper and organization endorsement announcements
- Filing deadlines
- Radio and TV air dates
- Benchmark poll
- Tracking polls
- All fundraisers and home parties
- Major candidate trips outside the district

- Press opportunities
- Door-to-door canvassing
- Direct-mail drop dates
- Important events
- Planned phone banks
- Community events and parades
- Yard sign blitzes
- Radio and TV time-buy deadlines
- Absentee ballot deadlines
- Candidacy announcement and kickoff
- GOTV activities

These deadlines give everyone a sense of urgency about the campaign, as well as allowing everyone to see the level of involvement that will be required to accomplish everything outlined on the timeline.

# Conclusion

The final chapter of the campaign plan revolves around the key points that will determine whether you win or not. What does this campaign boil down to doing?

Does it rest on fundraising? Does it rely on several other candidates getting in the race to cut down on a front-runner's lead? Does winning depend on the candidate actually walking to—and talking with—16,000 households over the next four months? Or does the campaign's success require your getting one of the two major newspaper endorsements?

Whatever your campaign must have in order to win should be summed up in the conclusion. This wrap-up gives you and your key players a chance to see in writing what the top worries are likely to be. It also outlines the support and solutions necessary to meet the challenges ahead. The conclusion should call for periodic reviews to ensure that these challenges are being met on target and in time for the rest of the plan to fall into place.

# Campaign Plan Review and Approval

The campaign plan is obviously a critical document. It requires research, evaluation, careful number-crunching, some inspirational message development and a creative slogan.

The plan should be a living document—one that you can come back to throughout the campaign to update, rethink, and rework as conditions demand.

Once the plan is written, it should be reviewed by your steering committee or kitchen cabinet for fine-tuning and acceptance. It should become the course of action. Now, everyone who touches the campaign can begin with a sense of direction that is hopefully the most efficient, doable path to a successful finish.

# Campaign Budget

| | Mar | Apr | May | Jun | Jul | Aug | Sep | Oct | Nov | TOTAL |
|---|---|---|---|---|---|---|---|---|---|---|
| **Voter Contact** | | | | | | | | | | |
| Graphic design | | | | | | | | | | |
| Printing | | | | | | | | | | |
| Labels, lists and postage | | | | | | | | | | |
| Newspaper ads | | | | | | | | | | |
| Radio and TV | | | | | | | | | | |
| Billboards and bus signs | | | | | | | | | | |
| Buttons, balloons and gizmos | | | | | | | | | | |
| **Fundraising** | | | | | | | | | | |
| Printing | | | | | | | | | | |
| Labels and lists | | | | | | | | | | |
| Postage | | | | | | | | | | |
| Events | | | | | | | | | | |
| **Campaign staff** | | | | | | | | | | |
| Manager | | | | | | | | | | |
| Fundraiser | | | | | | | | | | |
| **Consultants** | | | | | | | | | | |
| **Office** | | | | | | | | | | |
| Rent and utilities | | | | | | | | | | |
| Equipment and supplies | | | | | | | | | | |
| **Miscellaneous** | | | | | | | | | | |
| **TOTALS** | | | | | | | | | | |

*FORM 4: CAMPAIGN BUDGET*

# Sample Campaign Costs

## For Legislative or Statewide Races

### Staff & Consultants

| | |
|---|---|
| Campaign manager | $1,500 - $3,000 per month |
| Office manager | $1,000 - $1,500 per month |
| Press secretary | $1,000 - $2,000 per month |
| Consultants | $2,000 - $4,000 per month |
| Pollster | $10,000 - $14,000 for a baseline poll |
| | $4,000 for supervised volunteer polling |
| Photographer | $600 for a full-day photo shoot |
| | $350 for a half-day photo shoot |
| Debate/image coach | $2,000 for the campaign |
| Graphic artist | $500 for basic logo design |
| | $500 - $2,000 for brochure design |

### Fixed Costs

| | |
|---|---|
| Rent | Minimum $500 per month |
| Utilities | $100 or more per month |
| Phone usage | $250 per month for two lines |
| | $600 per month for four lines |
| | $600 per month for a cellular phone |
| Computer and printer | $2,500 minimum |
| Software | $1,000 minimum |
| Copy machine | $600 used |
| Furniture | $500 used |
| Fax machine | $300 used |
| Phone system | $600 used |
| Supplies | $250 per month |

FORM 5: SAMPLE CAMPAIGN COSTS

# In-Kind Contributions

## General Supplies

- ❏ Calendar
- ❏ Chalk board
- ❏ Computer disks
- ❏ Computer paper
- ❏ Copy paper
- ❏ Easels
- ❏ File Folders

- ❏ Glue
- ❏ Message pads
- ❏ Notebooks
- ❏ Paper clips
- ❏ Pencil sharpener
- ❏ Pencils
- ❏ Pens

- ❏ Post-its
- ❏ Scissors
- ❏ Staples
- ❏ Tape
- ❏
- ❏
- ❏

## Equipment

- ❏ 35 mm camera
- ❏ Answering machine
- ❏ Button machine
- ❏ Calculator
- ❏ Coffee maker
- ❏ Computer
- ❏ Computer printer

- ❏ Copy machine
- ❏ Dictaphone
- ❏ Fax machine
- ❏ Postage scale
- ❏ Radio
- ❏ Staplers
- ❏ Tape recorder

- ❏ Telephones
- ❏ Television
- ❏ Typewriters
- ❏ VCR
- ❏
- ❏
- ❏

## Furniture

- ❏ Bookcases
- ❏ Computer table
- ❏ Couch
- ❏ Desks

- ❏ Desk chairs
- ❏ File cabinets
- ❏ Folding chairs
- ❏ Microwave

- ❏ Refrigerator
- ❏ Work tables
- ❏
- ❏

FORM 6: IN-KIND CONTRIBUTIONS

# THE CAMPAIGN TEAM

## *PEOPLE, PLACES AND THINGS*

To get your campaign work done, you need a team—a good team. Your campaign team will consist of a few people who will be paid and at least three times that number whom you cannot pay. And those you do pay will be hired for salaries far less lucrative than similar jobs in the private sector. Whom you attract, how many people you hire, what your chain of command becomes, and how everyone works together will ultimately determine the direction—and the success—of your efforts.

Campaigns become a metaphor for the way people perceive you will run government. Does your campaign attract many diverse individuals? Do you have a strong budget and spend your money wisely? Do you have an open-door policy that encourages everyone to be part of the picture? All of this gives clues to the press and public as to how you will perform in elected office.

Your campaign team is composed of many people: staff, consultants, volunteers, endorsers, contributors, vendors and supporters from throughout the community. The level of support you get from each one is very different, based on the role each person assumes. For example, people who contribute to your campaign are not necessarily endorsers, nor is their home an automatic site for a campaign yard sign. If someone is a vendor to your campaign, you may not assume that she is also a supporter. A supporter may not be someone you expect to walk door-to-door with you. The goal of any good campaign is to determine which level of involvement each person will have, once attracted to your campaign. It is possible that a few people will fall into all these categories. The challenge is to determine who will do what, as well as to ensure you are not taking a person's level of involvement for granted.

It's your campaign manager's job to be able to determine within minutes of meeting someone where he or she might fit in your campaign organization. *How you assemble people is as critical as getting them.* The campaign that is best in organizing its volunteers is the one that's likely to have the most, as volunteers are drawn like magnets to good campaigns. Campaigns that wander—appearing to make up tasks as they go—lose both momentum and volunteers.

Although you don't need a royal palace or a 12-room headquarters from which to centralize your campaign work, you do need a place that works to anchor your campaign workers, supplies and tasks. Many campaigns seek the cheapest headquarters when, for a few dollars more, they might find a place that helps build visibility and actually attracts more volunteers.

Supplies need not be first-class nor extravagant, yet they should help you get the job of message delivery done as efficiently as possible. Seek free supplies wherever you can, but don't be penny wise and pound foolish by making do when, for a few dollars more, your output could be professional and your volunteers happier.

# *How Good Campaigns Are Run*

Campaigns that have a variety of people representing all kinds of diversity, parties and perspectives help make the team a better representation of the general community. Campaign organizations thrive on newcomers from every corner of the community. Effective campaigns:

- Do their homework and research before developing strategy.
- Rely on good—but not all—advice.
- Stick to the strategy, but allow for good ideas to be added.
- Have realistic expectations of what can be accomplished.
- Hire competent, experienced people and let them do their jobs.
- Have a chain of command that everyone knows and no one changes.
- Communicate from the top down and the bottom up.
- Attract a wide variety of volunteers from diverse backgrounds, ages, cultures and experiences.
- Have the candidate around every once in awhile, just to talk to folks.
- Have few meetings—but also have few secrets.
- Provide ongoing training for everyone, especially in fundraising.
- Are more fun than your first roller coaster ride.

A campaign that has a spirit of teamwork and making things fun, coupled with a determined commitment to get the candidate's message out, is one that can handle the tough and tense days to come.

## Watching Out for Trouble

Power struggles between the steering committee and the manager, the candidate's exclusive control over the checkbook, and failure to make decisions can hamstring the best of campaigns; yet you can avoid all the above if you simply get your act together from the start.

Seldom will you find so many people ready to fight to the death for total control—and yet there is usually no money in the checking account and few assets when the war for control breaks out. The perception of power in politics can make the mildest of personalities become a rude tyrant almost overnight. To minimize the migraines, make sure that everyone understands her or his role and responsibilities so you can get on with the plan.

# Getting Professional Help

Consultants, particularly political consultants, are considered one of the necessary evils of today's campaign world. *Campaigns & Elections* magazine lists some 56 separate categories for today's political professionals, most of them consultants. There are media consultants, fundraising consultants, direct-mail consultants, pollsters, speech and image consultants, event specialists, database and list managers, and general consultants who will help you determine which, if any, of the others you will need.

The number of consultants is growing faster than the national debt. As in any business, there are good ones and there are those who are probably not worth the precious resources you have raised. How do you determine what kind you need? What do you pay them? If it doesn't work out, will they automatically release critical information about you to the press or your opponent?

Most candidates seldom call a consultant; consultants usually find the candidates. It's important to remember that consultants are in the business of moving public opinion on behalf of their clients. Doesn't it stand to reason that they would be equally as good at marketing themselves effectively to you, particularly if you have no idea what you need?

Before you agree to one meeting with a consultant, step back and reflect on what you might need—and what you can afford. Too many candidates end up hiring high-priced consultants—whom they are delighted to have help them—only to find that there is no money left to get a simple brochure out the door to targeted voters.

## *What You Should Know About Consultants*

Consultants usually find out about you from party leaders, the press or the official filing office of the state, county or local government. They already know if your seat is held by an incumbent or if it's going to be a hot race. They will have learned a little about who you are, and that you don't yet have a full team put together. It is not unusual for a consultant to call you before you have even filed.

You should know much more about the consultants you talk with than they know about you. If you decide you want to talk to one, make sure you talk to at least two before you settle on any. Let consultants you speak with know that you are looking around, and ask them if there is competition they respect. Talking with consultants in the early days of your campaign can be more than just interesting, it can be great on-the-job training for you. These political professionals are usually the best institutional memory of the campaign world. Download as much free information from them as they are willing to give. Consultants are very good at assessing the big picture, but be careful of those who offer specific strategic advice before they see all the numbers (polling, targeting, etc.) and facts of your race.

Before a meeting with consultants:

- Find out what kind of experience they have in races similar to yours in scope, budget, the local area, etc.
- Delve into their reputation for working with the entire campaign team.
- Compare their rates.
- Talk to winners and losers they have had; find out their apparent recent win/loss record (no consultant ever admits to having a win/loss ratio that is anything short of 4 to 1).
- Find out how people feel about their styles (direct, brutal, dependable, intense, always shooting-from-the hip, etc.).
- Get a handle on their strengths and weaknesses.
- Find out who else they may be marketing in your area from other candidates who have been approached.
- See if any of your prospective funders have worked with them in the past.
- Find out who loves to work with them.

Talk to those who prefer not to—or refuse to—work with them.

Have your act together before meeting with a consultant. Make sure that you are ready with good questions. Many different consultants would make your campaign team better, but which ones must you really have to win? Knowing how hard it is to raise money, ask yourself if you'd be willing to spend a dozen hours a month on the phone raising money to pay for the information they provide.

Ask prospective consultants:

- How do you propose to win this campaign?
- What do you know about my district that I don't?
- Who are your local contacts, and what is your institutional memory of the politics, voter trends, fundraising PACs and key endorsements in the area?
- What other races in this area have you already signed or are expecting to sign?
- What do you feel is new this year that may or may not be for me?

## Check out your consultant's:

- ➤ Experience
- ➤ Reputation
- ➤ Rates
- ➤ Winners and losers
- ➤ Style
- ➤ Strengths
- ➤ Weaknesses
- ➤ Other clients
- ➤ Friends and foes

- What do you perceive your role to be? What isn't your job?

- What value would you add to the team that may not be billable hours? (Many consultants have specific expertise for which they are paid, but they may add other quality information such as targeting or opposition research—or help with certain donors that you should know.)

- What is your staff support? May I see their resumés?

- How much of your staff time will I get instead of your time? (Do not be offended by time spent by the consultant's staff. In many cases they are better than the consultant. They stay home and do the work while the consultant specializes in analyzing what the staff has done.)

- What will the consulting cost? How do you bill? Is there a markup on some services? Are there administrative costs that are added to the bill? How often do you invoice, and what has to be paid up front? (Radio and TV spots—and the time buys for both—and direct mail usually must be paid for before they are released to the campaign). All of these costs are legitimate; just make sure you know what they are so there are no surprises.

This business is all about spin. Make sure you are the client—not the target.

## How to Choose a Consultant

As in any business, there is a growing role for consultants. Consultants should be able to give you competent advice that can save you precious money, time and other resources. Anyone who has ever had an idea used in a political campaign has probably toyed with being a political consultant. The perception of the consultant jetting around the country spilling her or his brains on the table for a campaign to consume, then getting back on the plane with a pocketful of money is unfair. Most consultants don't last two years in the business. The seasonal and fickle nature of the consulting trade forces people to seek other jobs to fill in the weak months and off-year cycles.

However, the ones that do survive have to be good. You might not like their previous candidates, their style, or their fees, but they are worthy of your respect and consideration.

Consultants are paid in various ways. If you want a consultant to be the main driver of your campaign, complete with campaign plan, direct mail, radio and TV production responsibilities, then you may want to hire her through a monthly retainer. The retainer usually means that all services, but not products, are included in the one fee you pay each month (except newspaper, TV or radio time-buy placement percentages).

You can pay consultants for specific services and projects such as a fee for writing the campaign plan, a fee for developing your message, or a fee for working with the press. You can pay consultants hourly as you would pay for any other professional service. Most consultants prefer a more definitive commitment than a few hours of consulting here and there.

You can pay for some services as part of the voter contact materials that are developed. For example, a media consultant is paid through the production and placement of the TV ads. A direct-mail consultant gets paid through the development of the brochures and a cut of the printing costs. However you determine whom you hire, ask if they get cuts of other business they bring to you.

Some consultants offer to do campaign work for a relatively small fee plus a large bonus if you win. The number of consultants who work on the "bonus" plan are dwindling, and those who do demand a much heftier price for their risk than had the campaign simply paid them up front.

Consider all your options—and your cash flow.

Choose a consultant:

- Based on intelligence (not just a good spin doctor).
- With creativity (fresh approaches, not last year's boilerplate).
- Who has analytical skills.
- With the ability to inspire or motivate.
- Who has a good grasp of the facts and politics in general.
- With the expertise you need.
- Whom you can afford.
- With a client list of candidates like you.
- Who has political talent that you don't already have on your team.
- Who has a style you can work with.

Remember that any one of many consultants could get you successfully over the finish line. Try to choose the one with whom you and your team can work best.

## Consultants You Should Not Hire

There are few consultants still in the business who are bad for you. There are many who will take advantage of any situation and client to make as much money as they can. Your job is to know enough about how they work so that you don't end up paying for their clever marketing.

More important than not hiring an unscrupulous consultant is the potential unfortunate timing of hiring a consultant. It is important to have your full team aboard as soon as possible, but it's not necessary to pay them until you need their services. Ask them to suggest schedules for payment and services and then compare it to others before you choose.

Don't hire:

- Someone with a big name, but little time to spend on you.
- A consultant with no specific duties—or duties they define, with no spending controls.
- Anyone you will be constantly second-guessing.
- Someone who has exclusive control of your budget, including radio, TV and other voter contact materials they produce.
- A consultant who allows constant interruptions when talking with you. Find someone who will focus on you when with you.
- Someone who doesn't get back in touch with you in a timely manner.
- A consultant who can't explain his billing.
- Anyone you can't afford.

Hiring a consultant should be the first step you take in building your campaign team. She should be ready with advice, names of other campaign professionals you may need, and a timeline for completing key projects. Though most campaign consultants don't require a contract, it's a good idea to spell out the general rules the two of you will be operating under throughout the course of the campaign.

# Job Descriptions

## The Candidate

The candidate's first and foremost job throughout the campaign is to raise money. Of course, this is only one of her many responsibilities. But if she did nothing more than sit on the phone and raise money, her campaign would stand a better chance of succeeding than most first-time candidates. A candidate is Chair of the Board of the campaign, hires the key people and consultants, and she is continually in search of connections that can assist her in her bid for office. The candidate determines where she stands on critical positions and issue directions, but does not write the issue papers. The candidate sets the ethical tone of the campaign, and, though she delegates many tasks to others, is the final authority. She okays all voter contact materials: from brochures, yard signs, and newspaper ads to radio and TV spots. She also courts the press and seeks out key supporters and endorsers.

Throughout the campaign, the candidate must keep up on the news and stay informed about what is happening within the campaign. Her day-to-day activities include raising money (continually), making speeches, pressing flesh and making her best effort to get places on time. And, all along, she manages her time well, takes care of herself, looks her best, stays healthy mentally and physically, and tries to be pleasant at all times.

Being a candidate is not as tough as it is sometimes boring. How many people can you really enjoy talking with when you've had little sleep for days? And how can you cleverly discipline yourself to make more than 1,000 phone calls for money in less than six months' time?

Candidates frequently suffer from the "I can do this faster than I can explain it to others" syndrome. Other syndromes include the "Why don't we ..." one, where the candidate comes up with good ideas as a defense mechanism against making her high-donor phone calls. The last syndrome of first-time candidates is "Just let me tweak this for a moment, then I'll get back to ..." Candidates do need to be their own person. They do need to be informed, and they have the right to change things at the last moment. However, that right may cost the election if the syndromes become habits.

### Candidate Control

Many candidates by their very nature are high-strung people—often Type-A's who figure they didn't get where they are by taking orders from people half their age. Campaign managers and schedulers can expect their candidate to hold onto her schedule as if it were a loved family pet. However, attempting to wrest total time control from the candidate or trying to get him to do high-donor phoning all day every day probably won't work. The solution is to allow the candidate to do one or two detail projects. This should be scheduled at the end of the day after all campaigning has been done. Every candidate should have time every other week for his or her personal support group, masseuse, a night out with friends or whatever is relaxing.

The candidate's job is to listen to those who are more objective about her than she can be about herself. She might not accept all the advice, help and perspectives coming her way, but she has a duty to listen and comply with her campaign responsibilities most of the time.

# The Campaign Manager

The campaign manager is the alter ego of the candidate. Common characteristics include self-confidence and being a quick study, as well as inspiring, motivating, creative, hard-working, a good problem-solver and the essence of quiet competence. The manager is usually hired after the consultant is aboard. She should help write the campaign plan with the consultant. She sees that the campaign follows that plan, and she checks in regularly with the consultant throughout the campaign. The manager wears many daily operational hats, including devising the media strategy and organizing the day-to-day message spins, with the press person if the campaign has one. Along with the candidate, the manager helps raise money and attract volunteers to the campaign.

The manager is the one who decides what needs to be done by when, by whom, with what resources and for how much money. She sets the direction of the campaign and hires and fires the rest of the campaign staff, although the candidate often has veto power over any prospective hires. On a day-to-day basis, the manager sets priorities for both time and money and oversees the short-term and long-term budget. The manager continually keeps the candidate informed and on track.

Campaign managers have more than enough to do without the responsibility of writing checks and balancing the checkbook. If the treasurer is accessible, available and amenable, it is best to have the treasurer write all checks. Whoever writes the checks, detailed records and receipts for each check written must be kept for public disclosure reporting.

Needless to say, a campaign manager works long hours and must stay informed on all campaign aspects—having her own sources and contacts that are not tied to the candidate. Some of the responsibilities a campaign manager might end up with include: stepping in for the candidate if a last-minute conflict comes up (so the manager needs good presence and speaking skills); keeping the candidate's family informed of schedule changes; and refereeing between warring forces within the campaign. If a valued member of the steering committee is at odds with the fundraiser, then it's the campaign manager who has to work the magic to bring them back together.

And, through it all, the manager needs to take care of herself while reducing the stress level within the campaign and maintaining her natural sense of humor.

| **A campaign manager is:** |
| --- |
| ➤ Self-confident |
| ➤ A quick study |
| ➤ Inspiring |
| ➤ Motivating |
| ➤ Creative |
| ➤ Hard-working |
| ➤ A problem solver |
| ➤ Quietly competent |

## Choosing the Right Person for You

In choosing your campaign manager, look for a person whose personality is well balanced with yours. This does not mean someone like you, but someone you respect, and who respects you. The campaign manager is often referred to as the second most important relationship in the candidate's life—the spouse being the first. You need to have confidence in your manager's competence, honesty and professionalism. You must be able to be open with her, and her with you. Most candidates report that they worry about their manager protecting them more than they feel they need to be protected. Candidates search for trustworthy managers who will tell it like it is, but not overdramatize news. Being a candidate is a roller-coaster ride in itself; you need not hire a manager who makes you bounce emotionally from day to day.

As you search for your manager, it's good to remember that you get what you pay for: if you pay more, you will get more. You may be able to hire an excellent manager for less than she might make somewhere else by promising her a job on your staff upon winning the election. Or you might promise a hefty bonus if you win. Some candidates offer to help the manager find a job if the campaign doesn't win. Whatever the promise, suffice it to say that paying as much as you can for the near-impossible job you're expecting is always the best bet.

As with all of the people that will be working full-time on your campaign, Internal Revenue Service regulations require that you treat the manager as an employee, which means withholding for and paying federal and state payroll taxes. Historically, many campaign staff members have not reported campaign income, as most campaigns treated them as independent contractors and did not report their compensation as the IRS requires. However, most campaign staffers meet the IRS definition of employees, so campaigns are legally required to treat them as such. While some campaigns still think they will get away with not withholding and paying payroll taxes, many others have been burned, making it an unwise choice for you to try to cheat Uncle Sam.

## *Where to Find a Campaign Manager*

An obvious place to find a campaign manager is former campaigns; this way you get someone with experience and a track record. Other people who often make good campaign managers are those who have started various types of advocacy groups, organizations and non-profit institutions. Also consider former political reporters, event fundraisers, and people who have served on the staff of legislators or public administrators. Don't forget the Democratic and Republican Parties, the League of Women Voters, and the National Women's Political Caucus—all of which are places you will find people looking for campaign jobs.

Also, there are at least ten political management schools in the country, in addition to several colleges and universities with expanded political science departments. Check to see which students may be graduating from your area colleges, then check on others who have gone away to school but might be returning to your area when school is out. Young people of all ages flock to presidential campaigns. Find out from your party organization who these people are that have been involved in presidential politics.

Law schools and university public relations and journalism departments are all good breeding grounds for today's political pro. Some schools have even listed campaign management among the most popular emerging careers of the 21st century. Let the professors know of your interest to give these students some on-the-job training, and they'll probably forward resumés and/or intern candidates to you.

### Hiring Rules

The first rule of any campaign hiring is to hire the best, regardless of sex, color, age and other characteristics unrelated to job performance. Don't think that just because you are a woman running for office you must have a man running your campaign. It's also a poor move to hire someone you think has a prestigious name in the community, but has no campaign experience. Agree on a starting monthly salary, with perhaps an increase after a short probationary period. Be sure to include health insurance and the promise of a future job if it is deserved.

# The Key Players

## Fundraiser

A good fundraiser knows how to ask for money and has raised it for others—many times. She has a database of potential donors and knows where to continually get updated lists of more names. She is a good detail person (important for pledge followup and thank-yous), and perseveres without becoming a nag. She must move in connected circles so that she knows people with money, and she is not afraid to cut to the quick and ask for it. More important than knowing how to ask for money, she needs to be good at closure—and getting the candidate to reach closure on the hundreds of calls he will make to prospective, receptive donors.

Your fundraiser should be a research-based person who fits in with your campaign team, makes her own resources, and is not easily distracted. She must be good at getting people to do their jobs as part of the fundraising efforts. Above all she must have the time to do the job. See the *Fundraising* chapter for other aspects of the fundraiser's day-to-day tasks.

## Office Manager

The major responsibilities of the campaign office manager are to assure that the phones are answered, the lights are on and that work is going on. Ensuring that the office runs smoothly is seldom acknowledged as a high priority of a campaign. However, campaigns that are run efficiently also:

- Attract more volunteers.
- Have fewer mistakes that end up on the front page of the newspaper.
- Get more projects done—and more done on deadline.
- Help keep the candidate focused.

# Sample Employment Contract

## Campaign: _____

This is an employment contract for professional services between _____, herein known as the candidate, and _____, herein known as the campaign manager, for mutual services to be performed in conjunction with the _____ Campaign.

## I. Services to Be Performed by the Campaign Manager

A. Drafting of a campaign plan outlining the overall campaign strategy, including a press plan, budget, fundraising plan, timeline, field plan, organizational chart, targeting analysis and a scheduling strategy. The campaign plan will be completed within thirty days of the date of hiring the manager.

B. Assembling a campaign staff, full-time and part-time, paid and volunteer, to carry out the key responsibilities of the campaign. Hiring decisions will be made by the manager after consulting with the candidate. The manager will monitor the progress of the staff during the campaign and make any changes deemed necessary.

C. Managing the office, including setting priorities for personnel and financial resources, as well as setting office policies, making personnel decisions and maintaining quality control. The manager may delegate responsibilities to other members of the campaign staff as required by time restrictions.

D. Determining the consultants needed by the campaign, seeking appropriate applicants, and recommending specific consultants to the candidate. No consultant will be engaged without the consent of the candidate.

E. Being chief spokesperson for the campaign on matters involving the campaign finances, strategy, staff and all operations. The manager is responsible for accumulating information on opposing campaigns and generally being information central for the _____ Campaign.

F. Staying in contact with and being considerate of the candidate's family and their need for time and attention from the candidate and campaign.

## II. Services to Be Performed by the Candidate

A. Setting the theme, issues and message of the campaign to include the vision and tone of both the candidate and campaign, as well as the attitudes that will inspire and lead the campaign team. The candidate will also be the spokesperson on all issues and policies important to public administration and leadership for the district.

B. Keeping to schedule, which includes a skilled time-management commitment to making phone calls for high-donor contributions, attending community events and generally meeting voters, public speaking that is well thought-out and prepared prior to the event, and minimizing time not dedicated to the campaign.

C. Being the singular Board of Appeals on all campaign matters that supporters or constituents may not find resolved by the campaign manager.

D. Advising the campaign manager on strategy, personnel decisions, timelines and priorities for both personnel and financial resources. In addition, the candidate will take time to personally thank the staff and volunteers for their dedication, ideas and work.

E. Promising to keep up a strong, sharp personal appearance and healthy lifestyle so that we might all benefit by his determined example, and assuring that his car is in good repair throughout the campaign.

## III. Just Compensation

A. The campaign manager will be paid a salary of $3,000 per month plus expenses, as approved in the budget. The salary will be paid monthly on the last day of the month. In addition, if the candidate wins the general election, the manager will be paid a bonus of $3,000.

## IV. Final Clause

A. This contract represents an agreement between the campaign manager and the candidate to respect each other's opinions, to listen to each other's advice and to criticize and applaud each other's accomplishments throughout the duration of the campaign. This partnership allows for each partner to make three decisions during the course of the campaign that may stand without explanation or rationalization. We will both remember that we are each other's strongest campaign supporters, and that our personal successes are tied to the communication between the two of us.

Signed and delivered after a probationary period of working in partnership:

_____          _____

*Candidate*                                                              *Campaign Manager*

*FORM 7: SAMPLE EMPLOYMENT CONTRACT*

The office manager's chores are many, and they are important. The job includes opening the mail each day and making sure each piece of paper brought into the office gets to the right person. The office manager keeps tabs on all office supplies, making sure the campaign never runs out of anything crucial. He maintains a list of the names, addresses and phone numbers of all key campaign people, including vendors, and revises the information when appropriate. The office manager also makes sure that everyone who answers the phone knows what to say—and what not to say.

The office manager should be aboard early in the campaign to help with the innumerable details involved in finding and setting up an office. He also sets up all office systems and procedures, and then has the job of assuring that they are adhered to by the staff. The office manager should be someone who can handle the stress of doing many things at once, as he will be the person who knows where everything is and how everything works. Unfortunately, he's also the one everyone thinks they can turn to for help— at the same time. A good office manager is not superhuman, just super-resourceful.

# Scheduler

*The scheduler is the only person with the authority to commit the candidate's time.*

Perhaps the most stressful job in the campaign is that of the scheduler. She's the one who is responsible for pages of directions, dozens of phone calls to confirm and reconfirm details of times, dates and places—and she's responsible for the accuracy of hundreds of people who will call the campaign with their directions, dates and details of events.

A scheduler must have the patience of a saint, the fortitude of a gold-rush miner, a hide of steel, and the organizational capacity of a mother of triplets to handle the details.

The campaign scheduler keeps the master schedule for the campaign. No one else has the authority to commit the candidate's time. In addition to responding to all requests for candidate appearances, she seeks out invitations for the candidate to meet with groups of voters. She is responsible for getting all details about each event, advising the candidate on appropriate attire, and arranging the candidate's transportation. She briefs the candidate each day on any schedule changes, is always on the lookout for press opportunities, and generally keeps the candidate on track.

The scheduler reports directly to the candidate and campaign manager. In well-financed campaigns, the scheduler has a pager and a cellular phone that is reserved exclusively for the candidate and manager to call and check on details. Schedulers must be accessible, and they have to commit major portions of the work week to being in contact with the campaign and people who wish to reach the candidate.

Schedulers are best found in jobs that require the organization of zillions of details. Realtors, travel agents, secretaries, full-time parents and former campaign managers are all good places to look for help. If a candidate already has someone who is handling her scheduling, that person might be the best choice for the campaign scheduling job. See the *Scheduling* chapter for other details about the scheduler's job.

# Database Manager

An absolute must for any campaign is to have a well-maintained database of names, addresses and phone numbers of all people the campaign will need to contact through the course of the campaign.

The earlier in the campaign you start to put all this together, the better, and the database should be compiled—or at least supervised—by the person who will maintain it. The database will continually evolve over the course of the campaign, and will be an invaluable tool for many campaign functions. But before you determine what kind of computer your campaign will have, choose your database manager. Too many campaigns have wasted large amounts of time and money investing in computers and computer programs that are not appropriate for the campaign functions.

A campaign is no time to train a computer/database manager: time is too short for that. Make sure your computer guru has experience with a variety of programs, computers, and other features like the Internet, e-mail, modems, etc. Also make sure that she understands the critical nature of the data she is organizing and inputting.

Confidentiality, dependability, accessibility and the ability to make computer-illiterate volunteers feel welcome at the computer terminals are all valuable assets to find in a database manager. Although computer language is slowly filtering down to the rest of the world, your computer guru should be able to explain more than just why she needs to spend more of the campaign funds for upgrades, backups and new networking capabilities. And she will need to communicate well with the workforce who will be doing the data entry.

Computer people can be found in computer labs all over the place, or you may find your database manager through a previous campaign in your area. Ask your business database manager, or the person who works the computers for your political party to help you train a person who is already computer-literate, but perhaps a newcomer to campaigns. See the *Computers and Campaign Technology* chapter for more information about a computer/database manager.

# Media Coordinator

The media coordinator is responsible for all communication between the press and the campaign. Always on the lookout for press opportunities, she coordinates all campaign press releases and press conferences. In addition, the media coordinator is responsible for completing all campaign questionnaires accurately and on time. She coordinates the opposition research and issue research and helps brief the candidate before her speeches and debates.

The media person is as important in many campaigns as the manager. She must be ever-mindful about the facts the campaign and candidate are using that reflect issues and campaign news. She must have good writing, researching and speaking skills. She must be able to "spin" a bad situation within seconds, reflecting the best angles for her candidate. A press person usually has had some experience within the media itself—serving as a reporter, a public relations professional or as a spokesperson for an organization or other elected official.

You need to find a press person whom you can trust. A press person is someone you can tell the worst of all news. If there is something in your past that is likely to blow up in the context of the campaign, the press person needs to know it as soon as you have her confidence and she has your respect. Nothing can sink a campaign faster than a press person being caught not knowing an important, but negative, fact regarding her candidate. The press can sense if your spokesperson is getting and giving all the facts. She needs to be ready for anything and everything, which can only happen if she is well-informed and has immediate access to you. Since campaigns have a nasty habit of making the press person relate to the candidate those critical stories the press is writing, remember that the press person is on your side, even if she appears to be fending for the reporter. A good press person will interpret the press and give you strategy on how best to get good press. If you feel like punishing a reporter for continually giving you bad press, but your press person advocates keeping communication open, she's not just doing her job, she's doing a good job.

# Field Coordinator

The campaign field coordinator's responsibilities include organizing the phone banks, door-to-door canvassing, construction and placement of yard signs, participation in parades and sign-waving activities. He or she must be a planner experienced in dealing with lots of people and good at getting things for free, such as yard sign stakes or labor to assemble the signs. A good field person is familiar with the district, understands targeting and endorsement procedures, and is good with people and details. Ideally you will find for this job a friendly, hands-on person who is a good delegator, energetic and focused, but also can see the big picture.

Campaign field positions allow a person to learn about politics from the bottom up: doing the grassroots work that got political campaigns started two hundred years ago. Field workers are good with people, understand enough about math and numbers to stick with the targeting plan, and work in a disciplined manner so that the necessary work gets done.

You can find good field people by checking out past campaigns to see who the interns were, or young people who have just graduated from college. Since field work includes a lot of walking, phoning and mailing parties, it's good to have a coordinator who can do all these things herself. See more about the field coordinator's responsibilities in the *Field Operations* chapter.

# Volunteer Coordinator

The ultimate volunteer coordinator is a self-starting, enthusiastic, supportive, thoughtful person who cares about people and has lots of friends. A good listener, persistent, and a detail person, he or she moves in large circles of political activists and can size up people quickly. This ideal person works well with people of all ages, is fun, a great team-builder, and can instill a good work ethic in those volunteers she recruits.

The volunteer coordinator maintains a database of all campaign volunteers, their skills and their times of availability. In minutes, she can tell what people can do which tasks well. A good volunteer coordinator is a considerate person who remembers the little things about people, which makes people want to work for her.

Volunteer coordinators can be found in all organizations, businesses, and professional associations. They are the ones who put together the company picnic, the holiday celebration or the going-away parties. Volunteer coordinators like to phone people and don't mind asking them to do work, even if they just volunteered yesterday. These people are worth their weight in gold. Seek them out and sign them up. See more about volunteer coordinators in Chapter 12.

# Treasurer

The treasurer must be someone in whom you have utmost confidence from the beginning. She must be good with money, as the stakes are way too high to make a mistake. The treasurer is the only person in the campaign besides the candidate whose mistakes can result in serious fines and court dates. The treasurer must, therefore, be trustworthy, experienced (hopefully having

# Key Persons List

| | Name | Home Phone | Work Phone | Cellular Phone | Fax |
|---|---|---|---|---|---|
| **Staff** | | | | | |
| Campaign Manager | | | | | |
| Computer/Database Manager | | | | | |
| Fundraiser | | | | | |
| Office Manager | | | | | |
| Scheduler | | | | | |
| Treasurer | | | | | |
| **Coordinators** | | | | | |
| Field Coordinator | | | | | |
| Home Fundraiser Coordinator | | | | | |
| Mailing Coordinator | | | | | |
| Media Coordinator | | | | | |
| Phone Bank Supervisor | | | | | |
| Volunteer Coordinator | | | | | |
| Yard Sign Coordinator | | | | | |
| **Committee Chairs** | | | | | |
| Events Committee Chair | | | | | |
| Finance Committee Chair | | | | | |
| Issues Committee Chair | | | | | |
| Steering Committee Chair | | | | | |
| **Consultants** | | | | | |
| General Consultant | | | | | |
| Media Consultant | | | | | |
| Photographer | | | | | |
| Speech and Image Consultant | | | | | |
| **Other** | | | | | |
| | | | | | |
| | | | | | |

FORM 8: KEY PERSONS LIST

done the job in the past), accessible during the day, night and weekend to write needed checks, and willing to learn and understand all the rules and regulations of public disclosure commissions. See more of the details about the treasurer in the *Fundraising* chapter.

# Yard Sign Coordinator

Although yard signs are a part of the campaign's field operations, larger campaigns will have a yard sign coordinator in addition to the field coordinator.

Your campaign will need a band of trusty crusaders to hit the streets regularly looking for new spots to place those darling little yard signs. Good yard sign teams have three responsibilities covered:

- Securing and organizing all the supporters who will allow yard signs to be placed in their yards or windows.
- Construction of the yard signs so they might be placed with ease and consistency once the locations have been secured.
- Placement and maintaining of yard signs in the designated areas.

In all these cases, the yard sign coordinator needs to be a good task-master who will work weekends and evenings. The job requires about four or five hours a week, depending on how many signs you want to keep posted. A good campaign puts the signs up once after it is legally appropriate to do so (about 90 days from primary or general election day), and then usually has to replace each sign at least once before election day, due to vandalism or the weather.

# Mailing Coordinator

A person who keeps up on all the changes in postal regulations is someone you want to keep in mind for your mailing coordinator. These folks are usually called on every time you have an invitation to mail, a fundraising letter to send, or a piece of direct mail that the campaign can't afford to send to a mailing house.

The mailing coordinator may or may not be responsible for securing others to help with the mailings, but he must be available at the times volunteers are most able to work (nights, weekends and holidays). Depending on the nature of the campaign, the mailing coordinator is usually not needed every day—but is needed with more frequency as the campaign nears the final stretch.

Mailing coordinators should attend one of the trainings offered by the U.S. Postal Service on all the nuances of the mailing system. They are responsible for keeping a supply of the cardboard trays, special stickers, rubber bands, and mailing bags to sort and ready the mailings for the post office.

## Phone Bank Supervisor

If your campaign has lots of volunteers willing to identify supportive voters for your Get-Out-The-Vote program, or to remind people of an upcoming fundraising event, you'll want to operate a phone bank. Your phone bank supervisor is the person who secures the locations for phone banks—offices with at least five phone lines available in the evening. The supervisor oversees the phoning, making sure that the integrity of phoning undecided voters is maintained. For example, if a phone bank supervisor overhears a phoner arguing with a voter or recording responses too optimistically, given the actual response of the voter, then he or she should intervene and instruct the volunteer to do the job objectively, or reassign that volunteer to other needed work.

# *Campaign Committees*

## Steering Committee

The Steering Committee is formed at the beginning of the campaign to get things started, to assess the opposition, weigh the pros and cons of the campaign and devise pre-emption strategies. The members of this committee are expected to do real work, mainly raise money and help with PAC and other endorsements. During the campaign, this committee advises the candidate and provides a reality check from the community and various groups and organizations. The names of the committee members should appear on the campaign letterhead, and these people should be visible in various capacities throughout the campaign.

### *Hints for an Effective Steering Committee*

- Organize a steering committee by first identifying what you want the members to do. Put the desired qualities in writing.
- Do your homework before asking supporters to be a member of your steering committee:
    - ➢ What do they want out of being on your steering committee?
    - ➢ What rules or guidelines do they suggest?
    - ➢ What time do they have to give?

- What will they bring to the table?
- Where does this campaign fit in their list of priorities?
- What would they like to do?
- What would they like to learn?

- Define all committee assignments, including days of regular meetings, other committee members, the chairperson, and the time and other commitments expected.

- Let everyone know that each person will have to put serious time into fundraising, but that you will train them, then have a fundraising workshop within 30 days.

- Establish rules and a process for breaking them. Get familiar with Robert's Rules of Order or a comparable alternative.

- Have fewer large meetings, more small meetings, and always have a written agenda.

- If you want the big cheeses from your key organizations on your steering committee, be sure they delegate an assistant to attend meetings and do followup when they cannot.

## Handling conflict

For reasons as yet unknown to the human mind, steering committees tend to be a breeding ground for some of the most horrific battles over control of resources not yet accumulated. When the expected blow-ups come, be ready with a plan to handle the conflict. Remember that steering committees exist for too short a time to make use of a good therapy program; instead, try these hints:

- Appoint a chair who's fair and focused, with a good sense of humor.
- Delegate conflict points to a special subcommittee of trusted members who are skilled at conflict resolution. Appoint this group before the committee starts meeting.
- Structure the debate to allow conflict to be discussed rationally and logically.
- When quantifiable data or polling can be used to referee a point in question, use it.
- Watch for control issues, as opposed to real conflicts of direction, opinion or resources.
- Discourage whispering campaigns, secret side meetings or "my way or nothing" attitudes.
- Suggest that members with ongoing conflicts take a hike—together.
- After a tough meeting, summarize what happened, circulate it to members and ask how to improve the situation, should it arise again.

# Kitchen Cabinet

The kitchen cabinet is your group of personal advisors. This group consists of a handful of trusted people: usually the spouse, a few close friends, the consultant, the manager and perhaps a chief fundraiser or donor. You consult with them on such matters as whether to run, when to consider pulling out of the race, and how to respond to negative attacks from other candidates. They provide advice on key campaign hirings and financial matters, such as loans to the campaign, and they serve as a reality check on values.

This group may never have to meet, or it might meet only three or four times as emergencies suggest. But it's good to have these folks in mind and agreeing before the campaign is started.

# Finance Committee

The Finance Committee's number one job is to raise money for the campaign, which includes each committee member giving the maximum allowable contribution, if possible. Their names should appear on the campaign letterhead, and they should each hold home fundraisers and attend all major fundraising events. They raise money by getting sponsors and selling tickets to campaign events and recruiting contributors from among their political acquaintances known to be high donors. Committee members accompany the candidate to places where she can be introduced to high donors, set up conference calls with potential donors, and dial for dollars directly themselves. See the *Fundraising* chapter for other details.

# Events Committee

The Events Committee builds campaign momentum and injects the campaign with lots of fun and visibility. Committee members are responsible for the planning and implementation of events, which includes getting sponsors, selling tickets, decorating for the events and cleaning up afterward. They also collect money and in-kind contributions at the events. Other events committee responsibilities include phone banks and mailing parties.

# Issues Committee

It is the job of the Issues Committee to prepare the campaign's issue papers. There need not be an issue paper prepared on every issue of the campaign, nor even every issue the candidate has a strong opinion on. The committee should prepare well-researched and well-written papers on no more than five issues.

In addition to the issue papers, the job of filling out questionnaires falls to this committee, along with the media coordinator. There will be many of these questionnaires from many associations, newspapers and special-interest groups. Although each group will of course include issues specific to its interests, there will be a lot of overlap on the more general issues. Thus, the easiest way to answer these questionnaires is to do a lot of cutting and pasting in your word processor.

Other duties of the Issues Committee are: briefing the candidate before debates, newspaper interviews and other special meetings; writing the candidate's in-depth speeches (but not the key three-minute "stump" speech); and preparing the candidate's response to those difficult questions that will probably be asked of her when she least expects it.

Items not included among this committee's responsibilities are developing the campaign message and slogan and writing the candidate statement for the voters' pamphlet.

# The Campaign Committee

In smaller campaigns that don't have all the above committees, there may be only the Campaign Committee, with all the duties outlined for the separate committees described above. In other campaigns, it is a way to bring everyone together, communicate, bolster the candidate and rally the troops. The Campaign Committee consists of honorary chairs (two or three), all committee chairs and any campaign staff who want to be included, but no consultants. This committee raises money, teaches others how to raise money, builds momentum, and levels the playing field for everyone.

# Anatomy of a Good Campaign Meeting

No matter what committee may be meeting, there are some simple rules to keep the meeting moving and pertinent to those attending. Advance notice is a must, with a reminder call to each member. If the reminder calls reveal that fewer than half the people can attend, the meeting should be rescheduled. A good meeting always has a written agenda, distributed in advance if possible. A good way to energize any meeting is to bring a stack of contribution checks. Every meeting should consist of news given out and news brought in. There should be reports of campaign goals reached and those being worked toward, and a report on the opponent's campaign. Assignments should be given to each attendee (and to some non-attendees), and the meeting should be over in less than two hours.

# Campaign Organization Chart

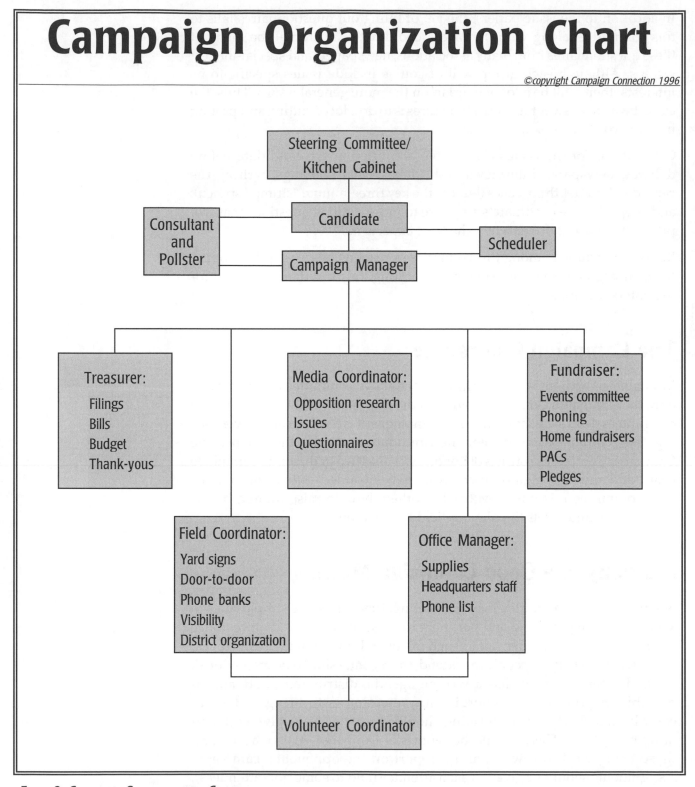

**Steering Committee/ Kitchen Cabinet**

**Consultant and Pollster**

**Candidate**

**Scheduler**

**Campaign Manager**

**Treasurer:**

Filings
Bills
Budget
Thank-yous

**Media Coordinator:**

Opposition research
Issues
Questionnaires

**Fundraiser:**

Events committee
Phoning
Home fundraisers
PACs
Pledges

**Field Coordinator:**

Yard signs
Door-to-door
Phone banks
Visibility
District organization

**Office Manager:**

Supplies
Headquarters staff
Phone list

**Volunteer Coordinator**

FORM 9: CAMPAIGN ORGANIZATION CHART

# *Choosing a Headquarters*

A campaign headquarters can be a fun place to work, retreat to, or create. It may be dirty, dingy and small, with few windows, but as magnetic in drawing volunteers and supporters as a yacht. Your job is not to find the cheapest headquarters; rather, it is to find one that will maximize your limited resources.

In the early days of a campaign, most candidates use their home or office (if not a government employee) as a campaign base of operation. However, soon after a campaign manager is hired, the search should begin for a decent headquarters. Warehouses, former headquarters for other campaigns, offices that have been vacant for a long time, empty houses, or the offices of a friend of the candidate that can be rented cheaply are common locations. Try to locate a headquarters that will allow you room to grow. Other factors to take into consideration for your headquarters include:

1. *A good place for volunteers:* Is the proposed location on a bus route? Does it have ample free or inexpensive parking? Is the lighting adequate? Is it in a neighborhood where people can feel safe walking at night? Is the location convenient for the candidate to stop by several times a day? Is it close to the printer, the post office, restaurants, etc.?

2. *A good place to be seen:* Is the location one that many people will see every day? Can you place signs on top of the building or in the windows? Do the city's "insiders" drive by this location frequently so they will see all the activity going on? Is it in an area that may give your campaign a bad name, such as near a strip joint or an area known for drug dealing?

3. *A good buy:* Can you get the landlord to donate a portion of the rent to the campaign as an in-kind contribution? Are the utilities included in the rent? Is there garbage service available? Can you expand easily as the campaign grows? Can you get insurance at this location? Most landlords will require you to have fire and liability insurance. In addition, you should consider theft and contents insurance, especially if a lot of people have loaned the campaign equipment and supplies.

4. *Good for campaign needs:* Is the building conducive to the wear and tear that campaigns usually exert? Is there enough electrical capacity for several TV cameras? Is there a telephone system in place, or will you need to install one? What about the configuration of the offices: are there places to have a discreet meeting and private conversations?

These and more factors go into securing a good headquarters. Remember, though, a good headquarters makes for very happy volunteers who are likely to be more ready, willing and able to help you when you call if the location is accessible, reasonably functional, and a fun place to be, as opposed to unsafe or about to fall down.

# Headquarters Daily Operations

Your campaign is a business, and as such it needs to have rules guiding the day-to-day operations of the headquarters. The pace of a campaign is always somewhat hectic, which can quickly lead to disaster if basic guidelines are not followed. The following guidelines should help you set up your own rules.

***Office hours:*** Though campaign workdays are always longer than the standard eight hours, the headquarters should establish official hours of operation during which someone will always be in the office. From 8:30 a.m. to 6:30 p.m. on weekdays, at least 10:00 a.m. to 3:00 p.m. on Saturday and a few hours on Sunday are good guidelines.

***Dress code:*** Most campaigns have casual dress codes or no code at all. However, even the most casual office will have days when something special is going on and everyone needs to dress up. These occasions should be announced a few days in advance and dress guidelines given.

***Opening the office:*** The first person to the office each day should unlock the doors, bring in any newspapers left outside, turn on the lights and put the coffee on. She should retrieve all messages from the answering machine and any faxes that came in overnight, making sure they all get to the appropriate people.

***In/out board:*** To keep the campaign running smoothly, it is absolutely necessary that staff members check in and out of the office as they come and go. People out of the office should make it clear when they will return. The campaign may decide to have a cellular phone or two so that some key people can be reached at all times.

***Phones:*** Establish a standard method of answering the phone. Always have message pads by each phone and a central place for phone messages. Also set strict guidelines on directing incoming calls: all invitations go to the scheduler; press calls go to the media coordinator or campaign manager, etc.

***Supplies:*** The office manager is in charge of supplies. She should set up a system that assures the office has the supplies it needs when it needs them while staying within the campaign budget. The system also needs to guard against supplies disappearing to places unknown.

***Housekeeping:*** Very few campaign headquarters have janitorial service, so the task of keeping the place clean falls to the staff. Every staff member should be responsible for keeping his/her area clean, and rules need to be established to keep the common areas clean. If you have a kitchen area, each staff person should wash his own dishes and clean up his own messes.

*Mail:* Mail delivered to the office is opened by the office manager and distributed to the appropriate people. It is crucial that no one retrieve the mail who does not know the office rules for distributing it.

*Reception:* The office manager also serves as the official receptionist. It is crucial to present a friendly and professional image to all people who come in the door. This can make a big difference in whether or not those who drop by the office become supporters, contributors and volunteers.

*Files:* The job of setting up a central filing system falls to the office manager. It is important to keep the files up-to-date and organized, as there will be constant demand for various items. Don't let anyone take files out of the office without making a copy first.

*Money:* The office manager is in charge of petty cash. The campaign treasurer is in charge of writing checks. Anyone needing to make a purchase should get it approved in advance by the campaign manager or the office manager. Campaign workers who purchase items with their own money will be reimbursed, but the expenditure must be approved in advance if the campaign is going to stay within budget.

*Invitations:* The scheduler is responsible for handling all invitations, which may come by mail, by phone, or occasionally in person. In the absence of the scheduler, someone else in the office should be familiar with the scheduling request form and how to respond to invitations.

*Daily activities:* There should be a bulletin board or other posting place advising of the day's campaign activities, especially those things happening at the headquarters. This would include staff meetings, which should be brief, but are absolutely necessary to keep everyone informed on campaign developments.

*Contributions:* There will occasionally be contributions delivered to the headquarters in person. It is crucial that these are given directly to the office manager to be processed in the same way as those that come in the mail. There is no excuse for lost contribution checks!

*Smoking/drinking:* Many buildings have no-smoking policies, and if yours doesn't, you should establish one in your headquarters. You could consider having a smoking area if you have ample space, but be aware that allowing smoking in your headquarters could cost you the services of a number of volunteers. Alcoholic beverages in the campaign headquarters should be strictly confined to special occasions, and then make sure that no underage people are served. The last thing a campaign needs is a felony charge for serving a minor.

# Headquarters Needs

## Supplies

- ❑ Aspirin
- ❑ Calendar
- ❑ Cassette tapes
- ❑ Chalk board
- ❑ Computer diskettes
- ❑ Computer paper
- ❑ Copy paper
- ❑ Correction fluid
- ❑ Dictionary
- ❑ Easels
- ❑ Envelope sealers
- ❑ File folders
- ❑ Glue
- ❑ Highlighters
- ❑ Marking pens
- ❑ Message pads
- ❑ Notebooks
- ❑ Paper clips
- ❑ Pencil sharpener
- ❑ Pencils
- ❑ Pens
- ❑ Post-its
- ❑ Push pins
- ❑ Rubber bands
- ❑ Scissors
- ❑ Scratch pads
- ❑ Staples
- ❑ Tape
- ❑ Thesaurus
- ❑ Writing tablets

## Equipment

- ❑ 35 mm camera
- ❑ Answering machine
- ❑ Button machine
- ❑ Calculator
- ❑ Coffee maker
- ❑ Computer printer
- ❑ Computers
- ❑ Copy machine
- ❑ Dictaphone
- ❑ Fax machine
- ❑ Kitchen utensils
- ❑ Lock box
- ❑ Postage scale
- ❑ Radio
- ❑ Staplers
- ❑ Tape dispensers
- ❑ Tape recorder
- ❑ Telephones
- ❑ Television
- ❑ Typewriters
- ❑ VCR

## Furnishings

- ❑ Bookcases
- ❑ Computer tables
- ❑ Couch
- ❑ Desk chairs
- ❑ Desk files
- ❑ Desk lamps
- ❑ Desks
- ❑ Diskette file boxes
- ❑ File cabinets
- ❑ Fire extinguisher
- ❑ First-aid kit
- ❑ Folding chairs
- ❑ In/out trays
- ❑ Message holders
- ❑ Microwave
- ❑ Refrigerator
- ❑ Tool kit
- ❑ Work tables

FORM 10: HEADQUARTERS NEEDS

***Closing:*** It may seem like the headquarters never closes, but when it does, be sure to close and lock all windows and doors, turn off the coffee pot, copy machine, printers and computers, and turn on the answering machine with an up-to-date, lively, outgoing message, like: "You've reached the Jane Harris campaign. We're all marching in the Lakeview community parade today with our wonderful candidate who was endorsed yesterday by the Municipal League ..."

# Furnishing the Headquarters

Ideally you will be able to borrow or have donated to the campaign all the furnishings and equipment you will need. Campaign staff often bring their computers and other items to the headquarters for the campaign to use, and seasoned campaign workers always have a list of sources of cheap or free furnishings and supplies.

For each item loaned to the campaign, be sure to label it with the name and phone number of the owner, so you can return it at the end of the campaign. Also, it is important to check with your public disclosure office to determine if the use of any of these items must be reported as an in-kind contribution.

# The Growing Campaign

Campaigns are very versatile organisms. They grow slowly at first, unsure of each step, but forging ahead nonetheless. They expand gradually and then grow in great spurts. In the process, they may mutate, lay dormant for spells, or spread in directions you never planned or ever imagined they would. However, they are a living thing. The best ones change with the people, talent, and resources brought (or not brought) their way. However, they have a direction and a plan.

Build your campaign as a living one. Follow the plan, but let it grow, and learn from that growth. It will make you much more apt to survive than those campaigns that refuse to grow even though people, places and things demand it.

# *FUNDRAISING*

## *GETTING YOUR CAMPAIGN MOVING*

Fundraising has been called the mother's milk of politics. You may not win with it, but you certainly won't win without it. More than all the other factors put together, fundraising determines today's winners and losers in the campaign world.

Fundraising is the cornerstone of getting your message out to the right voters. It is also the anchor which allows you to contract with the help you need to pull your plan together. Direct mail, radio, TV, yard signs and all the other avenues for getting attention cost money. And, in most cases, the money you raise in the early days of the campaign signals to the press who is a viable candidate and who isn't.

Despite all the campaign finance rules and regulations enacted in the past two decades, the cost of today's campaigns continues to skyrocket. Politics is no longer a spectator sport, nor is it reserved for a few insiders who get to call the shots just because they always have. The rough-and-tumble world of today's campaigns is growing more professional. From telemarketing phone banks to voter list services, the vendors who now service the political market comprise a list that's as long as your arm. And services that were once the exclusive realm of volunteers are now being paid for in many campaigns.

All of this costs money … lots of it.

Asking for money is commonly the least favorite job—and the most important one—that candidates assume when they declare for office. Unless you are independently wealthy and can buy everything yourself (and even then, voters are likely to look askance at such a person), your life on the campaign trail will involve much more dialing for dollars than asking for votes.

But, no need for despair. For every $1,000 you raise, there are hundreds of people who will get your message. And for everyone who contributes to your campaign, there are several more who will be influenced by that person's commitment. Someone who writes a check is definitely going to vote, and is likely to tell his housemates, office colleagues and friends about his choice.

If someone invests in your campaign, he or she is likely to be an honorary member of your fan club. In fact, reporters looking for an interesting approach to the money of today's campaigns usually look at two numbers: the amount of money raised, and the total number of contributors. In many state legislative races, it's frequently the case that the candidate who has the most contributors is likely to win, even if the other candidate has raised more money.

How much money do you need? It's hard to say, but there are lots of clues to determining what you will need to win:

- How much was spent by candidates who ran in this race last cycle?
- What has changed since the last race (new regulations, redistricting, incumbent in trouble, voters wanting change, etc.)?
- Are you a challenger? (The race will cost more.)
- Are you the incumbent? (It should cost less, but you will be able to raise more.)
- Is this an open seat with many candidates? (The campaign may cost less than a challenger race.)
- Were you appointed to this office to fill a vacancy, and now must run for election? (This could cost less.)
- How many people are in the race?
- What else is on the ballot? Is this a presidential election year, a gubernatorial election year or an off-year election?
- Who or what else is on the ballot with similar values or party allegiances that might compete for the money you will solicit?
- What base of support are you starting with, and how many votes do you think it will take to win?
- Will your preferred method of voter contact be direct mail, radio or TV?
- What else will influence the cost?

The answers to these questions will help you determine how much your campaign will cost. If you start with campaign actual costs from the previous cycle and the number of voters you must get your message to in order to win, you will have a good base upon which to begin the budgeting process. After you budget, then tackle the fundraising.

Raising money requires discipline. It requires organization. It means being persistent. Asking for money and getting it also requires good timing, a sense of humor and enough self-esteem that you can handle rejection as much as 70 percent of the time over the course of a campaign day.

It is not an easy job, but if you put time and energy into understanding the nature of fundraising, you can raise as much money as you need and more money than you think.

# Raising Money the Right Way

Candidates are always overwhelmed by the amount of money they must raise. Most hate the job long before they ever learn how to do it properly—and all too often candidates pick up poor habits in phoning for donations and make the process longer, more arduous and painful as they go. The unfortunate truth is that most candidates spend more time learning about superficial issues than learning how to ask for money. Campaign managers and steering committees routinely criticize their candidates for not getting on the phone and raising money, when the only assistance they provide is a phone book, a telephone and an ultimatum to raise $100,000.

*You may not win with money, but you certainly won't win without it.*

Some campaigns begin by determining how much money they think they can raise and then putting a budget together to meet those expectations. Such logic is fatally flawed. After all, if you only raise the money you think you can, and that's not enough to win, then all your efforts will be in vain from the start. A good campaign plan begins with a reasonable budget that assesses what it will take to win and then develops a fundraising plan to raise the needed funds.

Successful fundraising depends on many factors:

- A multifaceted, written campaign plan.
- A seasoned fundraising coordinator.
- Good research on previous high donors.
- Updated lists of prospective donors on disk.
- The right fundraising message.
- Enough time dedicated to raising money.
- Enough money to pay for mailings and events.
- The right attitude of the candidate.

Learning to raise money requires dedication, concentration and a lot of people. Though most campaign workers offer to help in many capacities along the campaign trail, few offer to help with fundraising. However, if half the campaign team were given a quick training on how to raise money the painless way, candidates would have more help, and more fun in accomplishing this critical campaign task.

# Who Will Help You Raise Money?

In today's campaign world, everyone needs to raise money. There should be no separation of functions between volunteers and fundraisers. Everyone should help with fundraising. What can a relative novice do to help? How can people help raise money when they have little time to do so? And how can fundraising be a less tedious chore?

## Who will give you money?

*People who:*

➤ *Know you and/or grew up with you.*

➤ *Give money to campaigns every year.*

➤ *Have worked with you on important issues or campaigns.*

➤ *Like what you have to say and what you stand for.*

➤ *Encouraged you to run for office.*

➤ *Know someone else on your campaign.*

➤ *Dislike the other candidate.*

➤ *Want to belong to the winning team.*

➤ *Will want something from you after the election.*

➤ *Think you are the candidate most like them.*

➤ *Have been well courted.*

➤ *You have thanked for help.*

➤ *You ask and ask and ask again.*

A campaign can use the talents of anyone who has a basic interest in helping to raise money to get the message out. Too often a candidate and a paid fundraiser are the only people dedicated to raising money. If a dozen people pitched in to help, more money would be raised more quickly—and more people would be attracted to helping. Every candidate should have:

- A researcher/organizer to gather names, addresses and telephone numbers of frequent campaign contributors in the area and other prospective donors referred to the campaign.

- A computer person to maintain the list of prospective donors and ensure that the candidate always has an updated list of names, with no duplicates, of good prospects to call.

- A scheduler to make sure that the candidate has plenty of time to phone for contributions.

- A coach to help the candidate develop her fundraising message, (different from the campaign message), then sit with her while she phones, to be sure that she has the process and the message down pat.

- A finance committee to help raise money by introducing the candidate to prospective donors.

- An events committee whose members will help organize, orchestrate and ensure attendance at fundraising events.

- Small-donor coffee hour hosts and hostesses who will invite friends and colleagues to their homes to hear the candidate speak, then make a pitch for contributions.

- People who formerly or presently serve on association or political action committees that endorse and disburse contributions to candidates.

- Other candidates and elected officials to offer moral support, interesting stories and clues on how to ask for money and stay on course in following the fundraising plan.

- A great fundraiser to coordinate the details of the fundraising process and make sure that all pledges are followed up.

The fundraising process requires that you scope out many different people, lists, organizations and insiders before you begin. A good fundraising drive begins months in advance of a campaign. However, once the campaign has begun, it's important that you make calls every day or at least three times a week. Failure to have completed all the research should not deter you from getting on the phone once the campaign begins in earnest.

# The Fundraising Coordinator

The first person most campaigns hire is a general consultant or campaign manager. The last person hired is often a professional fundraiser, usually after half the campaign is over and all the key people realize how far behind the campaign is falling in raising money.

Hire a fundraiser as soon as you know you are running for office.

Today's fundraisers are not easy to find, and they are traditionally more expensive than a campaign is expecting to pay. However, if they are good, they are worth your candidate's weight in gold. No decent fundraiser works for just a commission, though many will take a commission in addition to a monthly retainer.

A fundraiser should be part task-master, part people-recruiter, part confidant of the candidate, and full-time schmoozer—able to leap into powerful elite circles of high donors as well as able to stuff envelopes with volunteers on a Saturday afternoon.

A good fundraiser can walk into a law office or political action committee office with only her charm, and walk out with a list of prospective donors for the candidate to call, a commitment to hold a conference-room fundraiser, and a bag full of office supplies to augment the campaign's day-to-day needs.

Campaign fundraisers are not easily found, which is why you should begin early and in earnest to find the right person for your campaign. Track down last year's (and the year before's) candidates who made their budgets. You do not need to hire a campaign fundraiser from a winning campaign—in many cases a losing campaign will have a great fundraiser, who has learned more by losing than by winning. Other places to look for fundraising talent include state political parties, local women's groups, non-profit associations, former candidates and campaign managers, college students eager to learn about fundraising and people who have organized major community fundraising events.

> ### Wanted: Fundraiser
>
> Must be a self-starting, highly organized, determined professional with prior experience in raising money from individuals, groups and organizations. Applicants must understand the importance of deadlines and be good at coercing people to do what they don't yet know is fun. Responsibilities include developing a fundraising plan and budget, securing lists of potential donors, coordinating direct mail and phone solicitations, staffing a finance committee, and overseeing the events committee. The hours are long and demanding, but the reward is great: a better government (and a salary you get to help raise yourself).

# Campaign Fundraising Calendar

© copyright Campaign Connection 1996

| | Mar | Apr | May | Jun | Jul | Aug | Sep | Oct | Nov | TOTAL |
|---|---|---|---|---|---|---|---|---|---|---|
| Personal solicitations/ high donors | | | | | | | | | | |
| Direct-mail letters | | | | | | | | | | |
| Home fundraisers | | | | | | | | | | |
| Populist events | | | | | | | | | | |
| PAC contributions | | | | | | | | | | |
| Credit-card plan | | | | | | | | | | |
| Personal contribution | | | | | | | | | | |
| TOTALS | | | | | | | | | | |

FORM 11: CAMPAIGN FUNDRAISING CALENDAR

# The Fundraising Plan

A comprehensive fundraising plan is developed by the fundraiser (and perhaps a fundraising consultant) along with the candidate, prospective finance committee members and others who have helped put together written fundraising plans for previous campaigns.

The fundraising plan should be a diverse, interesting and layered plan that involves many people and many more prospects. Campaigns rely on reaching prospective donors in a variety of ways. High donors require personal meetings or phone calls. Mid-level donors require personal phone calls, letters and events. Low donors require letters and events. Insiders almost always give money at events or personal meetings.

However you court your prospects, cull them according to their potential giving power: high, mid-level or low donors. Then set your game plan to reach them through one of the following ways:

- Personal phone calls from the candidate.
- Finance committee efforts: personal meetings, conference calls or bundling of checks.
- Small donor mailings to interest groups and individuals.
- Peer-group fundraising.
- Credit card plans.
- Phone banks.
- Events: the campaign kickoff, celebrity evenings, populist events, coffee hours, etc.
- PAC fundraising.

All of these methods will need a budget and time allocated on the candidate's schedule to effectively implement. Equally important to the monetary budget is the volunteer and professional staff budget it will take to complete the fundraising plan. Campaigns are filled with great intentions, but seldom filled with really great fundraising. Start with a doable plan that seeks to raise at least 10 to 20 percent more than your anticipated expenses, as campaigns traditionally need more money than they initially think. In addition, some elements of your fundraising plan will simply not reap the amounts you think.

A fundraising plan includes four critical parts:

1. *A fundraising timeline* (see Form 1: Campaign Fundraising Calendar) that lays out how much money is to be raised each month through each fundraising method, so you can compare this anticipated income with your campaign budget.

---

*Look for early money and support among your:*

- Old college, high-school and grade-school classmates.
- Rolodex and personal address book.
- Neighbors—now and in your past.
- Business associates (your dentist, doctor, grocer, attorney).
- Colleagues at the office.
- Friends and associates with whom you have shared local concerns.
- Candidates to whom you have contributed or volunteered.
- Acquaintances from PTAs, church and civic organizations.
- Christmas card list.
- Family—even your long-lost and distant relatives.
- Colleagues from your health club, gym or sports teams.

2. *A short narrative on each* of the various fundraising aspects, with the names of the people who will be responsible for implementing the plan. It is customary at the start of campaigns that not all of the key people will be named, but it is important to note that a key person will be needed for each task.

3. *A short budget that allocates* money for each of the functions named in the plan. For example, the small-donor fundraising letters will require postage, printing and stationery. Events require money for location, food and beverages, invitations and postage.

4. *A human resources budget* that specifies how many people you will need for each event and when you will need them.

The fundraising plan should be drafted at least nine months before election day, reviewed by members of the prospective finance committee, and approved as revised by the candidate and fundraiser.

# The Candidate's Contribution

Most candidates put from 10 to 15 percent of the total budget into the campaign themselves. If you don't invest in yourself, how can you expect others to contribute or raise money? The days of expecting everyone else to shoulder the campaign expenses without putting in your fair share are dwindling, if not gone. No philosophical or good-government argument nor personal poverty will cut through the ice of high donors and political action committees who are looking for reasons not to support candidates. Personal commitment is judged in great part by your own cash contribution to the campaign.

The candidate usually pays for some campaign start-up costs—stationery, envelopes, the "campaign look" (logo) and perhaps a consultant to figure out what to do first. Computers, lists, photos, and a new phone line (and its exorbitant deposit) are also typical expenses that are incurred before the money starts flowing in from friends and early supporters.

Remember that it takes money to raise money.

# Asking for Money

The best step you can take to ensure your campaign is off on the right foot, is to learn how to make effective high-donor calls to people you know are likely to support you and have demonstrated their ability to contribute large amounts to political campaigns. In most campaigns, high-donor fundraising results in over half the money raised in the entire campaign. Consequently, if you are anticipating spending $60,000, then it is not unreasonable to plan on raising $30,000 through high-donor (more than $100) phone calls.

To begin this process, you need to do it right:

- Have the right approach and message.
- Be in the right mood with the right attitude.
- Acquire and build the right lists to call from.
- Engage in the right advance notice to prospects.
- Follow up on all pledges right away.

Candidates always wonder where they will get names of people to call in order to raise all the money in their budget. Money is raised in direct proportion to the amount of time you spend asking for it. If you only spend an hour a day raising money, you will raise a third of what you could raise if you spend three hours a day fundraising.

Doing the research to get ready to fundraise takes months; setting up the process takes weeks; setting up the contacts takes days; making the contacts usually takes hours; but making the pitch should only take a few minutes, and followup takes only seconds.

The goal in all good high-donor fundraising is to know more about the people you call than they will ever know about you (and you'll be on TV and radio as well as in direct-mail pieces and the newspaper). Through research, you'll learn that the same 10 percent of contributors fund 90 percent of all campaigns. The rest comes from those circles of people you know personally.

These high donors should give you a list of at least 100, and hopefully more than 200, people from whom you can expect to receive early money and support. Though they are unlikely to contribute large individual amounts, they give the campaign a boost by giving you added numbers of supporters, which helps encourage the traditional high donors to give you early money.

Your job is not so much to convince a prospective donor that she should support and contribute to your campaign. Your job is to negotiate an amount. If you get bogged down in the "why should I give to you," you'll never get off the phone with a contribution.

*Your job is not so much to convince a prospective donor that she should support and contribute to your campaign. Your job is to negotiate an amount.*

The goal in convincing someone to give you money is to first convince yourself. You are in this world of politics to make your community a better place. You must understand that you are not begging for money. Rather, you are asking people to invest in you and the pursuit of a better world. Believe the experts and current elected officials when they say, "Public service is no peaches and cream." It is a tough job where you will work day and night, with and for people who never think you do enough for them. The pay is never commensurate with the time and energy you have to give—particularly since you must sacrifice valuable time with your family, which you'll never get back.

You deserve every cent you raise. Believe it.

Asking for money gives candidates cause to rethink their decision to run. In many cases, you will ask people you may not even like. You will have to ask them four or five times to give you money that you would rather earn by waiting tables. And even the best fundraisers have days when 70 percent or more of their calls for cash result in rejection.

Understand the importance of putting together the right lists, in the right order, with the right backup information and the right timing. Your list should be arranged so there are some people you may know interspersed with those you do not. The data sheet detailing the names, phone numbers and basic background information on the person you are calling should also list that person's general or specific contributor history.

Remember, you need to know more information about your prospective donors than they will ever know about you—and you're the candidate.

The best information to compile comes from public files located in the city, county or state office that records campaign contributions. Most people don't know themselves how much they give to political campaigns. But if you research, record and then compile, you'll find that a single person listed as giving $50 to one candidate has also given $50 or more to others. You need to know the giving power of the people you call. If your research reveals that a person gave $250 total to four campaigns, you know that he or she can afford to give you at least $100—if you can make a compelling case.

Nothing is more of a lost opportunity than to ask a person for $100 only to have them agree in less than a second. Ouch. You should have asked for $250, or the maximum contribution allowed.

## How Do You Ask People for Money?

1. *Establish a quick, comfortable rapport.* Start with a friendly "hello," two or three sentences of introduction or, if you know the person, catch up from the last time you talked. Explain your purpose in calling and how you got her name, revealing that you know the prospect is a frequent donor with a line like, "I was reviewing the campaign contribution records and was happily surprised to see that you and I have shared the same interest in issues and candidates. I supported Jack Jones, Sandy Wienert, the school bond and those same three candidates you did for City Council."

2. *Explain why you are running,* what you have in common, and why the prospective donor would find you an exciting choice. Explain how you intend to win and what makes your campaign unique. This should be as interactive a conversation as possible. Don't drone on forever. If you've been talking for more than a minute, ask a

question, or at least check to make sure that your prospect is still alive on the other end of the line.

3. *Give him or her an "insider's" look* at what's going on in the campaign. Prospective donors are investors in a small business—your campaign. A candidate should have insider information about the campaign (recent polls, strategy plans, key people who have endorsed your candidacy, fundraising goals reached, etc.). If a person has not contributed to you before, then a few comments about your key issues and background can be added. Keep a sheet of these "campaign news tips" with your calling list.

4. *Ask for a specific amount of money.* Be very direct about your reasons for calling: a contribution of more than $100. Ask for more than you think the person can give. The information sheet from which you call should detail each person's contribution history. Remember that your time is valuable; don't demean yourself by asking for less than you are worth.

5. *After you have asked for $100, stop talking.* Even if the pause is seemingly forever, and you find the silence unbearable, resist the temptation to talk. Let your prospect break the silence. If he or she shows any signs of reluctance, go back to step four, but don't start negotiating down the amount in question.

6. *Explain why you need the money.* Have a list of expenses that need to be paid in the upcoming weeks. Donors prefer to contribute to media buys for radio and television, direct mail expenses, yard signs and things they can directly see or touch. Asking for money to pay staff salaries, rent or the phone bill is never as enticing to a would-be donor. Know the specific amounts that each of these things will cost and ask the prospective donor if she will contribute $100 towards the $4,642 needed for the 47 radio spots. Or ask for $132 to pay for the printing of your new fundraising letter.

7. *Instill a sense of immediacy* and follow up the pledge immediately. Once you have a commitment for a donation, thank the donor for the pledge and tell her what she will get for her investment. (She will receive monthly campaign updates, invitations to special events, victory party info, etc.)

8. *Then get that check.* Remember that only 80 percent of pledges ever come in. However, 100 percent of the checks you go get today actually make it to your checking account. Offer to send someone out to pick up the check right away. Some campaigns have found it more than worth their time and trouble to delegate a person to run around and pick up checks on days when the candidate is calling. If picking up the check is not possible, then follow up the call with a short thank-you letter within 24 hours. The letter should restate the amount pledged and the urgency for it and include a return remittance envelope.

# What if a Prospect Says She Can't Afford a Donation?

If you have given it your best try and still the prospect is not moving, don't hang up yet. If you can't obtain a large donation now, then try for a smaller one today and call again later in the campaign as you prove how well you are doing. You can tell the prospect that the press is judging this race not only on the amount raised but on the number of individual donors.

If a prospect can't give you cash right now, ask if she will join your pledge program—or better yet, part of the credit-card plan. She can contribute $25 today and another $25 each month until the election.

If that still isn't working, try asking the prospect to help you raise money. Perhaps she can ask a few people in her firm to meet with you, or have her spouse contribute. Ask if she can check her Rolodex right now and give you the names of three or four people that she will call and tell to expect a call from you. If you're still getting a cool response and no help, then ask if she can volunteer some in-kind service, equipment or supplies. This could be anything from staplers and scissors to computers or printing services.

If she's still playing hard-to-get, ask her for advice and tell her you will call her back in the future. Don't hang up until you have a win/win situation. You need to feel good (or at least not bad) about the experience, not so much for her, but for you, as you need to go on to the next call with an upbeat attitude.

Every time you succeed in getting a contribution, it makes the next one easier. Only experience contributes to good high-donor fundraising.

# Questions People Ask When You Ask Them for Money

1. *How is it that you expect to win?*
   You need to be able to explain (in less than five minutes) that you are a viable candidate who not only understands what it takes to win—but has what it takes to beat your opponent.

2. *How much money have you raised to date?*
   The universal question posed by every high donor, this question stops most candidates in their tracks if they cannot say they've raised a serious amount within weeks of their initial announcement.

3. *How much will this campaign cost, and how do you expect to raise it?*
   In addition to your own personal contribution, this is where you trot out all of your early pledges and explain how many people promised you, before you announced, that they'd be there for you.

Anticipate what lists you'll be able to get, and what political action committees are likely to be there for you.

4. *Who's helping you?*
Bring out those lists of endorsers who encouraged you to run. Have the names of as many VIPs as possible, along with their promises of money.

5. *Can you delegate? Who is your manager? Who is your consultant?*
Every campaign requires at least eight key players to allow you to focus on your job as a candidate. List your manager, your fundraiser, your finance committee chair, your volunteer coordinator, your media or general consultant, your pollster, and anyone who's helping organize seniors, women, the business community, labor, etc. Contributors want to know you're not going to try to manage your own campaign.

6. *How much time are you spending on the phone?*
If there is ever a question you must answer with conviction, this is it. People who give money to candidates know that there is only one way to succeed: you must be persistent, unapologetic and dedicated to getting on the phone to ask for money.

7. *What are you going to do that's different from others who have run and failed?*
This is where you talk about the weaknesses of your opponent, the change in the mood of the voters (as proven by recent polls or newspaper analyses), or your commanding lead in fundraising. Whatever your ace in the hole is—this is where you play it, convincingly.

8. *How many votes will it take you to win, and where will they come from?*
Most candidates have no clue as to how many votes they are looking for, but a crafty high donor knows that if someone on your team doesn't know the answer to this question, you probably haven't targeted your voters, and your campaign dollars will not be well spent.

9. *Are you going to campaign full-time?*
Candidates that have a full-time job they are trying to hold onto as long as possible need to be able to show they have a campaign operation that can accommodate the candidate's hours away from the campaign trail. A candidate should plan on spending at least the last three months prior to the election campaigning full-time.

10. *What's your message?*
Another trick question. This answer should not be limited to the slogan, but it should include it. Three practiced sentences will be fine. And no more than three issues should be mentioned.

> ### Questions you will be asked:
>
> ➤ *How will you win?*
> ➤ *How much money have you raised?*
> ➤ *How much will it cost?*
> ➤ *Who's helping you?*
> ➤ *Can you delegate?*
> ➤ *How much do you phone?*
> ➤ *How are you different?*
> ➤ *How many votes will it take?*
> ➤ *Will you campaign full-time?*
> ➤ *What's your message?*

All these questions are important in establishing a positive, insightful rapport with the prospect, but remember that the point is to get back to the subject at hand: raising money.

Remember that raising money is a process, it's not a courtship for marriage. Get to the point as soon as you can. Candidates often have a hard time getting to the point and as a result end up wasting their time—and more importantly, the time of the prospect. After all, you're calling people who give money to campaigns. They know the drill.

Some candidates start the asking process by sending a packet of information to a prospect. Then they phone the prospect and talk for a half hour. Instead of asking the question, they make arrangements for lunch. After the lunch (which the candidate wrongly pays for), still no direct pitch for money. They say they'll follow up with more information they will mail. Then they follow the mailed package with another phone call. Time spent: three hours. Money spent: $20. Contributions received: $0.

Get to the point. After you send a prospect a package, call. Follow the steps for asking for money. Ask. Ask again.

## What's the Worst That Can Happen?

Anticipate in advance all the creative, stalling and negative responses you might get in asking for money over the phone. Then have your own comeback ready for the debate. Some common negative responses from prospective donors include:

*Prospect:* "No, I'm supporting someone else."

*Candidate:* "I understand. In that case I would like to be your second choice."

*Prospect:* "No, I haven't got any money."

*Candidate:* "I know times are tough, which is why I'm not as interested in the amount as much as I'm interested in getting a check with your name at the bottom."

*Prospect:* "No, I haven't made up my mind yet."

*Candidate:* "I know how you feel, I've often felt that way myself. But I found that if I didn't invest early in good campaigns, then the best people wouldn't be the ones I'd be choosing among. I'm not asking for an exclusive endorsement here; I'm asking for enough money to build a viable campaign to get my message out. Will you help me?"

*Prospect:* "I can't take a stand until my PAC (or company, boss, organization, spouse or other entity) does."

*Candidate:* "I know how you feel, I've felt that way too, but to compete now, I need to have 100 contributors. No matter what your PAC does, I'm sure they understand my dilemma. I've talked with your people and feel confident that they're headed my way. However, if I don't get help now, their endorsement may come too late."

*Prospect:* "I don't feel I know enough about you."

*Candidate:* "I understand, and I'm willing to do what it takes to change that. Your contribution means a lot to me, to the point that I'm willing to head over to your office now to sit down and chat more. What I'm asking for is a contribution now to get this campaign off on the right track. You're a seasoned political watchdog. You know some of my key endorsers (name them), you know some of my key staffers and consultants (name them) and you know what we share in common. Unfortunately, campaigns don't allow for a lot of time to discuss the critical issues before candidates are ruled viable or not, based upon the money they have raised. All I'm asking for is a chance to compete."

*Prospect:* "I need to talk to the others in the race first."

*Candidate:* "I appreciate your democratic approach, but I'm hopeful that my initiative means something. I believe you to be an important bellwether. I realize the importance of early phoning, which is why I'm asking now, before my competitors. I'm not asking for your exclusive support, though I'm hoping to have it. What I know is that I need to have 150 contributors in the next 10 days to show the press and my competitors that I have the campaign that's setting the agenda. I'd like your name and a check now to be able to compete."

*Prospect:* "Send me some information and let me take a look."

*Candidate:* "I'll do better than that. If you'd be willing to write me a check today, I'll bring some material over myself." Or "I've sent you some material already, but if you'd like more, I'll bring it to you. I'm so serious about having a check from you this week that I'll stop by your house myself to pick it up."

*Prospect:* "I'm contributing heavily to other campaigns on the ballot and don't know if I'll have money left for this race."

*Candidate:* "I know how you feel. I've often felt that way myself when I looked at my checkbook and the causes I've supported. But I've found that these local races are just as important. If we don't have people like me pounding the pavement and building those messages important to the whole slate, then the top of the ticket's job will be harder. And I'm not asking for the maximum contribution, just $100."

*Prospect:* "I'm going to wait until filing deadline, or until the race heats up."

*Candidate*: "By that time, this race could well be decided. Right now the campaigns that are able to get their messages out early are the ones whom the press, the endorsing organizations, and the public will consider viable. I'm running this race the right way: getting my money now, when we must begin talking to the voters. You know as well as I that the public is in a challenging mood. We need to talk to them now, not wait until filing deadline."

The universal rule to take with you as the best comeback to any rejection, real or anticipated, is the "feel, felt, found" rule. If someone is about to reject you, say, "I know how you feel, I've felt that way myself, but I have found that …". Originally developed by Madalyn Schenk from New Orleans, it is the best tool to take with you to every solicitation occasion.

# High-Donor Phoning

If you call 15 potential donors an hour, you should connect with seven, and on a good day, you will get money from four.

With a donation of $100 from each donor, you could raise:

$400 per hour;

$1,200 per day (three hours);

$3,600 every week (three days);

$14,400 every month ( twelve days);

$86,400 by the end of a six-month campaign.

To accomplish this worthy goal, you would need to make:

15 calls per hour;

45 calls per day (three hours);

135 calls every week (three days);

540 calls every month (twelve days);

3,240 calls by the end of a six-month campaign.

This would lead to:

7 connects per hour;

21 connects per day (three hours);

63 connects every week (three days);

252 connects every month (twelve days);

1,512 connects by the end of a six-month campaign.

And it would bring your campaign:

4 high donors per hour;

12 high donors per day (three hours);

36 high donors every week (three days);

144 high donors every month (twelve days);

864 high donors by the end of a six-month campaign.


To make this plan a reality, you, your fundraiser and finance committee will need a list of at least 2,500 prospective donors, but the payoff is great: you could raise more than $80,000.

# High-Donor Calling Form

©copyright Campaign Connection 1996

**Name** _____  **Referred from** _____

Home phone _____ Fax _____ Home address _____

Work phone _____ Cellular _____ Home city, state, zip _____

Occupation/title _____ Company _____

Company address _____ Company city, state, zip _____

Contribution history _____

Notes _____

How much to ask for: $_____ In-kind _____

## Calling Log

| Date | ❏ Contribution: | ❏ Volunteer: | ❏ Referrals: |
|------|-----------------|--------------|--------------|
|      | Amount _____ | Task _____ | _____ |
|      | Item _____ | _____ | _____ |
| Notes: | | | |

| Date | ❏ Contribution: | ❏ Volunteer: | ❏ Referrals: |
|------|-----------------|--------------|--------------|
|      | Amount _____ | Task _____ | _____ |
|      | Item _____ | _____ | _____ |
| Notes: | | | |

## Followup

| ❏ Followup letter: | ❏ Contribution received: | ❏ Thank-you letter: |
|--------------------|--------------------------|---------------------|
| Date _____ | Date _____ | Date _____ |
|  | Amount _____ | |
|  | Item _____ | |
| Notes: | | |

*FORM 12: HIGH-DONOR CALLING FORM*

# Dedicating the Time for High-Donor Fundraising

If you spend a little time raising money, you raise a little money. If you spend a lot of time raising it, you reap the benefits. Most campaigns incorrectly assume they don't raise enough money because of a candidate flaw, or because money has just run out in town.

In fact, money is not raised and campaigns are lost because the candidate, the campaign manager, the fundraiser and the other staff members dedicate too little time to this most-important function of any campaign.

At least 25 percent of the candidate's time should be spent on the phone asking for money. Another 15 to 20 percent of her time should be spent asking for money in person, attending fundraisers, meeting with her finance committee or urging others to raise money on her behalf.

Time should be scheduled for fundraising activities, particularly high-donor phone calls, before the rest of the schedule is set. The candidate, campaign manager and scheduler should agree on the fundraising time goals for each month, and subsequently, each week. If the candidate is campaigning full-time, then up to 40 hours a week should be dedicated to fundraising activities. If a candidate is working a full-time job and also campaigning, then 25 percent of the available hours dedicated to campaigning should go to fundraising (about 15 hours a week).

It's important to break down your fundraising into bite-size pieces, rather than face the entire job at once, which can seem overwhelming, unreachable and too daunting to begin on any particular day.

## Hints for High-Donor Phoning

- The best times to phone are Monday and Thursday mornings to prospective donors' offices. Sunday and Thursday evenings are best to catch people at their homes, with Saturday mornings also being good.

- Send a packet to each prospective donor a week before you call. Explain that you will call on a particular day the next week, and include, with your personal letter of introduction, a brief bio or brochure and any positive press clippings. And, of course, don't forget a remittance envelope.

- Work from high-donor forms that list the prospective donor's name, address, business address, both phone numbers, recent campaigns she has given to and "additional notes," which record interesting information about the prospect. Be sure to record the prospect's response.

- When leaving a message on the recording machine of a prospective donor, make it an intriguing one, not one asking for money. And always include the times you will be available. Try: "Hello, there, Sam Hunt. My name is Jill Smith, and I need some political advice. A mutual friend of ours, Jim Kirk, suggested I call you this weekend. Could you give me a call either tonight between 6 and 8 p.m. or tomorrow afternoon between 3 and 5 p.m.? Thanks, and I'll return the favor."

- Or a more humorous approach: "Hi there. My name's Jill Smith and even though you might already know that I'm a candidate for City Council, please don't hold that against me. I need your advice, and no, I'm not just hustling for money, I need an answer to a few quick questions before I hustle you for money. Thanks."

- Give yourself daily goals of how many people you will call, as opposed to calling until you reach a certain dollar total. To do an effective, high-donor campaign, you should have a list of at least 500 names per month, or 150 people a week to call. Have someone keep a tally of the money you've received through high-donor phoning to give you the positive feedback you need to keep on calling.

- If a prospect does not call back after the first message, then call again the next day. If she does not call back after the second message, call the third day. Keep calling. Usually a prospective donor will respond to your persistence. If you have a mutual friend or contact that knows that person, have her call to see if she can encourage a return call to you.

- Designate one person on the campaign to do nothing else but ready your phone list of prospects. A prospective donor who can see you have done your research on her will be far more interested in investing in you than a person who knows she is just a name on a list of previous donors.

- Don't be discouraged. Always have a list of tough prospects interspersed with easy ones. Arrange your call list accordingly, so you take on the tougher calls at the start of your phone session and the easier ones at the close. This way, you feel successful at the end of the day.

## *The Finance Committee*

Few people volunteer to be on campaign finance committees. Finance committee members are responsible for raising money, but seldom do they have input in how it is spent. They are given goals, but seldom any resources. Finance committees are told about strategy, but are rarely consulted about strategic decisions.

Finance committees are usually not well thought-out, nor do their members produce commensurate with the goals they are given. And for good reason—the roles of finance committees are seldom well explained to prospective members.

People who serve on finance committees are not substitutes for the candidate. They cannot call high donors and get the same response the candidate gets. However, members can help raise lots of money through many different mechanisms.

The campaign staff and the candidate should be available to work with finance committee members, either through dedicated time on the calendar or through staff support for the projects and backup required to follow up on work done by committee members.

No two finance committees are the same. Some meet at 7 a.m. every Monday morning to be briefed on campaign updates or to plan new approaches. Some work very independently, sharing lists and sponsoring events themselves. Still others never meet, with individual members bringing bundled checks to the campaign office.

The best finance committees are the ones where members agree to bring in money the best way they know how. This includes:

- Giving the maximum contribution.
- Getting another maximum contribution from their spouses or other family members.
- Getting many checks from friends and colleagues and bringing them to a fundraiser or to the campaign office.
- Hosting a fundraiser at their office, a restaurant or a private club.
- Attending all important fundraisers and buying a table at some.
- Introducing the candidate to other proven high donors.
- Organizing conference calls among the candidate, prospective high donors and themselves.
- Hosting a breakfast with several prospective donors.
- Organizing several people to give through the credit-card program.
- Courting members of influential PAC boards to endorse the candidate.
- Signing a letter to friends and political insiders urging them to send a check.
- Sitting with the candidate as she makes calls to people known by the member.
- Securing in-kind contributions (phone systems, fax machines, computers, etc.).

Finance committees need to be given their charge: to raise a specific amount of money, both as a whole unit and as individuals. At the first meeting, the

> ### Finance committee member qualifications:
>
> ➤ Be able to contribute the maximum allowable amount to the campaign.
> ➤ Associate with people who can contribute large amounts to the campaign.
> ➤ Have a background of raising money, particularly political money.
> ➤ Have the time, staff, and desire to help raise it.

treasurer and fundraiser should explain and hand out all pertinent legal information regarding campaign rules and regulations. A short card should be prepared to remind members of the dos and don'ts of legal fundraising.

Most campaigns start off on the right foot giving the finance committee pertinent information and ambitious goals. Then the campaign—pressed by other business—leaves the committee alone to go its merry way. What happens then can be anyone's guess. If there is a good, self-starting organizer, or a committee member who has served as a ringer for similar groups in the past, then there's a chance that some money will get raised.

However, a better plan is for the fundraising coordinator to serve as the staff member who speaks with each member of the finance committee at least once a week, offering information, supplies and followup where necessary. The committee should meet to share and split up lists of prospective donors who should be amenable to a call for money. The fundraiser should also facilitate the scheduling of the candidate with finance committee members.

Generally speaking, both the candidate and the fundraiser work to add new members to the finance committee: it is the only committee on the campaign where there can never be too many people.

# Special-Interest Groups, PACs and Peer-Pressure Fundraising

It starts with who you know and then, who they know. Peer-pressure fundraising is little more than an organized chain letter that begins with small networks of professionals, special-interest groups and mutual friends. Just like a chain letter, the key is getting people to pass the message.

Start the chain reaction with a look at the professional people who are attracted to your candidacy. Create a master file of your contacts and sort them by type: professional groups (lawyers, nurses, teachers), labor associations (state employees, engineers, restaurant employees), business groups (chambers of commerce, downtown associations), special-interest groups (women, environmentalists, minority groups), and others who lend themselves to peer-group organization.

Identify a key person to be your first contact—a special-interest coordinator—in each group. Do your homework and find the most credible and influential person. Remember, you are soliciting an endorsement that will translate into thousands of dollars in contributions from the endorser's peers. In your first meeting, concentrate on impressing your coordinator with the campaign's strategy and with your chances of winning.

Once on board, it is important that your coordinator contribute at least as much money as others are asked to give. Once the coordinator invests in the campaign personally, donation requests will have far more conviction and credibility. The campaign should supply each special-interest coordinator with campaign brochures and a list of specific items paid for with solicited donations, and arrange for followup letters and return envelopes to confirm pledge amounts.

# Building a Small Group of Support

It should not be difficult to get a core group of colleagues—particularly among people who have past records of political involvement—to agree to divide up a list of peers and telephone or visit a specific number of them. In some cases, the special-interest coordinator will want to hold a "meet-and-greet" in the office conference room to introduce the peers to the campaign. The candidate may be asked to give a few brief remarks, and then the coordinator should make a direct pitch for donations.

# Getting the Group to Raise Money

Special-interest group coordinators should arrange for a phone bank one night a week at a colleague's office. Have the candidate stop by the phone bank early in the fundraising process to thank the phoners and urge them to expand their network of projected calls. Make sure each volunteer records the results of each call, and jots down any useful information about donors.

Most special-interest coordinators prefer to start with a targeted direct-mail piece outlining why their colleagues should support the candidate. It may also include why the group should not vote for the opponent. Several other colleagues should sign this letter of support. The campaign manager and fundraiser should approve the letter, and if they have any concerns, ask the candidate to review it as well. After the letter is prepared, the coordinators need to secure the names, addresses and phone numbers of everyone who will receive the letter.

The campaign will arrange to have the letter printed; however, some special-interest coordinators, who have the financial means to help, may offer to have the letters and envelopes prepared on their personal or business stationery. Personal stationery works better than campaign stationery to attract peer-group attention. If the peer coordinator pays for the mailing, make sure it is reported as an in-kind contribution to the campaign.

# Speaking at Meetings

There are plenty of meetings your peers traditionally attend to hear about important issues. Another job of the special-interest coordinator is to get the candidate on the agenda to speak at those meetings.

The candidate should talk about the campaign: her reasons for running, key issues and the nature of the race and campaign (mention the high cost of campaigning). The candidate should announce the role of the special-interest coordinator in organizing members of the professional or special-interest group present.

After the candidate speaks, however, there needs to be someone else to close the deal. The special-interest coordinator needs to have remittance envelopes and volunteer information ready to hand out at the close of the meeting. The sign-up sheet for the meeting, if available, is a valuable followup list for more contributions.

Underlying all of these peer-pressure strategies are two rules: target the special-interest groups that best fit your accomplishments, memberships and contacts; and make a great first impression.

# Political Action Committees (PACs)

Political Action Committees are the mainstay of big city-hall and federal campaigns. PAC power, an outgrowth of campaign finance reform from the '60s, is a major part of today's political landscape. Groups, particularly labor unions or business associations, form "committees" to become entities that can give money, time and energy to campaigns. Originally devised as a way to circumvent individual campaign contribution limits, PACs get their money from individual memberships or donations.

Labor unions frequently request deductions from their members' paychecks, whereas business PACs request sizeable donations each year depending upon the businesses' gross revenues. PACs then have political directors, endorsement review boards, trainings and recruitment projects. Their biggest job is to influence their voters on who would be a good choice for all the interests represented by the membership or its management.

PAC teams, loosely termed "member education" or "education committees," spend time and money influencing their membership and general voters—with campaign tools as sophisticated (or more sophisticated) than the candidate's own campaign.

PACs pay outright in the form of contributions to the candidate. They might pay for a poll or other big-ticket item, such as the production of a TV or radio spot. They could contribute staffing (a frequent contribution of environmentalists and social service groups); construction and placement of yard signs (firefighters and public safety PACs); phone banks (business and teacher PACs); sponsorship of several events around the district (trial lawyers, doctors and insurance companies); and magazine or newsletter mailings to the members (the National Rifle Association, gay organizations, women's groups and many others). Still others will develop their own brochures, TV or radio ads (such as the National Abortion Rights Action League and the AFL-CIO).

To avail yourself of the possible gold mine in help that these PACs offer, you need to know as much about them as possible.

- Know to whom they have contributed in the past, and what their average contribution to candidates like you has been.

- Know who controls the money (the PAC direction, coalition president, dominant business leaders, etc.).

- Know if there is a committee of members who interview the candidates before making a choice, then know the members on that committee.

- Know who else that committee or PAC director bases their endorsement upon (Democrats are supported by labor; Republicans by business).

- Know when they make their choice and the extent of what they contribute besides money so that you can ask for maximum support.

- Know people who know the important people so that you can be introduced to the important PAC people by the right folks.

To quote an old friend, follow the money and you can follow the road that leads to PAC power anywhere in this country.

# Small-Donor Fundraising: Direct Mail

Direct-mail fundraising is a strong core to any good fundraising plan. Candidates have lists of friends and relatives who should respond to a single letter with a check. However, for the rest of the people you target through direct-mail letters, it may take as many as five before you get your contribution.

Many campaigns don't understand the psyche of direct-mail donors. The truth is that the first mailing, if sent to a group of people who should be supportive of your candidacy, will only yield about a 4 percent return. That is, if you mail 1,000 letters announcing your candidacy, you can expect about 40 responses, with the average contribution about $25. If you make enough money on that first mailing to cover your expenses, you are doing well.

However, if you follow up that mailing up with a phone bank, and ask the prospects if they received the letter, your response rate will double to 8 percent.

After that first mailing, you're likely to be discouraged; don't be. Mail that same list again—making sure that you have made all address corrections, which you should request with any initial mailing. The second mailing should bring in more than your first, a 5 to 6 percent return. The third mailing will return about 7 percent, with the fourth and fifth securing even more, depending on how the race heats up.

> **Sample mailing schedule:**
> - At the time of your initial announcement.
> - Right after the official filing deadline.
> - Ten days before the primary.
> - One week before the general election.
> - After the election to clean up remaining bills.

Some candidates use a cost-effective means of thanking their donors and resoliciting at the same time. Every time a donor contributes, she gets a thank-you and a new request for another donation.

## Tips for a Small-Donor Solicitation

- Make the outside envelope unique, not a dead giveaway that it's a political solicitation. Remember that insiders will receive 40 to 60 requests a year. Put yours in a different-sized envelope. Put a teaser, in a color other than black, on the front, like, "the best news you'll get this year ..." If you can afford it, have the letters hand-addressed. Some firms now specialize in hand-addressing envelopes for less than a penny apiece.

- Long letters are better than short, one-page ones. Remember, these are going to insiders who actually look to see what you're saying and how you think you're going to win.

- Include recent newspaper clippings, a brochure, a list of endorsers, an invitation to an upcoming event, or something else besides the letter and the obligatory remittance envelope.

- Ask for money on every page. You should make at least a quarter of the copy of this letter asking for money. Repeat the need for money, the people who are already investing in you, and what the money will be spent on. And use a PS to again ask for money, in your most provocative pitch.

- The signature should not look like it was printed at the same time as the rest of the letter. It should look as if you really signed it. Also, don't send out a letter that begins with "Dear Friend." You're asking for money. People take their money very personally. If you don't ask personally, you won't get it.

- It's perfectly okay to write in the margins of your letter. You may underline or circle items. Anything that makes this letter look like you put some time and passion into it, as opposed to it looking like everyone else's letter, will improve your chances of getting a contribution.

- The solicitation must sound real. Many requests for money are dry and hollow, or they spend way too much time discussing the true issues of the campaign. Of course substance is important, but these letters are going to people you know or who you know to be political insiders. Time is better spent talking about the chances of you winning, or talking about the worst that could happen if your opponent wins, than discussing your eight-point transportation plan.

- Don't forget to place the required disclaimer on your stationery and envelopes, and include in your letter information about maximum amounts the donor is allowed to contribute.

Direct mail is an important element to your fundraising, but it really becomes significant once you have a plan that delivers five and six pieces of mail to a prospect during the course of the campaign. The clue: get started early and mail often.

# The Credit-Card Program

With all the ongoing changes in today's campaign laws limiting the power and financial influence of political action committees, there is a definite need to increase the number of smaller donors to your campaign. Small donors need not be defined as those who give between $5 and $50. They should be defined as those who give that amount at least once.

The goal of the campaign should be to move those donors from only one-time contributors to once-a-month donors. One of the most successful tools used in 1992 by hundreds of candidates throughout the country was to offer a credit-card program. This entails working with your bank and setting up the ability to receive funds through Visa or MasterCard credit cards. To the bank, your campaign looks like any other small business. When you become a credit-card merchant through the bank, you pay for the privilege of receiving Visa and MasterCard payments. You will pay a monthly fee to the bank for this service.

Although the charges will vary, most banks charge a yearly fee of around $30. In addition, a monthly charge based on the average donation amount and the annual volume of contributions will be billed. This monthly rate should be no higher than 6.95 percent. For example, if a person donated $25 a month for five months, her contribution to your campaign would be $125, and the bank would charge up to 6.95 percent of that $125, a total of only $8.69.

It's worth it!

Some campaigns have found it effective to hold events where you pay a small fee to get in, and then sign up for the credit-card plan as part of the program. Others have sent out letters with pledge forms that look like a credit card. And, still others have taken the credit-card machine with them every place they go in order to maximize participation in the program.

If you begin by asking 12 of your friends to subscribe to the credit-card plan at $25 a month, each of them ends up being a $150 donor by the end of the campaign. In many cases, campaigns have been blessed with more than 100 such donors, making their monthly intake from their credit-card program large enough to pay for all the standard bills that are due the first of the month.

## Credit Card Release Form

Name as it appears on your card —please print:

_____

❑ MasterCard     ❑ Visa

Card Number: ❑❑❑❑-❑❑❑❑-❑❑❑❑-❑❑❑❑

Expiration Date: _____     Signature _____

I hereby authorize the Jane Doe Campaign to debit my credit card each month by:

❑ $15 ❑ $20 ❑ $25 ❑ $30 ❑ $40 ❑ $50

for the months of:

❑ June     ❑ July     ❑ Aug     ❑ Sep     ❑ Oct     ❑ Nov

FORM 13: CREDIT CARD RELEASE FORM

# Events

Beware the event that requires 1,000 details for a $300 profit. Today's campaigns are learning that fundraising events are usually good for bringing people together and building important visibility, but are not as productive as high-donor phoning when it comes to adding to the checking account.

There are several different kinds of events you might consider, each with its own time frame:

- Auctions, celebrity speaker events, and multiple events on the same night (50 home parties for $50 each) all take at least two months of planning if you're going to do them right.

- Kickoff events where you hope to attract hundreds of people should be planned six to eight weeks in advance.

- A spaghetti feed, chili dinner, potluck, or picnic event takes a month to five weeks to organize, follow up and rally lots of people to attend.

- A high-donor dinner in a private home or an exclusive club should take three to four weeks to organize and secure people who will attend.

- A coffee klatch or wine-and-cheese hour takes three weeks to organize from the moment the host or hostess is secured.
- Selected breakfasts with members of the finance committee can be organized in less than a week, as long as the finance committee member agrees to shoulder the responsibility for accomplishing the work.

# Large Populist Events

From the kickoff breakfast to the chili feed, from the art auction to the fun run and picnic, from the spaghetti feed to the evening at a movie theater, these populist events have a way of getting out of hand very easily.

The good news: These events allow for people of any income level to attend. They provide an opportunity to use your volunteers. They raise needed visibility. They can bring in lots of new small donors. They give the candidate a feeling of leading a real team. They build momentum.

The bad news: They require lots of time, and usually the time that should be spent hustling people to attend is spent organizing the decorations, the food and booze, and other details of the event itself. These events also have a way of slipping on the schedule, with the all-important get-out-the-folks-to-attend phone calls waiting until it's too late.

Large-scale events require lots of organized people—not just the ones who will come to a meeting once every week to "strategize" the event. They also require some upfront money to secure locations, pay deposits on food and entertainment, and they require a lot of followup effort (phone banks, mailing parties, program design, etc.).

For any event that will involve getting hundreds of people to attend, you will need to engage an events committee to get you through the detail work that these entail.

# The Events Committee

A good events committee:

- Has a chair who is ruthless about deadlines, agendas and holding people to commitments to do work.
- Meets occasionally, but meetings are not the focus of the committee: the work gets done and people check in with accomplishments and a request for additional assignments.
- Outlines each person's duties in writing so that specific duties are the responsibility of someone other than "the committee."
- Has a checklist of all the important tasks that must be done.
- Has a budget that has been approved by the campaign manager and/or the fundraiser.

- Checks the community calendar to make sure the planned events are not in conflict with other important events.
- Keeps in touch with other members of the campaign team so that if an event is being planned at the same time that yard signs are being placed around town, the two interests can work together.
- Is filled with fun, energetic people of all ages who can bring new perspectives to the event.

## Setting Event Limits and Goals

Events can get out of hand in days (usually the days immediately prior to the event). You need to establish a goal for each event. Large populist events should raise at least $5,000, whereas your coffee klatches and meet-and-greets should bring in at least $500. For large events, you should ask for money to get in. For meet-and-greets, you ask for money before you allow anyone to get out. The approach and amounts may be different, but the goal is the same: fundraising for your efforts.

Each fundraising event should have at least one goal: breaking even or making money. Unfortunately, campaigns are filled with fundraisers that were lots of fun, but they cost so much the campaign had to pay out more than it brought in.

# *Tips for Successful Event Fundraising*

- Get sponsors for every major event. These sponsors should be secured in time to have their names on the invitations.
- Send out a remittance envelope with every invitation.
- Follow up every mailing with phone banks before the event.
- Have at least a dozen table captains or sponsors for an event. Each of them will bring another five to 10 people to the event.
- Have someone not on the events committee oversee the checklist for each event.
- Be sure you have obtained the proper licenses or permits for the event, including police or parking permits, insurance permits, liquor licenses, etc. If you are offering daycare services, make sure the people working are certified daycare workers.
- Make sure someone is singularly responsible for ensuring that no one under the legal age drinks, and that no one leaves who is legally drunk.
- Have the event at a location that is accessible, so that everyone can attend and no one can complain or accuse you of being insensitive to disabled issues.

# Event Checklist

**Name of Event** _____ **Coordinator** _____

**Date and location** _____

| Expenses | | Supplies | On hand | To order |
|---|---|---|---|---|
| Invitations and Mailing | | | | |
| Design | _____ | Brochures | _____ | _____ |
| Printing | _____ | Buttons | _____ | _____ |
| Postage | _____ | Contribution envelopes | _____ | _____ |
| Site Costs | | Liquor permit | _____ | _____ |
| Permits | _____ | Name tags | _____ | _____ |
| Decorations | _____ | Pens and markers | _____ | _____ |
| Food, drink | _____ | Contribution basket | _____ | _____ |
| PA equipment | _____ | Receipt book | _____ | _____ |
| Entertainment | _____ | Sign-in sheets | _____ | _____ |
| Rent | _____ | Table and chairs | _____ | _____ |
| Other | _____ | Refreshments | _____ | _____ |
| **Total Expenses** | _____ | Scissors and tape | _____ | _____ |
| **Revenue** | | Decorations | _____ | _____ |
| Advance sales | _____ | Yard signs | _____ | _____ |
| Sponsors | _____ | Volunteer cards | _____ | _____ |
| Door | _____ | Balloons and string | _____ | _____ |
| **Total Revenue** | _____ | Candidate bio sheets | _____ | _____ |
| **Net Profit** | _____ | | | |

FORM 14: EVENT CHECKLIST

- If the event is to be held in a private home, send a campaign worker, preferably someone from that neighborhood, around to all the houses in the area the night before to let them know what's going on and to invite them to attend.

- Budget for each event early and set the fundraising goal for the event to cover all event expenses plus a profit high enough to make all the effort worthwhile.

- Make sure you take all the necessary campaign supplies to the event.

- Always include directions and a phone number on the invitation, even if the event is located at the most popular hotel in town. Make sure you note where people can park.

- Have as many members of the finance committee there as possible, so that they can work the crowd for possible high donors.

- Make sure the campaign treasurer or someone who knows the fine details of campaign finance regulations is there to answer any questions about contributions.

# *The Importance of Thank-Yous*

Much ado is made by candidates about the thank you letters which follow a contribution to the campaign. In fact, failure to respond to contributors with a timely thank-you note is among the top beefs that candidates have with their staffs. Some believe that a timely thank-you gets you a better chance at an additional donation. Some staffers believe that a thank-you doesn't matter and should be left on the list of last things to do.

Thanking a high donor should be a no-brainer. Acknowledgment of a maximum donation should be timely and personal, with the candidate's signature or even a phone call, if the donation came unsolicited.

Thank-yous to low donors should also be timely. Any good campaign computer program today includes a mail-merge feature for easily tracking donations and sending thank-you letters. With each thank-you letter, include another remittance envelope and ask if the donor could find another person to match her contribution.

# Please Sign In

**Event:** _____

**Date:** _____

| Name | Address & Zip | Home Phone | Work Phone | Endorsement |
|------|---------------|------------|------------|-------------|
|      |               |            |            |             |
|      |               |            |            |             |
|      |               |            |            |             |
|      |               |            |            |             |
|      |               |            |            |             |
|      |               |            |            |             |
|      |               |            |            |             |
|      |               |            |            |             |
|      |               |            |            |             |
|      |               |            |            |             |
|      |               |            |            |             |
|      |               |            |            |             |
|      |               |            |            |             |
|      |               |            |            |             |

*FORM 15: SIGN-IN SHEET*

# Coffee Klatch Checklist

## Pre-Event Checklist

❏ Invitations budget

❏ Postage budget

❏ Map of directions to event

❏ Place event on candidate's schedule

❏ Invitations designed

❏ Invitations printed

❏ Invitations mailed

❏ Event checklist and agenda to hostess

❏ Phone bank followup to invitations

❏ Reconfirm time with candidate

## Event Checklist

❏ Balloons and signs outside

❏ Sign-in sheet

❏ Name tags

❏ Pens and markers

❏ Contribution basket

❏ Brochures

❏ Volunteer forms

❏ Contribution envelopes

❏ Refreshments

❏ Cups, plates and napkins

## Sample Agenda

5:00   Set-up begins

7:00   Start time

7:15   Candidate arrives and meets each guest

7:40   Candidate gives 10-15 minute speech

7:50   Q&A from the audience

8:05   Pitch for money and volunteers

FORM 16: COFFEE KLATCH CHECKLIST

# General Rules for Raising Money

1. *You need to spend money in order to raise it.* Budget for events, mailings and phone banks so that you can do them right. Volunteers are much more attracted to campaigns that look good and can afford to look better than the competition. This does not mean that a lot of money need be spent, but it does mean making your materials look sharp.

2. *Money comes in commensurate with the amount of time you spend raising it.* There is no limit to what you can raise. There is only a limit to your patience. Conquer it and you can raise the money that will help you win.

3. *Do your homework and know how much a prospective donor can afford* to give you based on their past giving experience. Always ask for a specific amount of money, and then be quiet. Let the prospective donor break the silence.

4. *Never send out an invitation to an event* or a fundraising letter without a return, self-addressed remittance envelope.

5. *No one wants to give you money.* You must ask for it. Ask again and again, and never exclude anyone. Train everyone on your staff, your volunteers and even your family how to ask for money.

6. *Keep a running total of what you have raised.* Break out goals for each day, week and month so that the high-donor fundraising is manageable.

7. *Don't let a pledge become a deadbeat donor.* If a person hasn't sent in the money he pledged after a week, call him back and say you're going to be in the neighborhood that day and will stop by.

8. *Learn how to fundraise effectively, don't just accept it* as a hated chore. Have experienced people with you as you begin regular high-donor phoning so that you might learn how to do it well from the start.

9. *Don't make fundraising the last thing on your list* of things to do each day; make it the first, or you'll never get to it.

10. *Ask for money everywhere you go.* Have a cellular phone for high-donor phoning in your car. Have an extra phone line installed in your home. Secure a phone just for you in the campaign office. And, phone every chance you get. Phone from pay phones during breaks when you're on a radio program. If people see you phoning for bucks, they'll be more willing to give you money, or at least talk about how determined you are at doing the most important job of any candidate.

11. *Have fun.* There's a reason they call it FUNdraising. If you're not having fun doing it, others won't have fun giving it, nor will they help you raise it.

# ENDORSEMENTS

## THE INSTANT LOOK OF CREDIBILITY

Campaigns look for high and low donors to fuel the campaign coffers. But often in the early stages of the campaign, donors are reluctant to come aboard until they can see that a candidate will be credible, viable, and competitive with others expected to be in the race. Enter the endorsers. These are people who provide the backbone of the campaign. They stand arm in arm with you, the candidate, to give an enhanced effect that says you're worth their time.

Simply put, endorsements provide a halo around you that makes others— those few who are paying attention in the first phase of the campaign— strongly consider your candidacy.

What are endorsements? They represent a type of guilt by association. When you are running for the first time, endorsements are people who are better known than you are. They could be former elected officials, local heroes, heroines, celebrities, or people well known to the swing voters you have identified as your target. Senior leaders, for example, are among the most popular people first courted in campaigns because they give the impression of being able to swing other seniors, clearly one of the most important swing groups of any campaign cycle.

Endorsements are also the most cost-effective means of increasing your momentum. Campaigns operate at different levels; there are four campaigns within your overall efforts to reach swing voters: traditional insiders, party insiders, the press, and key donors.

First, there's the race for the traditional insiders: those usual suspects whose names are found on the backs of campaign literature. These people typically contribute 90 percent of the money for every campaign. They are the political players. They can be the deciding factor in those open seat races where everyone running is either a little well known or not known at all. Courting these insiders may not have a significant effect on those voters whom you want to swing in the last days of the campaign; however, they play a major role in determining which contenders have credibility in making it to the sprint to the finish.

Second, there's the campaign you wage with the party insiders—the 10 percent of the population who are activists within the Democrat and

Republican parties and whose endorsements move early donors and start the momentum for party support and official (or unofficial) favorites.

The third campaign within your campaign is for the attention of the press. Though newspaper reporters love to extol the virtue of equal time in the context of a campaign, they frequently are the decision-makers in determining who is perceived to be ahead, more credible and waging the most competitive campaign. A prerequisite to getting attention is your list of endorsements, as well as the money you have raised.

The fourth campaign is with the people who funnel key money into campaigns:

- Political action committees, such as business PACs.
- Powerful organizations like legal and medical associations.
- Active professional organizations, such as teachers, police and firefighters.
- Special-interest groups that get good press and can contribute critical volunteer help, such as women's groups, minority associations and environmentalists.

Your overall campaign is to reach those targeted voters whom you wish to convert to your side. However, before you ever get a chance to compete for these voters, you must first do battle for viability, which is where the endorsement game is played. In all of the above campaigns within your larger campaign, you will need a special strategy and road map to guide you through this insider ball game.

Early endorsements come from people who:

- Have endorsed before. You can find them on campaign literature that either political parties or longtime pols have collected. Also, newspapers often keep literature from past campaigns in their libraries; public libraries are a resource as well.
- Are watching the political process. In the first several months, this is seldom more than a small percentage of the population, even in the largest cities.
- Are well known, such as former elected officials, people quoted in the newspaper as experts or informed sources.
- Are key to money, organization, in-kind help, volunteers, and independent expenditures—the political gurus who steer other insiders to a campaign.
- Represent key pockets of your targeted voters, such as seniors, environmentalists, small and large business representatives, neighborhood and labor activists, women's groups, etc.

These people do their work or their damage by bringing many helpful resources to your campaign. In many cases, they will take over certain aspects or projects of your campaign. In every case they bring credibility, which can translate into momentum that brings the press and voters into your camp.

# Endorsements to Pursue

Endorsements that are important are those that lead to something else. They will get you started, get you money, get you help or get you key advisers that will lead to other endorsements.

Those you want.

In the early days, key leaders, elected officials, former candidates for the seat you seek, and other individuals considered on the inside are your target for the first endorsements. These key people are the ones you parade out to potential finance committee members and staffers you wish to hire. Without the early crowd, you'll have a tough time bridging to the next layer of endorsers: the business, labor, professional organizations, and special-interest groups. These traditionally endorse after the filing deadline, and they provide you with your first real sense of momentum, in the form of newspaper headlines and money.

Endorsements in the last few weeks are especially important in a primary election and in open-seat campaigns where many of the voters may be clueless about the options they have. Those endorsements that come at the close of the campaign move those voters who wait until the last days of the campaign to make a choice. Newspaper endorsements, TV commentaries, neighborhood groups and others fall into this category. Municipal League ratings and other more objective-appearing civic groups rate high here also.

Endorsements you especially want are those you can garner that were supposed to go to your opponent. If you believe that he has been taking a special constituency of his for granted, and the core crowd is restless, then have at it. Don't delude yourself; most organization endorsements are not surprises; they go to the candidate:

- With the longest ties to the organization.
- Whose background is most like that of the organization.
- Who has worked the group the hardest.

# Endorsements Not to Pursue

The endorsements you don't want are those that cost too much to get, either in time and energy or in courting them at the expense of another rival interest. You don't want to drop everything else, like fundraising calls, to pursue these groups if they are not well respected by your targeted swing populations.

---

## What an endorsing organization can bring your campaign:

➤ Small-donor contributions from their membership.
➤ High-donor contributions from their PAC war chest.
➤ People to build, install and repair yard signs.
➤ People to make phone calls to undecided voters.
➤ An endorsement of your campaign in its newsletter.
➤ Volunteers to work on your campaign.
➤ People to write letters to the editor on your behalf.
➤ Sponsorship of a fundraising event.
➤ A mailing to its members for campaign contributions.
➤ Independent expenditures for direct-mail brochures, TV or radio spots.

It is common for candidates to pursue all endorsements with equal vigor. They delude themselves into thinking that these endorsements will be the start of other shifts in momentum. However, if a candidate sits day and night on the phone garnering support for a local party district endorsement, her high-donor calls don't get made. As this process goes on for weeks, the campaign succeeds in blocking another candidate's chances for endorsement. This can go on for district after district as the insider politics brings more important tasks to a standstill.

Leave those endorsements alone where the endorsing group is likely to do no more than lend their name to your campaign brochure. Choose the endorsements you want and leave the rest to history. Remember that most of your target voters are not impressed with insider endorsements as much as they will be impressed with the direct mail, radio and TV you send directly to them—and that won't get to those voters if you don't raise the money. Be practical in your decision to seek endorsements. If you think specific endorsements will mean a lot to your targeted voters, poll the popularity of those you might want to go after and use in your campaign material.

Many campaigns have learned after the fact that the endorsements they thought were so critical actually made little difference outside the circle of political insiders.

# Individual Endorsements

How do you get an individual's endorsement? It's best to ask a number of key people whether or not you should run for office. If they are part of the decision-making, then they will be more inclined to lend you support once you've decided. Hint: few insiders ever tell a prospective candidate that they should not run. In fact, most people are flattered to be asked, so they give you positive results. You can take those results and make them part of your endorsement foundation.

Find out who's important, who's the best link to others you cannot easily attract, and who is emerging as the new political talent of the district. Dedicate some time to this, as it will provide you a clue to building long lists of endorsers, who usually turn into lists of donors.

Always have a list of those people who are endorsing you, and continue to update it as more well-known and influential people join your list.

In asking for an endorsement, set the stage right. Send a prospective endorser a packet of information that lists your initial endorsers, your biography, any campaign material you have developed and something that has a photo of you. Recent newspaper clips also work to establish basic credibility. If you are courting a particularly important individual, then you might wish to send in some reinforcements before you sit down with the prospect.

Have someone who knows both you and the prospect call to set you up as the person to endorse.

Make your pitch directly. Go over your background, why you are running, how you expect to win and why you would be a better choice that any opponent. You need to convince your prospective endorser that you are the candidate most like him. Use whatever other endorsements you have to sweeten the approach. Don't settle for "I need to wait and see how this campaign develops." Go for the gusto. Practice your approach with supporters until you feel confident.

# Rules for Endorsements

If someone contributes to your campaign, it does not signify an endorsement of your candidacy. A person who attends your campaign kickoff or who has endorsed you in the past will not necessarily endorse you in your current race. Before you publish a list of your endorsers, you need to have on file a written endorsement of your campaign from each person on the list.

Most campaigns include a request for permission to use names for endorsements on either volunteer cards or campaign contribution envelopes. In other campaigns, just getting verbal permission is enough. However, it is better to be safe than sorry. In recent campaigns, some federal or state employees in high-level jobs have contributed to a candidate only to be threatened with losing their jobs because they were listed as endorsing a campaign, when they had not.

Though you do not want to get overly hung up on the bureaucracy of organizing your endorsement list, be aware that opponents will be looking for any people who did not properly endorse you and are willing to make a stink about being erroneously listed as endorsers. The public disclosure commissions of many states have laws on the books making it illegal to falsely lead people to think you have an endorsement that you don't have.

# Who Are the Key Endorsements?

There are many special interest groups in each legislative district, and not all have equal clout, financial resources, organizational ability and influence with the voters of your district. Research what they have done in the past by talking to the leaders of these groups. Find out what type of campaign support activities their groups have provided in the past and will consider this election. Some of the common special-interest groups include:

- Senior centers and organizations
- Environmental groups

- National Women's Political Caucus
- National Organization for Women
- Business and Professional Women
- National Abortion Rights Action League
- Other women's groups
- Teacher, parent and education associations
- Homeowners' groups
- Labor unions
- Bar associations
- Medical associations
- Police and firefighter unions
- Political party organizations

Find out what groups have endorsed candidates in the past, either formally or informally. Even though some groups may be prohibited from officially getting involved, in practice, strong leaders in those organizations often do, and members usually follow that lead. Ask what useful materials each might have on file. For example, teachers associations may have precinct maps and lists of all their members who have worked on previous campaigns. Labor unions may have phone banking locations and lists of people who can be counted on to make phone calls.

# *Top Coveted Endorsements*

In every campaign cycle, there are organizations which traditionally endorse a candidate. Find people from your own circle of friends who belong to these groups and ask how you might seek an endorsement. An endorsement process can involve:

- A questionnaire from the group.
- A personal interview with the board.
- A speech to the membership.
- A vote of the board or general body.
- A committee recommendation, to be ratified by the general membership.

Many groups traditionally have established endorsement processes. A number of these groups are listed below. Find out which of these are critical to your campaign and begin your endorsement process with them.

## Professional:

- Lawyers
- Pharmacists
- Trial lawyers
- Engineers
- Doctors
- Teachers
- Police officers
- Architects
- Firefighters
- Veterinarians
- Social workers
- Dentists
- Accountants
- Nurses
- Bankers
- Health care workers
- Computer programmers
- University professors

## Special-Interest Groups

- Homeowners' networks
- Seniors
- Youth groups
- Women's groups
- Gay/lesbian/bisexual groups
- Parents organizations
- Consumer unions
- Environmentalists
- Ethnic communities
- Peace organizations
- Historical groups
- Public-interest groups
- Pro-choice groups
- Physically disabled

## Labor

- Machinists
- Teamsters
- Longshoremen
- Transit workers
- Bricklayers
- Postal workers
- Carpenters
- Hotel and restaurant employees
- Painters
- Plasterers
- Seafarers
- Service employees
- Auto workers
- Rubber workers
- Laborers
- Electricians
- Airline pilots
- Boilermakers
- Textile workers
- Chemical workers
- Graphic artists
- Iron workers
- Plumbers and pipe fitters
- Steel workers
- Locomotive engineers
- Mine workers
- Communications workers

### Business

- Broadcasters
- Automobile dealers
- Developers
- Printers
- Oil & gas industry
- Funeral directors
- Restaurant owners
- Retailers
- Insurance agents
- Hospital administrators
- Farmers
- Downtown business associations
- Property managers
- Contractors
- Cattlemen
- Lumbermen
- Home builders
- Gas station owners
- Cable businesses
- Grocers
- Chambers of Commerce
- Realtors
- Travel agents
- Commercial fishers
- Health care providers
- Nursing homes
- Telephone companies
- Trade organizations
- Manufacturers
- Employment companies

# Getting Your Endorsers to Help You

It makes no sense to seek an endorsement if you are not going to use the endorsing group effectively. Once you have an endorsement, make sure you ask for the right kind of help from that group. Ask how you should identify the endorsement for use on your brochures. Then have a list of possible activities that the group may help you do.

## Speaking at Meetings

There are numerous meetings that your endorsing organizations either hold or put together. These luncheons are often called the "rubber chicken" circuit, but they do allow a candidate to be seen by the voters. A smile from a candidate, a warm inspiring speech or a handshake will be remembered on election day.

You should identify one person from the endorsing group to handle the organizing for members at any meeting or luncheon. That person needs to have campaign contribution envelopes and volunteer information ready to hand out at the close of the meeting. If you can obtain the sign-in sheet for that meeting, do so. These are people whom you should contact for campaign contributions.

# Phone Banking

Some endorsing groups arrange for phone banks, to be staffed by their members at their offices. You should stop by these phone banks early and often in the campaign to thank the phoners and urge them on. These phone banks can be used for voter ID, getting people to attend events or for GOTV. These phone banks should be supervised by a member of the campaign, with results returned directly to the campaign so that followup fundraising calls can be made.

# Direct Mail

Most special-interest endorsers will prefer to start with a direct-mail piece to their members announcing the endorsement and asking members to support the candidate. The letter may also include why the opponent should not be elected, based on his actions that may have been in opposition to the group's best interests. Usually, several key people from the endorsing group will also sign this letter of support.

The campaign should request from the endorsing organization the names, addresses and phone numbers of the people to whom the letter is sent. These are prime people for the campaign to contact for contributions and volunteer activities.

Endorsements are important to all campaigns. They give your targeted voters more of a chance to see who you are through the eyes of others they might know better. Plot your strategy well, and moderate it with the reality of other campaign priorities.

# RESEARCH AND POLLING

## GET THE FACTS, JUST THE FACTS

Despite all your instincts to go out and campaign, you need to exhibit some restraint until you have completed some basic research. Good research can save you time, money and a lot of energy.

Of all the research you can do, polling is the best. There is no sense spending your campaign running around trying to contact the right voters, only to have the wrong message for them. Research and polling gives you the best road map for identifying those voters most likely to respond to your profile and message, and it helps whittle down that long list of issues to a few the public will listen to.

There are four basic research elements in a campaign:

- Strategic research includes polling and helps you plot what your message should be and who should be your target population.
- Campaign operational research helps you run a more effective campaign, raise more money, and attract more volunteers.
- Issue research helps you look, sound, and be informed on the important issues of the day.
- Opposition research, the newest, most controversial area of research, gives you information on the worst about you and your opponent.

> **Research elements:**
> - Strategic
> - Operational
> - Issue
> - Opposition

## Strategic Research

Strategic research is background information research that comes from public sources. Look for district maps that provide geographic as well as demographic data. The latter hold a wealth of information on the areas where different groups of people live, such as working class families, the "rich and famous," ethnic groups, university students, seniors, and others.

Universities, libraries, state political parties, label and list vendors and your secretary of state's office are good places to begin your search. A good exercise is to visit to your county records office, look at the 1990 census tracts and find out all the information available to you about your district. The local city and county planning offices are also a must to visit. Check out studies, surveys, and other research they might have. Plaster your walls with legislative district maps so you can see the lay of the land where you will be working.

In most districts there are at least two businesses that offer profile information called "voter files." This information is put together from election results and other public information in your district. Voter files contain information on the age, sex, and ethnicity of the voters, how often they have voted, where they are registered, and other information giving you clues to their voting patterns and frequency. It is from these same companies that you buy not only your mailing labels, but walking lists, and phone lists of your targeted voters.

# Polls

The most important strategic information comes from polls. They should be used to provide a backbone for the direction of your campaign. Many first-time candidates, thinking polls are used to predict whether or not a person can win, fear they will do poorly until they have been campaigning awhile, and thus think the money spent would be wasted. While polling can test name recognition, the main purpose of a poll is *not* to tell you today what is likely to happen three or five months down the road on election day.

There are a host of misnomers that candidates say about polls.* The most common include:

*Polls are best used when helping you put your best message in front of the key voters needed for you to win.*

1. *"Polls tell candidates what to think."*

    It is not the job of a poll to dictate what a candidate should think or how to formulate public policy statements. However, to be a good candidate, one must be responsive to the opinions held by members of the district. A good poll can tell you what your district's voters think.

2. *"Polls cost too much money for a small campaign to afford."*

    The cost of a poll can range from a few thousand dollars to more than $20,000. However, by knowing whom you need to reach, you save money by concentrating on voting groups who will respond best to your message. Polls may cost money, but they prevent you from wasting more money on targets that are broader than, or wrong for, your message and profile.

    After you have based one campaign on facts, as opposed to group instincts, it is unlikely you will ever go back to a campaign without a poll.

*Special thanks to Bob Meadow and Heidi von Szeliski of Decision Research, a polling company based in San Diego, who helped develop this list.

3. *"Volunteers can do just as good a job on a poll as any paid pollster, and the candidate can use the savings on something else."*

   A good poll depends on the objectivity of the interviewers; campaign workers don't tend to be objective. They often argue with people supporting the opponent or try to convert voters to their side. Their talents should be used for persuasion calls and phone banks, not opinion polls.

   Since the accuracy of volunteer polls can not be guaranteed, donors may not accept the viability of your results. This can cost you money.

4. *"Polls just tell the candidates what they what to hear."*

   A good poll does not distort results. A pollster who manipulates data will not be in business long. Make sure you deal with a reliable firm. All of your campaign decisions regarding message and target depend on this, so make sure that the people you are working with are credible.

5. *"I already have a consultant; I don't need a pollster."*

   A pollster should be a member of, and a valuable complement to, your strategy team. It is the pollster's job to make sure the rest of the team has a strong message that stays on target. A pollster should continually review your campaign materials and make sure the message is consistent with the poll results. A pollster, however, does not replace a speech writer, campaign manager, media consultant or others.

There are a variety of different kinds of polls available to you—and there are many different ways you can use them.

## *Baseline Poll*

Costing from $12,000 to $20,000, a baseline poll is a 15- to 20-minute poll with up to 75 questions and a sample size of at least 400 people. It seeks to give you a backdrop of what the people are thinking and what is important to voters. It can gauge what recent headlines and "hot buttons" are moving people. Baseline polls test messages, themes and possible slogans that you are considering.

The baseline poll also might address the nature of the campaign by examining the types of candidates voters would be more or less likely to support. A baseline poll is done early in the campaign to give you a clue about the kinds of messages you should be putting forward. It also examines the voter populations you should be targeting with these messages.

Baseline polls, as all good polls, should come with a summary, recommendations and "crosstabs." Crosstabulations are a statistical look at segments

**Kinds of Polls:**

➤ *Baseline*
➤ *Followup*
➤ *Tracking*
➤ *Buying into*
➤ *Sharing*
➤ *Volunteer*

of the population and how they feel about the issues. For example, 65 percent of the population may think that education is the most important issue, but crosstabs could show you that 80 percent of the women, but only 30 to 40 percent of the men feel that way. This obviously gives you the clue to include education reform on materials targeted to women voters, but not necessarily to men.

### Followup Poll

Costing from $6,500 to $8,000, this poll would generally be done just prior to the last month of the campaign. It could be triggered by one of your opponents dropping out of the race or something major happening in the district. A followup poll would contact 400 voters with 8 to 12 minutes of questions that focus on just those special issues. An example of this could be a rash of murders of young people in the district, and one of your major issues had been education reform. Now, you might shift that message to safety in schools. You could further test the message with new slogans such as, "Safety first for kids in our schools."

### Tracking Poll

Costing from $2,500 to $4,000, a tracking poll would likely contact 200 voters a night for several nights in a row. "Tracks" are traditionally done in the last week to 10 days of the campaign. They not only track the momentum of the voters, they track the effectiveness of your voter contact (radio, TV, and direct mail). If you are using more than one media message, you may want to alter your time buys based on the information from this poll.

For example, suppose you are using a message of "service to the community" on stations that attract women viewers, and a negative message on another channel. If a tracking poll shows that your negative ad is moving women voters more than the positive one, you may decide to air the negative ad on other channels as well.

### Buying Into a Poll

Costing from $250 to $3,000, depending on the number of questions included, you buy a set of questions as part of a larger poll being conducted. These, of course, are less expensive than a regular poll, but they are also diluted by the other messages included in the poll. For example, if your questions go on a survey of consumer marketing issues, the people responding may be thrown off by political questions that seem out of place among questions dealing with lifestyle issues.

## Sharing a Poll

Costing from $5,000 to $10,000 total, your share might be only $2,000. This is the group approach to polling. Questions can become watered down, or you might be forced to ask blander questions to fit the mold of your partner(s). If your budget requires you to share, make sure you are getting your money's worth.

## Volunteer Poll

Costing at least $1,000, for a professionally-drawn sample of registered voters, this is also known as an in-house poll. If you are going to undertake this type of poll, you must insist upon basic polling standards. There has to be a sense of professionalism, without which this poll would not be worth the time and considerable resources it takes to conduct it.

1. *A competent, experienced person must develop the instrument* (i.e., the questionnaire) so that it is objective and not leading. Often, when people put together their own poll, the questions are designed to get very predictable responses. These polls may make everyone happy, but they provide little useful information.

2. *You must poll a professionally-drawn random sample.* These are available through your local label and list vendors. Your sample size should be about three times the number of completed surveys you are aiming for. For example, if you want 400 completed questionnaires, your sample size should be about 1,200.

3. *The calls must be made from a supervised phone bank of good volunteers* who take instruction well and will not skew the questions or responses. The phone bank supervisor must be vigilant in stopping volunteers who show any bias whatsoever.

4. *Your poll must be completed within a short period of time.* A poll that takes two weeks to complete will not be considered valid. To be credible, the poll must be completed within four days.

5. *Have the results interpreted by a professional.* The creative interpretation that inexperienced campaigners might bring to the strategy table could sink your political ship. Stick to the facts and the most conservative interpretations of your results.

> **Polling standards:**
> - Objective questions
> - Random sample
> - Unbiased phoners
> - Short time frame
> - Professional interpretation

You can save yourself lots of money by doing an in-house poll, but when you consider the time, effort and energy required, you may find that volunteer polling is not as cost-effective as you first believed.

### Mail Survey

These are often popular with incumbent candidates, who send them out as part of a legislative newsletter. They are very valuable constituency tools, but they are not valid feedback for the development of issues or messages for your campaign. If you send out 12,000 newsletters asking voters what they think about specific issues, you may receive only 350 replies. This small sample cannot be construed as representative of all the voters in your district.

### Focus Groups

Costing from $2,500 to $4,000, focus groups are scientifically-drawn samples of ten to twelve people. They are asked to attend an hour-long meeting in a room which may have a one-way mirror. A facilitator will ask them questions about the campaign, candidate, local issues or other matters. These groups are particularly effective in testing messages and gauging the effects of opposition research. Focus groups are seen as a luxury that most campaigns cannot afford, but they are a great reality check and honest amplification to what people feel about your message.

## The Elements of a Good Poll

*Random samples:* Finding out about your voters requires a clean start. Your random sample should be drawn from people who have voted in three out of the last four elections. Be sure that your sample is proportionate to the district's last election in terms of gender and ethnicity, so that it is representative of the people who are likely to vote in this election.

*Primary issues:* What are your voters thinking? The five issues that top almost every area's most important concerns are education, transportation, the economy or jobs, crime and taxes.

*Secondary issues:* Next in importance are issues such as health care, the environment, housing, mass transit, welfare, etc. Your goal is to find out what voters are thinking and how they rank these issues in order of priority.

*Attitudinal questions:* Questions like, "Do you think you are better off now than you were four years ago?" and "Do you think the City Council is doing a good job?" give you good clues as to what people are thinking. Some polls ask voters what they think about a candidate that has your profile, without mentioning names. Likewise, your opponent.

**Effects of endorsements:** A poll can explore the effect of certain endorsements on voters' decisions. These questions might include, "Would the endorsement of the local newspaper have an effect on the way you vote?"

**How would you vote today?:** The final question of a poll is often, "If the election were held today, would you vote for Candidate A, Candidate B, Candidate C, ... ?" making sure that the order in which the candidates' names are read is rotated evenly.

## How to Select a Pollster

Polling firms are not all alike. Some do market research, some specialize in a particular political party or issue. Some simply will never understand politics, whereas other firms do almost entirely political work. Decide what you want, and then who can provide it best. Do you want a firm that will provide you with a written report and then walk out the door, or do you want a firm that will become a part of your team?

> *Some pollsters will never understand politics, while other firms make politics their specialty.*

When choosing a pollster, it is critical that you choose experience in the type and kind of campaign you will be running. Know the range of races—local, state, and national—the firm has handled. Get references from former clients. Ask for the name of a client who lost, and ask that person about the pollster.

Ask each prospective pollster a range of key questions:

- Has the firm ever worked on races in your locality, or is their area of expertise in another part of the country?
- What kind of data packages are offered?
- How would he suggest cutting his services if you could not afford everything?
- What is the turnaround time from the commissioning of a poll to the presentation of the final results?
- Will you receive any kind of interim reports?
- What kind of client load does he have? You don't want a pollster with so many clients that you are just a face in the crowd.
- Does he have any clients who will conflict with your campaign's key funders? If a pollster is also handling a down-ticket campaign in your area, it could create the perception of conflicts or collusion.
- Is the information from his polls likely to wind up in anyone else's hands, like the press?
- Will he work with you on a volunteer or in-house poll by helping with the writing, supervision or interpretation?

When talking to a pollster about money, make sure you are not comparing apples to oranges. The kinds of services offered vary so much that you need to be quite vigilant about what items cost. Ask about baseline polls, followup polls, tracking polls and focus groups, as well as what it would cost you to call and ask how today's newspaper headlines fit into the overall message of the campaign.

Beware of the pollster who gives you lots of technical information, booklets and crosstabulations, but then is on the next plane to another client. If he can't interpret the information for you as it applies to the day-to-day operations of your campaign, then look elsewhere. Also ask the rest of your campaign team if they are comfortable with the firm's representatives.

The final thing you want to know is exactly who is going to be working on your poll. The top pollster in many firms is not the only person who is going to be out there working and making all those phone calls. You want to know that you are going to have access to the top brass, at least in getting the best interpretation of your polls.

# Campaign Operational Research

There are four different areas of operational research that will save you time and make you far more effective in managing your resources, volunteers and money. These can also give you a head start on your competition, who will probably not be doing much research.

## Field Maps

Check out the legislative race in your district two years ago. Find the candidates who ran in those races—both winners and losers—and see if they have the precinct maps they used to plot targeted strategy. Normally, during their campaign they would have prioritized which precincts to walk, phone and mail. See how they prioritized each precinct and compare that with your own strategy. Be careful! You have your hands on some very colorful maps, but you need to match them with the election results, precinct by precinct, to determine how effective the previous candidate was with his targeting.

## Targeting

In building a good targeting plan that is well tested and easy to implement, you'll need some basic information from your label and list vendor to start building your target. This information will tell you how many perfect voters there are in your district, how many voters vote most of the time, some of the time and almost never. It will also tell you how many women and how many men are registered in the district. It will break the district down by age, giving you the ability to target senior women and see how big that group is. All this is critical in building a budget. Know how many votes you need to win.

# Fundraising

Good research on whom to solicit for donations to your campaign can make a marginal campaign into a winning one. One of the first activities you should delegate in the early stages of your campaign is the collection of contribution reports from previous campaigns that are in any way like yours. These are available from your state or local elections office.

Also research the people who have contributed to your opponent in the past. Some of these people might be receptive to your message. Remember, every time you pre-empt a donation to your opponent, you not only receive that amount, you keep your opponent from having that money to use against you.

# Endorsements

Research who in your district are the "movers and shakers", the insiders, the elected officials and the general VIPs who have a record of endorsing candidates early and can move swing voters into your camp. Round up all the brochures you can from previous campaigns. Check out who was listed as an endorser. Ask former candidates for their endorsement lists.

# *Issue Research*

Of course it's important to have good information upon which the candidate and the campaign can build a profile. However, issue research can take on a life of its own if not controlled. Determine exactly what issues are of importance to the people of your district, the press and you. Focus on only a few (no more than three), but know them very well.

*Issue research can take on a life of its own, if not controlled.*

Candidates who believe they are running on the substance of issues are overrating the importance of issues to the overall success of their campaign. However, those who say, "Issues are like tissues; use them once, then throw them away," are also wrong in assuming that a candidate doesn't need to be well-versed on at least some issues. Issues give a candidate a much-needed bridge to the voters. Through issues the public can see a candidate's sincerity, style, thoroughness, approach, creativity and values. What a candidate must not do, however, is assume that information about issues will in itself persuade a voter to support the candidate. Too much information can turn off the voter.

Wait for your poll information, so you know which issues your swing voters need to have addressed in the course of the campaign, and then begin your issue research in earnest.

Put together a group of trusted people to advise you on specific issues. Have one person in charge of all your issue research, with a series of specialists who can delve into specialized subjects. These people should be respected by you as well as by their peers. Wherever possible, they should be considered leaders in the field. Make sure they have the necessary time to develop your position, and that they understand how the information is likely to be used.

Get the facts and the budgets on any issues you plan to highlight. In this day, everyone is concerned about the bottom line. Know what has been spent on this issue in the past, what the voters got for their money, and what your proposals will cost.

In developing issue papers, consider desktop publishing these papers. Hopefully, they will be no longer than the front and back of one piece of paper. It is good for the public to see the substantive side of your candidacy, but these papers are not intended for the masses. Have four or five well thought-out issue papers, instead of trying to do twenty and doing none of them well.

Issue papers give you the appearance of substance and make you appear ready to face the tough issues in the big league. The issues you choose will fill out your speeches and make you appear knowledgeable, as well as give you a core curriculum for the innumerable questionnaires headed your way from various organizations. Issues also provide you with visibility. You can have issue briefings for the press, where you and your advisors sit down and discuss the issue, educating the press and the public at the same time.

## Handling the Dreaded Questionnaires

Issue research also requires that you have someone available to help with filling out questionnaires. The first thing your questionnaire specialist (usually your media coordinator) should do when a questionnaire is received is log the due date in the schedule book. Costly mistakes can, and do, happen when you rush to meet a deadline or miss it entirely.

Enter all questions from the questionnaires, along with your answers, into your word processor. This gives you the ability to cut and paste answers from one questionnaire to another, ensuring that your answers are consistent from questionnaire to questionnaire. Also, in the final days of a campaign, when you are strapped for time, it's extremely helpful to have easy access to answers written earlier in the campaign—when you had time to research questions and answers thoroughly. Complete all questionnaires at least two days prior to the deadline. This will give you time to fine-tune your answers.

## Use Issue Research as a Reward

In most campaigns, the people who are attracted to issues can usually be persuaded to also work in other areas. Issues work can be used as a carrot: "If you work on the phone bank for three nights, you can help write the campaign's education statement." Issues committees are perceived as being far more prestigious than some of the more work-horse committees on a campaign, but they are actually the least critical to implementation of a winning campaign plan.

# Opposition Research

Opposition research is not only important in today's political climate, it is absolutely imperative if you are going to convince the public why you should be elected instead of your opponent. Ironically, most campaigns spend all their time researching their opponent and no time looking at their own candidate's record. And when they get hit with some horrible ad in the last days of the campaign, they wonder why—and have no ready response.

Anything you research about your opponent, you should also research about yourself. You cannot attack your opponent's voting record unless yours is exemplary. This research, on both you and your opponent, is best done by a professional opposition research company, but a team of independent researchers can be pressed into action.

*Opposition research includes:*

➤ *Public*
➤ *Private*
➤ *Personal*
➤ *Financial*
➤ *Political*
➤ *Family*

Six different records require opposition research examination:

1. *The public record:* It reveals any information that is accessible and easy to get, if not always obvious.

2. *The private record:* This is information you may think is private, but can be obtained for a price.

3. *The personal record:* It is the inside story that contains little-known facts about you.

4. *Your financial record:* This includes your credit history, real estate transactions and other personal financial data.

5. *The political record:* It looks at the record you have established in the political world.

6. *The family record:* It's heartbreaking to see in print your less-than-perfect behavior, but it's even worse to see that of your family members.

# Public Record

If you are an elected official, you already have a public voting record. What votes have you cast on specific issues? How might a single vote be taken out of context or blown out of proportion to negatively effect an entire constituency—like seniors?

What's your absentee record? If you have been elected or appointed to a position, and have missed a number of meetings, this could be used against you. Have you ever exhibited public arrogance? Have you voted to raise dues, penalties, rates or fees? Have you traveled extensively on the public dime (especially anywhere with palm trees)? Have you used franking privileges (free mailings allowed public officials) to excess? Have you ever been accused of doing campaign work on the public's time?

Your written and spoken record falls into this category. Any testimony you have given, legal opinions, books or manuscripts you have had published, plus any letters to the editor you have sent will be scrutinized. Also, if you have run for office previously, your issue papers from that campaign will be targeted.

Another area of potential controversy is the minutes of meetings. If you have ever been to a meeting in which the conversation became heated, you may want to go back to the minutes of that meeting to see how you were recorded.

Do a Nexis/Lexis search for any time your name has been in print in any newspaper or magazine in the country. Know what is out there, because you may have been misquoted somewhere, or there may be someone else with your name who could be confused with you.

# Private Record

Take a look at the associations, clubs and organizations to which you have belonged. Could your membership in any of these groups be used against you? At issue could be groups with racist or sexist membership policies or those that are just politically unpopular at the moment. The Sierra Club, pro-choice groups and the Elks Club all have been politically unpopular at some point.

Another potential source of difficulty would be people you have fired. Anyone in this position could spill his guts to your opponent about his relationship to you. Likewise, anyone you have run against in the past, be it for local boards or higher office, may not think highly of you.

Other public records could even include library books you have read and video tapes you have rented. Although it is illegal to give out this information, it has a way of surfacing. Your employment files can also appear, including your evaluations and any charges of impropriety.

# Personal Record

Given this country's record of honoring privacy, it is horrifying to know exactly how much information can be obtained about us through the ever-expanding information highway. The Medical Information Bureau, an insurance consortium, has collected medical information on you and everyone else in the U.S. and Canada. They distribute information to potential employers and doctors by means of computer network. If you have had any drug or alcohol problems, been treated for a sexually transmitted disease, or visited a psychiatrist, they probably know about it.

Dozens of information resellers will, for a price, supply your bank records, credit-card charges, unlisted phone numbers, telephone records, and other routine information, such as your social security number and IRS files. Also available is credit information, employment and salary history, mortgage records, tax liens, bankruptcies and court judgments, as well as any other financial settlements. These information brokers are growing in number throughout the country and will become more popular as opposition research grows.

**Check your personal record:**

- Bank records
- Credit-card charges
- Unlisted phone numbers
- Telephone records
- Social security number
- IRS file
- Credit report
- Employment record
- Salary history
- Tax liens
- Court judgments

Your criminal record is also something you should check. The National Crime Information Center computer system connects police agencies all across the country. Private investigators, lawyers and anyone who is willing to pay for illegal access can usually find someone connected to the system to track down information on anyone. The information available could include anything from parking violations to occasions where the police were called to your home.

If you are divorced, your divorce decree is public record. If you have ever missed a child-support payment, expect that it may become an issue.

Your academic records could become significant. If you did not graduate from college, but you have implied that you did, you may expect it to be "discovered." If you received a failing grade in a course on the state legislature, that could be embarrassing if made public during your legislative campaign.

Old resumés are also critical. Look at all your old resumés. Is there anything you exaggerated in your early quests for a job that could haunt you now?

Your sexual history can be used by an opponent. If you have a reputation for playing around, you could be viewed as a womanizer if you are a man or a "loose woman" if you are a woman.

Your religious practices may be examined. Are you a member of a church? Do you attend regularly? If your opponent is a fundamentalist, expect close scrutiny of your spiritual connections.

# Financial Record

What you own, what kind of car you have, what kind of lifestyle you lead (which is evident by your accumulation of goods), plus your mortgage—and who cosigned it—can be important. Credit and collection reports can also be used against you. Have you ever been late making payments? Are your student loans paid up? Are there any occasions in your life when you have not been a good manager of money? Have you ever filed for bankruptcy? Have you ever been denied credit or lost your credit cards? If you have answered yes to any of these questions, then be prepared for your opponent to use this information in a quick-and-dirty shot against you. Your income tax returns can also be obtained by the opposition. If you are going to talk about fiscal responsibility, you had better make sure that your taxes have been scrupulously prepared and paid. Your personal financial statement required by public disclosure laws will also give your opponent financial information about you.

# Political Record

Who have you supported in the past? On what committees have you served? You will be identified by those people and causes you have supported. Have you ever hosted a fundraiser? Have you been a significant donor to any campaign? What is your party registration? If you were ever a member of the Green Party, and are now running as a Democrat, that may hurt you. What about your voting record? Are you running for school board, but have failed to vote on the last two school bond issues?

# *Family Record*

Not only will you have to undergo intensive scrutiny, but your family will be under the microscope too. Is your spouse involved in any business deals that could affect you? Has any member of your family been involved in a criminal investigation? Have your kids ever been in trouble, for anything from painting graffiti to drug trafficking? Offspring who are perceived as problem children can work against a candidate, particularly against a woman candidate. It raises questions about your parenting skills and your priorities.

# Using Opposition Research

Once you have completed the opposition research on your opponent and on yourself, you must decide how, if at all, to use the information you have uncovered. Obviously, you don't reveal any of your opponent's shortcomings in areas where your record is also less than perfect. However, if your record contrasts well with your opponent's, make that clear to the voters.

# Opposition Research Checklist

You may think you have a "clean closet", but there could be some skeletons lurking. Before you set out to get your opponent, make sure your own house is in order. Use the following list to check yourself and your family before you check your opponent.

- ❏ Voting record in public office
- ❏ Absentee record at board/commission meetings
- ❏ Public arrogance
- ❏ Travel at taxpayer expense
- ❏ Misuse or overuse of franking privileges
- ❏ Campaigning on the public's time
- ❏ Public testimony you have given
- ❏ Contributions you have made
- ❏ Books and articles you have published
- ❏ Previous campaign issue papers
- ❏ Newspaper and magazine articles about you
- ❏ Club and organization memberships
- ❏ People you have fired
- ❏ Opponents in previous campaigns
- ❏ Books and video tapes you have rented
- ❏ Employment records and evaluations
- ❏ Medical records, including mental health
- ❏ Credit-card charges

- ❏ Telephone records
- ❏ Tax returns filed accurately and on time
- ❏ Credit history
- ❏ Mortgages and who cosigned them
- ❏ Salary history
- ❏ Tax liens
- ❏ Bankruptcies
- ❏ Driving and insurance records
- ❏ Court judgments
- ❏ Police records and reports
- ❏ Divorce decree
- ❏ Child-support payments
- ❏ Academic records
- ❏ Old résumés
- ❏ Sexual history
- ❏ Religious practices
- ❏ Campaign financial disclosure reports
- ❏ List of private business clients

FORM 17: OPPOSITION RESEARCH CHECKLIST

For example, point out how many bills you have sponsored that have been enacted, while your opponent sponsored only three pieces of legislation, and none of them passed.

If you choose to go public with some of your research, do so early enough in the campaign that it doesn't look like a desperate last-minute attack designed to reach the voters too late for your opponent to respond. Always be absolutely sure of your facts. Verify them independently, and have solid documentation that you can give to the press.

# Responding to Opposition Research

Opposition research is the most feared aspect of a campaign. Everyone has something in his past he wouldn't want broadcast to the public.

*Candidates do not lose campaigns because the negative hits are so nasty; rather, they lose momentum because they respond to negatives poorly or they don't respond at all.*

Most candidates seem to fear this scrutiny for a few basic reasons:

1. *They fear information about them may surface* that even their families might not know—information that could hurt their families, even though it might not be pertinent to their ability to hold office.

2. *They fear lies and distortion,* such as cases where a little bit of truth is blown way out of proportion.

3. *They feel opposition research is uncontrollable.* Once it gets out, it takes on a life of its own.

4. *They feel it comes too late to adequately respond.* Traditionally, the most negative thing about you will surface during the last three to five days of the campaign, when it is going to be difficult to answer.

5. *They fear it because it is particularly effective.* The negative aspects of someone's personality are easier to remember than the positive.

However, there is something you can do about it. After you have completed your research on yourself, and know what can be used against you, it is important to remember that practically nothing on the list will be used. You go through this exercise so there are no surprises, and so you will know how to handle anything that might come your way.

More than 90 percent of today's campaigns don't do opposition research on themselves; they are unprepared to respond to anything that is alleged. Candidates do not lose campaigns because the negative hits are so nasty; rather, they lose momentum because the response is poor or nonexistent. When unprepared candidates are hit with negatives, they tend to lambaste their opponent, do something irrational, or respond immediately without having a well thought-out plan to bring the focus back to their own message.

To avoid this, do your research and get your facts. Get the paperwork that supplies the background information on exactly what happened. Have there been similar scandals in your district before? Are your constituents likely to react differently to your situation than they have in the past? Prepare answers to every conceivable hit you might take. Consider an inoculation strategy. Is it possible that you might need to take the initiative and leak this information, in order to take the sting out of it? If you have the ability to "spin" it your way, you may be able to get ahead of the problem and get your campaign back on course.

Good opposition research does not stop, but is ongoing through the course of the campaign. Track questionnaires. Every time you answer a questionnaire, request a copy of your opponent's completed questionnaire. Check out your opponent's campaign practices. Is he getting a reputation for wild parties, guerrilla tactics (like tearing down yard signs), or making inaccurate statements to your targeted voters? Look at campaign literature, speeches, position papers, and anything in writing.

Opposition research has become the stinger of today's political campaigns. You can respond to negatives—and do so effectively—even if the information against you is accurate.

If your opponent is going to use something negative in the campaign, you usually get a tip-off early on. Write down any nasty little zingers your opponent says about you during the course of the campaign, because they will give you an indication of what he might use in the last three to five days.

Remember, the worst you can imagine that could be said about you seldom gets said. Traditionally your sex life, past indiscretions, or embarrassing moments are not revealed because of the obvious: if you start slinging mud, chances are mud will be slung back.

You can control much more than you think. Prepare for any eventuality and have a game plan. If you are prepared, your chances of controlling the situation—and the damage—improve dramatically.

# THE MESSAGE

## CATCHING THE WAVELENGTH OF YOUR VOTERS

I t's far too often an elusive thing, this magical word we call message. Yet it is one of the most important "make or break" ingredients of a good campaign. Candidates who have crafted clever slogans after toiling for days have been defeated by opponents who took a simple phrase from a hamburger joint and modeled it for their campaigns. Candidates with high-powered consultants have been defeated because their clever messages have gone over the heads of their constituents. Worse yet—your message may seem important to you and your campaign team; however, to the outside world, it could seem so generic or boring that it appears you don't have a message at all. The curtain falls forever on the campaign that is referred to by the press as having no message.

Your message is the anchor of your campaign. It is the simplest, most direct form of communication from your campaign to your targeted voters. In its simplicity, it answers the fundamental question, "Why should I vote for you?" In its complexity, it answers the question, "Why should I vote for you and not the other candidate?" Other equally important questions to be addressed in the space of a word, a slogan or sentence are:

- Why am I running?
- What have I ever done for my constituents?
- What will I do for them that they could not do themselves?

Pretty tall order for a few words, isn't it?

It can be done—and is done every election cycle. If you are thinking about running for office in the future, but not within the next few months, you can begin collecting brochures of other candidates. Watch the political ads on TV, and don't change the radio when one comes on your favorite station. Write down the phrases that resonate with you. See how the campaigns with messages you remember fare on election day. This will give you a good idea of what you'll need when you run.

Most campaigns struggle for months without ever really hitting the nail on the head. They can't find the message that sticks in the guts and minds of the people who will make their choice whether to vote for them or their opponent. If you cannot articulate the most compelling reasons for voting for

> *Your message is the simplest, most direct form of communication from your campaign to your targeted voters.*

you, then you might consider another profession besides public service. If you can't convince yourself, how do you expect to convince others?

Particularly in these days of increased public cynicism, it is important to bond with your voters. That bonding process takes place through your message.

How do you get a message? You can refer to that list you've been building for months or years and do a little fine tuning to fit the times and the district. You can buy one from a fancy political consultant. You can walk into it at the next community meeting when someone coins a phrase that sticks with you. If you've run and won before, you can use last cycle's message, giving it a new word or two that makes it just a little different. You can take a corporate or product slogan and tweak it to meet your needs. You can agonize for months, and one day settle onto one of the hundreds of slogans on your list.

# Once Upon a Message

*The best messages start with a methodical process.*

The best messages start with *a methodical process* that leads you through your district's population base, issues and idiosyncrasies. The process takes you through your own personality, your opponent's plusses and minuses, and the current events that provide a context for your campaign. A baseline poll and/or focus groups can help keep you in touch and in tune with voter attitudes, but if you cannot afford them, you owe it to your message to try and find some baseline polling data that gives you clues as to what your voters are thinking and what they think are the most important issues. After all this research, you need to evaluate honestly the fruits of your energy and test your instincts.

# The Importance of Polls and Focus Groups

Clearly, the best research begins with good, objective information. Polls give you a snapshot of how the voters are feeling about issues. The larger the poll, the more information you can break down to target specific populations. If you poll only 400 people, it's hard to isolate how specific neighborhoods are thinking about an issue (fewer than 50 people within a neighborhood provides for a large error factor); however if there are 200 women in the neighborhood sample, the error factor is not too high for you to gauge how women think about specific issues. A focus group allows you to hear firsthand what people really think. Many a candidate and professional consultant have been stopped in their tracks by listening to a focus group chew on the issues, slogans and messages forwarded by a campaign team.

# Putting Your Candidacy in Context

Your campaign never stands alone. There are usually lots of candidates and issues up and down the ticket. What is the top of the ticket saying? If you appear on a presidential ballot, and you are the same party as the president, it's important to know his message. He'll be spending a lot of money on TV to get key voters on his wavelength. You don't want to run at cross purposes with him (unless the polls tell you that's a good idea); you want to capitalize on the message and see if you can craft a nice fit with your own, while not looking like you're owned by the party.

In addition to the ticket, you'll want to be in step with the times. If you're the darling of the environmental set, yet the entire town is seething with concern about crime and violence, you'll need to get in tune with crime if you hope to have a chance come election day.

# The Message Must Fit the Messenger

Your message, as well as your blazer and shoes, must fit you. A candidate lip-synching a message only because it's in her speech is easily detected by the press and public. You have to be able to internalize that message and convincingly express it with enthusiasm and energy, or it will fall flat. Often candidates complain that the message doesn't appear to be them; rather it was driven by poll results or what the campaign steering committee thought was the issue of the day.

There are many messages that a candidate traditionally feels strongly about. The job of a good campaign is to find one of those issues that resonates with the public—not to take one that leaves the candidate, and probably her audiences, cold.

# Trusting Your Instincts

When a message connects with voters, it's a beautiful thing. Heads nod. The press takes copious notes. The candidate reflects the energy of a receptive audience. The opponent pales in comparison.

Good instincts play a strong role in campaigns. Too often candidates are beaten into submission when their opinions really should count. An intuitive candidate transmits reactions from audiences. People listening to a good message generate responses that only a candidate in the front of the room is likely to hear, feel and collect. Audiences should play a direct role in refining, fine-tuning or throwing out a message. The feedback they give is invaluable. Trust your instincts. If your message is hitting home, you will feel it. If you think it stinks, it probably does. Get your reality check from your voters, not your paid staff. If they developed it, they have a vested interest in having you stick with it. Bring back your results early enough to make needed changes before your message is codified in your brochures, press accounts and voter pamphlet statements.

# *Developing the Right Message*

Developing a message requires setting up the choice for voters in the middle of a lot of other noise and competition for attention. The average voter is not hearing only your message, but hearing it in the midst of a thousand other messages in the course of a week. Candidates often make the mistake of thinking that they are competing only against their opponents for the voters' attention and selection. Actually, if you're lucky, the voter is hearing at least one political message, making her aware that election day is fast approaching.

Candidates actually are competing with the high-priced, well-researched, constantly tested Madison Avenue corporate and product messages. It is a rare candidate who gets to compete only with her opponent, instead of Coca-Cola, Nissan automobiles, Budweiser Beer and the local TV cable company. You're trying for a market share of a person's mind. Your message needs to stand out in and among a lot more than politics.

Once you get their attention, then you have to convince the voters that you are the best choice. This is where candidates usually falter by trying to thrust their wonderful qualities onto the public without regard to the choice that voters are considering. People don't believe that candidates are the best thing since sliced whole-wheat bread. A message that extols one's virtues may seem self-serving, bragging and unreal to ordinary folks. You need to be able to talk about your plus points in a way that helps voters select you over your opponent.

This is particularly important—in fact, imperative—if you are running against an incumbent or better known, well-financed opponent. While you might be determined to talk about only your good points, the public is so cautious about all politics that it usually remembers only the worst things said. You can talk about the good points of your candidacy, but do so in comparison of your opponent—even if you do so without directly naming your opponent.

- Vote for the one you can trust.
- Change for the better, not what we got last time.

Aim for a message that is clear, consistent, relevant, and understandable. Keep it simple. Remember that you want a phrase that stays with the voters long after the TV spot is off the air and the brochures are recycled. As a test to see what kind of messages are retained, ask your high school children which messages they can remember hearing on TV last night. Ask them what they remember from the informal list you wrote down of commercials on during prime time. Hopefully, they will remember having at least seen ads from candidates, though they probably better retained the messages of all those food and car commercials. Check it out. The results will humble you and send you back to simplify your message, perhaps adding a little more verve and risk.

# The Elements of a Message

Just figuring out what a message is can be daunting. Is it a slogan? A sentence? A paragraph? A speech? Is it the same thing as a theme? Where does style fit? Is your message your strategy? When do you know when you've got your message?

There is no dictionary of absolute terms in this business of politics: what is often perceived as the standard changes with each cycle and region. Your message is what answers the baseline question of why a person should vote for you and not the other guy. That can be a word, a phrase, or a few sentences, but it is seldom more than a paragraph. Your message is not your strategy; your message explains what you will do; your strategy explains how you will win.

You should follow the process outlined below to find your message, and after settling on an effective, exciting answer to the baseline question of why folks should vote for you, then see if you can move from that paragraph back down to a sentence, then to a phrase that will become your slogan. And finally, see if you can find a single word that sums it all up.

If you can't find one word that says it all, settle for a favorite phrase—the slogan that will be your soul for the next nine months. That slogan should be the most creative, clever phrase that reflects your message; it will be your verbal calling card to every audience, every person and every potential donor you meet. It is sometimes called your theme, and it can reflect your values and your style. Whatever it is, get used to it, as it will drive you crazy before the campaign is through. Make sure you like it, because it will be the first and last thing out of your mouth every day on the campaign trail.

| **Building a message:** |
| --- |
| ➤ *Generic research* |
| ➤ *Issue research* |
| ➤ *Strength and weaknesses* |
| ➤ *Differences* |
| ➤ *Writing* |
| ➤ *Testing* |

# Building a Message

It takes patience and process to develop a good message. Some candidates start out with an interim message until the campaign develops, the research is completed and an opponent is in the race. Don't start your campaign by saying, "I don't have a message yet, but I will soon." Start out with something like, "I know this district; I respect this district. Given the needs that are growing each day, I feel that it is time to deliver services that make life easier for the hard-working families that live here. I want a government that will help you—not cost you."

Then, set about your plan of building a message that hits the wavelength of your people. This process needs to happen sooner rather than later because generic, interim messages will quickly become tedious to the early insiders who are sizing up your candidacy as it takes its first steps.

## Generic Research

Nothing will compensate for strong, objective general research. Know your people. There are all kinds of generic information marking district demographics. There are census and other government reports, neighborhood profiles, county and borough population reviews and institutional reports. Build your data bank with information on party profiles (Democrats, Republicans, Independents and other parties). If you are in a state that doesn't have mandatory party registration, then check with the party offices to get their reports from previous elections. Determine the racial makeup. Check the gender gap—are there significantly more women than men who are likely to vote? What's the age breakdown? Who are the primary employers? What is the level of education of the voters? Are there predominant occupations? Is this an urban, rural or suburban area? What about homeowners vs. renters? What's the role of public employees and unions? Is this a one-company town? Are there a lot of gun owners? Is there a large gay population? What churches are there and what role do they play? Are there issues that divide the district? Are there rich neighborhoods and poor ones?

Factor all this into your research as you move to the next step. Before you think you know the neighborhood, drive around it. Walk the areas you haven't seen in a while. Know the numbers and the neighborhoods before you even begin to find the right words.

## Issue Research

Good political research taps into voter trends. All of the message research seeks to answer that great line from *Camelot*, "I wonder what the people are thinking tonight." Find the important issues, remembering that you never educate a crowd, you only catch their wavelength. The goal of polls and focus groups is to determine what people think is important; if they are happy with the direction that "the government" is taking them; which elected officials they like and respect; and what's making them angry. You should focus your research on the people who will vote, not all registered voters. Remember that the general population may be quite different from the 50 percent who are likely to vote.

Through polls and focus groups you look for "the wedge." The wedge factor gauges those issues that are likely to keep traditional voters from voting with their safer block. Issues like choice, gun control, gay rights, property rights, welfare moms, etc., tend to push traditional conservative or liberal voters into voting against the direction they traditionally lean. For example, Republican women might be expected to vote a straight Republican ticket. However, if a pro-choice Democratic woman is running against an anti-choice Republican man and the majority of Republican women are also pro-choice, the issue creates a wedge between Republican women and their usual party choice. They might cross over and vote for the Democratic woman, which is why you need to know the pro-choice voter attitudes among those Republican women voters, in the event you want to send them a pro-choice message.

Good polling helps you find the best people to target. Once you know your target and what they're thinking, your message is easier to write. Remember, finding the best people to target will allow you to build the simplest, cheapest coalition.

## Strength and Weaknesses

In starting your campaign, you went through the humbling process of figuring out your strengths and weaknesses. Go back to that paperwork and review your plusses and minuses. A good personality reality check will allow you to gauge your honesty, openness, effectiveness, intelligence, fairness, etc. The ideological plus points gauge how you stand in comparison with your public. Do your positions on choice, gay rights, the death penalty, gun control, the environment, taxes, health care, welfare, etc., put you at cross purposes with the majority of your voters? And finally, review your strategic positives and negatives. Can you raise the money? Is your name recognition greater than your opponent's? Do you have a field force second to none? Are you likely to garner the key endorsements?

After you've reviewed your personal pros and cons, go back and do the same for your opponent. After you've done this homework, ask others who might be more objective, detached and likely to have a better idea of the true line-up between you and your opponent. If you can get a local reporter to do this reality check, do so, as it could be invaluable and may give you clues as to how the press sees your campaign in its formative stages.

## Find the Differences that Make a Difference

Finding the lines of distinction can be challenging, but this exercise is most important. If you are truly setting up a choice for your voters, make it as easy for them as possible. Find those mirror opposites that make a difference. If you fare better in the realm of honesty, trust, openness and effectiveness versus your opponent who has been accused of dishonesty, being an elitist, or controlled by special interests, then draw that distinction in your draft message.

In campaigns where you might be running against others in your own party, then you need to be careful and develop a message that relies upon your strengths, saving your mirror-image opposite tactics for the general election. Or, you might choose a message featuring your strengths that fly in the face of your opponent without saying so explicitly.

If you belief that your opponent will be going after you from the get-go, then you might choose a message that immediately inoculates you from the attack you expect.

In summary, first aim for the mirror-opposite message that pits your best suit against your opponent's worst. Second, craft a message that emphasizes your plus points. If the mirror opposite of you puts your opponent at an advantage, then go with a message that inoculates you against his charges.

## Start Writing

You start your creative writing and messaging after reviewing the above. Know your people—focus on your swing targeted voters. Know your own strengths and weaknesses, as well as your opponent's. Chart a course through the wedge issues of the district, and begin to write your message. Start with a paragraph that answers these questions:

- Why you and not him?
- Why do you want the job and what will you do with it?
- Why you, why now?
- What will you do for people in the district that they cannot do for themselves?

Often, putting your finger on what it is that is making people angry will be the first step in getting their attention. Particularly now, in these times of unruly, restless voters, take time to understand their anger.

## Test Your Message

How does your message stack up in the face of your targeted populations? Does it exemplify your strengths and exploit your opponent's weaknesses? Is your message specific and unique to you and this race, or is it just another message du jour for any candidate running anywhere? Does your message grab anybody, or is it too safe and too boring? Does the message touch a nerve with your voters, or is it too trivial, or one that just doesn't excite people?

Are you a credible messenger for this message? Remember that the right message delivered by the wrong messenger often helps your opponent. And finally, does this message inoculate against your weaknesses? If you are a young woman running for office against a longtime incumbent, you might offer energy, change, a fresh voice and not part of business as usual. This helps the voters find the difference between the two of you in a way that hopefully inoculates against your lack of experience.

# Pitfalls of Messages

It's always easier to dissect someone else's message than it is to develop a good one of your own. Beware the steering committee member who can tell you a message is wrong, without being able to suggest one that's right. Conversely, some campaign team members are great at suggesting clever phrases and may even make their livings at wordsmithing. However, you need more than a clever line or two to win over the hearts and votes of your targeted voters. Stick with the process; stay with the plan. If there is any place in the campaign where you may need a reality check from someone who is in the business, message development is probably it.

If your message just isn't sticking, then it may be time to find help. Many good campaigns that have been able to raise money have been stopped dead in their tracks because a cynical press person has declared that the campaign had no message.

Frequent pitfalls include messages that are too vague; too boring; too grandiose to be believed; too complicated; too overused; and too much. You can't get three issues, two visions for the future and a snapshot of your style in a short phrase. So don't try. Settle on one simple message and both you and the voters will learn to appreciate it.

**Message diseases that afflict candidates:**

- ➤ Too many messages
- ➤ No message
- ➤ A message that changes
- ➤ A message that is too complicated
- ➤ A candidate who is not convinced by her own message
- ➤ Candidates who just repeat others' messages
- ➤ A message that is too narrow
- ➤ A message that is too generic
- ➤ A message that sounds good but means nothing
- ➤ A message on target for the last campaign, not this one

# Different Kinds of Messages

Your voters want to know why they should vote for you. They also want proof that you are more like them than your opponent. And, they want evidence that you are not one of the same old, same old politicians who will tell them anything to get elected.

They also want someone they can trust—someone accessible. They want demonstrated proof that you are sincere, direct, unique and ready to jump when they call. And the list goes on. They are never satisfied, nor are they consistent. While they can demand anything and everything from you, they don't want you to promise too much, or they won't believe you anyway.

Running for office is a tough enough proposition without the growing antagonism and cynicism of the voters. Yet, your message is the one place where you get the chance to tell them what it is you offer that's worthy of their time, energy and vote.

Voters have strong opinions that you need to respect. There is just no time in the course of a campaign to educate massive numbers of voters to your way of thinking. Better to know what you think; know what they're thinking and find the perfect fit. To get you started, there are many traditional types of messages.

1. *Character:* People will almost always vote against a candidate who has demonstrated bad character. Clues to bad character include: cheating, lying, drug addiction, drunk driving, a criminal record, sexual harassment and public arrogance (using taxpayer dollars for personal use). Less obvious problems include inattentiveness, indifference and ineffectiveness, which can also be portrayed as affronting the public's trust. If your opponent is guilty of any of these, then your message starts with building a mirror-image opposite.

2. *Effectiveness:* Getting things done. In legislative races, this is key. People expect good constituent service from their elected representatives. Effectiveness is often defined by the voters as working on things that concern them. Bringing home the bacon and taking care of the district's families are defined as effectiveness.

3. *Ideology:* Voters tend to vote for a candidate with whom they share similar views on popular issues. Religious ideology, basic liberal or conservative ideology, Democratic or Republican party affiliations—all do more to determine how someone will vote than all of this year's trend-setting issues.

4. *Values:* Values are the backbone of one's soul. They decide what you think and feel about the fundamental (and most controversial) issues of the day. Pro-choice stands, gun control, the death penalty, recreational drug use, gay/lesbian rights, and environment vs. job development are all examples of value-driven issues that determine more votes than more popular issues such as transportation, education and economic development.

5. *Class:* Voters tend to seek out and vote for people who are similar to themselves. The class criteria refers to ethnic, racial, and socio-economic class. Examples can include labor communities, minority populations, low-income and working families. A powerful appeal to voters can be "She's one of us" or "He's in step with us."

6. *Geography:* Voters choose people who live where they do. The tribal mentality is still evident in most elections today. In general, people believe the folks who live in their own backyard, those who live on their street, in their town, or in their part of the district. They'll remember you more than someone who lives far away or who has never lived in the district.

7. *Gender:* The gender criteria operates on two levels. Women usually vote for women in higher percentages than men vote for men.

Highlighting women's issues also draws women in greater numbers to a woman candidate than men's issues to a male candidate. Women's issues include reproductive choice, health care, child care, education, pay equity, the environment, affordable housing and equal rights.

8. *Generation:* The power of generational voting is legendary. Baby boomers, seniors, even the youth vote have been effective targets of a good message from the right candidate. The age of a candidate can put a candidate in step with a whole core group of a voting population, and it can also contrast dramatically with an opponent's age. This criteria of age plays well when contrasting "new ideas" with "old ideas." Age can be used to create a split among those in power and those excluded from the insider's circles. A call for generation change can come from either young or older candidates—all that is required is a stark difference from what your opponent's story might be.

9. *Issues:* If there is one issue that is riveting the district, capturing the headlines and polling higher on everyone's agenda than the more thematic messages, then you may want to delve into that issue as your message. If a railroad, runway or other development is coming into the district and most of your targeted voters are against it, then you might want a message that aims directly at stopping the intrusion. Issue messages can be tricky, for they can change due to outside factors quicker than more style-related messages.

Each election rests on different criteria, but every election usually has many of these message points at play. Every campaign should concentrate on shaping the criteria to find agreement with the voters. Remember, the best election messages are those that weave your points of agreement with the public in dramatic contrast with your opponent's points of contrast. Your research will help you define what's good for you.

# Packaging the Message

Once you have the message, you need to get it out. The message, at least in its slogan form, goes on every literature piece, from brochure to handcard to stationery and envelope. Put it everywhere: billboards, bus signs, even yard signs. Entire speeches revolve around it. When you answer tough questions at a debate or in an interview with reporters, find a way to get that slogan into the mix of comments. If you can find a photo that captures the slogan, then go for it as well.

Obviously, your TV and radio will include a heavy dose of your message, as will your voter pamphlet statement. Once you have refined it, and your message begins to feel like a friend, then explore the opportunities. Your phone banks should weave it into their dialogue with voters. Your endorsers should adopt it as well, and use it when they refer to you. Your fundraising pitch, your door-to-door comments to voters, and even your bumper stickers should reflect that phrase.

## Sticking to the Message

*Don't abandon your message just when it's starting to work.*

It's tough to stick to the message. Most candidates grow tired of their message within weeks, and they start improvising on the central theme. They feel they've said it so often that their opponent can recite their entire baseline speech as they are giving it. However, just when you think everyone in the world has heard it and is as sick of it as you are, that's when it's probably just starting to make headway with voters. Stay the course. Don't start getting creative with that slogan.

It's okay to give yourself enough room with your message so you don't bore yourself to death, but don't stray too far. You will be judged successful if you repeat most of your basic message word-for-word at all events. Add more to the beginning, subtract from here and there and add enough to personalize the message to the group, but don't get too far out on that limb. You worked hard for that message; now don't abandon it just as it's starting to do its work.

## When to Change the Message

If the voters are moving away from your tested message, or if new data reveals that you need a revision to the message, then consider making the change gently. Some campaigns report that changing a message that seemed out of date or not pertinent was too drastic for the voters to catch in time for a successful election day. Make sure that your message is really not catching on before you attempt a major change.

Changes are best made sooner rather than later in the campaign. Message changes are among the most radical moves a campaign makes. Be sure that you have the data to back it up, and make sure you aren't succumbing to bad interpretations before you make the move. Don't announce the change; slowly do it in writing, then in speeches and finally everywhere you had the old slogan.

# Different Messages for Different Campaign Folks

Campaign messages are usually set in concrete. But that doesn't mean that you can't dress up the message differently in front of different groups. As we mentioned earlier in this book, there are many different kinds of strategies you run within the same campaign. The same is true of your message.

You may have one message for your base—those voters who are likely to follow you without much courting, cost and fanfare. Then, there's the message for your volunteers, family and key staffers. They can take more variations on the central theme, but still it's good for you to stay close to the subject. Perhaps use a humorous spin on the message to your team.

Your donors and prospective contributors may require strategic messages as well as your central theme. Donors need to know more about how you intend to win, not just the magical phrases that constitute your slogan and baseline speech. Your message to the fundraising community should always include how much you need to raise, how much you have raised, key endorsers, etc.

This message variation to donors is also important to weave into the message to the early insiders, including the press. You'll want to have a strategic message in addition to your powerful central voter message that is designed to capture the targeted voters who will make their choice on election day.

# Summary Truths of a Good Message

1. *The golden rule of all political campaigns:* you need the right message delivered to the right people at the right time, many times in a variety of ways. The message is the driver of the golden rule.

2. *Do not try to educate your voters to your way of thinking.* Either they are on your wavelength or they aren't. If they are not in tune to one message, then find another. There isn't enough time in a campaign to bring people around to an opinion they don't already share. Respect them enough to find a message they already share with you.

3. *Every message should answer the three basic campaign questions:* "Why am I running?" "How am I better than the other candidate?" "What will I do for you?"

4. *Keep it simple.* Only the foolish do not.

5.  *Constantly look for examples of how your campaign is a metaphor for your message.* Use examples of your message at work in the campaign in your speeches and in the press.

6.  *Good messages are both a science and an art.* The science relates to the research, polling and focus groups. The art is in the creative wordsmithing and energetic style you create with a good, solid message.

7.  *Don't complete your message exercise until you have completed your opposition research.* If you know the weak links of your opponent's profile, it will be easier to find a mirror opposite to your own profile. Good strategy allows you to build this mirror-opposite message long before you release the opposition research.

8.  *Remember that your competition for the voter's attention is more than just beating your opponent*—it is competing against all the other messages generated, from Madison Avenue to your local cable company.

9.  *Campaigns have three equal parts*—the message, the messenger, and money—each as important as the other two. Without each carrying its weight, your campaign is doomed to playing an eternal game of catch-up.

# SPEECHES AND IMAGE

## PRESENTING YOURSELF TO THE PUBLIC

You have your message; you have your team in place. The fundraising plan is up and running; the targeting is complete. You've read the best material on all the issues, and attended all the training sessions you could find. You think you're ready to go—ready to begin your conversation with the public.

You've done everything but look in the mirror. Therein lies some new truth along with the same old you. With all your readiness to face the campaign ahead, you're still playing the old tapes about that self-image of yours.

Image. Style. Confidence. Presence.

That's the name of the game in this business of politics. You don't have to look like a painted woman or a graying-at-the-temples kind of guy to win; but you have to look better than you have before—for many reasons. You have to convince voters you have the presence to command attention and get the job done. If you're a woman, there's even more to consider: you have to look better than the women you seek to represent.

Political reality dictates that you have seemingly endless conversations on the campaign trail. There are strategy sessions with staff and consultants, pitches to potential donors, debates with opponents, courtships with the press and the ultimate voter contact with the public—directly at the doorstep, in direct-mail brochures or on TV. Yet, before hitting the campaign trail, how many candidates make the investment of honing their communication skills? Are you as effective as you could be with editorial boards and key endorsing boards? How do you expect to handle that staff meeting with the grace and strength it demands, despite the fact you've had little sleep the past three days? Can you deliver the eloquent and inspiring speech needed to sway the undecided voters—in the face of a smearing attack from your opponent?

For most candidates, unfortunately, the answer is a clear-cut "no." Upon honest inspection of our communication habits, many candidates realize that not only could they be doing a better job, but if they don't get much better right away, they will lose the election. Campaigners all over the world have watched the most well-intending heroes and heroines lose support, volunteers, endorsements, donors—and elections—because they were not ready for the stump. Despite the apparent enormity of the task, learning to

communicate effectively with thousands is as simple as becoming proficient in communicating one-on-one.

One quality that effects every other in being an effective communicator is your ability to know yourself. Knowing yourself is more than memorizing a name and social security number. It's more than knowing you're a wife and a mom. It's more than knowing you want to be the next state representative from the eighth district. Knowing yourself is about knowing why. Why are you running for office? What motivated you to get involved in public service?

Without being too touchy-feely, this thing called presence is directly rooted to your core. What are your values? What do you cherish in life? When you figure out what's important enough for you to give your all, risk everything and do it every day, then you should be able to unleash an energy and enthusiasm that the public can feel.

People respond to genuine warmth and energy. When you combine a strong sense of self with other public-speaking and appearance skills, there will be no stopping you. Clarity, focus, and purpose can guide any conversation and make it more effective. The key to having a greater outward impact begins with you looking inward.

## *Being Real*

If there is one pervasive criticism of public officials, it is that they come across as being better than the rest—artificially better than the rest. The public craves genuineness. Voters want someone whom they can relate to, not someone who is trying to con them with promises and a demeanor that are transparent and forced. Successful candidates need to be intimate in front of total strangers.

> *The public craves genuineness.*

This means you *can* express emotion, you *can* show concern, and you *can* be perfectly genuine even when you are in front of an audience. It all goes back to knowing yourself. How do you feel about controversial issues such as reproductive rights, the death penalty, gun control, gay and lesbian rights, and other "wedge issues" that determine many voters' choices for office? Why do you feel as you do? These are extremely emotional issues that you need to be prepared to deal with—from the gut. People can sense when a candidate reels off rehearsed statements. If you are going to effectively communicate with your audiences, you need to speak from the heart.

With the growing complexity and proliferation of issues today, it is impossible for anyone to have heartfelt responses on every one. You don't have to. You do need to be in touch with those issues and values that matter most to you.

# Dealing with the Tough Issues

From taxes to term limits, there are issues that will clearly differentiate you from your opponent. Everyone running for office is against crime, wants their kids to have the best education, will work to create more jobs, and has something to say about transportation. But the "wedge" issues are much more touch and go.

In every campaign, regardless of whether you are running for governor or water board, there are subjects that go to the heart of your values. The most frequently mentioned emotional issues concern the following:

1. *Abortion:* Once the simple answer to whether or not a woman should be allowed to have one, this subject of choice now includes parental consent, spousal consent, funding for abortions for women on public assistance, counseling on birth control in high schools, sex education, etc.

2. *Gay and lesbian rights:* From codifying rights for all gay people to freedom from discrimination in jobs, housing, marriages, adopting children and educating our kids, gay issues abound.

3. *Gun control:* Debates proliferate over handgun ownership, gun registration, waiting periods before purchase, restrictions on convicted felons, and outlawing of rapid-fire Uzis.

4. *Death penalty:* Should there be a death penalty, and for whom? Cost implications and whether appeals should be allowed add to the debate.

5. *The haves versus the have-nots:* What should be done with welfare reform, housing reform, illegal immigrants, affirmative action and other easy targets in the war between those that have and those that don't?

6. *Jobs versus the environment:* In suburbia it's the new mall; in the cities it's urban redevelopment or gentrification; in the country it's farms versus development. Neighborhood values that run at cross purposes to development are at the core of this age-old fight.

7. *Battle of the sexes:* This includes discrimination, sexual harassment, funding for domestic-violence programs, equal employment opportunities, credit laws and pay equity. Despite the perception that women and men are equal, there are many battles that frame today's campaigns.

> **Wedge issues:**
>
> ➤ *Abortion*
> ➤ *Gay/lesbian rights*
> ➤ *Gun control*
> ➤ *Death penalty*
> ➤ *Haves vs. have-nots*
> ➤ *Jobs vs. environment*
> ➤ *Battle of the sexes*

With each of these seven deadly sins of politics, there are no right nor wrong answers, but there are considerations you need to figure into whether you choose one battle versus another.

1. *Determine your true feelings* about the matter. There are some issues that you may have a "feeling" about, but not so strongly that you

would go to the mat. The truth is that many candidates may feel differently from the majority of their swing voters on one or two issues.

2. *Ask your constituents* where they stand, and be clear that you may be inclined to disagree with the majority, but will represent their feelings, as this issue is not one that draws your strong convictions.

3. *Talk with respected people* from the district to get a better idea as to how the movers and shakers in the area feel about an issue that might surface in your campaign. Also, get their history as to how the issue has changed over the years.

4. *Consult the polls.* Learn the opinions of the people who vote on the matter; after all, you will be representing them. Determine how this issue sorts out with your voters, your opponents' voters and the all-important swing voters.

5. *Announce your convictions,* even if you know they fly in the face of the majority of your constituents. In today's political climate, it's all right to admit that you don't always feel the same as your constituents. The public will admire how you have been upfront with them.

6. *Announce your determination* not to be held hostage by any special-interest group that controls an issue. Attack the political process whereby these issues dominate the debate, as opposed to the real issues on which you will be voting.

Before you choose to take a stand or answer a question on these wedge issues, do your homework, know yourself and choose your battles. You cannot stand for everything that is right and just, particularly if you live in a district where the majority of voters think differently than you.

Be smart without selling out your values. If you keep in touch with the values that have brought you to this candidacy, you will have the power to communicate those ideals to your constituents despite the rocky road ahead.

# *The Makings of a Good Speech*

For millions of Americans the fear of public speaking ranks higher than the fear of death. Yet each day we talk with dozens of people without any problem. The key to successful public speaking lies not only in learning to be effective on the podium, but learning how to talk intimately with one person while hundreds of others look on.

It is nearly impossible to be 100 percent genuine to a large group. Meaningful interaction does not take place one-to-many. It happens as the result of two people connecting—sharing a moment or a thought together. The key to successful public speaking comes from a candidate's ability to sincerely reach out to one person after another, and through this process draw an audience into an exchange so that every person in the audience feels she is speaking directly to her.

## Keys to a good stump speech

- Begin powerfully. Emphasize your message at the beginning of your talk.
- Repeat your message regularly.
- Emphasize unusual points. Make your key points in humorous, outstanding or unusual ways.
- Seek maximum involvement from the audience.
- End powerfully. Emphasize your message again at the end.

### Keys to a good stump speech:

➤ Begin powerfully.
➤ Repeat your message regularly.
➤ Make key points in unusual ways.
➤ Seek audience involvement.
➤ End powerfully.

# *Organizing Your Presentation*

### *The Subject*

There is probably no term used more in campaigning than "staying on message." This important maxim holds true for every communication you encounter—an interview, a talk with supporters or an important debate. Unlike other settings, the most important step in preparing your presentation has already been determined. The subject—your message—is the point of your speech, whether you're talking for one minute or one hour.

Your message is your guide though every communication; however, there are many different purposes and approaches to be considered in figuring out how you use that message.

- Do you want the group to give you money?
- Do you want the person or group to endorse you?
- Do you want to share your message in contrast with your opponent on the same podium?

### *The Target*

Once you have determined your objective, begin thinking about the setting in which you will be speaking. To whom are you speaking? Where will you be speaking? Who else is speaking? What is the occasion? The tone, length, and tools you use to communicate are all dependent on the answers to these questions.

## The Length

Once you figure out the target, then comes the length of your presentation. It seems as though somewhere it has been written that once a candidate has been given a microphone, he or she can talk as long as possible. For the rest of us who have to sit through endless, drawn-out, wandering speeches, we would like to suggest an alternative.

Less is more.

Your goal as a candidate is to be effective—not long winded.

The more succinct and dynamic you make your presentations, the more favorably your audience will respond.

**Introduction:** The introduction needs to grab the audience's attention. Just as your appearance gives people their first clues about you, your initial comments signal the rest of your presentation. After gaining attention, it is important for you to establish a rapport with the audience. Show the audience you are open to them and look forward to an exchange of ideas. Finally, tell them what you are going to tell them.

**Body:** Support your message with facts, your experience, your vision or ideas. If your message is "getting things done," this is an ideal opportunity to inject personal stories that reveal your ability to overcome odds and make things happen in your community. The more dynamic and lively examples you use, the more your audience remembers. Think of it as drawing a picture for your audience: the clearer, more graphic and colorful, the better the understanding your audience will have of you and your presentation.

**Climax:** The climax is the point in your presentation when you grab your audience. It's the time to let the audience respond, making your case—hopefully a gift of knowledge from you to them. The information is now theirs to decide what to do with. This is the point you want people to remember, perhaps with a call to action.

**Conclusion:** Repeat what you have told them: your message. A good conclusion leaves the audience with a clear picture of what you have just told them. It summarizes your main points and gives the audience one last reminder of your purpose. For most candidates, the relief of getting to the end often leads to a speedy and haphazard departure from the stage. This is the time to wrap up your comments with energy and enthusiasm. Take in that applause. Establish eye contact with your anchors in the audience whom you relied upon during the speech.

---

> **Phases of a speech:**
>
> ➤ *Introduction*
> ➤ *Body*
> ➤ *Climax*
> ➤ *Conclusion*

Practicing your presentations is something that we all agree makes sense, but few people actually do it. If you are to become a great presenter, you need to invest time in practicing your presentations. Try practicing in front of people who match the target population you are courting on the campaign trail.

# Different Formats for Different Folks

Most candidates always want to say too much. They try to get their entire biography, their endorsements, their vision of the future, their key issues, their campaign plan and a few jokes into the space of three minutes. Perhaps you should say more by talking less. Try following the age-old advice: tell them what you're going to tell them; tell them; and then tell them what you told them.

There are many different ways to approach a public-speaking event. For a short substantive speech, do not try to cram your 20-minute speech into three minutes. Instead, try something that is more akin to a great introduction than a speeded-up version of your main speech.

> **The rule of communicating any message:**
>
> ➤ *Tell them what you are going to tell them.*
> ➤ *Tell them.*
> ➤ *Tell them what you told them.*

## Anatomy of a Basic Three-Minute Speech

1. *Introduce yourself* in relation to your background, experience and top posts you have held.
2. *Answer the question* of why you are running for office, repeating your message as often as possible.
3. *Ask for support*, money, help, etc.—whatever it is that you want from them.
4. *Repeat the message.*
5. *Sit down.*

Most candidates run out of time before they finish their thoughts—and leave the audience with little more than the impression they were hurried and didn't finish what they intended to say.

Remember that less is more.

## Anatomy of a Rousing 20-Minute Speech:

When you are the main course for a speech, you need to give it your best. It needs to be practiced, filled with enthusiasm and right on message. One approach is as follows:

1. *Have an attention-getting introduction* (your connection to the audience, a story, anecdotal material, humor).

2. *Present facts* the audience might not know—preferably setting the stage for your message.

3. *Deliver your message.*

4. *Present a problem* with government or an issue that is challenging your community today.

5. *Present the solution.*

6. *Give a clue* as to what your opposition is likely to say about this problem.

7. *Explain* why the opposition is wrong.

8. *Issue the challenge*—not only for yourself, but for government and for everyone in the room.

9. *Build* to the conclusion (restating your message).

10. *Deal with the applause,* or walk into the audience to shake a few hands, give a few hugs and then head back to the stage.

# Types of Speeches

The needs of the audience are as important as your needs in giving a speech. Let's look at your choices.

**The basic speech:** This is when you stay in the safety zone. This is for those occasions where you are sandwiched among the cast of many who must speak. You reiterate the basics of your message but keep it short, sweet and to the point. This requires more patience than preparation. While not a challenge to the brain, these speeches are a challenge to the soul. The goal is to break out of the safe zone even though you have limited time, not much interest on the part of the audience and not much incentive to sound creative about a speech you have given 30 times.

This speech requires a campaign demeanor—professional suit or dress and blazer. Consider what the audience will be wearing and don't be significantly more dressed up. These audiences are usually orchestrated crowds. In some cases, it is critical to remember to stick to your message and try to change the connection you have with the audience. Your goal is to move more of your speeches from the basic, safe zone to the informational or emotional zone.

**The informational speech:** This is the "I know what I'm talking about" speech where you impart analytical, practical, intellectual and insightful information. Intensity builds. You are highly persuasive. You look crisp and professionally dressed (conservative, with simple jewelry). Have charts; show a command of the subject; offer a five-point program; have a book available to be sold. Tell them like it

**Types of speeches:**

➤ *Basic*
➤ *Informational*
➤ *Emotional*

is—straight talk. Look and sound in control. This speech takes more homework and preparation than the basic speech. Leave a hand-out of the charts you presented during the speech.

This speech is usually given to audiences of prospective support-ers or swing voters. It is an important speech in front of reporters, a special-interest group or with your other opponents.

***The emotional speech:*** When you tell an emotional story, using an approach that is passionate, people oriented, and risk prone, you're talking about an emotional speech. This is the "go for the gusto" speech where you might be preceded by a great introduction or a five-minute video. You walk through the crowd after the introduction, skip briskly to the podium, and walk over to supporters after the speech is over. You make it memorable by your performance and warmth—perhaps asking for audience participation. Have some surprises in the speech. If you're a woman, you might wear bright colors and dress with a flair. Be daring, creative and personal. In-vite the audience to participate by asking questions. Leave an emotional call-to-action brochure, as well as volunteer forms.

This speech is for emotionally charged audiences, like your cam-paign volunteers, women, young people, hometown audiences or for news clips where you know only a few sound bites will be used.

# Types of Audiences

Before you set foot onto a stage, you can generally determine the anatomy of the audience. Simply put, an audience usually falls into one of two main categories:

***Leaders:*** Energetic, enthusiastic, eager to learn, challenged and challenging, ready to participate. They want to learn—or at least be inspired.

***Followers:*** They want to be entertained. You are their luncheon entertain-ment; you're better if you're brief, clever and humorous. Audience participation is good.

There's a lot to know about audiences. It's important that you know more about your audience than they will ever know about you.

- Audiences know your frame of mind when you make a speech—make sure you're in a good mood. Don't talk to the press before-hand, nor make phone calls that will depress you. Talk to "up" people, go for a walk, redo your makeup, get a glass of lemon juice and water and generally relax. Call someone who makes you laugh.

> **Types of audiences:**
> ➤ Leaders
> ➤ Followers

- Audiences know if you have attitude—especially if you have a chip on your shoulder about them. Reduce every audience to one or two people you know, respect and like. Make them your "anchors" in the crowd. Visualize the crowd as the first one you ever wowed.

- Audiences know if you have memorized every word of your speech. They also know if you're on the stump, delivering the same speech a hundred times. To keep it from being just another stump speech, vary the early portion where you connect with the audience. You won't bore them if you don't bore yourself. Reach for new lines that turn them and you on.

- Audiences know when you've given up and are just trying to get through a speech. When this happens—and it will—be honest with the audience. Say "I'm not going to finish this speech, as I've given it hundreds of times before. I'm going to do something different. I want to look you in the eye and talk straight from my heart."

- Audiences judge you by your body language, your voice, your energy level, your dress, your movements and hand gestures, your eye contact, your smile, the volume and variance of your voice, your walk to the podium, your presence in relation to the podium, and other communication cues that you can control before you ever get to say a word.

- Audiences make their decision in the first 90 seconds as to whether they will take you seriously. Make sure you pour a strong impact, a warm personality and a decisive presence into that first minute and a half.

- Audiences are not just a big, faceless crowd in front of you. They are a combination of individual faces. Find your anchors and play to them. They will give you clues to how you are doing. They will be energetic when you're good; ready to fall asleep or looking away when you're not effective; and they will tell you when it's time to stop with their body language and eyes. Listen to them.

## *Getting Ready for the Big Speech*

Getting ready for a speech requires adequate time for all aspects of it to evolve. The best advice is to set a general guideline for each specific speech. After determining what kind of speech it will be (time allotted, gender, age and interests of the audience, likelihood of press presence, the appropriate dress, other speakers, etc.), then you and the speech writer should organize the message.

The message and new material should be developed at least 48 hours before the speech. The speech should be written and completed 24 hours in advance of giving it; and you should have an hour free immediately prior to presenting it.

An advance person should check out the location to ensure all details are perfect (foot stool to stand on if you can barely see over the top of the podium, technical details like video equipment, charts, etc.) the day before the speech wherever possible.

# *Your Voice*

How you present yourself is more than just your speech and all its trappings. How you sound has a very dramatic effect on what people hear and how they evaluate you. The things people value as they listen to you speak include:

- Level of self-confidence
- Enthusiasm
- Posture—head, shoulders, torso, feet
- Gestures and facial expressions
- Eye contact
- Friendly manner
- Variations in voice volume
- Variations in rate; pauses
- Ability to speak impromptu
- Use of humor
- Voice tone
- Variations in vocal pitch
- Non-verbal communications

Your voice gives people many clues about you. Are you forceful? Can you keep up with all the other elected officials? Are you sincere? Are you honest? To judge your own potential, practice your speech with a tape recorder. Play the speech back and see for yourself how you might improve. Give the tape to friends and professionals who deal with speech, voice and image. What do they suggest?

Often, particularly with women, voice is an underestimated characteristic. Like other tools in your "presence" arsenal, you can improve your image by improving your speech and voice patterns. Like your other characteristics, your voice can be trained to be more effective on the stump. Try it.

# *Making the Best of Every Introduction*

Even when you are not running for office, you introduce yourself to more than 100 new people a year. When you're on the campaign trail, you may well introduce yourself to more than a thousand individual people. You can make an impression, or you can do what thousands of other candidates do—make it a totally forgettable experience.

The best of all introductions is well thought out, practiced and interesting while being on point. It can be written by the candidate, the press secretary or the campaign manager.

## How to Introduce Yourself and Not Be Forgotten

The five points of a powerful introduction can be accomplished in only three or four sentences. The most important, most effective self-introductions are done more with body language, enthusiasm and presence than with words.

### *Your Name*

Your name is your verbal calling card. How you refer to yourself is critical in getting people to sit up and take notice. "I am indeed Marilyn Mayers," or, "I'm the Marilyn Mayers you've known for years," will catch their attention.

***Introduce yourself in relation to the people in attendance.*** "I'm Marilyn Mayers—the person who once told Jack Smith I would never run for public office." Or, "I'm Marilyn Mayers, and I see my old friend, Joe Jackson, over there. He and I have served on many civic committees and burned many midnight hours trying to balance the budget for all our wonderful youth programs."

***Introduce yourself in the context of your goals.*** "I'm Marilyn Mayers, and I'm one of a number of women who are giving up staying home and staying quiet in order to make homes for all of us safer."

***Introduce yourself as an agent of change.*** "I'm Marilyn Mayers, and I don't take no for an answer."

### *Your Position*

After your initial introduction, mention something about yourself that keeps their attention. Typically, candidates mention their job, other elected positions they have held or been appointed to, or that definition that captures the imagination of the crowd, "I'm Marilyn Mayers, your local assembly member and owner of my own small business, The Information Place."

### Your Message

The next part of the introduction should either be a clever line or one that explains your vision. "My goal is to get you thinking about the changes that must come in our educational system," or, "My vision is to have women and men throughout the state stand for something more than boring business and petty politics as usual."

### What You Want from Your Audience

Ask the crowd for something you need. This can be a very specific need, such as support for your candidacy; it can—and should—be asking for campaign contributions; it can be volunteer time; or it can be a call to action: to get involved in the mission you espouse.

### A Restatement of Your Message

The final part of the introduction should reiterate your campaign message as a statement of your vision or your campaign slogan.

# How to Talk to Anyone

Most people who run for office are thought to have the gift of gab. They seem to love to be in front of a microphone and appear ready to talk to anyone. In reality, it is astounding how many candidates are frequently at a loss for words when talking with people they meet at fundraisers, luncheons, community fairs and even at their own campaign events. Perhaps they are consumed with other things on their minds; perhaps they are stressed. Or—more often—perhaps they are just shy and unwilling to start a less-than-genuine conversation that is likely to be interrupted within seconds.

The most common conversations start with a simple handshake and a strong, unusual introduction. It's important to establish good eye contact—don't get caught looking past the person you're speaking with in search of more important people. Before you end the conversation, touch the person on the shoulder or lower arm, if it seems right and an appropriate close to the moment you spent together.

## Common Conversation Topics

When you're stuck for something to say:

- Inquire about a person's job, family, children, where she lives or how long she has resided in the area.

- Discuss current events (newspaper or radio headlines you heard that morning), or the guest speaker at the event.

- Conduct an unscientific poll. Ask people which issue they think is most important in the upcoming election, or ask about an issue they are likely to feel as strongly about as you do.

- Talk about your campaign. People love to hear about the inner workings of campaigns, even though they may profess to think all politics are somewhat sullied.

- If you want to impress a person with endorsements, that's okay, but never, never, never drop names. It sounds—and is—pretentious.

- Find one story from your past that exemplifies your ability to get through tough times. "I grew up with a single mom, and that's probably how I got to be so independent."

- Ask what you can do for them. "If there is one thing you would want me to do after I am elected, what would that be?"

**Conversation topics:**

➤ *A person's job or family*
➤ *Current events*
➤ *Conduct a poll*
➤ *Your campaign*
➤ *Endorsements*
➤ *A story from your past*
➤ *What you can do for someone*

# *Remembering People's Names*

1. Ask for a business card from everyone you meet.

2. Insist on name tags at all your campaign events, and take name tags to other people's events in case the hosting organization forgot them.

3. Keep a pen and paper with you at all times, so you can have a person write down her name and address to refresh your escaping memory.

4. Set yourself up to remember a few critical names before walking into a room. Don't be afraid to ask a person about her occupation or where she lives. The pause may help you remember her name.

5. Take someone with you who can be the fall person who says, "I'm sorry, but I don't believe I know your name." The candidate then can say, "Oh, I'm sorry, I thought you two knew each other."

6. Remember something special about the person, perhaps something that rhymes with her name or is characteristic of her: slim Jim, chatty Cathy, sweet Amy, etc.

7. Remember where you met the person or where she works. Should you get stuck forgetting a name, you can always introduce the person with a phrase like, "This is the big cheese from our state's education association."

8. Know someone in the room or remember the name of the first person you were introduced to in a long line of people. Then go up to that person and ask her the name of the person you can't remember.

9. When you meet someone new, repeat his or her name in your conversation several times. Not only will this help you remember the name, but it also will help you associate the name with the face.

# How You Look

You never get a second chance to make a first impression. Your appearance speaks thousands of words before you utter your first. Like it or not, the way you look is a part of your message.

A study conducted at UCLA reveals much in terms of what we believe when listening to speakers. The results:

- The verbal message (what you say) accounts for 7 percent of what is believed.

- The vocal message (how you say it) accounts for 38 percent of what is believed.

- The visual message (how you look) accounts for 55 percent of what is believed.

The way you dress is an important communication tool. Use it to your advantage.

## Matching Your Appearance to Your Appeal

### Color

Color, and its proper use, can make a tremendous difference in how you look. It is one of the first things people notice about your appearance. Once you discover which colors look best on you, you can begin to make impressive changes in your image impact. Male candidates have only recently determined that they also look better in certain colors. Given the restrictions that many men face in their official "campaign attire," most welcome a few hints for looking better.

The following is a very brief summary of the four seasons represented in standard color charts:

1. *Winter skin* has pink or blue undertones. Most people with winter skin have dark blue or brown eyes, and many have dark or silver gray hair.

2. *Summer skin* has a blue undertone with pink visible in the complexion. Eyes are blue, green or gray and hair is usually blond to brown.

3. *Autumn skin* has a golden undertone, complemented by golden brown eyes and hair ranging from auburn to strawberry blonde to golden or warm brown.

4. *Spring skin* has delicate golden undertones with hair ranging from honey blond to golden brown and blue, green or teal eyes with golden flecks in the iris.

There are numerous resources available to help you determine which season you might be and what colors are best for you. Once you begin purchasing clothes that work with your coloring, you will soon discover that this mumbo-jumbo about colors and seasons is actually based on thousands of people who have looked better because they tried it. It also can offer wonderful flexibility in your wardrobe and a delightful delegation to a few simple rules that make your clothing and appearance easier to coordinate.

## Clothes

Your clothes make a tremendous statement about you. While quality, tidiness and style are important for all of us, women's options are vast, making the selection you choose even more important. While a male candidate can make it through a campaign in suits and khakis, a woman must choose her outfits with great care.

During a campaign your wardrobe must meet several demands. First, it must communicate a professional manner. Second, it must be flexible to get you from your 7:00 a.m. fundraising meeting to your last coffee klatch at 8:00 p.m. Third, it must be functional and comfortable. Last, and certainly not least, your wardrobe must include clothes you enjoy wearing. Your clothes will contribute to your overall feeling of well-being on the campaign trail.

You can begin building that winning campaign wardrobe by clearly identifying your goals. How will you be spending your time on the campaign trail? What types of events and activities will dominate your days? For most candidates, the answers will include a wide variety of undertakings. Once you have inventoried your potential schedule, develop a sense of the types of clothes you will need for each activity and how they blend together. Also keep in mind the image you want to convey. When you have completed these exercises you should have a good idea of the types of clothes you will need.

The next step requires an honest assessment of how you look. Check out that profile of yours. Do you have short legs? Long legs? Are you tall? Short? Is one part of your body out of proportion with another? The goal is to present yourself in the best way possible. Once you understand your challenges you can build a wardrobe to highlight your strengths. Color, fabric, patterns, and accessories are all tools you can use to help overcome your challenges. Once you have identified areas you want to improve, seek the help of a professional to guide you in selecting the items best suited for your body.

**Your wardrobe must be:**

➤ Professional
➤ Flexible
➤ Functional
➤ Comfortable
➤ Enjoyable

One last wardrobe hint: try to build your wardrobe around three core neutral colors. Each season has neutral shades. The most effective way to integrate these colors into your wardrobe is to have a jacket, pants, and a skirt in each of your three neutral shades. With matching shoes, you are on your way to an extremely versatile wardrobe. From this point, each blouse you purchase should work with each color and provide you with endless mix-and-match options.

## Accessories

As a candidate the statements you make with your accessories will be closely watched. Does your broach have a hidden meaning? Is that scarf so glamorous that it cheapens you? Regardless of the outlandish speculation and interpretation that the public and media might engage in regarding your appearance, it is important that you keep in mind that people are more likely to remember what you wear and how you look than your message. If you give your clothes or accessories a reason to stand out, they just might—to your disappointment.

Jewelry reveals a great deal about the person wearing it. Keep jewelry to a minimum. No more than one ring per hand, one necklace, and small- to medium-sized earrings that do not dangle.

Shoes are one of the most important items in your wardrobe. Finding shoes that are both comfortable and complimentary will go a long way toward maintaining a well-respected appearance. Shoes should be purchased for quality, comfort and durability. This is especially true on the campaign trail. Purchase shoes in your core neutral shades and always keep them well maintained and polished.

Eyeglasses, if you must wear them, need to coordinate with your total look. The color and shape should compliment your natural features. Avoid colored lenses, as they prevent people from being able to look you in the eye. If you wear glasses during a television appearance, make certain to ask the crew to adjust the lights so your eyes are not in the shadow of your glasses.

Briefcases are imperative on the campaign trail. From the cellular phone to your fundraising lists and makeup, they contain essentials. Whenever possible, a woman candidate should not carry a purse while campaigning. It is distracting for her and gets in the way of impromptu pictures, etc.

## Makeup

Your face is the key to your image. Your eyes, your smile, even the glow of your face make a tremendous impact on people. Hence, the importance of makeup in your daily regime. With the proper tools, products and application your makeup will help you put your best face forward. The general rule with all makeup is to use more than you typically do in professional life or

**Tips for image building:**

➤ Do not get trendy.

➤ Buy the best clothes you can afford.

➤ Do not out-dress your constituents.

➤ If you wear glasses, buy non-reflective.

➤ Have makeup on hand for touch-ups.

➤ Don't wear anything distracting.

➤ Avoid revealing, flashy clothes and jewelry.

➤ When in doubt, go conservative.

➤ Avoid alcohol.

on the job. The best advice is to head to a department store makeup counter—with someone from the campaign accompanying you—and try several approaches.

The following steps will help you through a typical daily makeup routine of a woman candidate on the campaign trail.

**Makeup tools:** A good set of makeup tools is a must for effective makeup application. Powder, blush, eye shadow, brow and lipstick brushes are the basics.

**Foundation:** Evenly dot foundation on your face to give it a smooth, clean look. For oil-based foundation use a cosmetic sponge and for the oil-free, your fingertips.

**Concealer:** If minimal, cover under-eye dark areas and blemishes after applying foundation. If you have a more severe problem, apply concealer before applying foundation.

**Powder:** Choose the powder that is best for you, loose or pressed, and apply evenly over entire face.

**Blush:** Apply blush along cheekbones, beginning under the outer edge of the iris, and brush into hairline near the top half of the ear. Blend edges with a contour brush.

**Eyeliner:** Apply eyeliner on upper and lower lid, blending to soften the line.

**Eye shadow:** Visit your local makeup counter for assistance. Depending on your eyelid and eyebrow proportions, there are slight variations in the application of your eyeliner and shadow color. Don't be too colorful.

**Eyebrows:** Avoid using shades darker than your hair; chose a pencil one shade lighter than your hair color.

**Lipstick:** Apply red lipstick several times a day. Most women find it better to use a lip liner with regular lipstick on the soft portions of the lip, which keeps the lipstick on longer.

## Tips for Image Building

- Do not get trendy. Stick with a classic look.
- Buy the best clothes you can afford.
- Do not dress fancier, flashier or much more expensive than your constituents.
- If you wear glasses, buy non-reflective lenses. You don't want to interfere with people seeing you.
- Women should keep light makeup on hand for touch-ups before going in front of audiences or cameras.

- Do not wear anything that distracts from who you are and what you are saying.

- Women candidates should avoid low necklines, tight clothes, short skirts, noisy or flashy jewelry and jeweled nails.

- When in doubt, it's always better to go conservative. You will be more believable.

- For your energy's sake, avoid alcohol at events. It is very unappealing to voters if the drink affects your speech or thinking, and your opponent can—and no doubt will—use this against you.

# Health on the Campaign Trail

An important part of the candidate's image is maintaining her physical and mental health. It is important to include the following in your routine:

**Exercise:** Contrary to popular belief, exercise is invigorating rather than exhausting.

**Diet:** A balanced diet is essential to maintain peak energy. Avoid overloading on junk food at events.

**Makeup:** Include time for a makeup session and for repairs throughout your busy schedule.

**Hair:** Keep looking and feeling good with regular appointments for haircuts and styling.

**Sleep:** Write sleep into your schedule. It is essential to have adequate sleep, especially before TV appearances.

**Family:** Family time is important for you and your family members throughout your campaign.

**Quiet:** Remember to take time for yourself to think, read or just unwind.

**For your health:**
- ➤ Exercise
- ➤ Diet
- ➤ Makeup
- ➤ Hair
- ➤ Sleep
- ➤ Family
- ➤ Quiet

# FIELD OPERATIONS

## TAKE ME TO THE VOTERS

I n today's political world of expensive prime-time TV ads, Internet campaigning and paid phone banks, one might long for the "good old days" when most of the voters would meet their candidates at their own front door. It seems to most voters that campaigning has become impersonal, generic and out of touch with their everyday lives.

Nothing should be further from the truth.

Campaigns that don't have a human "touch" with their targeted voters are missing the best bet of their strategy. Field operations—the term that defines getting out of your office and meeting the voters one on one—are on the rise again. With voters becoming more disillusioned with politics in general, the best antidote for campaign cynicism is looking voters in the eye and talking with them directly— not over the airwaves, but in person.

Despite all the new politically-sophisticated tools, the most compelling move you can make to convince a person to vote for you is to meet her personally. Going door-to-door, calling voters on the phone or meeting them at a public event are the best ways to make a favorable, memorable impression. The problem is that one person cannot hope to meet thousands of people personally over the course of a nine- or ten-month campaign.

Enter the campaign's field operations. Field means getting your message to your targeted voters (not everybody in the district—but those targeted voters you have to move to your side in order to win). Creating a visibility where people live, work, commute and play: that's the job of a strong field operation.

Field operations primarily involve door-to-door campaigning, organized phone banks, yard sign strategies, and specialized mailings. Personal appearances at county fairs, hometown parades, and other important local events are also part of the field organizer's realm. It's the field team that must generate and use your volunteers well; it's the field force that determines whether you have the momentum to win; and it's your field operations that determine how successful your Get-Out-The-Vote efforts will be.

Get-Out-The-Vote (called GOTV) can easily make a three- or four-point difference in the outcome of an election, particularly in low-turnout areas or off-presidential cycle years. Getting out the vote means collecting the names and telephone numbers of all those voters who have said they are going to vote for you. The weekend before the election, you call and remind them that you're counting on their votes. However, the most important task of GOTV is calling your identified supportive voters on election day and asking them if they have voted. Sophisticated, well-staffed campaigns have election-day poll watchers who, every four hours, collect the names of those who have voted and check them off the list of identified supporters, leaving other volunteers in the office to phone those who have not yet voted.

Instead of being a lost art, today field operations and GOTV are taking on new meaning. Field now includes networking in cyberspace through targeted populations you can reach on the Internet. By keeping the names of those who are on the "Net," you can reach them periodically and keep them informed of your campaign's progress, urging them to volunteer as you go.

# *Designing an Effective Field Plan*

A good field plan requires enough people to do more than just write a plan. Many field plans fall flat because a campaign has reached beyond its means to plan too many activities for too few volunteers. As a result, the volunteers burn out and you have no plan, much less a good field plan.

The field plan is directed by one person. It has one target population of voters from which an integrated plan and timeline is built, detailing the phone banks, doorbelling, visibility schedule, voter-registration drives and absentee-ballot strategies.

The ingredients of the plan include:

- The job description of the field coordinator and the priority that field will have in your campaign.

- The number and the nature of the volunteers, supervisors, and paid staff you will need to accomplish field projects.

- How many times you intend to reach your targeted voters through direct mail, doorbelling, phone banks, yard signs, visibility events, etc.

- An analysis of other campaigns in the area and how your campaign might coordinate efforts with them.

- A review of the traditional grassroots efforts—and tolerance of such efforts—demonstrated in the area in the recent past.

- An assessment of your opponent and his likelihood of running a strong field campaign.

*The field plan is as important to the successful outcome of a campaign as the fundraising plan.*

Once the field plan has been up and operational for several months, then a separate Get-Out-The-Vote plan is written, usually created by the field staff who know the realistic capabilities of the campaign team.

The field coordinator or director is the spark, energy and verve of the campaign. The field coordinator is the candidate's local alter ego. She knows the local movers and shakers who make a difference. She knows the lay of the land, the important community events, and the places that can be converted to free phone bank locations with a single phone call. A field director keeps the local folks happy and feeling like an integral part of the team, even when the candidate never seems to be around. These people are a special sort; find one with an even temper, good people skills and a willingness to take risks. If she comes with great detail skills, so much the better. Field coordination is where most campaign professionals get their start. It's where the pros began and what the old-timers talk about when they refer to the way campaigns used to be.

A field coordinator's job is to balance the resources of the campaign to all districts, ensuring that the focus of those resources is aimed at the targeted voters—not just the local volunteers who yell the loudest. Focusing attention on swing voters gets a campaign closer to winning—and the field coordinator never loses sight of that goal.

# People Resources

Just as you need to know how much money it will take, you should know how many people it will take to accomplish the activities within your field plan. The volunteer budget—requiring both an assessment of the money and people resources needed—is a must for any campaign. It requires that you determine the number of volunteers needed to reach your targeted populations by specific task.

If you want to reach your targeted voters both by phone and by going door-to-door, you need to know how many volunteers it will take to do each. Once you survey the area where your targeted voters live, you might project that doorbellers could reach about 25 households an hour, if the area is suburban and the houses are fairly close together. To reach 5,000 voters you'll need 200 hours of volunteer doorbelling. If each volunteer works one five-hour day, it will take 40 volunteers to get the job done. If those volunteers will work two days, then you only need 20 of them and can reach the entire target on a single weekend. If you plan conservatively, expecting that only half the volunteers will accomplish what they initially promise, you would secure 60 volunteers for a weekend, hopeful that 10 would do two days of doorbelling, 10 would do one day, 10 would do half a day, and 20 wouldn't do anything that day, but 10 of those could probably be persuaded to do a day the following weekend.

If you want to reach those same voters through phone banks, you probably won't be able to reach as many per hour; however, you can usually attract more people to work phones than to canvass a hilly neighborhood. Depending on your script, you might be able to complete 12 calls an hour. Ironically, it's easier to reach people by phone than by going door-to-door, since a growing number of people leave their answering machines on even when they are home. To reach 5,000 households, you will need 417 hours on the phone. If each of your phoners will work a three-hour shift, you'll need 139 shifts. With ten phones that you can use five days a week, you'll be able to schedule 50 shifts a week. At that rate, you'll need about three weeks of phone banks filled to capacity. To fill the 50 shifts, you'd need at least 75 people each week who promise to phone bank for the campaign. These people would need to be reminded at least three times before each shift that you are counting on them.

In each of these cases, you would need another four volunteers just to commit to calling the volunteer workers to show up for doorbelling and phone banking. Each volunteer budget should also have at least one supervisor per night to oversee the work.

## *Monetary Resources*

Field campaigns require more than just people to make them successful. Although the blood, sweat and tears of your volunteers will drive the field effort, there are expenses to consider before you rev up the spirits of would-be campaigners. Field expenses include phone bills, mileage, supplies (from clip boards to pencils), stationery, name tags, maps, candidate bio handcards, flyers, invitations, thank-you cards, and other basic necessities (occasional refreshments and pizza)—all part of the plan for getting the word out. Volunteers should get the word early that the campaign will not reimburse expenses after the fact. All volunteer costs should be accounted for in the budget, approved in advance and reimbursed only after the volunteer fills out an appropriate form and attaches receipts.

Other major costs of field operations include lists. No successful field plan is complete without printouts of the campaign's targeted voters. Once you have determined the core voters whom you wish to reach, you must insist that all field activities revolve around it. Going back to the Golden Rule of Politics, all campaigns should be directed to getting the right message to the right folks, at the right time, a number of times in a variety of ways. Once you get the names of your targeted voters on one list, you can set about the task of delivering your message through phone banks, mailings and doorbelling. It's important to stick to the list, no matter what.

- No one should be phoned who is not on the list.
- No one should be doorbelled who is not on the list.
- No one should be mailed brochures who is not on the list.

Budget for walking lists, phone lists, labels, and a computer program or label/list vendor that will do the work for you.

# Grassroots Campaigns Make a Comeback

Field work is hard work. Doorbelling homes with nasty dogs, calling hundreds of people and asking them the same question without sounding bored, and labeling thousands of letters—none of this is your basic fun job-of-the-day, but someone's got to do it if your campaign is to have a look of genuine grassroots.

*The goal is to be considered grassroots and have the money to complement your efforts with paid media.*

Grassroots is the universal term for campaigns that take politics back to the neighborhoods and away from slick, insincere-appearing ones. Grassroots means you have enough magnetism to attract people to join you; you don't have to buy your workers. If you build a strong field operation, your momentum is seen as honest and growing. If you have real people walking many neighborhoods to endorse you, voters can put a friendly face on your candidacy.

Grassroots, field, neighborhood, individual voter contact—all of these terms give your campaign a sense of being real and not "spin." It is why we are seeing such a return to "grassroots campaigning." Grassroots means your campaign is good; people want campaigns that are supported by people more than dollars. However, if a campaign gets a reputation for being grassroots, it also usually means it has no money. The goal is to be considered grassroots (where volunteers are doing more of the visible work) and still have the money to complement your efforts with paid media.

# Voter Contact Plan

Once you have a field coordinator, a plan, a budget and lots of volunteers, you can plot your campaign strategy to reach your targeted voters. Refer to the *Paid Media* chapter to determine which of the major mediums you will use to get your message to your targeted voters. Perhaps it will be on broadcast media such as radio and TV; perhaps you'll target direct mail; if you're in the right race that's well-funded, you may well do both.

**Your voter contact plan:**

- ➤ Candidate schedule
- ➤ Voter registration drives
- ➤ Event mailings
- ➤ Voter contact mailings
- ➤ Event phone banks
- ➤ Voter ID phone banks
- ➤ Doorbelling
- ➤ Local press events
- ➤ Absentee-ballot strategy
- ➤ Coordinated campaign events

On your central calendar, place the dates when the major medium voter contact pieces will hit the streets. If you have TV to run for all three weeks prior to the primary, place it on the chart. If you have radio planned in specific markets for the last two weeks, write it down. Add the direct-mail pieces you think you need and can afford.

After these basic pieces are plotted on the calendar, begin your voter contact plan.

*Candidate schedule:* You need to be visible throughout your district. From county fairs to the largest non-profit fundraisers, these events should be put on your schedule as soon as you know about them.

*Voter registration drives:* Add the dates when you expect to solicit groups, mail to special lists and snag people at community events. Remember to record the deadline for registering new voters for the election.

*Event mailings:* In the early days of the campaign all events, from campaign kickoffs to headquarters openings, will require a volunteer mailing party. As soon as you know of the events, add the mailing dates three weeks prior to the event date.

*Voter contact mailings:* Any mailing to more than 2,500 voters might best be handled by a professional mailing house. However, these mailings that target your key voters should be listed on the voter contact plan.

*Event phone banks:* Whenever you have fundraising and other important events, you will need to have a phone bank followup. If you have invested money in mailing an invitation or a solicitation for money, you double your response rate by following the written material with a phone call.

*Voter ID phone banks:* Calling voters to determine whether they are supporters, opponents, or undecideds is one of the major tasks of any field operation, usually beginning six weeks before election day. Place these phone banks on the schedule as soon as you have a commitment from enough volunteers.

*Doorbelling:* Volunteer doorbelling usually takes place in the last month before an election, but candidate doorbelling traditionally starts as soon as the snow melts, the legislative session is over, or when the target has been determined.

*Local press events:* There are many opportunities to make a statement in the communities you want to represent. Once you have the candidate secured for public events (county fairs or special non-profit association events), consider scheduling a press conference.

*Absentee ballot strategy:* The date that absentee or vote-by-mail ballots are mailed to the voters is as important as the election day GOTV. This date and any action contemplated prior to the mailing (phone banks, voter contact mailings and doorbelling) should be placed on the calendar.

***Coordinated campaign activities:*** If there are major team-building rallies, events, fundraisers or GOTV projects that bring supportive or party members together to help certain candidates on the same ballot, these coordinated campaign activities should be listed.

As you can see, you have much from which to choose in putting together an effective, doable voter contact plan. The important factors surrounding your choice, however, include your ability to have enough volunteers, time and money to accomplish those choices. Do not attempt to do everything, especially in your first campaign or in the primary, for to choose all means you will surely do nothing well. Choose fewer voter contact items, but do them very well.

# Doorbelling

Meeting your voters on their front steps is an age-old tactic that still brings candidates the most likely voters. No matter what your opponent says about you, if a voter has met you on his own property and liked what he saw and heard, it's likely he will stay with you. Doorbelling requires quiet stamina and persistence, good shoes and a list of those important targeted voters.

Doorbelling works because it has a genuine tone of humility, sincerity, and direct communication. Too much of politics these days rings of "spin" and phony promises to voters. Doorbelling allows a candidate to look voters straight in the eye and tell them the truth. It also builds momentum. Nothing spreads the good word about your candidacy more than the actual siting of you in the neighborhood. In fact, talking to one person has a great multiplying factor. It's widely believed that making one contact in a neighborhood reverberates positively to at least 10 other family members, neighbors, friends and social acquaintances. A candidate on a voter's doorstep is more than just a conversational item; it's news to her entire circle of friends.

## Candidate Doorbelling

It's always most effective to have the candidate "do the doors." There's an element of excitement in seeing a candidate live and direct in front of you. If you are running a low-budget campaign; if you are facing an entrenched incumbent; if you are a newcomer in a large field of candidates seeking an open seat; or if you love meeting the voters and have a lot of energy, then doorbelling is for you. In state legislative campaigns or urban district races, doorbelling is one of the first logical moves a candidate can make.

In the early days of a campaign, the candidate should plan at least three days during the week and one weekend day to introduce herself to the voters. As people like to see and talk with the actual candidates running for office, you'll find it takes the candidate longer to cover an area than it does her volunteers. But the extra time is worth it.

Also, take a pile of yard signs with you, as it's easier for candidates than for campaign volunteers to secure locations for signs. People who may not even vote—or vote for you—are easily convinced to let you place a yard sign on their property.

# Volunteer Door-to-Door

There are three different approaches to hitting the streets: canvassing, doorbelling, and literature drops.

1.  *Canvassing* involves asking your targeted voters about the issues, their candidate preference, and open ended questions about what they want their representative to do. This is by far the most preferable door-to-door activity, as it maximizes the information back to the campaign and gives you a chance to focus on getting that person's vote. Canvassing allows you to follow up immediately with a letter and brochure that further expound on the subjects the voter has identified that are important to her.

2.  *Doorbelling* is the more popular form of voter contact. It involves knocking on the doors of your targeted voters and introducing yourself as a candidate for office or a campaign worker for a specific candidate. Hand them some information about the campaign, making sure it has the election date posted on it. Ask if they have any questions. Thank them for their time and move on.

3.  *Door drops or literature drops* are preferred by most campaign workers, as it doesn't require interacting with people. Lit drops require that you stick to the list of targeted voters, but it requires far less time per household. You simply drop a brochure or handcard on the front porch, or attach the piece to the door handle.

## *Finding the Best Neighborhoods*

After determining which form of contact you'll take to the streets, devise your plan.

Assign values to the precincts that house your targeted voters. Head first to those precincts that house the largest number of your undecided voters. Particularly if you live in an area where many of the voters vote by mail, you want to meet them first. When the first vote-by-mail ballots arrive, they usually find a population just waking up to the notion that an election day is looming. And, since campaign schedules get cluttered and hectic as the campaign gets closer to the finish, make sure the largest number of your most important voters see you first.

Be realistic about your doorbelling. Don't ask your more sedentary volunteers to traipse up 45-degree hills to reach targeted voters. Don't plan to cover rural areas on foot. Don't expect to get into every apartment complex on one day. Most have rules regarding "solicitors" which you are when you're soliciting for votes. Good apartment house strategy requires that you secure one person who lives there to let you in and walk with you to people's doors.

As the campaign manager or field coordinator, be sure your doorbelling volunteers are equipped with the following supplies and instructions.

> ### Door-to-door supplies:
>
> ➤ *Lists*
> ➤ *Precinct maps*
> ➤ *Campaign materials*
> ➤ *Poll Information*
> ➤ *Personal ID*
> ➤ *Tally sheets*
> ➤ *Pencils*
> ➤ *Plastic bags*

***Lists:*** Start with your list of targeted voters— a computer printout or stack of index cards with just the people you are to visit, or a list of all the people on the block, with those you are to visit highlighted. Stick to the targeted voters, remembering that only one in four households (at the most) has a voter whom you might realistically expect will vote for you. This may seem un-American, but trust the process: it is proven.

***Precinct maps:*** Better than county or party precinct maps can be updated neighborhood maps from a local taxi dispatch office. Most communities have taxicab guides; some even have private vendors who sell maps with households blocked out on them. County auditors, local and state parties, the local post office, former candidates in the area, local map vendors or your public library may have what you're looking for.

***Campaign materials:*** No matter where you head, have your trusty campaign brochure with a picture of the candidate, the message, the phone number where the candidate can be reached, and the address of the headquarters. Take along the voter pamphlet statement, a copy of important questions and answers the candidate has answered, or issue pamphlets if the campaign has them. Also carry contribution envelopes.

***Poll information:*** You should be able to tell people where they vote in their neighborhood, should they ask, so keep a central polling list in your car and refer to it before you start in each precinct. Also have absentee-ballot applications with you, in the event you run into supporters who want them.

***Valid personal identification:*** You need identification so that the police can call your family when they find your remains after they were dragged away by some fierce dog. Actually, ID is more important in case someone wonders whether you are staking out their home for a burglary. Carry a personal ID (driver's license, student ID, voter registration card, etc.) and something that identifies you with the campaign (T-shirt, button, letter from the campaign, etc.).

***Tally sheets, pencils, waterproof bags:*** All of the wonderful information you want to report back to the campaign needs to be recorded as you go—not after you've walked 200 homes. Jot notes about each home as you go (nice roses, cute kid, good question about recycling, send more info, call again, etc.). Make sure that you have waterproof containers or envelopes so that all that good data doesn't end up ruined.

## Doorbelling Script

Keep the script short, sweet and to the point. Once you ring the doorbell, you have about four minutes before their patience wears thin. After ringing, wait a minute or two before determining that no one is home or that no one will answer. If someone comes to the door, the standard script goes like this:

- Say hello.
- Explain you'll only take a minute.
- Introduce yourself, and state the office your candidate is seeking.
- Ask if you can leave a piece of literature for them to read.
- Give them a chance to ask questions.
- State the campaign message.
- Ask for their vote.
- Thank them for their time.

*"Hi, my name is Sandy Bradley, and I'm campaigning in the neighborhood. I promise I'll take only a minute. I'm working for Judy Baker who's running for the State House.*

*"May I give you her brochure? People are really cynical about politics these days, which is why we all encouraged Judy to run. She's one of us, having grown up here and run a business here.*

*"Are there any questions or issues I can address that might give you a better idea of where she stands?*

*"If not, Judy Baker and I would sure appreciate your vote on Aug. 27th. That's the primary. If she wins, we'd also like your vote in November.*

*"Thanks for caring enough to listen."*

## Doorbelling Dos and Don'ts

As the campaign manager, you must be sure everyone is well trained before anyone hits the streets. Volunteers who are properly trained feel confident, happy and more likely to finish the job that they've committed to do. Campaigns lose volunteers when they don't take every volunteer task seriously enough to organize the details for their team.

1. *Have an evening that you dedicate* to training, role-playing and anticipating problems. Even the most seasoned doorbeller can learn new tricks of the trade—or at least share funny stories with others.

2. *Make sure the doorbellers know* the importance of looking good. They are living, breathing examples of the best of your campaign. Although jogging shoes and jeans are allowable, it's best to have a sports jacket or blazer to reflect the seriousness with which you take the campaign.

3. *Dress like the people you will be meeting.* Sending young students with torn jeans to a seniors' home is not good voter contact. Sending a Caucasian team to an Hispanic neighborhood also misses the mark. Coats and ties in blue-collar neighborhoods are as taboo as a lack of coats and ties in communities of people coming home from Sunday church.

4. *Drive the area before you walk it.* Know the rough spots (you might decide to team up with someone else); know the spots where you're likely to make a rest stop; and plan your goals of where you hope to be by what time.

5. *Park in a location central* to where you are walking, or if you can, park at the end of your route and get a ride to the beginning. In this way you can use the car as a goal for your day's work.

6. *Approach dogs as necessary evils,* but don't push your luck. If there is a sign alerting you to a nasty dog on the premises, make your entrance cautiously. If you have a cellular phone with you, and have the phone number on your walking list, call ahead and see if the owner will come to the door for a moment. Although canvassers have been bitten, those cases are quite rare.

7. *Respect people's property.* Don't walk on landscaped lawns. Under no circumstances litter; in fact, pick up stray pieces of paper and throw them into your own pack, as the watchful eyes of the neighborhood may log this as a random act of kindness from your campaign.

8. *If voters are friendly and inviting,* ask what their most important issues are and venture your candidate's thoughts on them. If you're getting a warm reception, ask if you can count on their vote. As soon as you leave the house, jot down what you heard and/or saw.

9. *Don't spend more than a few minutes* talking with each voter. The point is to put a face and a warm voice on your campaign. You should not be registering people to vote, nor getting them to fill out absentee-ballot applications. Leave that information and follow up later with a phone call. If the voter is truly interested in the issues, then leave additional information or send it later.

**Doorbelling dos and don'ts:**

➤ Have an evening of training.
➤ Know the importance of looking good.
➤ Dress like the people you will be meeting.
➤ Drive the area before you walk it.
➤ Park in a central location.
➤ Approach dogs as necessary evils.
➤ Respect people's property.
➤ Ask about their most important issues.
➤ Don't spend more than a few minutes with each voter.
➤ Don't guess at answers.
➤ Always tell the truth.
➤ Don't doorbell after dark.
➤ Stick to your goals.
➤ It's okay to accept refreshments.
➤ Follow up with a short note.
➤ Encourage the candidate's family to participate.
➤ Apologize if you interrupt.
➤ Leave a note for those not at home.
➤ Don't use the mailbox.
➤ Report your results promptly.

10. *Don't guess at answers.* If you don't know an answer, ask what they think. Then, promise you'll look into the matter and get back to them. However, you should be well versed on obvious hot issues which face the community, even if your candidate will not have any direct jurisdiction over the matter if elected.

11. *Always tell the truth.* However, this doesn't mean being "in your face" stupid. If you detect someone is anti-choice and you're representing a pro-choice candidate, you need not argue Roe vs. Wade. You might instead explain that where you differ on this one issue, there are many other issues where you probably do agree. Move on quickly.

12. *Don't doorbell after dark.* Once the sun has hit the horizon, it should be time to wrap it up for one day. Doorbelling after dark is dangerous in some areas, and many people prefer not to answer their doorbells after dark.

13. *Stick to your goals.* Don't use excuses to quit early. Rain, snow or boiling hot weather should be anticipated. Remember that voters are more likely to respect you if they see you persisting despite a few raindrops. Also, keep your break times to a minimum.

14. *If you find a friendly face* along the way who offers you a glass of lemonade or cookie, it's okay to take them up on their offer, but do not stay more than a few minutes. Remember, you have a list to finish.

15. *Follow up your doorbelling* with a short note. The best doorbelling followup includes a personal message. If a volunteer went to the door, then a note from the candidate might state that "my friend Jeff told me about your concern about the new recycling schedule," or, "I heard about those roses in your front yard from Jeff. I recognize that politics is not a bed of roses, but wanted to thank you for talking with him."

16. *Encourage members of the candidate's family* to go door-to-door, as people are very impressed when family members campaign. Also, people are always curious about a candidate's family members. Voters often ask them questions about what it's like to have a family member running for office.

17. *If you interrupt* a person's sleep, apologize and excuse yourself quickly. If they are scantily-clad, do the same—and certainly do not go inside the house. If they begin telling you their life story, politely listen for a few minutes, and then insist you have a schedule and goals to keep before sunset.

18. *Leave a note* if no one answers the door. Say that you are sorry you missed them, but you hope they'll take a moment to read the brochure.

19. *Don't use the mailbox.* It's against federal postal service regulations to use mailboxes, and people don't like it. The same is true for newspaper boxes. Affix the campaign literature to the doorknobs with an elastic band, or stick it between the screen door and front door.

20. *Report your results* to the campaign promptly. Most campaigns will want you to return your doorbelling notes, supplies and lists that day so they don't get lost, destroyed or misinterpreted. Supplies that you don't use should be returned so that others can use them.

# Volunteer Phone Banking

Volunteer phone banking is a thankless job that must be done—the volunteer assignment that no one wants. It is the area in a campaign where we most frequently overestimate our expectations; yet it is also the single most critical place where we can double the amount of money coming into today's legislative and local government races. Volunteer phone banking is the workhorse of every campaign.

Volunteer phone banks are becoming a rare breed. In today's mechanized world of professional politics, the old volunteer phone bank is becoming less and less dependable. However, there are places where the volunteer phone bank is still critical:

- Following up on invitations to events or fundraisers.
- Identifying favorable and unfavorable voters so you can concentrate on the undecideds.
- Executing GOTV efforts.

Secure the best phone bank locations in town as soon as you know you will be doing phone banks. The best locations are professional offices such as law offices, travel agencies, real estate offices, teachers' associations or union halls. Locations that have done campaign phone banks in the past are good places to start your search. Check out locations now so that you can have the first crack at the best ones. Those will:

- Have plenty of free parking.
- Be close to bus stops.
- Have individual offices or cubicles for phoners, to limit interference between phoners.
- Include kitchens, preferably filled with free coffee and soda.
- Have phone systems that are easy to use.
- Be available for more than a few days in a row.

> **Volunteer phone banking is critical for:**
>
> ➤ Following up on invitations.
> ➤ Identifying undecided voters.
> ➤ Executing GOTV efforts.

Avoid allowing volunteers to make phone calls from home. Often the best intentions to make calls at home end up being calls that never get made. Efficiency increases with the number of phoners in one location. Phoners who can see how well everyone else is doing are driven to those standards as well.

# Supervisors

It is extremely important to have a strong supervisor at every phone bank location every night you call. Supervisors are the quality control you need to be able to rely upon the phone bank results. Supervisors should be people who have run phone banks previously, and they should be detail-oriented. Their job includes:

- Securing the keys, directions, security information and any other instructions for the evening's phone bank.
- Checking in with the campaign manager or field director to get the campaign updates that she can relate to the phoners.
- Calling other phone bank supervisors to gauge how things are going, measure results and set appropriate goals.

Bringing needed supplies:

1. Instructions and phone scripts.
2. Tally sheets.
3. Lists or index cards of the targeted voters to be called.
4. Precinct maps and local polling location information.
5. Voter registration and absentee ballot information.
6. Brochures and info on the candidate's positions and background.
7. A calendar of important campaign events.
8. A list of the key campaign people and their telephone numbers.
9. General supplies such as pencils, pens, clip boards, etc.
10. Coffee, tea, soft drinks, water and snacks.
11. Music or radios to give a more festive air.

Supervisors are also critical links in your voter contact chain. They can spot any volunteer phoners who don't work out. People who argue with your targeted voters aren't putting a good face on the campaign. Also, phoners who tend to believe everyone is for their candidate often record information too optimistically. Phoners who distract others or are not serious about the task at hand need to be reassigned to other campaign tasks. Supervisors should be trained in how to correct phoners' behavior, but they should also be given authority to let certain phoners go. Supervisors also can watch for workers who may be hard to understand, rude, too talkative or just wrong for the target audience in question.

Many phone banks today are trying to match the phoner with the target population to be called. For example, phone calls to absentee-ballot holders will be mostly directed to senior voters, so wherever possible, try and secure senior-sounding voices to make those calls. The same idea applies for people who might be calling into ethnic communities. If your phone banks are aimed at younger voters, consider having the young people of your campaign call them.

To determine how many phone calls you have to make to secure a safe margin of victory on election day, start with a little math. In a given area, you could expect that 35 percent of the population traditionally votes Republican/conservative/in line with the top of the ticket. Another 35 percent votes Democrat/liberal/in line with a key issue or initiative on the ballot. Figure out who the remaining 30 percent might be and target from there.

In a low-budget race, to make a 10 percent difference in the outcome of the vote would be an ambitious but doable phone banking goal. If you expect 50,000 voters, you need to identify 5,000 swing voters who will vote for your candidate.

# Your First Phone Banks

As discussed in the *Fundraising* chapter, whenever you mail an invitation or a solicitation for money, you can expect about a 3 percent return, with an average contribution of between $20 and $25. However, if you follow the mailing with a phone call, you can double the return and increase the amount of the average contribution. The same is true of invitations to events: no campaign event will be successful without a followup phone call after the invitation is mailed. Event and fundraiser phone banks traditionally get your campaign up and ready for larger voter ID phone banks that follow later in the campaign. These also give your early volunteers a chance to secure good locations for phone banks, with some of them progressing to supervisors before the larger phone banks begin.

*You only have so much time, energy and money in a campaign, so you must focus your efforts on those whom you really need to convince.*

# Voter ID Phone Banks

Phone banking to identify your key voters gives you a leg up on your opponent. You need to determine those people who are the most undecided—not the voters who most likely are going to vote for you and not those who have a demonstrated history of voting for candidates like your opponent. You only have so much time, energy and money in a campaign, so you must focus your efforts on those whom you really need to convince in order to win.

Targeted phone calls for voter identification do two things:

1. They help raise the name identification of your candidate.
2. They allow you to whittle down the list to those candidates whom you need to send additional mailings or call again.

# A Sample Phone Bank

Model your phone banks after this example. It should leave little to the imagination and allow everyone to feel as if they are ready to go, once they familiarize themselves with the script.

*Thanks for agreeing to be part of our phone bank. As you know, the campaign for Judy Baker for State Senate is moving full speed ahead. So that we might best stretch our resources to their highest and best uses, we're calling voters so that we might better focus attention upon the undecided voters. You'll be calling from the script below. Please try to stick to it as closely as possible. Our goal is 5,000 calls in the next three weeks, and to ensure the most accuracy, we want everyone saying the same thing.*

*If you are asked questions, you may address them. If you know the answer, please give only a short response. If you don't know the answer, ask if you may take their number and have the supervisor get back in touch with them. Keep a record of these voters on a separate list and hand it to the supervisor at the break. You have a brochure and a short question-and-answer sheet that we've prepared for you, based upon earlier questions Judy's been asked.*

*You'll find that most of the people you call will be undecided. That's good. As soon as we know a voter is a supporter, her or his name goes directly into our database for election-day GOTV phoning or leafleting. Names of identified opponents are removed from our lists so that we don't waste money on them in future calls or mailings.*

*The undecideds will get more mailings (some personalized that will focus upon issues they have identified as important), another phone call, and perhaps a doorbeller who will talk with them personally.*

*Let's get started with the instructions:*

1. *Be familiar with the script. We've tested it, but you might find we missed a word or two that you find difficult to get over. We'll be happy to change anything if you find it too cumbersome.*

2. *Know the right code for the result of each call.*

   | | |
   |---|---|
   | *CC* | *Completed call* |
   | *WN* | *Wrong number or no one there by that name* |
   | *NA* | *No answer* |
   | *IC* | *Incomplete call (survey begun but interrupted)* |
   | *B* | *Busy signal* |
   | *R* | *Refused to answer* |

| D | Disconnected, with no forwarding number |
|---|---|
| AM | Answering machine |

*If you get a machine, leave a clever message such as "Hi, I'm calling from the Judy Baker campaign for State Senate, and you've managed to miss the one call this evening that won't cost you anything. In fact, we're trying to give you more effective, better government that will cost you less. You don't have to call back, as we'll try to reach you tomorrow night. My name's Sandy and I promise we won't take more than five minutes of your time."*

3. *Don't be rude, but you may be firm. If someone is trying to provoke you into an argument, state something like this: "I'm trying to change politics for the better. I recognize a lot of what you're saying comes from the same frustration I have with politics. If I can't convince you, I'll let you get back to your evening and I'll go on to my other calls. Thanks anyway."*

4. *Keep reference material at your fingertips: the brochure, polling locations, dates, deadlines for absentee ballots and voter registration. Don't get into long-winded conversations. Remember, we have lots of calls to make.*

5. *We're only working on this campaign—not others. Please don't discuss other candidates you might be working with or supporting. To focus attention on this race, we're asking everyone not to stray into other campaigns. You never know who's on the other end of the phone.*

6. *Review the tally sheet before turning it in. Make sure that all your notes are decipherable and that false lines are crossed out or erased. Also be sure that all codes are dark enough to be read.*

7. *If you can help us with phone banks another night, please let us know. We'll take one break midway through the phoning when we'll give you an update on all the other facets of the campaign. We'll take questions then. If you have really serious questions, you can stop phoning and find the supervisor. Please limit these questions, as we have much to do.*

8. *Our phone bank hours are usually Monday through Friday, 6:00 p.m. to 9:30 p.m. We phone no later than 9:00, but we tally the results and straighten the room out in the last 30 minutes. On weekends, we call on Saturday from 11:00 a.m. to 6:00 p.m., in two shifts. On Sunday, we begin calling at 1:00 p.m., using three shifts to phone until 9:30 p.m.*

# Sample Phone Bank Script

*"Hello, my name is _____ , and I'm calling to see if you've decided whom you're going to vote for in the State Senate race. I promise I'll only take a few minutes. I'm working to try and bring back some good old-fashioned one-on-one campaigning to a process that's already way too impersonal."*

*"Have you decided whom you're voting for?"*

*"If yes, who?"* _____

If they can't remember the names, jog their memories with the list:

❑ Judy Baker          ❑ Kenny Baring          ❑ George Allen

If they say they are voting for either Kenny Baring or George Allen, thank them for their time and hang up.

If they say Judy Baker, proceed to #1, if undecided, go to #2.

**#1.** *"That's great. Actually I'm calling from her campaign now. You can imagine how happy we feel every time we get a response like yours. And we've sure been getting a lot of them lately. We're starting to see real momentum.*

*"Would you like to get involved in her campaign? There's so much help we can use–and it's not limited to any one task. If you have about three hours a week, you could be one of us who's trying to change the way we politic by getting back to basics and working with voters one-on-one. It's very rewarding. Would you like me to pass your name on to our volunteer coordinator for her to get back in touch with you?"*

If yes, ask when they would be available:

❑ Weekdays          ❑ After work          ❑ Evenings          ❑ Weekends

In any case, ask if they will contribute to the campaign:

*"Campaigns, as you know, require money so that we can get our message out to people who are still undecided. Our campaign is different, in that we are appealing to more people whom we're asking to write small checks as opposed to just going after large contributions from special interests. Could you help by sending us a $25 check?"*

If no, then ask for $15.

*"Thank you so much. Judy and I both really appreciate your support. My name is _____, and the number here at the campaign is _____. If you have any questions in the future, or want to get more involved, please feel free to call me."*

**#2.** *"That's fine. Most people are just like you. Are there issues which you think are important that you wish the candidates would address? What issues would they be?"*

❑ Education    ❑ Transportation    ❑ The economy    ❑ The environment

*"Thanks for telling me know about your concerns. Would you read additional information from the candidates on the subjects you care about?"*

**If no, then thank them for their time and wish them a good night.**

**If yes, then respond as follows:**

*"I work for Judy Baker. She has very decided opinions about _____ (whatever issue they mentioned above). I'll ask her to send you her views on that issue.*

*"Thank you for your time. My name is _____, and if you have any additional questions, I hope you'll call me personally. We're trying to put the personal touch back into politics. And talking with you makes it easy to do so.*

*"Thanks again and good night."*

FORM 18: SAMPLE PHONE BANK SCRIPT

# More Aggressive Messages

Most campaigns are personalizing communications whenever possible (requesting that volunteers identify themselves and leave their name and number in case people they call want to get back in touch with a real member of the campaign). It takes some of the perceptions of "political machine" out of phone banking. Also, you might change the script to a more forceful one. Most phone calls should start out as "blind calls" (calls that do not identify which campaign is calling). However, many campaigns opt for "persuasive messages," as they leave callers with a sense of whom they should be voting for and why.

Campaigns that rely on volunteer phone banks must realize that there will be good times and bleak times. However, the campaign needs to focus upon being persistent. Once you begin the phone banks, persevere, as they are a real link of positive connections with the voters.

# Yard Signs

It is 7:00 a.m. An exhausted field director is aroused from a deep sleep by a phone call. It's the candidate. Without even so much as a "Good morning," the candidate goes into an exasperated tirade: "Why aren't there yard signs on 23rd Street? I gave you a list two week ago! At this rate, I'm going to lose this election!" Click!

So begins another morning as the field director of a low-budget city council campaign.

Yard signs are truly a campaign's necessary evil.

There are many factors that drive a candidate's insatiable desire to see his name in people's front yards. Few of these desires stem from targeted strategy. Most stem from complaints: complaints from the steering committee that they never see their candidate's signs; complaints from supporters that they haven't received a sign (even if they live on a dead-end street); and from his own observations, as he drives to and from work, seeing his opponent's signs everywhere.

As a yard sign coordinator, you have many options. One strategy is to saturate the areas near the candidate's home as soon as yard signs are constructed. Usually the candidate's neighbors are easy to tap and can suggest others in the area who would happily display a sign.

Common sense dictates that you concentrate on yard sign locations near the homes of the steering committee members, local politicos and the reporters who will be covering the race in the local press. These are the people who will notice signs and will tell others about your growing name visibility.

A field director cannot hope to coordinate the yard sign strategy alone. Find good precinct workers and promote them to yard sign captains. There are three jobs for yard sign workers: finding locations, posting the signs onto stakes and then putting the signs up (or repairing them).

There are two major ways to get new yard sign locations.

1. Work your campaign lists: phone all supporters who haven't already requested a sign and ask them to put signs in their yards. Add to these by asking for sign locations from supporters whom you identify during phone banks and doorbelling.

2. Ask supportive candidates who aren't running or have no real contest during this election cycle for their lists of sign locations with phone numbers. Longtime campaigners usually have a gold mine of locations on key arterials that are available for the asking.

The bulk of your campaign signs should appear to spring up overnight in key locations in your targeted precincts. This is intended to give the candidate maximum visibility impact. As the campaign progresses, you will continually place more signs, neighborhood by neighborhood, which shows momentum. Keep about 10 percent of your signs for sign waving and for placing in highly visible locations the night before election day. You also will need to repair and replace stolen signs and signs destroyed by the weather.

Though some polls put a heavy emphasis on yard signs as the basis of voter contact, conventional wisdom puts them a distant fourth in effectiveness behind direct mail, phoning and doorbelling. However, the smaller the race, the more important the yard sign strategy.

Early planning, delegation and followthrough are the keys to success in the necessary world of yard signing. See additional information regarding yard signs in the *Paid Media* chapter.

# Alternative Voter Contact Strategies

The way we campaign is as much in flux as campaigns themselves. Many states are trying to make getting to the polls easier for the public. Other states are launching aggressive vote-by-mail or absentee-ballot programs. And all states now allow citizens to register to vote when they renew their driver's licenses or motor vehicle registrations, or when they sign up for federal entitlement programs, such as Aid to Families with Dependent Children.

A good field director is not only responsible for outlining a strong voter contact plan for traditional voters, but she should also be on top of the voting process and changes that may alter the turnout.

## Voter Registration Drives

Time was when voter registration was the strategic rage of the land. From industrial communities in the North to minority communities in the South, community activists would mount months of pre-election work to register people underrepresented on election day.

There were just two problems:

1. Most of those registered did not show up to vote. In fact, organizers found that it was critical to register fewer people, but then concentrate on getting them to the polls.

2. Since little was done to determine voting preferences before launching a huge campaign, some well-intended activists registered scores of citizens who ended up voting against their preferred candidates.

These strategies evolved before the start of the National Voter Registration Project, an ambitious project launched by the League of Women Voters. In

**New voters to target:**

➤ *Truly new voters*
➤ *Fallen-away voters*
➤ *New residents*
➤ *New citizens*
➤ *Native Americans*
➤ *Vote-by-mail voters*

less than two years, the national project has registered more than 8 million voters through special registration drives and automatic registration options at Department of Motor Vehicles offices.

These new programs have all but made it fruitless to attempt your own new voter-registration drives, but its success has opened up the doors for field coordinators throughout the land.

Topnotch field coordinators should:

- Obtain the names and addresses of those newly registered folks by the way they were registered. You might want to know if these new folks were registered at the motor vehicle office so that you might send them special messages related to being a "motor voter."

- Plan a mini-campaign to focus upon those new voters. They usually constitute about 10 percent of the vote. Mail to them. Call them. Go door-to-door. But hound them with tender loving care, as they are most important for you to deliver to the polls.

There are pockets of new voters whom you can target through voter registration plans.

**Reaching targeted voters:**

➤ Identify
➤ Mail
➤ Radio
➤ Walk
➤ Make notes
➤ Follow up
➤ Open headquarters
➤ Collect names

## Truly New Voters

Target new voters at your local high schools: We know that kids who vote within two years of their 18th birthday usually vote the party preference of their parents. If you have feisty, energetic young campaigners, you might send them into schools to organize a voter drive that is coupled with a GOTV plan.

## Fallen-Away Voters

Each year most elections offices purge their lists of people who have not voted in awhile. Call your elections office or local list vendor to see if you can obtain a list of those who have recently been purged. Send them a notice that they have been dropped (most will be grateful), and encourage them to re-register. Send them a new registration form.

## New Residents

In any district there are some new developments, subdivisions, or redeveloped areas. These are perfect places for concentrated change-of-address registration drives. These are very defined drives, as they usually take place in very specific areas and can be organized with few resources and in a short time period.

### New Citizens

Every fourth of July most cities have new-citizen ceremonies. People who have just become American citizens have an enormously high voting record, at least the first year after they become citizens. Your campaign and candidate should attend these ceremonies. Meet the new voters and get their names and numbers so that you might add them to your targeted voter roles.

### Native Americans

Native Americans have one of the worst voting records. Yet, when organized, particularly by Native American organizers, they have a very high response rate. The same is true of other minority communities who have become increasingly disenfranchised. If they are worked by their own representatives, results can be very rewarding.

### Absentee-Ballot or Vote-by-Mail Campaigns

The West is full of states that are revolutionizing the way we campaign and vote. In more than 18 states, extensive vote-by-mail campaigns are not only allowed, but growing rapidly. In these campaigns, voters who comply with certain rules and regulations, or who apply for an absentee ballot, are mailed a voting ballot approximately three weeks before the actual election date. This increasing number of vote-by-mail campaigns means you have two election days per primary and general election: the date the absentee ballots are mailed to voters and the real election day.

# A Sample Neighborhood Field Strategy

To run a credible neighborhood campaign, you must dedicate time and money to the neighborhoods. Your goal is to increase the number and quality of times that you will interact with targeted voters. If a particular neighborhood has a reputation for voting for people like you, but seldom turns out in great numbers, then it might be a perfect target for your field program.

Lay out a strategy that either compliments your paid-media efforts, or substitutes for them because of limited funds. Some campaigns concentrate on neighborhood field strategies when:

- There are lots of talented, hard-working people who are used to being involved in grassroots campaigns and require little direction or encouragement.

- The area is critical to your efforts and there is not enough money to attract them through TV, radio and direct-mail plans alone.

- The campaign is very competitive and the area so critical that doorbelling and phone banks will help deliver those swing voters still "on the fence."

# Neighborhood Plan

Reaching targeted voters in critical areas can also produce other advantages: it can be a visible sign of momentum for the press and prospective donors who are watching for a sign that the campaign has its act together.

To begin a special neighborhood plan:

1. Identify the voters you want in the selected neighborhood.
2. Mail them an announcement that you will be walking in their neighborhood.
3. If funds allow, run radio spots telling the public you will be walking in the neighborhood.
4. As you walk door-to-door, leave your bio sheet and an invitation to the opening of your neighborhood campaign headquarters.
5. Note little things about the households where the perfect voters live (roses, big black dog, little boy, friendly neighborhood feeling, etc.).
6. Follow up your door-to-door efforts with personalized letters thanking each voter for talking with you. Include any appropriate issue statements and a short note acknowledging that special something about each person's home.
7. Open a headquarters in the neighborhood, which will be:
   - A location where neighbors can get yard signs.
   - A resource location, where all campaign materials can be picked up, ordered or replenished.
   - A central location for dropping off contributions.
8. Collect the names of early supporters and continue to build the list of voters whom you can count on for GOTV, come election day.

All of this should be coupled with your efforts to reach targeted voters through direct mail, radio and TV.

# Diary of a Perfect GOTV Program

## Friday: The Weekend Before Election Day

### 6:00 p.m.    The Rally

The candidate delivers a strong, fiery speech. A news team arrives for a live feed to catch the crowd and the candidate's comments. Two hundred volunteers show up eager to walk, phone, wave signs, watch the polls, and do "whatever needs to be done." Everyone signs up for two or three jobs, and all your team leaders show up, ready for the big push. The door-to-door crowd gets their packets for the weekend doorbelling, and phone bank teams get their instructions.

## Saturday

### 9:00 a.m.    The Door-to-Door Brigade

More than 150 people begin their precinct walks. These volunteers will contact voters who most often vote for the candidate's party. As seasoned doorbellers, the workers ask each prospective voter if he or she intends to vote for their candidate and appropriately records the responses. Doorbellers go in pairs and cover a minimum of two precincts on Saturday and two precincts on Sunday.

### 10:00 a.m.   Phone Banks Begin

The less physically-inclined will phone precinct locations where doorbellers are not apt to go: senior housing complexes, apartment buildings, condominiums and rural areas. These 50 or so volunteers are supervised by an enthusiastic captain, and the phoners compete with each other to see who can make the most calls.

### 2:00 p.m.    Candidate Visibility

The candidate goes door-to-door in the local business district, greeting voters and talking with store proprietors. She is accompanied by a team handing out literature and waving signs. The press runs a story on last-minute efforts to woo voters.

### 6:00 p.m.    Evening Phone Banks

The evening shift of phoners arrives with its own supply of coffee and sandwiches. The day shift made great progress, and the supervisor issues new lists of persuadables who have not yet been reached. Three volunteers call the volunteers scheduled to phone tomorrow and remind them to show up.

### 9:00 p.m.  *Candidate Visibility*

The candidate and a new team of loyal volunteers decide to hit Saturday-night hot spots. They stop by fast-food restaurants, the local dinner-dance club, the square-dance hall, a softball banquet and even the local police dispatch office. Every place there are people, the campaign crew makes it their business to stop and talk.

# Sunday

### 8:00 a.m.  *Campaign/Candidate Visibility*

The candidate begins a well-orchestrated schedule of morning church services, while campaign workers attend the major churches where ministers may be urging voters to vote for another candidate. At those locations, the team already has a flyer under the windshield wiper of each car at the service—giving your side of the story.

### 11:00 a.m.  *Phone Banks*

The sedentary supporters arrive, having seen the local newspaper endorsements of the candidate. They begin calling targeted persuadable voters who have been hard to reach throughout earlier efforts. By evening, all have been called, and the supervisor hands out lists of supporters identified in July and August. The callers start phoning them to remind them to vote.

### 12:00 p.m.  *Doorbelling*

The campaign has fewer doorbellers than yesterday, but manages to have 50 volunteers ready to seek out new precincts of targeted voters. They show up on time, and they are walking by noon. The campaign projects a strong family image when volunteers show up to walk with their kids in strollers and baby carriages.

### 1:00 p.m.  *Candidate Visibility Squad*

The shopping-mall blitz begins. Cars decorated with campaign signs, balloons and streamers drive from mall to mall, delivering campaign workers. The squads hand out literature and talk to everyone who will listen, and a few who won't. Before they leave, they place campaign flyers on the windshields of all parked cars.

### 3:00 p.m.  *Yard Sign Construction*

The field director gathers her sign crew together to build the remaining signs needed for waving tomorrow and Tuesday. After the signs are made, the captains take a dozen or so each and head for those key locations where signs have been vandalized or stolen.

### 5:00 p.m.    *Strategy Session/Quality Control*

Phone supervisors, doorbell captains and yard sign coordinators meet to assess the weekend's efforts and to make midcourse GOTV corrections. All doorbellers' packets have been returned. An inventory is taken of supplies needed over the next two days, and all project directors go over their plans of action.

# Monday

### 6:45 a.m.    *Sign Waving*

The early-morning crowd breaks into groups of three to six and digs in at four key intersections to wave signs and catch the attention of drive-time voters. The waving goes on until at least 8:30 a.m.; then the volunteers head to their jobs.

### 10:00 a.m.  *Candidate Phoning*

The candidate makes last-minute fundraising calls to bank that last dollar before election day. She asks for money to pay for the drop piece still sitting at the printer's. All high-donor contributors who have not contributed the maximum allowed are fair game for this last push.

### 12:00 p.m.  *Absentee Voter Phone Bank*

Campaign phoners target absentee-ballot voters who have not yet mailed in their ballots. The list of voters who have requested absentee ballots has been obtained from the county election office.

### 4:30 p.m.    *Sign Waving and Candidate Visibility*

Volunteers arrive at key intersections to wave signs during rush hour. Other campaign workers head to major buildings and bus stops to pass out flyers, reminding voters that tomorrow is election day. The candidate walks through the most populated commuter areas to be seen by the voters. The press is informed about the visibility schedule and meets the candidate to get a few election-eve sound bites.

### 6:00 p.m.    *GOTV Phone Banks*

The phone banks assemble some 50 of your best volunteers and begin to phone those precincts with the highest number of supporters and traditionally high turnout. They ask voters when each is planning to vote. This forces the voter to pick a specific time when she/he will go to the polls, hence reinforcing her/his commitment to vote.

### 8:00 p.m.   Election Day Checklist Meeting

All phone bank supervisors, poll watchers, sign-waving captains, coordinators for drivers and baby sitters, the office manager, the door-drop leaders and all key personnel go through a checklist of supplies, key volunteers and lists of things that must be done to make election day a maximum-effort/maximum-success operation. Volunteers call remaining field workers to let them know of last-minute changes.

### 10:00 p.m.  Guerrilla Yard-Sign Blitz

All remaining yard signs that are not needed for sign-waving are placed in key targeted precincts. Remember that yard signs placed along major right-of-way corridors are illegal, and the campaign can be fined up to $500. The key is to place them no farther than a block apart, leading to precinct polling places.

# Tuesday: Election Day

### 4:00 a.m.   Literature Drop

About 50 people rustle out of bed before the crack of dawn, and in the campaign version of the milkman's matinee handle the early morning drops. A simple card with a rubber band or special doorknob hook reminds voters where their polling place is. They work until 7:00 a.m.

### 6:45 a.m.   Sign Waving

Key intersections are filled with volunteers reminding voters to go to the polls. Banners are draped on the overpasses, signs drag a slogan over several blocks, and the candidate works the busiest intersection.

### 8:00 a.m.   The Candidate Votes

The candidate heads to her local polling location to cast her vote.

### 8:00 a.m.   Child-Care and Driving Services Begin

Not many people take advantage of these services, but the campaign gets good press for offering voters rides to the polls and child care while they vote.

### 10:00 a.m.  GOTV Phone Banks

Your volunteers are back in the saddle, making sure that your reliable core of voters is just that by calling identified supporters to make sure that they vote.

### 12:00 p.m.  *Visibility Squad*

Car caravans with loudspeakers cruise the precincts, driving through the main business districts as workers head to lunch. These cars do not hold up traffic; rather they bring attention to the campaign and then move to those precincts where turnout is usually strong for your party.

### 2:00 p.m.  *Increased Phone Banks*

The campaign phoners continue, as supporting business offices and other locations where there are a lot of phones are the staging sites for large phone banks.

### 4:30 p.m.  *Sign Waving and Candidate Visibility*

Bus stations, government office buildings, factory entrances and places where large numbers of voters are likely to pass on their way home are key targets for visibility. The candidate and the loyal sign wavers hit as many locations as possible with brief handouts, instructing voters to vote on their way home.

### 5:15 p.m.  *High-Volume Phone Banks*

Everyone not working sign-waving assignments is on the phone, making final GOTV phone calls before the polls close. The candidate also picks up a phone and makes calls. It inspires the volunteers to push onward.

### 8:00 p.m.  *Polls Close: Let the Victory Party Begin*

By 8:00 p.m. the campaign headquarters is transformed. The candidate shares the first hour with the staff and key volunteers before the general public comes at 9:00 p.m. The press secretary stays close to the phone all night.

## Wednesday

### 8:00 a.m.  *Fielding Followup Victory Phone Calls*

The press secretary and campaign manager return to the campaign head-quarters to receive press and well-wishers.

# The 10 Most Common Problems in Getting Out the Vote

**GOTV problems:**

➤ Trying to do too much
➤ Not enough volunteers
➤ Lack of leadership
➤ Candidate overload
➤ Staff burnout
➤ Not enough supporters identified
➤ Extra expense
➤ Solo volunteers
➤ Lack of preparation
➤ Lack of information

1. *Trying to do too much* results in doing everything poorly. Instead of planning on eight different volunteer projects (phone banks, doorbelling, sign-waving, lit drops, etc.), plan on two or three and do them very well.

2. *Not having enough volunteers* will burn out the ones you do have, resulting in everyone being exhausted, irritable and/or sleeping until noon on election day when you need them most.

3. *A lack of leadership* means that confusion and chaos will be the standard instead of priorities and accomplishments. A chain of command, voice of authority or designated decision-maker is needed for each project.

4. *Candidate overload.* The campaign manager or scheduler should watch the candidate's stress level and not overload an already pressure-packed schedule.

5. *Staff burnout* can cause stupid mistakes and turn off a large number of volunteers who need to be encouraged, not discouraged.

6. *Not identifying enough supporters* in time for the GOTV is one of the most common GOTV problems. Nothing is worse than having volunteers ready to phone on election day with no names to call.

7. *Expensive supplies.* Items are always more when you order them "rush" than if you plan ahead. Know what you will need before GOTV begins and see what you can schmooze.

8. *Solo volunteers.* Beware of the volunteers who want to work alone going door-to-door, or want to phone from home. It may appear to be more convenient, but it is also far less productive.

9. *Lack of preparation.* Planning ahead and walking through possible problems early will save you lots of time, which is the most important resource you have in the waning campaign hours.

10. *Lack of information* at your finger tips can shut down an entire GOTV operation. A good office manager will have the home, fax, car and work telephone numbers of all staff, campaign advisors and key volunteers.

# What a Candidate Does on Election Day

How to keep the candidate from driving everyone else crazy on election day? Her every moment is scheduled.

With all the hustle and bustle of election day; with all the stress and pressure, with the press of people and the lack of time to think, it is important that the candidate's day be as bearable as possible for everyone. Here are ideas of what you, the candidate, can do to increase visibility, as well as keep your momentum going strong.

- Vote early with trusted neighbors (the local minister, the little old lady down the block, next door neighbor, etc.) and family members. Remember, this is often a photo opportunity.
- Wave signs at key intersections with volunteers.
- Call all top contributors and thank them for investing in you and personally invite them to the victory party.
- Drop by local newspaper and TV stations with a newspaper you have designed that has your name as a winner in the headline; show them how you can have grace and a sense of humor under pressure.
- Make GOTV phone calls with the volunteers; thank the phoners for all of their hard work; bring flowers to those who have identified the most supporters.
- Take your spouse for a quick lunch in a public place and thank him for standing by you during all the campaign trials and tribulations. And tell the press—the public loves romance.
- Head to the entrances of key government buildings early in the morning, at lunch time or after work to greet voters and ask them to vote.
- Drop by the senior center for breakfast or lunch; we know there is almost a 100 percent voting record at these group homes.
- Go by the biggest department store in the district and buy a victory scarf or tie to wear for good luck. Greet voters on the way in and out.
- Keep a cellular phone with you all day so the campaign can call and let you know of schedule changes; you can also call your steering committee and other campaign VIPs to thank them for all their hard work.
- Take a moment out to go to church (you may need all the help you can get). Do not hand out brochures.

# VOLUNTEERS

## THE REAL UNSUNG HEROINES AND HEROES

Volunteers can tell you much about a campaign. The number of volunteers a campaign has tells you how well the campaign is organized. The quality of the people can tell you about the depth of the candidate and the personal draw she or he must have to attract such volunteers. The diversity tells you what kind of reach the candidate and the campaign have. The willingness of the volunteers to do anything for the good of the team tells you how effective the campaign is likely to be in the long run. The good humor and sense of fun of the volunteers also tells you whether or not the campaign is likely to grow, as the campaign that generates its own good feelings is the best natural magnet for more to join.

What is a volunteer?

Well, it's the working mom who gets up at the crack of dawn to assemble kids to walk in a parade; the college kids who stand in the freezing cold to wave yard signs; the teachers who make the same tedious phone calls to voters night after night; the party insiders who take abuse as they go door-to-door from people who hate politics; the political newcomers who try to get contributions from their friends and families for their candidate; and they do it all while juggling a job, family and the other survival skills of life.

Volunteers make a campaign go around. They give you the field power to get your message out; they add spunk and pizzazz to the chaos and confusion that comes with any campaign.

In the not too distant past, campaigns seldom had a single paid person on board. In these days, when the professionalization of politics has netted a wide array of paid jobs in campaigns, the role of the volunteer has changed somewhat. But for every paid position in a campaign, there should be at least 20 key volunteers who can be called on to do day-to-day tasks, as well as the all-important field chores such as canvassing, phoning, mailing parties and events.

There are just a few basic rules in the management of volunteers:

1. Use them or lose them.
2. Never make work for them just to get them out of your hair.

3. Treat them as if they were paid staff, with responsibilities and commitments they will acknowledge and accept.

4. Call them, re-call them and call them again before expecting them to show up.

5. Whenever possible, feed them.

6. Give them access to you, the candidate, on a regular basis.

7. Offer them more options than just the first job that needs to be done.

8. Thank them, and thank them again and again.

9. Don't ask them to do anything that you wouldn't do yourself.

10. Remember their names.

11. Don't wear out your welcome too early; pace the requests you make of volunteers.

12. Assume that only a third of those you call will actually show up as planned.

Every seasoned political junkie can tell horror stories of how a great campaign lost its steam—and its volunteers—because the management either wouldn't delegate real jobs, or because the volunteers were never organized to perform meaningful tasks. It's one thing to pay someone to do the grunt work and detail tasks; it's another thing entirely to ask a volunteer to do the same without instructions, authority, or the necessary equipment and supplies. Every campaign will need at least three distinct levels of volunteers:

- Volunteers who accept a general responsibility that is ongoing, such as the management of events, researching the opposition, filling out questionnaires, getting needed office supplies, advancing events for the candidate, etc.

- Volunteers who accept a project responsibility, such as helping to put on a specific fundraiser, waving signs at sports events, helping with a specific endorsement, or getting the candidate ready for key debates.

- Volunteers who fill in where they are needed for important field assignments, such as walking door-to-door, phoning undecided voters, or putting up yard signs.

A good volunteer coordinator can determine, sometimes within minutes of meeting a prospective volunteer, in which of the three categories the volunteer might fit. She also has a list of assignments she needs to fill, as well as times, dates and locations of the next field project where many other volunteers will be present.

The most frequent complaint a volunteer will echo throughout a campaign is, "No one ever calls to ask me to help." This not only signals a dysfunction within the campaign, it has a chilling effect on others who were thinking of volunteering, but now hear that no one ever contacts prospective volunteers.

# The Campaign Workhorse

Many people are attracted to campaigns. A lot of them are hoping that the campaign will be able to pay them, but a lot more will stick around for the "psychic pay" if there's no hope of monetary payment. And that's good. The campaign that has more paid people than volunteers can have a chilling effect on the press and public. Both are looking for leaders who can inspire others, not just buy their way into office.

Who is it that a campaign can typically expect to attract as its volunteer army?

- People who are bitten by the political bug, especially in these skeptical times when government and politics as usual are going through a great change.

- People who want to run for office themselves someday.

- People who are disenchanted with the system or upset by the incumbent's actions or inactions.

- People who have time on their hands and are looking for something more meaningful to do than watch *Oprah*.

- Newcomers to your town.

- Political junkies who have been involved in politics for years and love the excitement of it.

- People unemployed, under-employed, or unhappy with their job.

- People in the midst of a personal struggle: divorce, empty nest, job loss, etc.

- Young people looking for experience they can build on for future reference or networking.

- Friends, family and acquaintances of the candidate.

| **People who volunteer:** |
|---|
| ➤ *Political aficionados* |
| ➤ *Future candidates* |
| ➤ *Disenchanted citizens* |
| ➤ *People with spare time* |
| ➤ *Newcomers to the area* |
| ➤ *Political junkies* |
| ➤ *Unemployed people* |
| ➤ *People in life changes* |
| ➤ *Young people* |
| ➤ *Candidate's friends and family* |

This is the first tier of people who will be attracted to a campaign. These are the people that you have to be ready to attract, organize and follow up on as the campaign begins. The next tier are those people you might want to go after, with reasonable assurance they will be receptive to your overtures to help.

# Where to Find Volunteers

Campaigns who wait for the field force to find them are going to have a lot of work that won't get done. Good volunteer coordinators begin looking for people to join the team long before the candidate has filed for office. There are legions of people who will get involved in politics if asked to do so—and if their first experience is a good one. Where do you find these people?

- Volunteers from previous campaigns, perhaps against the same incumbent you face, or another recent race in your area.

- People who have been party activists with the local Democratic, Republican or Perot's United We Stand parties.

- Young people in high school or college, perhaps majoring in political science.

- Seniors who would like to continue contributing to the community, or at least get out and meet interesting people.

- Professional organizations, such as teachers' groups, the Chamber of Commerce, trade unions, firefighter and police unions, neighborhood groups and environmental groups.

- Key friends and relatives the candidate and her family has known for years and have helped in the past.

- Good-government groups, such as the National Women's Political Caucus, the League of Women Voters, the Municipal League, Common Cause, etc.

- People you may have met at health clubs, Weight Watcher classes, softball clubs, etc.

- Civic organizations, such as Kiwanis, Rotary, Elks, Veterans of Foreign Wars and others.

As your campaign grows, and as the momentum begins to shift to your campaign, you will have people who will be attracted to your campaign. They see you in a parade or at a public event and talk with you. Sharing a personal moment with someone who has been thinking about getting involved in a campaign can result in getting a great new volunteer *if* you ask her *then*.

Get ready for these people; they represent the third tier of volunteers. They are reinforcements.

They will call your campaign, offering to help, after:

- You receive particularly good press, or an important endorsement.

- A current volunteer asks them to come aboard.

- Their organization endorses you and they feel encouraged to get involved.

- It's down to the last two weeks and the momentum is in your court.

- Negative hits to your opponent convince those on the fence to get involved.

Be ready for them, and when the last-aboard comes around, have your Get-Out-The-Vote plan ready to go, with times, dates, places and assignments for them to choose from.

# The Pact with Volunteers

The best advice for establishing a relationship with a prospective volunteer is to ask for some basic information—some preferences as to what she would like to do and what time she might have.

First, the information: get the basics, such as the correct spelling of her name, her address, work and home phone numbers, fax number, e-mail address and her cellular phone and pager numbers. Find out what her personal background and expertise might be. Check out her technical skills (computers, e-mail, fax, video, desktop publishing, fixing equipment, etc.). Understand her management skills (personnel, diversity training, leadership, project management, etc.). Ask her to explain any volunteer skills she has developed (other campaigns, civic organizations, company events or fundraising drives).

Learn what professional, personal and family situations might impact a volunteer's time commitment to the campaign. Determine the times, days and periods each might be available. All of this information should be collected on one simple card from which it can be entered into your volunteer database.

Most volunteers end up in the job that most needs to be filled when they walk in the door, not what they might be best doing over the long haul of the campaign. Rather than doing this, find out the type of activities each volunteer would like to do. The most common include:

| **Popular volunteer tasks:** |
| --- |
| ➤ Phone banking |
| ➤ Placing yard signs |
| ➤ Doorbelling |
| ➤ Mailings |
| ➤ Office work |
| ➤ Research |
| ➤ Writing letters |
| ➤ Fundraising |
| ➤ Waving signs |
| ➤ Escorting candidate |
| ➤ Data entry |
| ➤ Errands |
| ➤ Campaign visibility |
| ➤ Endorsements |
| ➤ Registering voters |

- Phone banking
- Putting up yard signs
- Canvassing door-to-door
- Mailings
- Working in the office
- Research
- Writing letters
- Fundraising
- Waving signs
- Accompanying the candidate
- Data entry
- Running errands
- Attending festivals and fairs
- Working on endorsements
- Securing yard sign locations
- Registering new voters

After finding out what they want to do, ask if there are areas in which they would not want to work. Be careful here, as almost everyone claims not to want to be involved in fundraising. You might explain that you have a topnotch fundraising effort—one that will train people to be able to raise money on their own after this race. Too many campaigns lose great potential help in fundraising because they do not attempt to break down the stereotypical, negative attitudes about raising money. Try, "You know, the fundraiser is the only person in this business that you can be sure will always have a job." The best fundraisers seldom ask for money, they organize others to do it.

Appeal to your volunteers' sense of adventure in being part of your campaign effort by reinforcing their idealistic reasons for getting involved. Talk about the importance of your race. Let them know your basic strategy for winning—as well as your chances. Do not be afraid of explaining your less-than-perfect chances of winning, as prospective volunteers are more likely to work longer and harder—and make more of a commitment—if they know the challenge is real and your campaign is not considered a shoe-in.

Don't limit your conversation just to the ideological, however. Tell them the practical ways their help will make a difference. Explain the training that you will be willing to provide to help them become well-versed in what you're asking them to do.

## *What Volunteers Get Out of a Campaign*

In the event you begin negotiations with a prospective volunteer who could add much to your team, and you're faced with the question, "You think I'd be pretty important to your success, and you can't pay me. Why should I volunteer?" you might respond, "Look, I would love to pay you, but we have to pay to get our message out to our targeted voters. If we could, we would pay everyone, but as it is, we are putting everything we can into direct mail (or TV, or radio). That isn't to say that there isn't something you would get out of this besides cash. There's a lot in this for you, besides just electing a great person to office."

For example, tell them:

- You'll meet people who might be able to network you into groups—perhaps even jobs—that you might want in the future.
- You'll meet new friends, and even be rolling up your sleeves and working with people you've read about in the newspapers.
- You'll add to your resumé, and be able to point to your campaign role as a reference for any promotion or appointment you might seek in the future.
- You could get training on equipment that will be very useful in the future (Internet, e-mail, computer programs, databases, new phone technologies, etc.).
- You'll get a chance to learn about issues that may have seemed complicated, out-of-reach or just too "insider" for you to care about.
- It's exciting; you'll have a front-row seat on political change in an environment where you can see how the process works.
- You get your chance to change the direction things are going; most people never have the opportunity to influence the "big picture;" through campaigns you can.

- You'll get a chance to be creative and perhaps even have a project of your own.
- You may even see firsthand that politics appeals to you, and you may want to pursue it further yourself.

As a candidate, always carry volunteer cards with you so that when you meet a prospective volunteer, you can ask all the right questions. Also, if time is limited, you can leave the prospective volunteer with a card that she or he can fill out and return to the campaign. If the prospective volunteer is having a hard time determining whether or not she wants to join your campaign, you should reveal a little more of yourself, then about the campaign. Have a short kit for enticing the prospect into your camp:

- A recent set of press clips about the candidate and campaign.
- A biography or brochure which sets the tone.
- An endorsement sheet with names of key supporters.
- A list of the key people working on the campaign.
- A list of upcoming speaking engagements or other events where the prospective volunteer can see the candidate in action.
- A list of jobs the campaign needs filled.

The dance to bring a volunteer aboard need not be long and boring, but it should be well thought out. Remember that most volunteers do not determine whether or not they will work with your campaign on the first meeting; they usually have already made that decision. However, they are judging how well organized the campaign is, and they are weighing how much time and what level of commitment they will give the campaign.

Wow them, and they are yours for whatever you can empower them to accomplish.

> **When you meet volunteers, have:**
>
> ➤ Recent press clips
> ➤ Bio or brochure
> ➤ Endorsement list
> ➤ Key campaign people
> ➤ Schedule of events
> ➤ List of campaign jobs

# The Volunteer Coordinator

This person is the walking, talking definition of "a people person." She likes people, she's organized and she has been around campaigns for awhile. Volunteer coordinators are seldom paid, but they are among the most important first players you can have on your team.

A volunteer coordinator is good with people from the start. She doesn't mind making phone calls; in fact she lives on the phone, calling, re-calling and then calling people again who have said they will show up for a particular assignment.

She is genuinely interested in people, frequently reminding the candidate about the insider wealth aboard the campaign that should be tapped for special assignments. She does it all, from ensuring that each targeted voter has been walked, phoned and mailed, to organizing staff and volunteer birth-day parties. She is responsible for collecting the name of anyone who wants to be involved in the campaign, and she is the front person who makes the snap decisions about who should be assigned to what key projects.

Many candidates look for a volunteer coordinator before hiring a campaign manager, and for good reason: the people-resource person has to begin as-sembling the field force as soon as possible to compete with other campaigns that are looking for the same people. In the world of politics, it's important to start recruiting key people soon, as the campaigns most friendly to your candidacy are the ones most likely to steal your best prospective volunteer workers.

What does a good volunteer coordinator bring to the team?

- Enough time to devote 20 hours a week to the campaign in the last two months.
- Lots of people she knows who might be willing to join the campaign's efforts.
- An organized mind and a penchant for details.
- A sense of the political process, to know what campaign tasks to prioritize.
- An ability to judge people and to know how to allocate responsibili-ties.
- A great sense of humor and an unflappable sense of optimism.

Once you find your volunteer coordinator, never let her go. Even after the campaign is over, keep this person close to the inside track of your political and professional operations, as she is the bridge to all the people who were part of the campaign momentum.

# *Volunteer Training*

Many campaigns make the mistake of not having general campaign training days on the schedule. Do not assume your volunteers know how to best complete an assignment, even if it is something as basic as doorbelling, phone banking or mailing. Start every committee meeting or project with a briefing that includes:

- The point of the project or meeting.
- The key people who will be involved.
- What will be asked of the volunteers.
- The budget allocated to the project.

- The equipment available and necessary.
- A schedule of project deadlines.
- The detailed process of what needs to be done.

All projects, meetings and staff sessions should begin with presenting a creative way to ask for money. Some of the most proficient candidates unfortunately never train their own people how to ask for money. It is assumed that only special people are raising the money—and that most people attracted to the campaign want to do anything but raise money. However, if you train your volunteers how to ask for money, at least you will have tried to empower everyone on board to help with the most fundamental task at hand: raising money.

Campaigns also have the right to issue rules, within reason, for the good of the team and public perception.

# Attire

While campaigns are usually thrilled just to have people who show up with clothes on, there may be a need to require certain standards of dress if the campaign headquarters are likely to be visited by TV crews, and you are worried about your campaign being perceived as too young, too casual, or not very serious.

# Roles/Responsibilities

Be clear with your directions and the roles you are empowering others to assume. A written statement of commitment is frequently used to clearly outline what you expect and what a volunteer is willing to deliver. Keep it simple, but outline exactly what the commitment between you and the volunteer entails.

When assigning a specific task to a volunteer, be sure to clearly define the task itself, the responsibilities of the volunteer and what support she can expect from other members of the campaign team.

# Language

Campaigns can be very stressful and bring out the best rhetoric as well as the foulest language. If you are trying to encourage seniors, more reserved folks, or even those who simply demand a more professional environment in order to do their best work, then you might have to insist on a basic cordial language for day-to-day order.

# What Volunteers Shouldn't Do

In the course of the campaign, you will be constantly amazed at the energy, creativity, spirit and commitment of the volunteers who will make up your field force. In addition to the ground war, they are responsible for spreading the word in places your campaign literature will never reach. Also, volunteers give the campaign its attitude and *esprit de corps*.

But, in this business, remember that it is seldom your enemies who get to you: you know them and what they're capable of doing to mess with your plans. However, your friends (usually your volunteers)—well, you may never know what they'll do next, all in the name of helping you.

To minimize problems from the well-intended, it's good to know how volunteers in other campaigns have inadvertently gotten themselves, their campaign, and their candidate in big trouble. These simple instructions for volunteers have helped many a campaign manager start the volunteer army out on the right foot, and it has allowed them to go back and jerk the chain of a volunteer who has gotten out of line.

*Your friends: you never know what they might do next, all in the name of helping you, so make sure everyone knows their roles.*

1. Don't speak on behalf of the campaign in front of anyone but your very best friends, colleagues and family. Most important, never talk with the press or in front of a crowd unless you are authorized to do so.

2. Do not incur one penny of expense that has not been authorized in the budget or approved by the manager.

3. Loose lips have sunk many political ships. If you are having a beer with a friend from another campaign, do not talk about the campaign.

4. Don't take on too much. Every well-intended volunteer who takes on more than he or she can accomplish can put the campaign agenda on hold.

5. Don't be afraid to ask for help, particularly if you know just enough to get started on a project and others are following you. Stop and ask for help.

6. Don't hog the candidate's time in public; you should let undecided voters and prospective donors talk with her in public. You can see her back at the headquarters.

7. Don't control a project so tightly that it discourages others from helping or investing in the campaign's team efforts.

8. Show up for those commitments you make. The most dreaded people problem of all campaigns is the failure of volunteers to show up for projects they agreed they would do.

9. Don't undercut the management. If you don't like something the manager or consultant has suggested, then talk to the manager or the volunteer coordinator; don't go to the candidate to complain.

10. If you cannot get along with people assigned to work with you, ask for another assignment, or ask for a job that will put you in another location—perhaps even your home.

11. If someone on your project is bringing everyone else down, bring it to the attention of the volunteer coordinator or campaign manager.

# How to Fire a Volunteer

In every campaign there is at least one person everyone has a hard time tolerating (hopefully this is not the stressed-out candidate). There is no rule requiring that you keep all volunteers who come your way. In fact, some campaigns determine way too late that they should have fired a volunteer. Of course, every campaign should try its best never to lose a volunteer, but if the circumstances warrant a change of scenery for a specific volunteer, then the manager should step up to the plate to handle the matter.

You should consider letting a volunteer go if dealing with him becomes too time consuming, with few positive results. If you have to clarify his role and continually restrict his comments, actions or plans, then sit down and attempt to talk through the problem. Be clear about what you will tolerate and ask for a commitment from him that his behavior will change. Common tactics for restricting the damage that an unpopular volunteer may be inflicting on the rest of the team include the following:

- Assign the person to a special project, like watching the evening news, clipping newspaper stories or reviewing issue papers of the other candidates. Projects requiring a problem person to work alone have a chilling effect on inappropriate behavior, and may get your volunteer back on track.

- Have others on the campaign whom he respects talk to him about being a team player.

- Have the manager talk with the person about what exactly he is doing that makes others not want to work with him. Offer suggestions on how the behavior might change and offer to help him fit in.

- Give him a specific project that keeps him out of the office or working with people who are more tolerant; if this still does not work, then try uninviting him to the next few insider meetings or staff get-togethers, but be clear and explain your actions to him.

- Never be mean nor belittling, even to the most obnoxious volunteer, as your actions could ricochet, with an ill-tempered volunteer going to the other side or simply telling others about the treatment the campaign gives its trusted volunteers.

- Never have the candidate be the heavy-handed one; let the manager handle that chore.

# Tips on Types of Volunteers Who Like to Do Specific Jobs

Every campaign outreach person should be looking to bring the widest variety of talent to the campaign. Frequently campaigns stereotype the kind of work that certain people are asked to do, without ever asking the volunteer. As a volunteer coordinator, be sure to ask each volunteer for her preference, and explain what the campaign needs most before you get 30 people volunteering for the ever-popular, ever-useless issues committee. But there are specific tasks that certain kinds of volunteers typically offer to handle. See if you can create a campaign that breaks up that record:

***Seniors:*** Good office workers; they love to do mailings and will sit for hours with the right company (and cookies) to get out your invitations, special mailings, etc. Make sure you have transportation worked out to get them to and from the mailing parties.

***Women:*** Typically good volunteers for projects that involve other people. You will attract more women, more often if you arrange for daycare facilities at the campaign headquarters or wherever you want them to show up.

***Young people:*** Excellent doorbellers. They have that unbounded energy to trek up steep hills, fight off dogs and finish the entire list of households to be targeted.

***Kids under 10:*** Great parade participants. Parade watchers love to see little kids biking, riding in a decorated truck, or just plain having fun with the candidate on the route.

***Teachers:*** Good phone bankers, GOTV workers, and great helpers in filling out questionnaires. Teachers throughout the country have a reputation for being dependable, willing and organized workers. And a teachers union endorsement means all kinds of teacher volunteers for your campaign.

***Firefighters:*** Great sign-builders who can sometimes also be counted on to distribute your campaign flyers. Again, wait for the endorsement, and then let them do their work.

***After-work helpers:*** Able phone bankers, mailing-party workers and general visibility helpers at evening meetings. These after-five folks can be the advance team for your fundraising events.

*Government employees:* Great researchers and press insiders. Make sure these folks aren't doing your campaign work on the taxpayer's dime, as the public seldom forgets a candidate who inappropriately uses government resources to get elected.

Campaigns require increasingly more time from volunteers as election day approaches. You will probably be doing well if you have 20 volunteers to start your campaign. You should double that number by the halfway point, and for the last month, you'll need 100 people to sign on for at least a couple of hours a week. Some campaigns have way more, some way less. Candidates: remember that from the moment you declare your candidacy, you should begin collecting (and committing) volunteers to work with you in the last five days for the GOTV momentum.

> *The best way to recruit new volunteers is to have your volunteers bring in their friends, colleagues and family. People who already like being together are more likely to respond to an invitation to help.*

# The Volunteer Budget

Before your campaign determines what it will accomplish, make sure each project has a people budget—the number of people you will need to work how many hours in order to get the project done. Campaigns are filled with great ideas and dreams of thousands of wonderful volunteers who will miraculously descend upon the campaign just in time for an event to be organized; but unless you have a written volunteer budget—as well as a written monetary budget—you shouldn't be planning anything.

A volunteer budget starts with realistic expectations and honest assessments of how much time it will take to accomplish the job. Some examples:

*Phoning for Money:* A seasoned volunteer can make about 15 phone calls per hour to ask prospective supporters for money or if they plan to attend a fundraising event. To reach a mailing list of 1,200 supporters, you'll need eight people working four nights, two and a half hours each night.

*Phoning for Support:* A well-trained volunteer can reach about 12 people per hour to ask if they are supporting the candidate and if they would like specific issue information or other followup material. To reach 6,000 voters as part of your GOTV efforts, you'll need ten volunteers phoning two and a half hours a day, five days a week for a month.

*Mailings:* A focused mailing party of five people will require about an hour to stuff 1,000 one-page letters with return envelopes into letter-sized envelopes, affix mailing labels and sort by zip code for mailing. For a mailing to 10,000 voters you'll need ten hours of five people working the process, or five hours with ten people working.

**Doorbelling:** Door-to-door canvassing requires the strong-of-spirit and legs to get through the long lists of identified voters. In a rural area, you may reach only six or seven homes per hour. In urban settings, you might do 25 per hour, depending on whether you are knocking on doors and establishing eye-to-eye contact with voters (the campaign preference) or simply leaving a flyer on the doorstep. If you have 250 targeted households per precinct, one person would need 10 hours to get through the entire list—five hours on Saturday and another five on Sunday. If you have 70 precincts, you'll need 35 dedicated people to accomplish the district canvassing for two weekends in a row, both Saturday and Sunday.

**Yard signs:** Yard sign strategy requires four squads of people to get the job done right. First, form a construction team of at least two people to assemble the signs. Two people can construct about 50 yard signs per hour, once equipment and supplies are obtained. Then it requires a dedicated squad to go door-to-door to obtain permission to place the signs where you want them to go. Two people should aim for getting 100 permission slips along key arterials over the course of a four-hour afternoon. Then the third yard sign squad can be dispatched to put the signs up. An efficient two-person team can place about 50 signs in a three-hour afternoon trek into the neighborhoods. The fourth yard sign squad is composed of those volunteers who replace signs that have been damaged or stolen. As these locations are few and far between, it may take an entire afternoon to replace 25 signs.

**Events:** An event requires some creative—and varied—volunteer work. In addition to a mailing party and phone bank before the event, you'll need two people to advance the event with the proper supplies, yard signs and sign-up sheets. In addition, you might need someone to enter data gathered from people at the event or to phone them later for additional contributions.

Whatever your great plans, know the number of people each project will require. Campaigns die on the vine because an overly zealous manager reaches too high and comes up with the failure of a project or event. It makes little sense to plan a great GOTV strategy of phone banks, door-to-door walking and a great rally on election eve if you have only four people to phone, eight people to go door-to-door and 25 people at the rally. Better to put them all into one project, than to do many that will have little effect on the election outcome.

Also, know when not to ask your volunteers for help. If you are asking 25 people to show up for a mailing that will take eight hours, and you could pay a mail house $250 to do the same, wouldn't it be better to ask the 25 people to do something you couldn't get done for a reasonable price?

When you have to mail over 10,000 brochures or call more than 2,500 people, consider using your local mailing house or telemarketing company. These people charge less per piece or call than you might think. Of course, if you're trying to build up your volunteer force and have little else for them to do—or no money—then go ahead and organize your work parties. But beware that many volunteers want their time to be spent wisely. Often they know that their time would have been better spent on another project—and would have chipped in the $200 to get the mailing done quicker.

# The Rights of a Volunteer

Volunteers are truly the unsung heroines and heroes of a campaign. They make candidates look good—sometimes even better than they are. Volunteers have rights, too.

1. To be told when they are doing a good job, as well as how they can improve.
2. To be given the inside scoop on most campaign information and strategy, at least before it hits the airwaves or is given to special-interest groups.
3. To be able to keep their area of responsibility until the end of the campaign, as long as it's being done appropriately.
4. To hear from the candidate, or at least spend time with her.
5. To be listened to, even though their advice may not be taken.
6. To expect that their names will be remembered.
7. To be thanked early, often, genuinely, and profusely.
8. To be remembered after the campaign is over.

No, the candidate does not owe all her volunteers a job, but she does owe them the courtesy of a return phone call, at least once-a-year letters or invitations to get-togethers for old times' sake, and a few references for future activities.

> *Volunteers make candidates look good—sometimes even better than you might ever imagine. Volunteerism spurs people to great heights.*

# PAID MEDIA

## GETTING THE MESSAGE OUT

So, you say you have the "silver bullet"—that one thing that will blow your opponent out of the race. You package it for the press, leaking it to the largest newspaper. When they refuse to bite, you repackage it for the TV stations. They don't take it either. You beg the weekly newspaper—and still no luck.

The silver bullet? And no one in the free press will buy it?

It's time for *paid media.*

Paid media is the phrase commonly used for the radio, TV, and direct mail that is used to mass circulate your positive message, as well as the "silver bullet" information that the public should know before they consider voting for your opponent. Going back to the golden rule, paid media is how you deliver your message to your targeted voters at the right time and in a variety of ways. Most (70 percent or more) of your campaign budget should be dedicated to these forms of media.

Of course, if the candidate could walk to each home in the district, and personally talk with each of the targeted voters, then there would be little need for paid media. Even if you are able to walk door-to-door, it still is a very brief introduction, not enough to convince a skeptical voter to vote for you. And, for those "silver bullet" pieces of information, it's unlikely that you would want to assault your targeted voters with that information at the door—which is why we have seen the development of radio, TV and direct mail as an alternative to that personal touch of campaigning.

Within the definition of paid media, there is a division between media that is "hot"—and media that is "cold." "Hot" media is radio and television. It's real, direct, and right there in front of you on the TV tube or on your car radio. It's moving, emotional and can easily push your hot buttons. The "cold" media is direct mail. If done well, it can catch your attention, but it must be very good and provocative before it will move voters. It appears colder and less personal. However, because of campaign costs and the need to reach voters several times, direct mail is traditionally the preferred voter contact method in most state, county and local campaigns.

Other means of voter contact include door-to-door contact, yard signs, bumper stickers, buttons, bus signs and other gizmos that don't really get you votes, but help in building name recognition and reinforcing the messages delivered by radio, TV and direct mail.

# What Does Paid Media Do?

At its very best, paid media gets the attention of your undecided voters and helps persuade them that you are the best choice for the job. With good paid media you get the best bang for your buck.

Paid media seeks to establish that special wavelength between you and your voters, making them feel confident that you are talking about the issues that are most important to them and that you have the kind of solutions they will want to buy. Good media can move undecided voters to feel comfortable enough to make a decision and vote. It is also the most effective—and most dependable—way you can deliver messages about your opponent's shortcomings. Your paid media will give voters a reason to fire an incumbent or not hire your opponent. Paid media can also reinforce those who are leaning in your direction and thinking about voting for you, but haven't made a definite commitment.

In most campaigns a major portion of the undecided voters have not made a decision regarding for whom to vote even as late as ten days before the election. It is in those last days when the majority of people who are going to vote start paying active attention to the races on the ballot. Hence, most of the paid media is broadcast or mailed in those last days of the campaign.

Paid media is many things, but it should not be everything at once. Keep the message simple. You cannot tell the entire life story of the candidate, all his issues, and take a whack against his opponent in one 30-second spot—or even in one direct-mail brochure.

At its worst paid media can take most of your hard-earned money and not hit the voters you need to move in the last days of the campaign.

Paid media that is cheap-looking gives voters the impression that you are not the kind of person who can handle the job. Paid media can also be boring, tedious and uninviting. In this media age you are not competing with just your opponents, or even the other candidates further up or down the ballot. When you mail a brochure or place a broadcast ad, you are competing against Coke, Pepsi and all the other advertising giants from Madison Avenue and Disney World. The public will see dozens of advertisements every day, of which three or four may be political. Your brochure must be provocative enough that your message gets read before it goes to the recycling bin.

# Types of Voter Contact

Before you divide up your budget, consider what you are trying to accomplish. In most cases where money is tight, you'll want most of your money going for those expenditures that are most critical for moving your targeted undecided voters. Don't buy the most expensive yard signs in town and get T-shirts with matching baseball caps for every volunteer if you can't afford the kind of media required to get voters' attention. In reaching voters there are three general types of voter contact:

## Persuadables

Radio, TV and direct mail—these are the hot and cold media. Persuadables allow you to get your message to undecided voters or leaning voters; they convince voters that you are the best candidate for them. Persuadable paid media also allows you to show off your background and experience to voters—as well as demonstrate why your opponent would be wrong for them.

## Name Recognition

This includes billboards, bus signs, bumper stickers, yard signs, etc. Name-recognition paid media allows you to simply keep your name in front of the voters. This will hopefully raise your name recognition among your voters.

## "Keeping the Family Happy"

Items in this category include buttons, T-shirts, matchbooks, balloons, pot holders, sponges, key rings, message pads, pens, pencils, hats, and all the other gizmos with your logo on them that you give away. Traditionally, the people who want these things are your own volunteers and your campaign "family." Few votes are ever earned by these trinkets. Your best strategy is to pick one of these items for your campaign and hope that it's availability will keep the "family" satisfied.

# Voter Contact Plan

A voter contact plan is a narrative, a calendar and a projected budget of what money you'll need by when for your paid media. It shows the relations among the media you are using and helps you see what people will be getting in the mail while they are hearing something else on the radio with yet again another reinforcing message on TV. Your voter contact plan explains what targeted populations will get what forms of paid media at what time.

It discusses the general strategy of your campaign and how all the elements fit in with the message-delivery system. This plan becomes the backbone of your campaign and allows you to know in advance what has to be done by what date, projecting your cash-flow needs.

Also included in the voter contact plan is the delegation of responsibilities—who's going to do what. It clearly defines who is responsible for the scheduling and production of your spots and your direct mail. It will also include cost breakdowns, with per-piece estimates as well as total cost. The types and sometimes the specific radio or TV shows on which to air your spots will be examined, as well as the number of direct-mail pieces to be distributed to each targeted population segment. Critical deadlines are posted on a calendar.

Issues are also featured in the voter contact plan. You will decide which issues and messages you will be directing to your targeted voters. Polling and research will dictate which message goes to which target. It will be the foundation of your plan.

A typical voter contact plan is three to four pages in length. Many campaigns skip a voter contact plan altogether, thinking that when the time comes and all their consultants are on board, then there will be time to decide these issues, since most of the TV or radio spots and direct-mail pieces will not be needed until the end of the campaign. Many campaigns never correlate the messages of their direct mail to their TV or radio spots. It is critical that all of this be done in an early and cohesive way, so that you are not rushed into producing less-than-first-rate materials. Four months before the primary is not too early to be addressing these issues.

# Making the Decision

In today's campaign you could well be spending 70 percent or more of your campaign budget on paid media. How do you determine whether to spend your money on radio, TV or direct mail? Let's look at some considerations.

## Money Limitations

If you don't have the money to produce a good TV spot, you certainly don't have enough money to place the spot. What is going to reach your targeted voters? How are you going to be able to deliver your punch more than once in the last ten days of the campaign? If you don't have a minimum of $25,000 to $50,000, then in most media markets it is foolish for you to even consider going on TV.

# Historic Profile

What kind of races have been run in the past? If you are running in a city council race, and no city council candidate has ever gone on TV before, it's probably because it was cost-prohibitive for the amount local campaigns traditionally raise, or because the market was too broad to be considered effective.

# What Can You Do Best?

In taking on an opponent, make sure you choose the media where you can be the best. You need to dominate the market. If your opponent has a war chest that allows him to purchase TV, even though he cannot saturate the market, then perhaps you'll want to focus on six or seven direct-mail pieces to hit those voters that you need to reach. The same principle applies to the lower end of the scale. If you are considering doing bus signs or billboards, make sure you can dominate that media.

# Frequency

If you are going to place your message on TV, conventional wisdom says that you will need to hit a minimum of 600 to 1,000 gross rating points a week. (Gross rating points gauge the effectiveness of your spot; they measure the number of times an average family is likely to see it.)

Frequency is also important in direct-mail strategy. You can't mail only one piece of mail to a voter during the campaign and expect to win. You need to plan for at least three pieces in the primary and three pieces in the general if you are running as either a challenger to an incumbent or for an open seat. If you are the incumbent, you may be able to reduce that to two pieces in the primary and the same in the general. Even if you have no opponent, you should still be mailing in both the primary and the general to keep people aware that you are their elected official.

# Targeting Enough

How frequently will voters get your message? One of the reasons many candidates choose direct mail over radio and TV is that the latter hit broader markets. Television hits the largest market. If you place a 30-second ad on a local station, the truth is you will hit thousands of voters who don't live within your district. And, of the people within your district, many will be non-voters or staunch supporters of your opponent.

To avoid spending money on this broad spectrum, many candidates choose to dedicate their advertising money to radio. In large markets there can be as many as thirty different radio stations. Candidates can focus on the target population they want by learning the demographics of each station and then placing ads on those which most reflect their target. For example, classic radio shows and basic news shows are favorites of seniors. Because seniors are very dependable voters, you might want to target some of your seniors through a radio strategy. However, keep in mind that the radio brush is also a broad one, in that you will still hit many people who are not your focus or target.

Direct mail allows you to target your voters specifically. Targeted mail is the most popular option of voter contact and paid media that candidates use. It may not move voters as directly, quickly or strongly as TV; however, it does the trick for many campaigns.

# *Getting Help With the Media*

To determine who will help you produce your media, examine your budget. What can you afford? In many campaigns where the candidate wants to do a little bit of everything (TV, radio and direct mail), she or he feels that one consultant ought to be able to handle everything.

Although media consultants traditionally do a number of special services, few do everything. Take a look at those who have past experience producing the medium you want to use, and examine their products. If you have chosen a general political consultant, she will either refer you to the right media producers, or do the work herself. (See the section on choosing a consultant in the *Campaign Team* chapter.)

When it comes to making your final decision on what media to use and which media consultant you should choose, take a look at what's out there, what you can afford, what's best for your market, and, most importantly, who you will be best-suited with in the medium that will have to dominate when the going gets tough.

In the case of a direct-mail consultant, you need to make your choice early in the campaign, because they can help you choose your campaign logo, design your stationery and assist you with all those early decisions that show you are a serious candidate.

When it comes to radio and TV consultants, you will be pressed to make a decision well before you need to go into production. It is good to have your team in place early (if it doesn't entail a lot of cash upfront). Then, as you ready your campaign plan, your media consultant can be part of the early message development and campaign plan process.

# Television

Television spots, both the 30-second and the increasingly popular 60-second spot, are an important part of today's campaign climate. Television is provocative. It is emotional, and it can definitely be damaging. It also requires complete professionalism and seasoned expertise in its production. You will need a general or a media consultant to help you translate your message to TV.

## TV: the Advantages

If you can afford it, TV goes right to the heart and soul of your targeted voters. If you have done your time buying adequately, and your production is topnotch, then nothing can be as persuasive as TV. Television is alive, it is a "hot," emotional medium. It allows the public to see the candidate and relate to her. The easiest way to move voters is with TV. It allows for a relatively quick response to negative hits. A spot can be produced and on the air in less than 24 hours, although you may pay dearly for rush production.

> ### Advantages of TV:
>
> ➤ *Most persuasive*
> ➤ *Hot, emotional medium*
> ➤ *Can see candidate*
> ➤ *Quick response to negatives*

## TV: the Disadvantages

TV costs a lot of money. The initial investment may seem overwhelming, because the production cost is high for a first-rate product. Placing your ads on prime time (peak viewing times) is also costly. And, if you place your ads during off-hours, you risk missing your targeted viewers. TV is not the best targeted medium, as you may hit many people outside your target. All things considered, it's the money that always looms as the biggest obstacle.

> ### Disadvantages of TV:
>
> ➤ *Costs a lot of money*
> ➤ *Not well targeted*

## Typical TV Spots

Traditionally, there are more than a dozen kinds of common television spots. The most popular are:

*Biography:* The first and most frequently used is a biography spot. This spot introduces you to your voters. If you're an incumbent, it reminds them of the hard work you have done. This spot usually shows images of you hard at work, at play, with voters and generally being a leader.

*Issue:* An issue spot is the next most popular bet. Contrary to popular belief, an issue spot does not detail all the facts, information, solutions, and anything else you care to say about the issue. What an issue spot does do is seek to establish the most important aspect of a problem that you want to address—the one aspect the voters find most important.

**Endorsement:** Next you might have an endorsement ad. In these ads your core constituents talk about your virtues and effectiveness. It lets people know that you have done the type of work that keeps you in touch with them.

**Constituent story:** A favorite constituent success story is also popular. It features a constituent who details the trauma she or he has faced and how you came to the rescue.

**Campaign trail:** Another effective spot might show the candidate on the campaign trail shaking hands, walking through a whole collection of scenes: the candidate going door-to-door, walking down a hall (faster than everyone else). The whole feel of the spot is fast paced.

**Family:** The family spot is also fun. It can show humor, a personal side of your character, or highlight something either the candidate or a family member might say. It tries to say, "I'm one of you."

**Candid camera:** The "candid camera" spot has also had its successes. It affords you an opportunity to use something your opponent has done, and perhaps exaggerate it.

**Cartoon:** Some spots use cartoon-type characters. You use the character in the cartoon to explain what's going on. Near the end of a campaign when all political ads seem to look alike to the voters, a colorful cartoon ad can stand out from the others.

**Comparative:** The famous comparative spot helps bring out the differences between you and your opponent.

**Hit:** The "hit" spot is usually used in the last weeks of the campaign, and it takes whatever "silver bullet" you have and dramatizes it for full effect.

## Cost and Production

TV spots can range anywhere from $2,500 to more than $20,000 to produce, depending on who your media consultant is, what kind of spot you want and how technically demanding the filming requirements are to complete your spot.

When your consultant presents the budget projection, you can ask for an outline of what TV spots are anticipated during the entire campaign. However, the last month of the campaign is no time to determine that you have a consultant too expensive for the campaign. Choose a consultant, ask for a media budget projection, and then make your inquiries about cost-saving alternatives.

Production begins with the concepting of a spot, its copywriting, and the placement of that copy on story boards that explain the visuals alongside the words. After the story boards, the producer will begin to arrange for the actual people, backdrops, props, equipment and technicians necessary to complete the production. A 30-second spot can take three days or three hours to produce, depending on its concept.

Once you have a spot's concept and story boards, you should know what is going to be said and be able to approve or suggest changes. Try to trust your consultant's opinion. You're paying for it, but the consultant can be much more objective about its effectiveness than you will be.

The most popular complaints candidates have about their TV spots typically involve how little is said and how vague it appears to be. TV is a very tough market. Impressions and images are everything. Resist the urge to play director, producer or minister. Thirty seconds is a very short time. Less is better, and least is best when it comes to words, ideas or visuals.

# Timing

The timing of a good TV spot varies as much as candidate brochures. Most campaigns place a biography spot on the air early in the campaign to establish name recognition and a positive message. Near the final few weeks before the election, you may have several spots focused on specific undecided voters (women, seniors, minorities, etc.), or those voters who may be slipping from your side.

# Time Buying

Placement of your TV spots is generally based on the universal standard known as the Nielson ratings. The Nielson ratings, which are compiled four times a year gauge prime-time viewing as well as all the other shows throughout each day. They tell you who, as well as how many people, are watching. This demographic information helps you determine where and when you should place your spots and is available directly from the stations.

In today's political arena there are professional political consultants who concentrate on analyzing time-buy information for different areas. These time buyers place your spots in front of the voters you have targeted. The fee for this service can range from 6 to 15 percent of your total time-buy costs.

In major campaigns it is not unusual to hire a staff person to handle just the time buys. This person is generally more motivated to solicit the best available deal for the candidate. In many cases, campaigns who have their own

time buyer get great deals because the staff person is on constant watch for new "avails" (the cancellation of other spots), and can snap them up as soon as they appear.

Media consultants who produce TV spots might require that they also place the spots. Usually this is the most lucrative job in the political consulting business. For the effort and expertise required, the payoff is great.

First the time buyers identify which programs attract your target. Next they negotiate with the station for time on those shows. If a campaign is looking to place many ads, a good time buyer should be able to get better than standard rates.

Knowing what your opponent is doing with his TV time-buying schedule is immensely important. Public files that list the time buys of every candidate who places ads are located at every TV station. A good time buyer will keep her campaign manager current on the opponent's time buys—and analyze what it means.

Time buying is more of a science than an art. Understanding your targeting, the Nielsons and the flexibility of each station are the keys to success. A good time buyer will get a candidate the right placement at the right cost and bring back information on the rest of the field.

# Cable TV

Cable TV can be a valuable part of your TV voter contact strategy, particularly as it relates to selected target markets that you wish to reach. In many urban and suburban areas, over half the population is served by cable TV. This gives residents access to from 15 to more than 40 stations. A candidate should be able to buy ads on at least four of these stations, and the price for placing an ad on these local cable stations is very reasonable. Prices can be as low as $10 for a 30-second spot. Because cable companies serve very specific geographic areas, it is easier for candidates to selectively reach their targeted audience with different spots.

In many communities candidates can purchase time on Lifetime, ESPN, CNN and Nickelodeon. Demographics show that a lot a perfect voters watch CNN and CNN Headline News, while high-turnout seniors and women watch Lifetime. Men obviously watch a lot of ESPN, and women watch Nickelodeon. You can check the Nielson ratings of any of these stations to find out their viewership in your area.

Cable TV is becoming a more popular voter contact tool. Look for all local candidates to consider using this avenue of message delivery more frequently in the future. However, don't expect it to match the numbers of voters reached by prime-time TV.

While cable TV lets you geographically select your viewers, it gives you fewer viewers to reach. In fact, cable viewer numbers are closer to the numbers of radio listeners than to those of network TV viewers.

Even though placing ads is cheaper on cable TV, the production costs for the spots will still be high. A talking head goes about as far on cable as it does on network TV, so do not assume you can get by with low-quality ads. High-quality spots are still a must.

Cable ads will not stand alone in reaching targeted voters. Because viewership is more limited, candidates will have to supplement this strategy with other forms of voter contact, like radio and direct mail.

## TV: What Can Go Wrong

**Wrong placement:** Your message is on the wrong station or program to reach your targeted voters. This can happen when someone in the campaign has a favorite program and insists that spots be placed on it, disregarding demographic information.

**Technical difficulties:** Your spot runs, but the first ten seconds are inaudible or nonexistent, or the picture is distorted. It could be any one of a myriad of technical snafus.

**Shoddy production:** If you are going to commit precious funds to buying TV time, you must insist that the actual product be of "air quality." The talking head, self produced, amateur camcorder TV spots will not do.

**Bad image:** This can range from a bad hair day to Nixon's infamous five-o'clock shadow. Still shots or footage of a candidate looking bad will be detrimental to a campaign.

**Message mistakes:** A cute, clever or humorous spot may be absolutely wonderful; however, if your message is missing, the spot is of little use. If you have the wrong message on the air, it doesn't matter how brilliant the spot looks.

**Money shortage:** Many campaigns go ahead and book time buys on the assumption that money will be available in time to pay for them. If the funds don't materialize as expected, the campaign loses its momentum.

**More is not better:** In some campaigns there is an abundance of good ideas for campaign ads. The problem arises in trying to use them all. If you put four spots on the air and the average one runs only five times, you have diluted their impact.

**Too complicated:** If an ad is too wordy, has too many messages, and the people are talking faster than the general population can understand, then

> **What can go wrong with TV ads:**
>
> ➤ Wrong placement
> ➤ Technical difficulties
> ➤ Shoddy production
> ➤ Bad image
> ➤ Message mistakes
> ➤ Money shortage
> ➤ More is not better
> ➤ Too complicated

remote controls will be activated as the viewing public escapes. The message must be kept simple. In this case, less is not only better, it is the only game.

# *Radio*

Radio is often overlooked in the world of broadcast political commercials. TV is the dominant broadcast medium, and radio thus becomes it's younger sibling. Radio is usually viewed as a second choice when you need a "hot" medium, but television is beyond your budget's reach.

When choosing radio as a part of your media plan, keep it simple: one thought per spot. Have an understanding of the instrument you are using to broadcast your message. Why do you listen to radio? Do you listen for news? Do you listen for music? Do you listen for information, or do you listen to be entertained for short periods of time?

Most paid media on radio is heard during drive times: those early morning and late afternoon hours when people are traveling to and from work. These are the hours with the highest listenership, and they obviously cost the most. These hours have the highest ratings, though the people listening are generally doing other things. They are driving, doing housework, watching their children, jogging, or taking the dog for a walk.

Music is the dominant force that keeps most people listening to most radio stations. Music helps your radio spots keep people tuned in and listening to what you say. In addition to music, repetition of your message typifies most political radio spots.

When you choose your radio message, pick one that supports your other media messages, such as your direct mail and TV. Stay with your overall strategy.

## Radio: the Advantages

**Advantages of radio:**

➤ *Quickest response*
➤ *Spot markets*
➤ *Easier decision process*
➤ *Great for humor*
➤ *Effect of music*

The biggest advantage of radio is that it is the quickest way to get a message on the air in order to respond to an attack. You can literally cut a spot in the morning and have it on the air in the afternoon. Because the production can be done so quickly, radio becomes increasingly important in those critical last days of a campaign.

Radio allows you to hit spot markets. Spot markets are very specific groups of your target that you might not be able to easily reach in any other way.

Cost is a financial advantage. Production costs are minimal compared to TV, and placement is also inexpensive by comparison. You can buy radio time with targeted listenership that is outside the prized drive times at bargain prices.

With radio comes an easier decision-making process. There aren't as many choices to make. You don't have to worry about the visual side of production—there isn't any.

Radio is a great place for humor. The best spots are those which combine humor with message and leave the listener thinking.

In a medium where the audience is listeners, music can be a great ally. It can create interest in your message and keep voters tuned in to hear you. It can give your spots a uniqueness that will help them be remembered.

## Radio: the Disadvantages

In radio there is a tendency to try to do too much, and to say too much. The end result is that it can be very boring. When that happens, the audience tunes you out.

Radio lends itself to being amateurish. Campaign managers look at the radio process and think, "How hard can this be?" Many try to write and produce their own spots. These in-house radio spots can come across with as much élan as the morning announcements at the local high school. This is why it is critical to have a professional involved.

One of the biggest disadvantages of radio is that it is not given proper respect. Candidates try to fit it in instead of planning to use it to its highest and best capabilities. Radio is a medium that will grow in use as people judge its true potential.

> **Disadvantages of radio:**
>
> ➤ *Tendency to do too much*
> ➤ *Inspires amateurs*
> ➤ *No respect*

## Typical Radio Spots

There are as many kinds of radio spots as there are TV spots. On radio, creativity is at a premium because the listeners must supply the visual image.

*Biography:* A bio spot is usually a 60-second ad introducing the candidate and explaining her background. It is typically accompanied by lots of rah-rah music, but you could use mellow music that sets a backdrop to your life story.

*Endorsement:* Endorsement spots feature a familiar, strong voice, either a woman or a man, talking to the voters explaining why she or he is supporting you. It can be an elected official, a local personality, or an actor or actress who does voice-over work for local accounts. Other approaches to this kind of spot use seniors or children whose voices identify their age.

> **Types of radio spots:**
>
> ➤ *Bio*
> ➤ *Endorsement*
> ➤ *Issues*

*Issues:* In producing issue spots, the specific issues are not as important as the approach you use. For example, if you are going to talk about crime, instead of reeling off facts and figures, it is better to talk about how crime has affected you or people you know. Explain how you plan to make a difference.

# Cost and Production

Compared to TV, rates for radio are very reasonable. You can target your message by choosing a station whose demographics match your targeted voters. If you are focusing on seniors, you might choose classical or news stations; if you are focusing on men between 18 and 49, you might choose the best sports station or maybe a country and western station.

When it comes to radio production costs, you will be charged by the amount of studio time necessary to produce your spot. A typical amount of time to produce a spot is one hour. You need to have your script in hand before you walk in the door, and you need to follow it. It is always good form to practice in advance of taping. Remember that many good spots do not feature the candidate. They may feature two people chatting over coffee or someone talking about what is important in the campaign. These types of ads are generally more successful than those which just feature the candidate talking straight into the microphone.

To obtain good production quality on your tapes, each spot must be recorded in a soundproof room on reel-to-reel tape. You should tape several readings and then select the best one to which you add your disclaimer and any appropriate sound effects. It is helpful to have professional help with this latter part—picking the music and selecting and adding the sound effects.

The cost of producing your spot can range anywhere from $100 to $1,500. Even very expensive radio spots will be cheaper to produce than a mediocre TV spot.

# Timing

Radio is similar to TV in that it is used toward the end of the campaign cycle. Although there are increasing strategies that use radio buys early in the campaign to introduce the candidate, in the majority of cases, radio spots will begin to air in the last three weeks of the campaign.

It is often a good idea to buy spots around big events. For example, you might air a bio spot during the mid-summer all-star baseball game, or during the broadcast of your local high school's first football game.

It is not unusual for a campaign to develop three or four spots for use during a primary and another five for use during the general.

Project the time necessary for production of your spots, and add the timeline to your campaign plan so that the production and placement can be completed well in advance. Spots may be produced a month in advance of their actual air time.

## Time Buying

As TV stations have their Nielsons, radio stations have their Arbitrons. Arbitron ratings tell you who is listening and when. They not only tell you how many people listen, they also tell you what kind of people listen. This information helps you determine how much money to spend at each station to maximize reaching your targeted voters.

## Radio Stations: Who's Listening?

Who is listening to radio and when do they listen? There are many different kinds of formats; let's review some.

**Radio formats:**

➤ *Top forty*
➤ *Easy listening*
➤ *Country and western*
➤ *News and information*
➤ *Sports radio*
➤ *Classical*
➤ *Talk radio*

***Top forty stations:*** This is everything you would expect, from the very loud to grunge to the best-selling pop artists of today. The average listening age for these stations is often under the legal age of voting, therefore these are not good stations for reaching targeted voters.

***Easy listening:*** These stations usually attract the yuppie crowd—anyone in the baby-boomer set. They can be very useful for targeting women.

***Country and western:*** This format more heavily attracts men, especially those between 26 and 55. It appeals to a more moderate, conservative set. If you are targeting Republican voters, this might be a good buy for you.

***News and information:*** This is often the very best buy for reaching core targeted voters. Seniors and perfect voters are often attracted to this format. These stations also tend to attract high listenership during morning and afternoon drive times.

***Sports radio:*** Although sports radio tends to attract younger male audiences, many of whom may not be voters, it can be useful in a strategy designed to attract male swing voters. It gives you an opportunity to place ads during those sporting events that you know will attract a wide listening audience.

***Classical:*** This is a good buy for reaching senior voters, particularly women. These stations often have a high listenership of perfect voters.

***Talk radio:*** The newest rage and the best reason to be born-again audio, these radio stations have an increasing Ross Perot/ independent and more conservative voter profile.

There are many other emerging types of radio stations, but most will have some kind of stable format, meaning the format stays the same throughout the day.

## Radio: What Can Go Wrong

**What can go wrong with radio:**

➤ Boring image
➤ Wrong placement
➤ Buying too soon
➤ Changing too often

**Boring image:** A candidate errs when he talks straight into the microphone, saying too much in a boring way. Your spots will be competing not only with your opponent's ads, but with all the other advertisements run by the station. It is critical that they be interesting enough to hold the audience's attention. Radio that is light, that seeks only to deliver one message, that entertains the audience and then leaves one message is best.

**Wrong placement:** Missing your audience is another grave error. You must do the work upfront to make sure your targeted voters are your audience. Remember your audience when placing your spots. It's probably not a good idea to place a spot with classical music in the background on a country and western station.

**Buying too soon:** When you try to beat your competition onto the airwaves, you risk spreading yourself too thin and not having enough money to compete in the final days. You can also spread yourself too thin by trying to place ads on too many stations.

**Changing too often:** Changing your ads too often is also a mistake. You need to air each spot for at least a week in order to enter a listener's consciousness.

# *Direct Mail*

In our country today, the most popular and cost-effective form of voter contact is direct mail. Direct-mail brochures allow candidates to specifically target the exact voters they wish to reach with a very specific message. It is also affordable, so you can get your message out several times during the course of the campaign.

Direct mail at its worst is just another form of junk mail that arrives with all those other ads and solicitations, only to last as long as it takes to get from the mailbox to the recycling bin.

Direct mail at its best is provocative, colorful, unique and thoughtful. It pulls you into its substance before you realize that it is political in nature. The goal in today's direct-mail market is to produce material that gets read. The average voter gets between forty and fifty pieces of political or community non-profit mailings a year. A candidate's goal is to produce those four or five pieces that a voter actually reads. To accomplish this, a political mailer has to be the best piece a voter receives that day. This means it has to be more interesting than the department store mailings, the direct-mail catalogs and the grocery store flyer. A candidate's political mailing must stand above all the other so-called junk a voter receives.

Good direct mail is never junk mail.

Direct mail allows you to focus on the individual voter you wish to reach at any specific time in the campaign. With direct mail, a campaign can put a key message in the voter's hand within forty-eight hours. It is a very cost-effective means of turn-around response for anything your opponent may say about you.

A typical piece of direct mail has a turnaround time of about two and a half weeks. This includes concept, copywriting, production, printing and delivery from mail house to voter. Shorter times are possible and have been accomplished many times, but whenever possible, allow for the direct mail to be done in an efficient and not stressful time frame.

# Direct Mail: the Advantages

Direct mail is cost-effective and allows you to explain your message many times in a variety of ways that can be unique and persuasive. It can be produced quickly, and it works well in delivering a negative message about your opponent to specific targets, so that not everyone gets the "hit" message.

# Direct Mail: the Disadvantages

For direct mail to be effective, you need to ensure that it is part of a package and done correctly. Direct mail has to compete with a lot of other noise out there: the true junk mail and all the bills, catalogs and coupons that come in the mail every day. Good direct mail must have professional graphics done by people who know how to do political direct mail. (This does not mean someone who has only had experience working for a public relations or marketing firm.) It also has to be coupled with good targeting and quality printing.

Caution: where a candidate wouldn't think of interfering in the production of a television spot, with direct mail candidates tend to get more involved than they ever should be. The purpose of a direct-mail piece is not to put everything you ever thought or knew into it. The purpose is to leave the voters with a simple message that will persuade them to vote for you. In direct mail, as is the case with all voter contact material, *less, less, less is much, much more.*

> **Advantages of direct mail:**
>
> ➤ *Cost-effective*
> ➤ *Delivers the message many times in a variety of ways*
> ➤ *Quick turnaround*
> ➤ *Good for negative hits*

> **Disadvantages of direct mail:**
>
> ➤ *Lots of competition*

# Types of Direct Mail

There are more than a dozen forms of direct mail that are typically used in a campaign. A good voter contact plan allows a candidate to determine at what time which piece and which theme is going to dominate. Among the most frequently used types of direct mail pieces are the following:

*Biography:* The bio brochure tells a candidate's life story, her qualifications and experiences. The shorter the biography, the better.

*Endorsement:* An endorsement brochure explains how you are most like the voter. Endorsements are listed. Some list everyone who has ever signed an endorsement card, some list elected officials and key campaign players, along with names from the general population, and some list only celebrity endorsements.

*Accomplishments:* A candidate's accomplishments are used to show how the candidate has been helpful to people. This is not just a long list of what the candidate has done, but an exploration of what the candidate has meant to people.

*Issues:* In today's political climate, experience dealing with issues is a very common theme. Among the issues commonly spotlighted are crime, transportation, education and the economy.

*Values:* Who you are, what you do and what you stand for are all likely themes to be used in a values piece. Values are the backbone of the soul. They tell you what a candidate believes in, what she will work for and how she will accomplish her goals.

*Style:* Style points, such as working honestly, bringing consensus, listening, taking on the status quo, and bringing a new voice to the table, are something the public likes to see in a brochure.

*Demographic:* A demographic approach allows a candidate to focus on different lifestyles. This could be seniors, same-sex households, women or working families. Targeting senior or women voters is a traditional demographic theme.

*Geographic:* In campaigns where there are issues specific to a particular part of a district, a geographic brochure is appropriate.

*Letter:* Although not as effective as a brochure, the letter format is just what you imagine—a letter, usually typewritten, using both sides of a single sheet of paper. One of the most effective is a handwritten letter from the candidate's mother explaining why you should be voting for her daughter or son.

*Ethnic:* In areas where there are clusters of diverse populations, a candidate may want to do a piece that is directly focused at specific ethnic communities. Two or three members of the community may be pictured on the front.

---

**Types of direct mail:**

➤ Bio
➤ Endorsement
➤ Accomplishments
➤ Issues
➤ Values
➤ Style
➤ Demographic
➤ Geographic
➤ Letter
➤ Ethnic
➤ Absentee
➤ Slate card
➤ Comparison
➤ Attack
➤ Response

**Absentee:** Most people in this country who vote absentee are seniors. Thus brochures to this targeted group usually take on a more conservative message and often feature pictures of seniors.

**Slate card:** Slate cards or sample ballots have become very popular in California and are increasing in popularity elsewhere. These cards recreate the ballot so that voters can see in advance how it is going to look. In California these cards may be produced by organizations or even by mail houses. Candidates pay to be on these cards, which could include races from U.S. President down to local dogcatcher.

**Comparison:** Comparison pieces are very popular. They are sent out in the last days of the campaign and feature pictures and points of difference between the candidates. Comparisons are made on issues, experience, contributions, and anything else you might find useful.

**Attack:** Attack pieces focus on why your opponent should not be elected. It uses your opposition research or other negatives that you have discovered. It graphically depicts your opponent's defects as larger than life.

**Response:** If in the last four days of the campaign you find yourself under attack, you need a response piece. This piece can attack the attack, divert attention by attacking your opponent on another issue, or humorously dismiss the attack and get back to your agenda.

# Printing and Production Process

Many candidates have misconceptions about the time involved in preparing a direct-mail piece. They mistakenly expect a one- or two-day turnaround after they have signed off on a piece. There are many steps to a good production process.

1. *Determine the concept* of the piece, as well as its copy. A good direct-mail consultant will talk to you directly about the concept. You will see a rough draft of the copywriting as it will appear graphically in a brochure. Other considerations include:

   ➤ Colors: how many colors and what colors?
   ➤ Bleeds: will the design bleed off the page or have borders?
   ➤ Size: how big and how many folds?
   ➤ Printing dynamics: how many pieces can be printed on one sheet?
   ➤ Run size: how many pieces will be printed?
   ➤ Stock: what kind of paper will be used, will it be glossy or matte, and will it be recycled?
   ➤ Printer: who will print the piece, and will a union shop be used?
   ➤ Ink: flat or metallic?

---

## Tips for good direct mail:

➤ Remember that the average voter reads fewer than 25 words.

➤ Rely more on headlines and subheads than on paragraphs.

➤ Understand the importance of photos and cutlines. A picture is worth a thousand votes.

➤ Color is important. Use bright, unique colors, and more color than text.

➤ Make sure your brochures are friendly. White space is allowed.

➤ A cluttered look with mixed messages is detrimental.

➤ Use short sentences; long sentences will not be read.

➤ Use words like you or we to personalize. Avoid generalizations.

➤ Don't make promises you can't keep.

➤ Don't exaggerate your accomplishments.

➤ Use bullets and graphic organizers, but only a few.

➤ Put the important information in the first two sentences; they may be the only ones read.

➤ The best direct mail teases the voter inside. It does not look political, giving the reader an excuse to discard it.

➤ Don't put your biography, a hit on your opponent and a major issues statement all in one piece.

➤ Keep it simple so voters will remember the message.

2. *Design the layout* of the piece. All told, determining what the finished piece is going to look like can take from three hours to three days.

3. *Assemble the photographs* and add them to the piece. At this point the copy goes to the campaign to be proofed for accuracy. The campaign manager is usually a better judge of a piece than the candidate. This is not to suggest that the candidate be kept out of the loop. The candidate should have an opportunity to view a piece at least twice in the development process, but after a final review, the campaign manager should be the one to sign off on the piece.

4. *Prepress and printing.* Once the layout is finalized, negatives are produced and sent to the printer. Printing, cutting and folding can take from one day to a week or more depending on the complexity of the brochure and how many are printed.

5. *Labeling and sorting.* When the brochures have been printed, they go either to a mail house for labeling and sorting, which will take at least a day, or they go to the campaign for volunteers to label and sort, which could extend the process by days.

6. *Delivery.* Once the piece is labeled, sorted, and bagged, it is delivered to the post office. It can then take up to three or four days for a bulk-rate piece to be delivered.

The time between developing a concept and getting the finished piece in the voters' hands averages two and a half weeks.

## Costs

Good direct mail can cost anywhere from $0.25 to more than $1.00 per piece depending on the complexity of the design and the number of pieces you print. Of course you can produce direct mail that comes straight off your local copy machine for 6¢ to 10¢ per piece, but remember that you get what you pay for. With direct mail, your goal is to put something in front of the voter that she will actually read.

Ask your direct-mail consultant for ways to cut costs. Many direct-mail houses will give you a break on costs if you schedule your work in advance. They can also give you design clues that can save money.

Many campaigns will ask a direct-mail house or graphic artist to help devise the voter contact plan, which gives the candidate the ability to see where each piece will fit in the overall plan and how efficiencies can be incorporated into producing the whole package. If you are coordinating the printing of any piece, always get at least three quotes on how much the printing will cost.

# Direct Mail: What Can Go Wrong

*Overload:* You put too much information into the piece.

*Long turnaround:* The production takes longer than you anticipated.

*Too much process:* The effectiveness of a brochure decreases in direct proportion to the increase in the number of people involved in reviewing it.

*Overzealous candidate:* Candidates who write their own brochures tend to write for themselves rather than for their targeted audience.

*Printing errors:* Anything can go wrong in the printing process, from wrong or faded colors to brochures printed with one side upside down.

*Omissions:* Forgetting to include on the piece the bulk-rate permit number, or political disclaimer. Either of these can send a campaign into apoplexy.

*Rush charges:* Lack of pre-planning adds rush charges, which can double your costs.

*Wrong target:* The piece is mailed to the wrong voters.

*Bad timing:* The piece goes out late.

*Mixed or no message:* There's no central message or there are too many messages. Keep it simple and to the point.

*Poor graphics or photography:* Sloppy graphics or bad photos make for a brochure that is likely to go straight from mailbox to recycling bin. On the other hand, eye-catching graphics and professional photos significantly increase the chances that the piece will be read.

*Boring:* The final travesty is to put all this time, effort and money into producing a piece that is boring.

> **What can go wrong with direct mail:**
> - *Overload*
> - *Long turnaround*
> - *Too much process*
> - *Overzealous candidate*
> - *Printing errors*
> - *Omissions*
> - *Rush charges*
> - *Wrong target*
> - *Bad timing*
> - *Mixed or no message*
> - *Poor graphics or photography*
> - *Boring*

# *Newspapers*

Newspapers are seldom the place where undecided voters see a campaign unfold. In recent years, newspapers have played a very minor role in campaign plans. In major cities there often are fewer than a dozen newspaper ads for candidates during the last weeks of a campaign.

However, there is a resurgence taking place in the role newspapers play in a campaign. Triggered by newspaper publishers who have decided that politics is growing into a major emerging business and market, major daily newspapers have drastically reduced the cost of ads for political candidates. More than a half million offices are up for election every two years. Given that most of these races are contested by two or more candidates, there is a very large potential market for newspaper ads.

Newspapers are a "cool" medium. They are not as exciting as the TV and radio markets, but they represent a form of mass marketing that will become increasingly more popular as the new rate structure is put in place.

People read the newspaper to get news. They read it for the sports page, the comic strips and the advertisements. They don't usually read it to determine whom to vote for. But as newspapers reexamine their interest in emerging markets, there is a new feel in their marketing strategy. Publishers are trying to lure candidates back to their pages by offering other services, such as free messages on voter hotlines for candidates who place ads in their newspapers. Some newspapers offer inexpensive ads in special voters' guides that are published during the last days of the campaign. They are also offering to do your actual production and graphics for free. In pulling out the stops, they will probably succeed in making newspapers competitive for your budget dollars.

Newspapers are better at handling the more complicated issues in a campaign. Newspaper ads can handle more information than TV or radio ads. Conscientious voters are likely to spend more time with their newspaper than they will spend with TV and radio ads.

In some communities more than 75 percent of newspaper subscribers are registered to vote, as opposed to 55 to 65 percent of the general public. We also know that newspapers attract readers who want more information than is available through other media.

# Newspapers: the Advantages

*Advantages of newspapers:*

➤ *Higher percentage of voters*
➤ *Reinforces other media*
➤ *More than a sound bite*
➤ *Perception of style and substance*

One clear advantage of using newspapers is that a higher percentage of newspaper readers than of the general population actually votes. The reduction in ad prices is also significant.

Creative, well-done ads that are graphically pleasing do have an impact. And they can reinforce other media you are using.

Newspapers also provide more than a sound bite for those undecided voters who, in the last weeks of the campaign, are looking for more information than is available on glitzy TV spots.

Newspaper ads can give you a perception of substance as well as style. They provide you with an opportunity to compete with the news pages. Although readers do differentiate between the two, those voters who are likely to be influenced by news reporting will generally take time to read the ads and consider them in making a decision.

# Newspapers: the Disadvantages

Newspapers are still a re-emerging market for political dollar expenditures. The fact that you still see just a few political ads—and they are not very creative—leads to the conclusion that not many campaigns are taking this medium seriously.

## Typical Newspaper Ads

*Endorsement:* Probably the most popular newspaper ad is the endorsement ad. It consists of anywhere from 100 to 1,000 names in minuscule type listing endorsers of the candidate. One effective use of endorsement ads is to place one the week before the filing deadline. Candidates have found this to be a strong pre-emption strategy—in some cases scaring an opponent out of the race.

*Event:* Advertising a fundraiser, community event or speaking engagement does more than just announce the event. Announcing fundraisers lets people know that your campaign is financially viable. Advertising events not only draws a bigger crowd, but it also paints you as a candidate on the move. Advertising a debate or TV call-in show gives your voters a chance to see you in action or to participate by calling in questions. You could also advertise the time you will be walking through a certain neighborhood, to let people know you are coming. Even if the voters never see you in their neighborhood, they will know that you were there.

*Response:* In the last days of the campaign where time and money are at a premium, sometimes it is quicker to respond to any negatives that have been printed on the news pages by placing an ad that counters the negative charges.

*Reinforcement:* A reinforcement ad restates the message played out in other media, such as direct mail radio or TV.

*Issue:* Frequently, campaigns that want to appear more substantive will choose to run newspaper advertisements featuring one issue each week. This allows voters to see more of the candidate's positions and action plans.

## Costs and Production

Your newspaper ads should be eye-catching: they should look good and make your message sing. To accomplish this you will need professional help. In many cases, the newspapers themselves will have staff trained to help you. Although newspapers allow you the luxury of expanding the content of your

ads, that doesn't mean you have to tell your life story. It is still best to keep it short and simple.

In most major cities, the new low political rates are your best bet. However, other discount rates are frequently available. These rates are offered to candidates based on how much is bought. For instance, if you plan to buy four or five full-page ads during the course of the campaign, your "per column inch" price will be less than if you purchase only one.

You need to determine early in the campaign what your strategy will be and how much it will cost. This will allow you to buy your ads in blocks at reduced prices rather than pay the higher costs of buying each ad separately.

## Placement

Newspapers have distribution numbers similar to Arbitron and Nielson ratings for radio and TV. These numbers tell where the newspaper goes. One of the benefits of newspapers is that in large cities you can target very specific parts of town. Whether you are printing an ad or a tabloid supplement, you may be able to pick the areas of your city to which it is distributed.

You can also pick the days on which your ad will be published. It is important to time your ads to the days on which most of your targeted voters will be reading. Monday and Tuesday are traditionally high readership days, particularly for those who read political stories. Does your newspaper publish a political notebook column? If so, that would be a good day to have an ad, preferably placed near that column.

## Newspapers: What Can Go Wrong

***Wrong section:*** Your ad can be buried in a section of the paper where it will not be read. If your targeted audience never reads the sports page, and that is where your ad appears, then you have wasted your money.

***Graphically uninteresting:*** Your ads may not be graphically interesting enough to be noticed. When ads are too wordy or cluttered, they are often overlooked or purposely skipped.

***Not unique:*** Another problem arises when the newspaper's graphics department designs all campaign ads. The ads take on a sameness and fail to grab the reader's attention.

## Tabloids

At present tabloids are a controversial aspect of the political print business. Not really newspapers, but not traditional direct mail, tabloids are a four- to six-page insert that goes into the newspaper for delivery. These tabloids can be printed by you or by the newspaper, but you design them.

Tabloids can be colorful, with lots of pictures, and because of their newspaper-like format, they are relatively inexpensive to print. However, they are also more likely to be discarded than a direct-mail brochure. People are so used to the overwhelming number of inserts already in their newspaper that they are likely to overlook yours and simply recycle it.

## Weekly Newspapers

Like regular newspapers, weekly newspapers give you more of an opportunity than radio or TV to get your message out.

However, weekly newspapers have one distinct advantage: they are much more targeted. Usually geographically or demographically targeted, weekly papers stay in the home longer than daily papers, and their ads cost less. Daily papers usually find their way to the recycle bin fairly quickly. Weekly newspapers hang around the house longer because they often contain schedules of upcoming community events. During its week-long life span, a weekly newspaper may be read twice by three or four people.

Advertising in a weekly paper also has the advantage of raising the level of awareness of your campaign with the paper's staff. It may increase interest in your race. And reporters and editors on the larger stations or TV may actually see your handiwork in the weekly newspapers and assume your race is on the move.

A major disadvantage is that no matter how many good voters read the paper, you are still reaching a very small group of people. A direct-mail strategy will impact a significantly higher number of voters.

## *Yard Signs*

Yards signs are a universal battleground of campaign insiders. There's the old school of pols who think that yard signs are among the most important expenditure in a campaign. And then there's the new school that thinks yard signs should be scrapped in favor of putting every cent into TV or direct mail.

Yard signs are a constant source of grief and aggravation from the time they are first proposed, through choosing their colors, to determining how many to order, where they should go, and then who should take them down. It doesn't matter what race you are in—from dogcatcher to U.S. President— yard signs will be a point of contention.

The function of a yard sign is to increase name familiarity and candidate voter recognition. They do not persuade your voters. They are, however, the modern kitsch of campaigns, and are often done for the simple fact that everybody else is doing them. In thousands of campaigns across the country, consultants are advising candidates not to put a lot of time, money and effort into these signs, only to be overruled by the candidate and her inner circle. They are every season's "hottest toy," and usually a "must-have" of every first-time candidate.

Yard signs do have a function. In part, they convince the "movers and shakers" in your district that you are a significant player in your race. Visibility, in the form of yard sign distribution in key areas, tells your supporters and interested voters that you have early organization.

Yard signs are important for what they tell about your early organization more than they are for your increased name recognition. Early, good sign strategy says your campaign has the finances to pay for printing—and the field organization to get them up. Your sign placement also gives out clues about your campaign's strategic capabilities. Blanketing major arterials shows that there is a thought process behind your sign placement, where placement at the end of a cul-de-sac says there is an "anyone who wants a sign should come pick it up" strategy.

Besides building name recognition, a good yard sign campaign can help build interest in campaigns that fall further down the ticket. They also help the development of your field organization, giving volunteers something tangible and visible to do.

## Typical Yard Signs

| Typical yard signs: |
| --- |
| ➤ T-design |
| ➤ H-design |
| ➤ Sandwich |
| ➤ Flag |

Yard signs can be constructed in many ways.

***T-design:*** In a T-design, the top of a yard sign is stapled to a lath (a narrow flat piece of wood the width of the sign placard). The placard and lath are then attached to a stake. A second placard may be attached to the opposite side of the stake, for a double-sided sign.

***H-design:*** An H-design sign is constructed with a stake along each side. The sign itself is the cross-piece of the H. These signs can also be made double sided. This design is most often used on large signs.

***Sandwich:*** The sandwich sign uses two large wooden signs attached at the top and spread open at the bottom to sit on the ground. The tops are generally held together by hinges.

***Flag:*** The flag design features signs that have been printed with both sides off-center, allowing the sign to be nailed along one side to a stake. It then resembles a flag flying from a flagpole, with both sides visible to passing voters.

There is an ongoing debate about one-sided vs. two-sided signs, and the rising costs of stakes and laths have fueled this debate. In reality two-sided signs are only important when both sides of the sign can be seen. One-sided signs are great for hillsides and areas where only one side will be visible.

Before you place your yard sign order, you need to determine in advance how many you will need. As with any printed material, the per-piece cost goes down as the number printed goes up. Therefore, make sure you order enough signs in the beginning. If you are using two-sided signs, remember that you must order twice as many placards as you want to have signs. Most state legislative campaign orders range from 500 to 1,000 signs.

Businesses that specialize in yard signs often have off-seasons when you can get your signs done at a discounted rate. If you know in January that you are going to run, it might be worth having your signs printed then.

## Cost and Production

Campaign signs should be bright, colorful and easy to read. They should have few words, yet convey an energy about your campaign. The trend today is to add your slogan to the yard sign, even though most still have just a professionally designed logo and the name of the candidate. There is an ongoing debate about how many colors yard signs need to be effective. One color is just fine if the design is bright and eye catching. Two-, three- and four-color signs can be equally effective.

Yard signs are becoming folk art, and they can be very endearing to campaign aficionados. However, the average voter is not likely to notice how many colors your signs have, nor appreciate the hours that went into their design. Being realistic, the voter will probably only notice how many signs there are.

When you are having your yard signs designed, you need to take your name into consideration. Decide whether you wish to emphasize your first name or your last name. If your name is Belinda MacPherson, and being a woman in the race is an asset, you may want to just highlight Belinda. If gender doesn't matter, the size constraints of a small yard sign may force your choice. If your name is Ruth Bell you don't have to choose between your first name and your last. Your goal is to give voters something to focus on: one word, one message. Your name, position sought, and any disclaimer required by law are all that is necessary. If you include a slogan, keep it to five words or fewer.

If you are doing a one-color yard sign, try using a colored background with white letters. When considering design, remember: more color, less text.

Yards signs are becoming increasingly expensive. In areas where the weather is hostile (windy, rainy, snowy), campaigns often depend on laminated or plastic signs. These can cost from $1.00 to $2.00 per sign, depending on the size, number of colors and number of placards printed. You have the option of printing on both faces. The standard yard sign in use is made on a polyethylene-coated cardboard. A 22" x 28" sign runs between $1.25 and $2.00 a face. These signs are not as durable as plastic and are unlikely to withstand the gale-force winds of Juneau, Alaska or the hurricane-driven rains of south Florida. In addition to the printing cost, yard signs also require wood laths and stakes for their completion. This adds an additional $0.50 to $1.00 per sign.

As wood stakes become increasingly scarce, other methods of yard sign construction are on the rise. One new design employs a metal frame which is placed in the ground. The sign itself is actually a printed plastic bag that is slipped over the frame and secured at the bottom. At present this is still a fairly expensive alternative, but it's on the right track to tomorrow's options.

Another alternative to yard signs is large plastic sheets that fit over a front door, transforming the entire door into a campaign sign.

These are among the new approaches to increasing the name familiarity of a candidate. As they become more cost-efficient, their use will increase.

# Strategy

If you decide to use yard signs in your campaign, you need a plan, and you need at least four types of volunteers to handle the roles associated with yard sign strategy. First, you need people to solicit yard sign locations. Second, you need people to construct the signs. Third, you need volunteers to go out and put up the signs, and you need a repair crew.

Important note: Before any yard signs are placed, check for local rules governing sign placement. There are often legal restrictions on the times and places signs may be displayed.

Your goal is to place your signs in areas where you have permission and where they will be viewed by large segments of your targeted population. To do this you must develop a strategy. Among the plans that are successful are:

***The overnight blitz:*** After determining your targeted neighborhood, solicit locations throughout the neighborhood. Then over the course of the first weekend when signs may be placed, blanket the area.

***Arterial saturation:*** In every community there are specific travel patterns that people must follow to get where they want to go, whether on the way to work, school or shopping. Covering these areas is one of the best uses of yard signs. You may even place yard signs outside your district if large portions of your voters travel those roads.

**Burma Shave:** As with its namesake, this strategy employs cute slogans intermittently placed over the course of a mile or so.

**Wall Drug approach:** Signs may read, "Ten blocks to Kim Elton," "Five blocks to Kim Elton," "One block to Kim Elton," then the candidate appears waving to voters behind a sign that says "Kim Elton." As voters drive on, they encounter signs that say "Kim Elton one block back," etc.

**Sign waving:** Candidates in many areas wave signs on election day and perhaps the day before. However, there are no set rules about when you can wave them. There is no reason for you not to employ this strategy earlier than the last weekend before the election.

**Message signs:** Delivering a message via signs is also a possibility. Some campaigns print stickers that can be attached to yard signs. The stickers carry various messages such as, "Vote Nov. 3rd," "Vote Tomorrow," "Vote Today," and "Thank You" (for the day after the election). These require a lot of upkeep, but they do keep voters looking at your signs for new messages.

**Big signs:** Large 4' x 4' and 8' x 8' signs play a critical role in sign strategy, particularly if you can get the supplies donated. Signs this size are very expensive, both in construction and maintaining, but they can dominate key locations and overwhelm smaller signs. This gives candidates a psychological advantage.

# Repair

Although every campaign team thinks that they have been personally targeted by their opponents every time a sign is destroyed, the truth is that most yard sign damage can be attributed to vandals or inclement weather. You need a dedicated crew to handle the necessary repairs. Damaged signs reflect negatively on a campaign. It is very important that they be repaired or replaced quickly.

Every campaign must deal with yard sign thefts at some point. You should make it clear early on that this will not be tolerated of your campaign workers. There are no winners in yard-sign wars, so it is best to avoid participation.

# Permission

It is very important that you obtain permission from individual property owners before you place a sign. If you do not have permission from the owner of a vacant lot, it would be better to avoid placing a sign there. The public will know that it is likely that you do not have permission, and no one likes the visual blight created by yard sign forests that spring up in these locations.

# Removal

As soon as the election is over for you, whether it be after the primary or the general election, get your signs down. By this time, the public is sick to death of campaigns and they want any reminders removed promptly. Lingering signs can reflect badly on your campaign. In some cases candidates have been publicly chastised in local newspapers for not quickly removing their signs.

There is also a financial incentive for removing signs. Many parts of your signs can be used again. You may want to call losing candidates and offer to collect their signs in exchange for keeping the stakes, laths and plastic-coated placards.

# *Bus Signs*

Bus signs are a good way to build name familiarity in areas where your targeted voters live. Although these signs are not good at message development, they can support the message of your other voter contact media. Bus signs are great for hitting drive-time audiences. Buses traveling the main drive-time routes during rush hours find captive audiences behind the wheel.

Bus signs are not very expensive, and for candidates who cannot afford more expensive forms of voter contact, they are a good buy. They are particularly useful in down-ticket races such as municipal court positions. One advantage of bus signs is that they show you support the community, since fees generated from their placement are funneled back into the local transit systems.

## Typical Bus Signs

***The whole thing:*** You can paint the entire bus. Although this is more often found with commercial accounts, it is available for use, and if you have money to burn, a bus can be turned into a giant traveling logo.

There may be a required minimum display time of as much as one year.

**Side or back:** It is more customary for campaigns to choose signs for the back or side of a bus. You can do many creative things with bus signs. "Another busload of people for [name of candidate]", is one clever bus-sign strategy.

**Inside:** You can also buy small ads that are placed on the inside of the bus. These obviously have a much smaller audience than those on the outside of the bus.

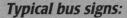

**Typical bus signs:**

➤ *Entire bus*
➤ *Back of bus*
➤ *Side of bus*
➤ *Inside*

## Cost and Production

When designing your bus signs, keep it short—under ten words. Don't get dramatic with complicated slogans or copy, because people will not have time to read them. Use a lot of color: as with your logo and other signs, you want more color than words.

These signs do have a long production time, so prepare for it. They may take from four to six weeks to produce, and you must pay for them upfront.

The cost of each sign depends on its size and how long it will be displayed. There is a one-time cost associated with the production of the sign, and the rest is based on the duration of its display.

## Targeting

It is important when buying bus signs that you choose routes that will be frequented by your targeted voters. You must be selective when choosing the bus routes that will carry your signs. Don't select only the routes that are cheapest; choose the ones that your targeted voters see, or your money will be wasted.

# Billboards

Billboards certainly attract attention. You can imagine the grief of a first-time candidate when she drives down the road and comes face-to-face with a larger-than-life smiling photo of her opponent. Billboards also have a place in today's campaigns, but like yard signs and bus signs, their purpose is mainly to develop name recognition. While they do not persuade voters, they can give legitimacy to a campaign. Billboards are often used in low-budget campaigns in lieu of other, more expensive types of voter contact.

First-time candidates often use billboards as an introductory tool. They place them strategically through the district early in the campaign to get voters used to seeing the candidate's face and recognizing the candidate's name.

Billboards mostly support other strategies. If you have a strong direct-mail strategy, if you have strong TV and radio, then billboards become just another brick in the foundation of your campaign.

# Typical Billboard Ads

***Logo or photo:*** The most common political billboard features a candidate's logo. Photo billboards featuring a smiling and sincere candidate are also common. A photo billboard featuring a key endorser is also a worthwhile gambit.

***Tickler:*** An emerging style of billboard is called a tickler. It employs humor or intrigue. The billboards are updated every week or two with a new message to capture people's attention. The downside to this concept is that it costs money every time billboard vendors touch the signs, so this strategy is expensive.

# Cost and Production

Once again, it is important to keep it simple. Your name, the office you seek, a short slogan and any required disclaimer is all that is needed. Big and colorful are still your goal, but billboards also lend themselves to humor. Mostly, however, they should support your message and be placed in areas well traveled by your targeted voters.

The cost of billboards is determined by the size of their audience. If you buy "40 percent coverage", that means that your billboards will be seen by 40 percent of the population in that area during the time it is displayed. You can purchase billboards with a smaller percentage. Remember that the cost is determined by the size of the audience.

There are all kinds of strategies when it comes to placement of billboards. There are neighborhood vs. freeway strategies, downtown vs. suburb strategies, city vs. rural strategies. Once again, the question you should ask is: where is my target? It doesn't matter how many people see your billboard, it only matters if your targeted voters see it.

There are many creative types of billboards available today. There are three-dimensional boards, revolving billboards that show more than one message, digitized billboards where letters change as you are driving. These gimmicks can be expensive; the best plan is still to choose a simple, but clever one.

# Gizmos

In addition to the types of voter contact that persuade or move voters, there are also those things that are merely intended to increase name familiarity.

This category includes those things you purchase for the campaign that keep your "family" of volunteers satisfied. These gizmos are the balloons, T-shirts, bumper stickers, buttons, refrigerator magnets, fans, buttons, stickers, candy and any other item your name could be printed on for distribution to the public. Volunteers, the press and political insiders love to discuss these gizmos, but they will never win you an election.

*T-shirts:* These cost anywhere from $7.00 to $15.00 per shirt, depending on the fiber content and whether they are printed on one side or two sides and how many colors are used. T-shirts are good for volunteers who are going to be participating in community events like parades, fairs and picnics. It is a good idea to sell your T-shirts instead of having the campaign supply them. You should mark up the shirts to at least 50 percent above cost. Remember that if you sell the T-shirts, you will owe sales tax to your state, if it has one.

*Balloons:* Balloons are festive and brighten any campaign. But in addition to the balloons, you usually need to get a helium tank to get them in the air. Balloons can cost anywhere from 6¢ to 30¢ each, depending on the type and what you have printed on them. Try to keep your cost as low as possible.

*Bumper stickers:* Bumper stickers are fading fast from the political scene. In many cases they are what is first cut from a budget. In a district that is heavily populated by apartment buildings and multiple housing complexes where you don't use yard signs, bumper stickers may be a good alternative. Just make sure that any stickers you purchase are easy to remove. Nothing is worse than taking off paint with your bumper sticker.

*Lapel buttons and stickers:* Many people believe a campaign is not a reputable one if it doesn't have buttons. However, a sticker strategy is cheaper. Buttons can cost more than $1.00 apiece, and they are almost always used once and then discarded or added to someone's collection. Buttons are good for your inner circle who will be wearing them frequently, but for most events you should use stickers. Stickers are sold in rolls of 500 or more, and are a fraction of the cost of buttons.

***Pot holders, sponges, etc.:*** For some communities where your voters are spread over great distances, and it is unlikely that you will have any other means of communication, it is acceptable to use these types of gizmos to raise your name familiarity. They can be expensive: from $0.50 to over $1.00 apiece. But receiving a usable item may give these far-flung voters a reason to remember your name.

***All the rest:*** Fans, magnets, and any of hundreds of other gadgets should be a one-time buy at most. It would be reasonable to suggest that volunteers who feel strongly about one of these be given the task of raising the money to pay for them.

The general gizmo strategy is that if you are going to use one, budget for it and only do that one. Have your "family" make a choice. When possible, see if you can get your volunteers to pay for it. Make it clear that the campaign will only pay for one gizmo, because it is more important to use funds in a way that will bring you votes.

A gizmo that gets you press can be a good investment. A veterinarian passing out pooper scoopers might attract press attention, as may candy bars proclaiming a candidate as the sweet choice, or Asian Americans using fortune cookies. Veterinarian Dr. Joyce Murphy of Anchorage, Alaska, passed out dog leashes that said, "We need to control our dogs and our government."

With all the voter contact options you have, it is difficult to determine which ones and how much of each to use. The best plan is to look at your target and determine how you can persuade those voters.

# THE PRESS

### ALL THE NEWS THAT'S FIT TO PRINT—AND MORE

## *The Nature of the Press*

Most political insiders look at the morning news and assume that reporters sit up all night trying to create the perfect story to discredit their candidate. Not true. Today's reporter is overworked, underpaid, and expected to accomplish more than his or her counterpart of ten years ago. The reporters you will encounter are just trying to get "new" news in a very contrived political market.

Put yourself in their shoes and imagine what it must be like to get 20 press releases from candidates in the course of a week, all of whom are trying to say the same thing in a new way without answering any of the questions reporters think are pertinent.

Reporters are decent human beings, which may seem to be a novel concept to most candidates. They live in neighborhoods, have families, send their children to public schools, and they even have passionate feelings about public policy. Generally their feelings about government accountability run stronger than those of the public at large. Many of the best journalists think of themselves as representing an average slice of the American public, believing that their task is to ask the questions that the public would ask in their shoes. They see themselves as playing the watchdog in a democracy that is always being tested.

Their job is to know what's going on. As a consequence of their professional experiences, they might not see things your way. Most, but not all, are objective and can separate their personal opinions from their professional assignments.

Reporters have a natural distrust of all politicians; they feel politicians only tell the public what it wants to hear, and they are even more distrustful of the whole political consulting/campaign management business. They see politics as "spin" (cleverly crafted one-liners) oriented, as opposed to their view of the world, which is "truth" and substance oriented.

As chummy as one might appear, remember that no reporter is a friend, but neither is he an enemy. He or she is put on your campaign beat to watch for weaknesses that might tip off the public that you are not fit to serve.

Despite the natural tension between the press and politicians, there is a way you can build a relationship that can serve both the reporter's interests as well as your own.

## Handling the Press

To expect good press coverage for your campaign, start by taking a media inventory. You need to know more about the media—the reporters, editors, columnists, photographers, copy editors, and television anchors—than they will ever know about you. Get to know them and understand what their professional responsibilities are.

What are their own stories? Understand what they consider important. Seek out their professional style in covering stories. Know who their contacts are and what they are responsible for covering in addition to politics. A reporter's time may be split covering the courts and the police beat, as well as local government.

Determine who actually will be covering your race. Depending on the size of your campaign, there could be anywhere from five to 25 reporters on the beat of your campaign. They are the most important target group you need to impress. Do not fear them. Do not be intimidated by them. Do not mistrust them. And most of all, do not try to con them.

During the first phase of the campaign, you should get to know who they are. Call them. Sit down with them, if they are amenable. Ask to at least meet them in person. If you see them at a local meeting, talk to them. Give them information about who you are and what you are doing, and slowly start the process of courting their trust.

Meet them, yes, but don't be a pest.

You must learn the hours they work and the best way to get materials or messages to them after hours. Get their fax numbers and, if possible, their home phone numbers. Keep copies of this information at your office, in the glove compartment of your car and on the refrigerator at home. There is nothing worse than knowing a reporter is trying to get in touch with you for an official comment and not being able to make contact. Candidates have lost major ground by being cited as "unavailable for comment" on a big story.

Although it is good to have all this information, you must use it judiciously. You should never call a reporter during the heat of an angry moment, particularly after reading about a negative attack aimed at you. Too often, if you immediately call a reporter, your comments will not be well thought out and may provoke the reporter to push you to comments that show your anger or loss of control.

What can you do if the press errs at your expense? Your options include:

- Have someone else from your campaign committee call (preferably a VIP who knows the reporter). Have that person explain the problem, while offering to become a conduit to the candidate if the reporter feels there is a problem.

- Fax a memo to the reporter that clarifies the information, while sounding as if you aren't angry—just hoping to get the information right.

- Write a letter to the editor, but ask that it not be considered for publication, as your intent is only to straighten out the problem.

- Appeal to other media (especially competing media) to tell the whole story, and not just a piece of it. Do not demean the original newspaper story, as reporters are suspicious of any politician who approaches them about a story that was allegedly inaccurate in another media outlet.

- Don't do anything. It is not wise to argue with an entity that buys ink by the barrel. Let the problem go, and get back to your message and agenda.

In compiling your media inventory, understand the hierarchy within the press. With newspaper reporters, it is important to know the editors, the headline writers, the copy editors, photographers and even the business editors who may be responsible for input. And, of course, you need to know who sits on the editorial board. Understand the structure of your newspaper's operations. The same goes for other media outlets, such as radio and television. In the TV news business, there are assignment editors, news editors, reporters, camera men and women, news anchors and news writers. All play a part in the 60- to 90-second stories that make the evening news.

All this takes less than a few weeks to complete, and it will help you know who you're actually dealing with in the media.

# What Makes News

To begin the courtship of the press, understand the basics of the business. News is not what you would like to see quoted; it is what the press thinks has not been said until they write it. News is:

***Exciting and dramatic:*** If there are good guys and bad guys, mention them. News thrives in "the story" of conflict, and good overcoming evil. Create an enemy: if not a person, then an issue.

***Lights, camera and lots of action:*** Just having an audience doesn't necessarily have news. But if there is a camera rolling and lots of action taking place, you have a good chance of making it into the newspaper headlines, as well as the evening TV news. Anytime a TV camera is scheduled to show up, let the written press know they will be there.

***Filled with VIPs:*** If you have high-powered folks around, trot them out for the press to see as you outline your plan for solving a problem. Important people make the news more often than common folks do. If there are celebrities coming through town, get your picture taken with them.

**News Is:**

➤ Exciting
➤ Action
➤ VIPs
➤ To the point
➤ Timing
➤ Photo ops
➤ "Aha"s
➤ Superlatives
➤ Anniversaries
➤ Humorous
➤ Tragic
➤ Scandalous
➤ Fun

***Short, sweet and to the point:*** Lengthy statements don't work in any medium: radio, TV, special publications, nor newspapers. Be as succinct as possible, then cut your statements in half before you approach the press. And make it sweet. There's a reason sound bites work: the more clever your words sound, the more clever you'll be in getting press coverage.

***Timing that reflects the moment:*** News is news if it takes place as you perform it, not recite it. Live on the noon news, filled with action and a great backdrop or controversy works best. Projecting what's likely to take place tonight is more newsworthy than what happened yesterday.

***Filled with photo opportunities:*** News needs to have charts, pictures, film that moves people, and a backdrop that doesn't put you to sleep. Talking heads, no matter how important the message, are still talking heads to a viewership who wants to see the news, not just hear it.

***Lots of "aha"s:*** News is new information filled with zingers and astounding tidbits you didn't know. Messages that combine interesting, little-known facts with your thoughts on how to make things better make for good press.

***The superlative game:*** Be the first, the most, the only, the "hottest", the one who points out the worst, or the last, such as the ugliest pothole, the scariest sidewalk to kids, the largest travel budget year of your opponent's incumbency, etc.

***Anniversaries or important dates:*** Announce your candidacy on the fifth or fiftieth anniversary of an important event in history. Present your plan for better schools on the first day of classes, and from inside a school bus loading kids up for school.

***Humorous, tragic, scandalous, or fun:*** Stories that tickle the funny bone or make folks get teary-eyed are often newsworthy. Emotion, more than facts and figures, is news.

# Campaign Stories That Get Covered

Candidates and campaign staffers are often upset by their lack of success in getting stories picked up by the press. Nothing can be more discouraging in a campaign week than working out the details of an eight-part program to stop crime, and not a single reporter shows up at the press conference. News is just that: new. As creative as all your platform statements might seem to you, it is unlikely that a reporter will think so.

Press stories that often do work include:

- The announcement of your candidacy.
- Press conferences or important proposals that pit you against a popular official, project or program.
- Contributions you have collected (stories about the campaign often cluster around public disclosure reporting deadlines).
- Negative attacks on your opponent's record, particularly if you can prove the candidate has been hypocritical or deceitful.
- Key endorsements, particularly a roomful of them, especially if they are doing something mediagenic, like rollerblading.
- Community or televised debates.
- Controversial special-interest group questionnaires, especially if you choose not to answer them.
- Briefings where candidates bring special guests and experts into the press room to discuss specific issues.
- Your reaction to another hot news story on the day it breaks, such as at a major crime scene, the site of a natural disaster, the closing of a large business or manufacturing site, etc.
- Your position on key bond issues or initiatives, particularly if they're on the same ballot as your candidacy.
- Humorous incidents that may have happened to you or your campaign workers.
- Press conferences you put together in front of grade-school children or very elderly seniors.
- Events with lots of high-profile endorsers, including those who have held the same seat in the past.
- Changing your mind on a subject or getting caught changing your position, and you make it a story, rather than wait for it to be discovered.
- When you hit a milestone in the campaign, such as your thousandth contributor or doorbelling your thousandth household.
- Announcing your own opposition research—if you know your opponent has paid for a high-priced opposition research consultant, do your own research and release what they're likely to find.

- A steering committee meeting where you invite the press and agree to be honest in discussing the actual issues that come up at these inner circle meetings.

These are the main items you should consider packaging for the press. You should not expect that every time you breathe, add a new campaign staffer, or get a new endorsement, reporters will think it is newsworthy. Conflict creates stories. Those items that pit you against your opponent are the most likely press stories. In the absence of that, make your own news where you can, and do so realistically.

# Knowing Your Target Audience

To determine the importance of specific newspapers, or radio or television stations to your targeted voters, understand who the regular readers, listeners and viewers are that make up their audiences.

Newspapers, dailies and weeklies, have an audited record of their readers. This includes the geographic neighborhoods where they circulate, a demographic breakdown of their subscribers and a business breakdown of who advertises and why.

Radio stations have Arbitron ratings that are released quarterly. They give a profile of the people listening at any time during the day. You should look for radio stations serving your target groups. For example, if you have targeted senior women, you need to know which radio station has the highest number of senior women listeners.

When it comes to TV, the Nielson ratings also are released quarterly. These reflect the same kinds of information as the Arbitrons, only for TV. In the TV market, look for what kind of people watch what shows and what demographics reflect the viewer styles you need to target. The Nielson ratings are the key to what air times you should be buying, not what shows are most popular among your volunteers.

All of this is crucial information to any campaign, not just for the "paid media" (newspaper, radio and TV ads) you will buy later in the campaign, but also for what is called "free media." As you set about putting together your media inventory and strategy for attracting more press, know which stations, particularly radio stations, reflect the kind of voters you need to reach.

# Understanding the Reporter's Job

A reporter's job is to get the news, to get the facts, to separate the truth from the exaggerations and spin, to treat each candidate fairly, and to present the candidates with approximately equal time and treatment. This is sometimes frustrating for candidates and campaigns, because lesser candidates sometimes get press you may think they don't deserve. Reporters try to give them some degree of equal access.

Reporters have deadlines. You should know what they are. When a reporter calls asking for a response, you should know in advance how much time you have before her or his deadline. If the subject is a difficult one, you may get better press by calling a reporter back later to answer the question, even if your response sheds less-than-perfect light on the subject. Responding to the media is far superior to ignoring them. If you ignore them, it will eventually catch up with you—if not in this story, then in the next one.

Also, when it comes to reporters' questions, answer the question they ask. Consultants are frequently accused of telling candidates to answer questions by simply repeating their "message." When you answer a reporter's question by only repeating your message, you are simply creating a high frustration level in the reporter. This is a poor way of dealing with reporters. If a reporter asks you a question, answer it. If the question is a difficult one, hopefully you will have thought of it earlier and formulated an answer that fits. You should still add your message, but answer the question first.

If a reporter calls for a comment, instruct your staff people who answer the phone to solicit the subjects the reporter wishes to discuss. Then you can call back after having time to think through your response.

In order to make a radio reporter's job easier, find out if each station will accept pre-recorded "actualities." An actuality is a tape-recorded clip you make and play back to them. This may require special equipment to ensure the recording is clear, but in these days of one-person news departments in some radio stations, a prepared radio actuality will do the trick in getting you some quick press.

It is equally important to ascertain if your local television station will accept prepared video-taped clips. In many parts of the country there are special video services that will tape your press conference and package it such a way that you can just drop it off at the TV station. Much of the TV media don't like to rely upon pre-recorded, "canned" news, but in cases where there has been a downsizing of news departments, or in small media markets where news departments are always short-staffed, these pieces do get used.

It is to your advantage to find out if there are local people who can help you produce these tapes. Start finding these production firms now, as this will continue to be a growing market for campaigns.

> *A reporter's job is to get the news, to get the facts, to separate the truth from the exaggerations and "spin," to treat each candidate fairly, and to present the candidates with approximately equal time and treatment.*

# The Media as a Constituency

Frequently campaigns spend lots of time and energy determining their target populations. Senior voters, women and even white males under 40 are popular targets. Campaigns almost always determine what issues are important to seniors and how they best can reach them, as seniors are often the last swing votes to decide whom they will choose.

If you were to treat the media as a constituency at least as important as seniors, you would find it extremely productive. This requires a major change in how most candidates view the media. For example, what issues are important to the media? You might think the media are equally objective about all issues, when in fact that is not the case. The media often care passionately about issues the rest of the public may not consider a priority.

Some examples of key media issues are:

- Access to public records now kept closed.
- Threats to freedom of speech.
- Open meetings, such as union negotiations.
- Open legislative caucus meetings.
- Ethics reform.
- Term limitations.
- Campaign finance reform.

In addition, there are local issues about which the media will feel strongly. Routinely, newspapers and some TV stations will outline the concerns they think are of great importance and publish them in a New Year's list of issues to be addressed. Clip these editorials, tape the TV lists and file them away for future reference. Then review them before you meet with editorial boards. Consider these issues when developing your media plan. Talk about issues of particular interest to the press as well as the community. Be the first to announce that there will be no more closed-door meetings. Talk about ethics reform. Call for debates. Ask for more give-and-take sessions with your opponent. Create open forums and other opportunities that make the media's job easier.

Know as much about a reporter as you can. Find out where each one lives. When you put together plans that include yard signs, doorbelling, phone banks and direct mail, make sure that the media, *all* the media who touch your campaign, are included in those plans. Reporters need to be among those targeted voters you doorbell, phone, send direct-mail brochures and impress with yard signs dotting their communities. Your campaign activities must be clearly evident to them. Let the media see firsthand that not only are you a substantive leader, you have a strong campaign.

> *If* you were to treat the media as a constituency at least as important as seniors, you would improve your press coverage.

Party pols frequently report that journalists covering a race readily admit when one candidate appears to be head and shoulders above the others, but they don't expect to cover that person if she or he does not have the makings of a strong, competitive campaign.

# Tools of the Trade

To make your relationship with media better, easier, more effective and hopefully more creative than your opponent's, there are some traditional tools of the trade that work.

## Media Packet

Put together a comprehensive media packet that will serve as the first file folder reporters will collect on you. You can make life easier for the reporters covering your campaign by pulling together the following information.

1. *Your biography:* This should be no longer than one double-sided page that gives your basic resumé. In chronological order, this should include previous employment and titles, your responsibilities and accomplishments, and your educational background. Never make it look like you have a professional degree if you don't. There are unfortunately many candidates who have been tripped up by exaggerating their experiences, such as implying they have a degree from Harvard when in reality they only attended a six-week summer class. Make sure to add a couple of paragraphs about your personal background. Name each member of your family and give the ages of your children. Include where you were born and grew up. You might include any extensive travel or the countries where you have lived.

2. *A statement about why you are running:* This could be a copy of your announcement speech. It should include information on what you have done for your constituents that prompts you to think you should be elected. It should point out your unique qualifications and position you against your opponent. It also introduces your message. It should identify no more than three issues you feel are critical, and end with your slogan.

3. *Campaign materials:* Enclose a flyer, a brochure, anything that gives you the appearance of having a clean, professional campaign. You need to look sharp from the very beginning.

4. *A photograph:* This should be a 5"x7" head shot. Write your name on the back so you don't get mistakenly identified as a mass murderer.

5. *Your campaign "facts":* This lists the key people of your campaign, their titles and their telephone numbers—work (if not public employees), home and fax.

6. *Press clippings:* Include any clips that reflect your positive involvement in the community

7. *Your campaign press announcement:* Be sure to print it on your campaign letterhead so people get used to seeing your bright clean logo.

Once you have assembled all the pieces for your media kit, enclose them in brightly-colored file folders with your name on the outside. You can then give the folders directly to the reporters and they can easily add them to their own files.

# Press Releases

Another tool of the trade is the trusty press release. Today, press releases are frequently considered much ado about nothing. Reporters tend to look at press releases as, "Oh, oh, another spin-doctor-generated, non-news news release designed for the circular file." Obviously, any reporter with this opinion will not see your press release as worthy of his time and the paper's ink and space.

However, there is a place for press releases, even if they aren't provocative news.

Press releases can be used to announce a special event, special endorsements or special programs about to be initiated. They could also be about the money you have raised and spent (timed to the filing of your disclosure reports). You would also use a press release to respond to negative attacks. This last use is more common than all the previous uses.

The logistics of putting together a press release are fairly simple. Follow the format shown in Form 19: Press Release Format.

The best press releases are short. One page is best. Make absolutely sure there are *no errors*. Have it proofread by two people who are good spellers and know proper grammar and punctuation. There is nothing more embarrassing than having your press release show up as an item in a political column chiding you because you spelled your opponent's name wrong—or worse yet, your own.

In the course of a campaign you can expect that every four or five press releases will result in one actual story. Remember that even if your press release does not get used, it is likely to have an impact on campaign coverage; for example, if you issue a press release a week on a particular subject, it is likely that not only the reporter covering your campaign will read it, but the editors might also read it. It will surely go into the file to be read prior to any editorial board meeting regarding endorsements.

# Press Release Format

← *(your campaign logo)*

## *Anthony for Senate Campaign*

A solid record of effective leadership

## FOR IMMEDIATE RELEASE: ← *(Always begin with these two lines.)*

**For further information contact Sharon Herman  234-5678**

**February 1, 1999**

## Anthony to Run for Senate

↑ *(Your headline should be something a copy editor would write.)*

Oklahoma State Representative Carol Anthony today declared her candidacy for the U.S. Senate …

*(The release should read like a newspaper story. Start with the most important information up front, and keep the sentences short and easily understandable.)*

### ← *(Include this at bottom.)*

12345 Campaign Boulevard                                   Electionville, OK 77777-7777

*FORM 19: PRESS RELEASE FORMAT*

# Letters to the Editor

Letters to the editor are often among the best-read features of any newspaper. They reflect what real people are saying about real issues. A crafty strategy often used by conservative right-wing organizations relies heavily on a highly organized letters-to-the-editor campaign.

A good letter to the editor speaks to one issue; it should be only three or four paragraphs, and leave the reader with a simple message that is repeated. Concentrate on those issues that lend support to your positions, if not directly to your candidacy. Have supporters write letters about you and the issues you have been espousing. Be somewhat discreet, as editorial page writers obviously are aware of the organized patterns that campaigns may use to overwhelm the letters-to-the-editor mailbox. Send only a few well-crafted letters.

During the course of the campaign you could have a few good writers draft letters for other people to sign and send. These letters would discuss different aspects of your candidacy or your favorite issues:

- Issues you think are important that reflect the hot subjects of the day.
- Why we need people of your experience to tackle these issues.
- A clarification of your position on an issue.
- An attack your opponents' position, pointing out his flaws, but not mentioning you.
- Getting readers to think about your issues, without leading the voter to the doorstep of any particular candidate.

# Op-Ed Pieces

Early in the campaign a candidate or incumbent might be allowed to examine an issue at length on the editorial page. These pieces are often published as a long column, accompanied by a picture and an explanation of the candidate's expertise. These pieces should be to the point, not overtly political and no longer than three typewritten, double-spaced pages. They should outline how you see a problem, then explain the factors which led to the problem and, finally, they should outline your plan to solve the problem.

# Editorials

Editorials about politics in general and your campaign specifically are usually written throughout the campaign cycle. They may examine how money is coming in, how issues are evolving, what expenditures are being made by the campaign, and what issues aren't being addressed. Editors love to comment on how campaigns are progressing. Make sure that the editors know as much as the reporters do about the state of your campaign. Always keep them in the loop of all campaign literature, radio and TV spots that you produce. Pre-release your materials to the working press and editors before you send it to the general public.

## Questionnaires

In addition to newspapers and local civic groups, there are many special interests that will send you questionnaires. Often these questionnaires are long, tedious, a pain to complete and take time you don't have. Questionnaires are seldom the tool which will win you an endorsement; however, they can become a vehicle to deny you an endorsement. If you don't complete them correctly, it can give the endorsing organization the perfect excuse to withhold their support of your candidacy. These questionnaires, along with the candidates' responses, are often printed in either the newspaper or special publications.

## Political and Other Columns

In many newspapers you have numerous opportunities to get fun information about your candidacy—as well as nasty little digs about your opponent—into print. These social, political or community columns often collect interesting information about political campaigns and report tidbits that bring a human element to the campaign. Some of the best-read political stories in any race are often found in these columns.

Know the columnists, and provide them with information that is current, interesting, and might even poke fun at yourself, showing the public just how really human you are. These columns are traditionally printed once or twice a week. Like all good journalists, these columnists will want to verify the facts as you present them. Provide them with the story as you see it, and also the telephone numbers of people who can verify the story, as well as the numbers of any other persons mentioned.

## Photographs

Nothing is more tragic in today's campaign world than seeing the vast amount of money that candidates spend to make themselves look bad. Make  sure that your photographs are professional—no more, "I have a friend with a camera who takes really nice pictures." Regard photos as the best way to translate your personality.

Photographs that show you blurred, in a bad profile, not smiling, or pictures that are just unflattering will actually take votes away. You need photos that relay confidence and a caring personality. They need to make the best of what you have. Professional photographers know how to bring out the best in you through lighting, poses and appropriate backdrops, and can put you in the right mood for the perfect shot.

Budget for a professional photo shoot; it may be among your best investments. Think of photos as a critical component of your campaign packet. Pictures to take include the following:

*Portrait:* This picture shows you from the shoulders up. Look straight into the camera, chin down, and smile from within, softening your eyes and not necessarily grinning with your mouth. This should make you look serious, but at the same time caring.

*Full body shot:* This full-length photo should show you walking into the camera, as if you were walking up to the door of a constituent.

*Family time:* A family shot is a required shot. Seniors, particularly, want to know that somebody loves you. Voters will love that you are part of a family. It makes them feel safe and gives them a connection to you.

*On the job:* It is particularly important for women candidates to include a shot that shows them as an active member of the workforce. This shot says you are professional, competent and can be in charge. Be careful of pictures that show you typing, as it may cast you in a subservient position.

*At play:* Get a shot of you doing something recreational. Voters love the opportunity to see someone as a whole human being. This could be a jogging, walking, biking or other active shot, even if it's the first time in years that you have done such a thing. Avoid elitist sports like golf or tennis and high-priced sports like diving or yachting.

*Over the shoulder:* For this shot, stand with your back to the camera looking at the wall. Then quickly look over your shoulder at the camera as if someone just called your name. This is a very attractive, active picture that hides the dreaded double chin.

*You've got to love kids:* You and kids. This could be shot at a playground park. It could include your own children or grandchildren. Try a shot of you nose-to-nose with a child. This shot shows you as someone who has seen the future and is going to do something about it.

*Listening:* Another must is a shot demonstrating that you know how to listen. It is particularly effective if the person you are listening to is a senior. Most seniors want to know that their experience counts for something, and that you will give consideration to their voice.

> *If a picture is worth a thousand words, then a campaign photograph is worth a thousand votes.*

**The big cheeses:** If you are going to be endorsed by any elected officials, it would be beneficial to get photos of you with them. If there is an event where dozens of your supporters are likely to be in attendance with your campaign yard signs and T-shirts, get a group shot of you leading the crowd.

**Man and woman's best friend:** If you have a favorite pet, consider taking it for a walk, sitting with it on your lap, or just snuggling. To convince the voters that you're a kind, normal person, have a shot of you, with a cat in your lap, reading the evening paper.

**Doing what real people do:** Try a photo of you in your car. You could be getting in or out. You could be driving by giving a thumbs-up signal. These are cute, fun, action shots that can be used on announcements or invitations.

**Reading:** You with your morning paper and latté. Or burning the midnight oil reading a report late at night. These photos show you as a round-the-clock, driven worker.

Photos need to be regarded as an integral part of the media packet. If you are not satisfied with your first photos, shoot them again. Women candidates should stop by their favorite beauty shop before any photo shoot and men need to be recently clipped. This is no time for shabby hair. These pictures could rate right up there with wedding photos for the impact they can have on your life.

# Media Plan

The media plan is what you create to get good press. It anticipates the natural stories that are likely to come up during the course of a campaign (financial reporting deadlines, budget announcements from the government, tax mailings, etc.). It also contains your plan of attack to create news that will accentuate your issues and positions. The plan puts these stories on a backdrop calendar with other potential issues you want to highlight during the campaign.

This plan should be developed by the press person, the candidate and the campaign manager. Outline every milestone, from the announcement of your candidacy to election day. All the different stories you think you can generate during the campaign cycle should be placed on it as well. Craft stories around disclosure reports. This is a good time to think through the three main issues of your campaign and when each of them might be highlighted. Chances are these dates will change, but they will start you thinking. Consider scheduling a couple of press conferences outdoors with active backdrops that will creatively put you in line with your message. Include time for neighborhood debates and community forums.

Your media strategy should include plans on how you handle endorsements—those you get and those you don't. Schedule time in the final two weeks to deal with negative press. Include time to deal with your opposition research.

This plan does not need to be long, but it should be written, with all deadlines and events placed on a calendar.

# Press Conferences

Press conferences are an opportunity for you to get your message, as well as key news about your campaign, to your target voters. They also provide the media ample opportunity to talk with you about things that might not be on your agenda. Before you go into a press conference, you need to understand all the questions they are likely to ask. Be ready for anything. When you open the door and hold a press conference to talk about your issues, the press may insist on talking about their issues.

There are many clues to hosting a successful press conference:

> **For a successful press conference:**
>
> ➤ *Be prepared*
> ➤ *Convenient time*
> ➤ *Key players*
> ➤ *Fax in advance*
> ➤ *On time*
> ➤ *Handouts at end*
> ➤ *20 minutes maximum*
> ➤ *Open to questions*
> ➤ *Thank everyone*

1.  *Be prepared for all eventualities.* Determine all the points you wish to cover, and have all your facts in hand. You may want to have experts in attendance to validate your assertions.

2.  *Schedule your press conference at a time convenient for the media.* Take their deadlines into consideration. Choose a location that is easy and accessible, preferably with a photogenic background.

3.  *Have all the key players there.* Your key supporters and those who have strong identification with the issues should be present. Have a few staff people there.

4.  *On the day before, fax to the press information on the content of the press conference,* including time and place. Then make followup phone calls and ask if each reporter will attend.

5.  *Convene on time, but have a staff member on the lookout for late arrivals.* Understand that you might have to repeat your message for these latecomers.

6.  *Distribute your handouts only at the end of the conference.* You don't want to give reporters any reason not to pay attention to you.

7.  *Complete the conference in less than twenty minutes.* The best press conferences have ten minutes of performance, and 20 minutes of questions and answers.

8.  *Open the meeting to questions after your presentation,* and remember the basic rules: always tell the truth, answer the question, and then get back to reiterating your message—the point of the conference.

9. *Remember to thank everyone for coming.* Make sure your team has recorded the names, telephone numbers, and media identification of all those attending. Include in your handouts your schedule for the rest of the day, in case someone needs to get in touch with you.

It is not unusual for candidates to bring their own radio and TV equipment to a press conference. It's good to have people who look like they are scribes and reporters in the audience, to give the impression of a packed house. It is also important to record radio actualities or tape video clips if you can afford them. Then you can deliver copies to stations that were not in attendance.

# *Parameters of the Press*

In today's media folklore there are truths, and there are myths. In taking a look at how you can best work with your press corps, understand the parameters of the media.

## Off the Record

There is no such thing as truly off the record. However, most reporters do allow a candidate or campaign manager the opportunity to go off the record and give information they would otherwise not want to reveal on the record. Determine the trust level of each reporter. Know their track record. Most reporters will keep the information confidential and not attribute any quote to you, but may include the information anonymously in a story. In other cases, they will find someone else to confirm the information you gave them, and quote the second party. Usually reporters use the off-the-record information as a catalyst to find or confirm a story.

## Leaks

These are pieces of information that you deliver to the press, similar to off-the-record information. It may come in the form of a brown paper envelope delivered in the dead of night to a reporter's office or as an item slipped into a conversation with a reporter. The press is not stupid. They know that leaks are contrived information meant to damage your opponent. Reporters are rightfully suspicious of anyone who leaks information. If you have information that is too good to be ignored, yet too hot to have attributed to you, give the information to the reporter with the agreement that she or he does not attribute it to you without your permission.

# Exclusives

In today's ever-competitive media markets, exclusives are becoming far more popular than ever before. Exclusives consist of taking a story, such as your five-point program on crime that includes the endorsement of the police chief, and sitting down to talk about it with one reporter. Do not continually use the same reporter for every new press opportunity you create. However, in an age where news releases and press conferences are considered over-used, offering an exclusive may work. After an exclusive story has been read or aired, other reporters may pick it up and run with it.

# Fax Mania

The fax revolution began about ten years ago, and since that time a plethora of faxes rain into newsrooms from campaigns, overflowing the recycling bins. Faxes may be used legitimately to announce a press conference, announce goals you have reached, or to distribute the candidate's schedule. Contact a reporter to let her know a fax is coming. Make a return call to ensure the fax arrived. Do not overuse your fax machine. Early in the campaign you should not be faxing more than one sheet of paper a week to any reporter. In the last days of the campaign this may increase to three per week.

# Bugging the Press

It does little good to become a pain in the neck to your favorite reporter. These people have very busy schedules. Contact them when you have something to say, not when you just want to fish for information about your opponent.

# Buying Off the Press

Conventional wisdom used to be that if you placed lots of ads in your local newspaper, the owners would be happy, and that would ensure good coverage of your campaign. Nothing could be further from the truth. You can buy many, many ads, and it won't make a particle of difference in how your story is covered on the news page. The same truth applies in television and radio. Just because you drop a bundle on advertising, don't expect any special favors or coverage.

# *Other Media Sources*

## Neighborhood Newspapers

These papers are especially important in state legislative and community campaigns. They are traditionally published weekly and remain in the home at least a week, whereas a daily paper is usually tossed daily. Weekly newspapers tend to be more widely read within the household as well. Because weeklies tend to have smaller staffs, well-written press releases and stories you deliver to them have a better chance of being used. Make sure you know the reporters, the editors and the deadlines. Check out their circulation and determine how many of your targeted voters are served.

## Newsletters

Large organizations and groups such as seniors, women, labor, teachers, chambers of commerce, small business associations, social service agencies, and pro-choice groups often publish monthly newsletters. These newsletters do not cover traditional news, but if you have a particular perspective on an issue important to their constituency, you can get your message out, or at least publicize upcoming campaign events.

## Banquet Programs

During your campaign you will be asked to buy space in programs for many events held by important organizations. These ads are a waste of your resources. You may be tempted to place an ad in them because you know these people (they are your friends) and you want to keep them happy. However, this is not a medium which will sway voters and allow you to fully discuss your issues. Forgo this expense. One note, however. If this is the only chance you have to thank your friends for past "extra special" help, then the $200 may be worth it.

## Talk Shows

Today's new art form is the radio or TV talk show. There is not a media market in the country that doesn't have at least a few hours a day devoted to call-in shows. You know who they are. From Rush Limbaugh to Larry King, these shows give you the ability to address many subjects in the course of an hour or two. In most urban centers, these talk shows invite both sides of an issue or all the candidates for an office to appear on the same show. They want all the controversy they can get. While these shows have large audiences and cost a candidate nothing, they can be detrimental to your campaign.

If you decide to participate, be sure to be well prepared. Some clues to talk-show success include:

1. *Arrive on time with an information packet* explaining the issues you will focus on. Also have your message in writing. This is a good opportunity to acquaint the talk-show host with accurate data—something they don't always have.

2. *Make sure your supporters are ready to call.* Have them ask you tough questions to which you have already formulated answers. Don't let your supporters call and ask only softball questions, as it irritates both the host and the listening public.

3. *Be prepared to answer hostile questions* on issues that are most embarrassing to you. Remember, there is no rule that talk-show questions have to be based on truth. Questions could be fabricated for the purpose of getting your goat.

4. *Be succinct in your answers.* This is not the time for a soliloquy on your campaign theme. Be short, sweet, and to the point.

5. *If a tough question is asked, be the first to answer.* Don't leave an opening for your opponent. Get in there and be aggressive, but stop short of a fight. Use humor instead of anger to answer questions. It is important that you act in a cool, calm, and collected manner.

6. *Make sure you have the opportunity for a concluding statement.* Instead of thanking just the host and your opponent, make sure you thank the viewers or listeners for taking time to learn all the points of view. Give them your telephone number so they can contact you after the show.

In summary, these talk shows end up being great entertainment for their audiences. If the audience of a talk show includes your targeted voters, you need to put more time into preparation than you will ever spend on the air. Arrive with all the information at your fingertips—and don't forget your message. Be entertaining without becoming the butt of your opponent's or the host's jokes.

## Cable TV

In many communities public access to cable TV provides the opportunity to put together a special interview show about you and your campaign. Cable access is a wonderful new medium; however, you must be cautious when you use it. Don't prattle on for thirty minutes as a talking head trying to give the impression that you have all the answers to every problem. You could hurt yourself by looking foolish. Or worse yet, you could be totally boring.

In using cable you should answer very specific questions. Put as much energy into looking good as you do into preparing what you are going to say. Remember that these TV shows focus on a very small market, but their viewers are often the voters who go to the polls in every election.

## Voter Pamphlet Statements

Some people consider voter pamphlet statements to be the best-read means of influencing voters. A few studies have been done on the impact of these pages and pages of small print about hundreds of candidates and lots of issues, and they have shown that seniors recall getting their initial information about a candidate from these pamphlets more than other voters. Even though most voters don't recall reading much of the pamphlets, they recall it as having helped them make up their minds.

Voter pamphlets are mailed out earlier than most campaign direct mail. They set the stage. Plan for these statements. Put the most important information in them, allowing for some white space. (You do not have to use every word you are allowed.) State your message in a simple paragraph. Have another paragraph highlight the key parts of your resumé, and another include some key endorsements. Conclude by going back to your message. Use boldfacing, capital letters, and whatever else is allowed to make it graphically unique and appealing. And finally, make sure your photograph is clear and professional.

## Voter Video Statements

Similar to printed voter pamphlet statements, many municipalities are now using public-access TV as a way to provide voters with the opportunity to view statements from candidates. It is critical that you have professionals coaching you, so that you don't ramble on or get into things you do not want to talk about. Have an outline of what you intend to say printed large enough to be clearly visible as you speak. It should be placed close enough to the camera that you can see it as you look into the camera. These two- to four-minute statements may air several times during the last few weeks of a campaign.

# COMPUTERS AND CAMPAIGN TECHNOLOGY

## POLITICKING IN CYBERSPACE

There was a time when there were no computers in political campaigns. That time was a mere two decades ago. Since then a veritable revolution of computers has begun to redefine how you campaign. Though your campaign may not have ten computers, you will wish you did—particularly if your opponent has made the giant step and financial commitment to using computers as they will be used in campaigns to come.

Today we sit on the cutting edge of the computer-driven campaign. With California's Silicon Valley also being the heart of the country's most advanced campaigning technology and techniques, it's easy to see how candidates in our most populated state have tamed technology to give them an edge up on less-well-financed campaigns.

Technology offers you strategic as well as tactical advantages. Not only do today's campaign managers track their campaign's progress through specially-designed computer programs, but campaign field forces are now aided by computer programs that identify those targeted voters who live in great yard sign locations, giving the campaign an added incentive for personalizing any interaction with that voter household.

Just twenty years ago more than 95 percent of the campaigns in this country had no computers. As the microchip charged into most every field, it limped slowly, by comparison, into the campaign world. First, as public disclosure of campaign contributions became mandatory in every state, there was a need to simplify the record-keeping and reporting procedures. The first campaign needs were—and still are—the accurate tallying and reporting of campaign contributions that is required by law. Most public disclosure agencies either sell computer programs to record, calculate and report the required information, or they will refer you to one or more vendors of such programs.

From record-keeping and reporting needs, computers moved into the volunteer business, taking the place of the trusty shoebox filled with 3" x 5" cards containing data on each campaign volunteer. And, as computers became part of every office worker's life, they also became the tool for all campaign staffers who deal with the written word, to the point that many campaigns do not hire staffers unless they can provide a computer (or the staffer owns his or her own).

And computer science is not the only frontier of the technological age that is vastly improving campaign efficiency. There's the Internet for special online conferences with constituents, special phone machines that can deliver a message to your volunteers every week, fax machines that can target the people you wish to send press releases, cellular phones that can double the efficiency of candidate phoning, pagers to keep your scheduler always within a phone call of the candidate, and video tapes you can send to key endorsers with special messages from your high-level supporters. The list goes on, adding new technical breakthroughs almost daily.

In fact, technology can solve many of the big and little problems that plague campaigns. In a survey of more than 200 candidates who ran for office in 1992, the top pet peeves of their campaigns were listed as:

- Not being able to promptly get back in touch with volunteers who offer their services.

- Inadvertently sending out duplicate or even triplicate fundraising or event mailings to the same people.

- Not being able to send thank you letters to contributors in a timely manner.

All of these pet peeves can be resolved with computers. Campaigns can use the mail-merge function of any good word-processing program to send a personalized "welcome-to-the-campaign" letter to all potential volunteers. The campaign must simply designate someone to be responsible for collecting those names and then mailing the letters.

On the second point, all lists that the campaign acquires for mailings should be combined into one database, and then that database should be carefully checked for duplicate names. This can be a tedious task, but there are some campaign database programs that will do a reasonably good job of this almost automatically. It is worth the effort, because mailing duplicate pieces not only wastes money, but it sends the wrong message (inefficiency) to those who receive them.

The third peeve is also easily handled with computer technology. Most computer programs designed for campaigns have a function for automatically producing a thank-you letter each time a contribution is recorded. You must write the letter initially, and you should update it frequently, but it is an easy task. Some of today's programs also allow for you to add a signature and hand-written note, giving the impression that the candidate took time to jot a personal note to the donor.

Not only do computers help you through these pet peeves, they are also your most efficient connection with your voters. Computers are no longer the future; they are the required present, or your campaign will be strictly past tense. Where you need not (and indeed, should not) be the computer guru of your campaign, you should allocate the necessary resources, understand what computers can do, and have your own cyberadvisor to bring you up to speed and push some technological limits.

# Computer People for Your Campaign

Usually a campaign is hell-bent on using every single thing that is offered it for free, especially and particularly computers. Candidates often start scouting for a free computer or two before they even tell their families they intend to run for office. After securing or buying a computer, a candidate may read about a new campaign program that can do just about anything—all for an amazing $99.95. Then, after determining what the campaign should do with its computers and programs, he finally gets around to looking for a person to put in charge of all that hardware and software.

This process is the reverse of what it should be. Instead, you should find your computer coordinator and then consider what computer functions you would like to, and can expect to, incorporate into your campaign. Next, the computer coordinator, with input from the people who will be using the computers, should embark on finding the right software to accomplish the designated tasks. Finally, the hardware, with all the specifications necessary to accommodate the software, is borrowed, rented or bought.

The most important person on your computer team is your computer coordinator (alias database manager, computer guru, cyberadvisor, or technological whiz kid—whatever you choose to call her or him). The ideal person for this job:

1. *Has professional experience with computers,* preferably with campaigns, and a variety of computer uses.

2. *Has the necessary time to dedicate to your campaign* so that she or he can do more than set up the operations and stop by during times of computer crisis.

3. *Knows the limitations of the hardware and software* you are using and can help everyone determine computer time priorities.

4. *Is knowledgeable enough to make minor hardware repairs* and quickly learn and teach others how to use new software.

5. *Can speak a common language with the rest of the staff,* as opposed to only cyberspeak.

6. *Knows how and where to get the best prices* on hardware, software and anything else needed in the computer department.

7. *Is familiar with the Internet* and can help you devise a few key uses for it in your campaign.

**Your computer guru:**

➤ *Is experienced.*
➤ *Has time for the job.*
➤ *Knows your hardware and software.*
➤ *Learns quickly and can teach others.*
➤ *Speaks a common language.*
➤ *Knows where to find bargains.*
➤ *Is familiar with the Internet.*
➤ *Knows about political campaigns.*
➤ *Does not frustrate easily.*

8. *Knows about political campaigns*, preferably having worked as a volunteer on many.

9. *Does not frustrate easily*, as there will be people working on the campaign who know little about computers, but will expect a lot.

The computer coordinator has many responsibilities. She or he:

- Determines what hardware and software are needed, taking into consideration all freebies offered the campaign.

- Determines what should be purchased, and often negotiates the deal with computer companies or individual sellers.

- Decides the best place for the computers to be located in the office, considering the available light, security, electric power sources, etc.

- Determines who uses what computers and when, taking into account the overall campaign priorities.

- Sets up the rules and regulations for using the computers, including sign-on procedures, file backup schedules, and who is to have access to what information.

- Is the first person called if there are any problems with the computers, the databases, the programs or the people using them.

Listen to your computer manager. She understands the possibilities—and the probabilities—of handling specific chores.

In addition, you'll need people who are good at training others so that you can enlist a large number of people to do data input. People who design programs or supervise computer operations may be great at those jobs, but often they are less than patient with people who have few or no computer skills. There are people that will wander into your campaign who may never have worked on a computer. These folks need special help from a kindly computer-literate organizer.

You'll need lots of computer-literate people for your campaign. You'll need people who own computers and can use them for campaign work, so that they don't compete for the few computers the campaign can afford. And, of course, you'll need lots of user-friendly volunteers who are willing to learn and input all those names of targeted voters whose votes you will need to win.

# Uses of a Computer in Today's Campaign

The ideal campaign has a computer for every basic function or key person. The treasurer has a computer for recording all campaign contributions and can, with the push of a few buttons, determine how much each contributor has given. The fundraiser uses a computer for developing lists of prospective high donors to phone, as well as lists for low-donor mailings. The scheduler has a computer to input all requests for candidate appointments, as well as to determine if the candidate is using good time management. The press secretary has a computer with faxing capabilities that allows her or him to target special press releases to the right reporter, editor or constituent.

The field coordinator manages the list of targeted voters and can produce mailing labels, walking lists and phone cards of the exact voters targeted by the campaign. There's a computer for desktop publishing that allows the campaign to design simple coffee-hour or other fundraising invitations. The volunteer coordinator has a computer to maintain information about volunteers, so she can always access the people available to help on a specific day or specific task. And, of course, the campaign manager needs her trusty computer to be able to plot direction, craft new messages for specific needs, monitor the cash flow and simply react to the daily crises that effect all campaigns.

> **Computers can help you with:**
>
> ➤ Fundraising
> ➤ Contributor records
> ➤ Volunteer coordination
> ➤ Budget and cash flow
> ➤ Voter targeting
> ➤ Voter contact
> ➤ Candidate scheduling
> ➤ Press and media

Given that few campaigns can afford more than two or three computers, it's important to assess all that can be done with today's computer people, programs and hardware. At the very least, consider renting computer equipment. If you are looking for a long political lifeline, however, you will want to start investing in serious computer equipment. Remember that some campaigns are now investing more than 10 percent of their entire campaign budget in computer hardware, software and staff.

This will be the future trend, as computers help define the cutting edge of reaching targeted voters.

# Fundraising With Computers

## Developing High-Donor Prospect Phoning Lists

More than 50 percent of the funds you raise will come from asking people for money individually, one on one. To do this well, you need to know the best people to ask. Computers can help you find, track, solicit and resolicit important prospective donors.

The best high-donor prospect list you can build is one of demonstrated high donors from several campaigns. Almost every political jurisdiction has public files of campaign contributors. From these files, you can get the names and addresses of those people who have given to campaigns similar to yours in the past. By combining the lists of donors from several campaigns, you can see the total amount contributed to those several candidates by various individuals.

To save hours of tedious work, contact former candidates for public office who have already done this work and ask them for their lists, preferably on computer diskette. Or at least see if you can find someone who will scan the lists into a computer. Many law offices have the equipment to do this, and may be willing to let your campaign use it.

# Developing Low-Donor Prospect Mailing Lists

You will need to get names of prospective donors and members of organizations you belong to for mailing low-donor campaign materials. Ask for these lists on computer disks to save your volunteers hours of inputting time. Then use your word processor and its mail-merge function to send personalized letters requesting contributions to your campaign. Be sure to include a return remittance envelope in each letter sent.

For at least those people who have been politically active and have given at least $25 to previous campaigns, either the candidate or campaign volunteers should follow up that mailing with a telephone call.

Low-donor lists are also important for mailing invitations to rallies, populist fundraisers and coffee hours. At the very least you will want one list of at least 2,500 people to whom you will mail each month. This list will include your friends, family, colleagues, interest associates, etc. Remember that you will gather many important lists with potential for low-donor fundraising (organizations who endorse you, for instance). A fundraising letter and a remittance envelope should be sent to every person on these lists.

# Managing the Donor Lists

Campaigns require a lot of repetition, both in delivering your message and asking for contributions. In fundraising, it is critical that you first know how much a prospective donor can afford to give. Then you should keep track of when you contact each one, what she says, and when you should call back. Today, most campaigns have a volunteer in charge of maintaining a three-ring binder with this information for the candidate. However, some candidates have already graduated to sitting in front of their laptop computer from which they are instructed to call specific people on certain days. Background data is already prepared for them to review prior to calling, and the candidate herself updates the information after the call is made.

Whether a fundraising staffer or the candidate updates the donor files is not as important as having the best lists from which to call. Following up the calls with pledge letters, envelopes and more followup calls, should the check not arrive within a few days, is critical and easily handled if you are monitoring this entire process with your handy-dandy computer.

# Campaign Management

A good campaign computer program will use what is called a relational database to store information valuable to many areas of campaign management. A relational database is actually made up of several sub-databases, such as volunteers, contributors, voters, etc., that are related and refer to each other. In a relational campaign database, a person may actually belong to more than one of the sub-databases, but that person's name, address and other information is entered only once.

The alternative is to have separate databases for volunteers, voters, contributors, prospective donors, etc. These databases don't talk to each other, and require that the name and other information for a person who is a contributor, volunteer and voter be entered separately into all three databases.

For both everyday use and maintenance purposes, the relational database is much more efficient. Any change of address, phone number or anything else is entered only once, rather than separately into each appropriate database, and a relational database will take up less space on your computer's hard drive. Regardless of how you choose to set up your system, it is important to remember the primary rule of all campaign technology: have someone in charge who knows what she is doing and has the time to do it.

## The Treasurer: Keeping Track of Contributors

Computers can help you keep close track of all contributors to your campaign. You need to record what they have given, when the checks came in and all changes in addresses and telephone numbers during the course of the campaign. And, of course, you need to be able to generate accurate contribution reports to be filed with the proper public disclosure agencies. Needless to say, anything that does this much work for you is worth a lot. Computer programs that handle these tasks start at around $500 and go up to as much as several thousand for those that also perform several other campaign functions. A good campaign treasurer will probably insist on having a program to track at least contributions, and perhaps expenses, too.

It may be tempting to accept an offer from a local computer guru who volunteers to design a database program especially for you and save you $500 or $1,000. You should resist. The time involved in designing, developing and testing a program makes this approach impractical for a campaign that will last less than a year. Many of the commercial programs available have been on the market for years and have the benefit of being upgraded after input from many former campaigns just like yours. Go ahead and spend the money and get something that works immediately.

> **Computers and campaign management:**
>
> ➤ Keep track of contributors.
> ➤ Know which volunteers can help when.
> ➤ Manage your cash flow.
> ➤ Determine which voters to target.
> ➤ Get your message to the right people.
> ➤ Target the candidate's time.
> ➤ Communicate with the press.
> ➤ Research public files.

The contributor information you keep because you are required to is valuable information to your campaign. Anyone who has contributed to the campaign, particularly early on, is a prime prospect for another donation later in the campaign, especially for items like a last-minute radio response to an attack by your opponent. And your records will clearly show those contributors who have already given the maximum allowable amount, so that you do not contact them again.

## The Volunteer Coordinator: Knowing Who Can Help When

As mentioned earlier, one of the most frequent quality-control points that frustrates candidates in all campaigns is the inability to respond in a timely manner to those who want to help. By organizing your campaign to record all the volunteers as they find their way to your campaign, you stand a good chance of getting the best work from them. Computers can help you keep track of the time of day these volunteers will be able to work, where they will be available to be dispatched, what they want to do, and how much time they have available to give.

You can also keep track of how often you have used each volunteer's services, and continually check to see that no people who have volunteered their help have fallen through the cracks and not been contacted by the campaign. The quickest way to lose volunteers is not to use them. And be sure to send thank-you notes to everyone who volunteers on your campaign. Your computer can help with this task, also.

## The Budget: Cash-Flow Management

All good campaigns require money, and they require money management as well. A budget is the most fundamental strategic document of a campaign. If you do not formalize a budget, you will never know if you have the money to accomplish the most critical voter contact tasks of your campaign.

Budgets also give you key cash-flow information. If you plan to raise $100,000 in the course of the campaign, and you plan to spend $15,000 of that within the first few weeks of the campaign, you should realize that most contributions will come in at the end of the campaign, close to election day. Thus, the candidate may be forced to lend the campaign money to get the basic expenses paid for as needed to get the campaign up and running.

Budgeting requires tracking your fundraising goals at the same time you are gauging expenditures. Campaigns frequently find themselves awaiting those checks arriving in the morning mail before being able to pay the postage on a mailing to more prospective donors. A strong budgeting program, or even a simple spreadsheet program, can help you plan the campaign's cash flow.

# Targeting: Knowing Whom to Reach

Targeting holds the key to personalized, focused communications with voters who want more than generic political messages. Very affordable programs allow you to purchase voter files from a label vendor and extract from them a file of your targeted voters. Some programs allow you to download the entire database; others just concentrate on the information needed to build a realistic target.

Once you have the voter files, you can run a count of the specific subsets of voters you want to target. For example, if you need 20,000 votes to win, you may start with a base you believe to be about 10,000 voters. To get the additional 10,000, you may target women who have voted in three out of the last four elections. In addition, you might target senior women who live in rental units in certain areas of town. These programs allow you to determine whether there are enough people in these groups to give you that additional 10,000 voters. If not, then you could include Hispanic voters, or senior men, or a whole host of other targets.

# Voter Contact: Getting the Message to the Right People

Once you figure out who your best voters will be, computers can help you concentrate all your voter contact efforts on them. It is far less productive to reach all potential voters once or twice than to reach more-likely voters four or five times. Remembering the golden rule of all good campaigns, you need to get your message out to a very targeted number of most-likely voters several times, in a variety of ways. To do this, a computer comes in very handy and actually helps you save money while maximizing your impact. It can help you focus your mailings, door-to-door canvassing, phone banks and even your yard sign strategy to the voters you have targeted.

The first contact from a candidate to the voters is typically a direct-mail brochure or computer-generated personalized letter. These letters are easily generated using the mail-merge feature of your word processor, along with your database of names and addresses. The recipient's name and address can be at the top of each letter, and the letter can include any other personalized information you may have in your database. You can also print mailing labels from the database, making the entire process quite easy.

Other voter contact tools available through computer programs include walking lists for door-to-door canvassing and phone cards for phone banks. In most cases, you might be able to afford to purchase walking lists from a local list vendor, but you probably would not budget for phone cards. However, a campaign that has a sophisticated computer program can do both for pennies, thus easily keeping field and voter contact operations focused on the same people.

Telemarketing (phone calls to your targeted voters) uses advanced computer technology that you can take advantage of if you have a large enough volunteer force to phone for you. The phoners sit in front of computer terminals displaying their script and the questions to ask. In addition to the "Who would you vote for?" question, you also can ask the undecided voters about their concerns. To those who say their most important issue is economic development and jobs, you can send a letter, already written, from the candidate about jobs and the economy. To those whose number-one concern is education, a letter about schools can be sent.

When a campaign is ready for its Get-Out-The-Vote efforts, the entire list of those people identified as supporters will be printed out for the campaign volunteers or the telemarketers to contact, reminding them to vote.

Yard sign strategy also is helped by computers. Once you know your targeted voters, you can determine the ones that live on key arterial streets and call them first as part of your phone bank operation. Calling key folks about yard signs also allows you to begin your voter contact communication with them, in addition to efficiently finding good locations for yard signs.

## Candidate Time Management: Targeting Your Time

More candidates are turning to computers to help regulate their time, which is the most limited resource of a campaign. The candidate has only so much time to campaign, given other important activities such as working, sleeping and family responsibilities. A candidate needs to determine her available hours for campaigning and then determine what her highest priorities will be during that time.

Campaigns that record all incoming requests for speaking engagements from constituent groups can then track the time allocated for each demographic or geographic group. For example, if you have 30 requests for the candidate's time, you can schedule more strategically if you know what targeted groups you want to reach more often, and then allocate a specific percentage of her time for that group. And, if you monitor the candidate's time as a whole, you can ensure that she spends the necessary 30 to 40 percent of available campaigning time on raising money.

There are several excellent scheduling programs on the market for $50 or less. These programs keep track of the date and time of all events, as well as supplemental information such as directions to the events and what is expected of the candidate once she arrives. You can keep a master calendar of all campaign events and every item on your candidate's daily schedule, then print out customized calendars for different individuals with only the appropriate events listed.

For example, the candidate needs only information about what she is supposed to do. She doesn't need to know when headquarters staff meetings are or when phone banks are scheduled. On the other hand, the campaign staff does not need to know where the candidate is every minute of the day. The press would only need to know about the candidate's public appearances and not when she is scheduled to make her high-donor phone calls or attend meet-and-greet fundraisers.

Having the schedule computerized makes it easy to print an up-to-date schedule for the candidate and other key campaign people each day. You can also print weekly and monthly calendars to easily see upcoming events.

## Press & Media: Getting on the Right Wavelength

In working with the press, there's much to be gained by having the right information to the right reporter in record time. Although press releases are hardly what every reporter is awaiting, releases do serve their point. If you specially release news to certain reporters based on their individual interest or past stories, you can make a favorable impression. Most campaign press secretaries with computer faxing capability can program their computers to fax to specific lists of reporters. As soon as a press release is ready and approved, it can quickly and easily be sent to the reporters that count.

This becomes especially important when the response is directed at negative information released about a candidate in the final days of the campaign. At such time, the efficiency and technology of computerized faxing are worth their weight in gold.

When it comes to filling out questionnaires, a standard word-processing program can help the campaign remain consistent in responding to tough questions. If you get in the habit of entering all questions and their answers into the computer, you can then easily use the same answers in the next questionnaire sent your way. By the end of the campaign, when time is at a premium, a last-minute questionnaire takes only minutes to complete.

## Research: Knowing How to Use Public Files

Even though it takes special expertise to analyze public records for opposition research (both on you and your opponent), there is much data that you can track yourself, saving time and money for the opposition research talent you hire. Court records can be accessed from most online services, or you can trot on down to the local courthouse to look at the files in person. Nexis/ Lexis searches of stories from the past about you or your opponent will also reveal much about the race. Voter files that reveal when your opponent first registered to vote and how often he has voted since then are also online, or soon will be. Public disclosure records that detail a candidate's financial records and all campaign contributors are now available online from the Federal Elections Commission (for a fee), and in a smattering of states. All this, plus an ever-increasing list of opposition research, will be increasingly available from the privacy and comfort (or discomfort) of your own computer.

In addition, libraries have a wealth of research and data on almost any issue that can be accessed online, saving valuable issue research time—and it usually can be accessed anytime, not just during the time the library is open.

## Computer Cautions

Although computers mark the future of campaign efficiency and strategy, they are still in their infancy stage. Too often campaigns are eager to get everything at once, acquiring hardware and software to perform almost any task. However, if the campaign must learn how to use the technology at the same time it is learning how to campaign, a compromise is usually made that leaves the technology in the dust. In putting together your computer potential, go cautiously into the future:

1. *Beware of custom-built systems* designed by well-intentioned people, but not thoroughly tested. You cannot afford to be constantly dealing with programming omissions and bugs.

2. *Don't choose a simple spreadsheet* or database program to handle contribution data just because you already know how to use it. At least check out the political software available. Often it costs the same and has many additional and time-saving features.

3. *Don't bite off more than you can chew.* If you have a computer manager who can only spend a little time with the campaign, or you have someone who's not very familiar with either politics or computers, then you should not buy a sophisticated system. Stick with a simple one.

4. *Build your system slowly.* Don't go for the whole list of options in your first campaign. Buy what you need, but buy with a mind towards building the software and hardware systems you will need for your kind of political career.

5. *Back up your data regularly.* As you continue to grow in computer capabilities, learn the number-one rule for all computer users: back up everything at least once a week. If you are doing complicated computer voter contact tracking, or if you are recording many contributions, then back the system up daily.

6. *Make sure you have reliable and competent* computer people, not just people who know a little more than you do. Have your computer

coordinator talk with other computer gurus before you purchase either hardware or software.

7. *Accommodate the computer novice.* Your campaign undoubtedly will have volunteers who are not familiar with computers. Seniors, women who have been working out of the home and people new to this country are often among them. Have other tasks for them to do, but have special tutors available to train them for computer tasks if they are interested.

8. *Be aware that security risks are ever-present* with the growing number of people and computers in any campaign. Passwords should be set up for each person, such as the scheduler, media coordinator, treasurer and manager, as well as data entry volunteers, to assure that people can access only that data necessary to perform their jobs.

9. *Remember that computers can't do everything.* Computers are indispensable in many campaign tasks, but they are no substitute for other tasks, such as fundraising. A candidate can have computers full of valuable information that no other campaign has—but if she only spends half as much time as she should raising money, the state-of-the-art system means very little.

10. *Use your computer as a tool*—not a slave driver. If it helps you make more money, get more votes, and utilize more resources, use it to its highest potential, but don't let the wonderment of the technology captivate you to the detriment of the rest of the campaign.

# *Other Campaign Technology*

## The Internet

Technology doesn't stop at your computer table. In fact, it can require subscriptions to a half-dozen computer magazines just to keep up with the revolution now in front of today's campaigns.

The Internet, commonly referred to as "the Net," is blooming as one of the newest crops of computer technology to move from a cute story of campaign entrepreneurial spirit to one that actually might move targeted voters. Obviously only a small, though increasing, number of voters are presently hooked up to the Net. Yet home pages—described by some as a personal or corporate billboard on the information superhighway—are definitely the new rage in campaigning. Set up on the World Wide Web portion of the Net, home pages offer voters access to you and important campaign information, whether it be family photos, detailed position papers, or how to volunteer for your campaign. The cost is relatively cheap, the access amazing, and your ability to play in the politics of the 21st century is at hand.

To "get on the Net," the campaign should, at the very least, have its own e-mail address, which should be checked daily. A local Internet service provider can provide you with a site and address for a home page (called a "URL"), in addition to your e-mail address. Though home pages can often be put together by an Internet service provider for a fee, creating and maintaining a home page should not be beyond the capability of your computer expert. Print your home page's URL on all campaign literature and volunteer sheets, along with your e-mail address. Keep in mind that thousands of "Net-surfers" will see your page before the end of the campaign, so upkeep and quality control are imperative.

Examples of Internet uses:

*Fundraising:* Holding fundraisers, from auctions to other more personalized solicitations, is already being done. The home page advertises the date and time of the live event, and pictures of items to be auctioned off are shown on the screen. Web users can access your page and either pledge money or have it immediately charged to their VISA or MasterCard. The same idea, without graphics, can be accomplished by sending information to a designated list of e-mail subscribers.

*Speeches:* After important candidate speeches, the text and/or the actual delivery of the speech can be relayed through the Net, giving campaigns the ability to reach reporters, key potential endorsers, supporters with specific interests, and even the campaign central staff itself, who might not have been able to attend.

If you do this, be advised that your opponent may scrutinize all your speeches looking for inconsistencies or other things to embarrass you with.

*Volunteers:* After people access your home page, receive information on issues, talk with the candidate, or use any of your services, you might have them on line as a likely volunteer. In fact, soliciting and successfully enticing volunteers into the campaign after a home page communication has proved to be the most profitable use of the Net to most campaigns.

One caution, however: make sure that you do not fall victim to the heavy merchandising now starting in relationship to campaigns. Several entrepreneurial folks are selling speeches, campaign information and other gizmos while not being directly associated with a campaign at all. Printing your "official" e-mail address and URL on all literature can help alleviate this problem.

# Faxes

Every campaign must have at least one fax machine with a dedicated phone line to send and receive information. The candidate should also consider getting a fax machine for her or his home, as there will surely be several opportunities when it will be a great alternative to driving across town to approve a last-minute brochure.

Fax machines are also important for press, endorsers and key supporters. The names and fax numbers of these important people can be programmed into the machine for quick distribution of "blast faxes"—basic campaign summaries, key press releases, updated campaign contribution totals, etc.

# Cellular Phones, Pagers and Telephone Technology

Cellular phones are the greatest single fundraising machine invented. A candidate's job is to go everywhere her targeted voters are located. However, this often puts the candidate in a car for hours each day. Trapped in traffic, what can you do to be effective? Get on the phone and call, call, call. Talk with those hard-to-reach prospective donors. For some reason, calling from a cellular phone has a more immediate, attention-getting appeal. Cell phones can help you stay (for good or bad) very accessible:

> **Cellular phones keep you in touch with:**
>
> ➤ *Contributors*
> ➤ *Reporters*
> ➤ *Your scheduler*
> ➤ *Campaign staff*
> ➤ *Your family*

- You can be within reach of reporters on deadline—or reach them, even though your schedule is impossible.

- You can reach your scheduler or the people hosting an event, should you be lost and wandering around unfamiliar neighborhoods.

- You can call for backups of people and materials if you arrive at an event and find your opponent's materials everywhere and you have none.

- You can even call home to talk with those folks who haven't seen you for days. Leaving thoughtful messages on the home phone machine may keep everyone a little more cognizant of what's going on.

Cellular phone prices are coming down so rapidly that you may want to consider giving other key campaign people one also. For example, a willing and enterprising campaign manager can be the entire headquarters with just one cellular phone. Should you have a small staff, or have a headquarters that is away from the downtown core, the manager can have the campaign phone forwarded to her or his cellular one, making the headquarters—and the campaign—always appear to be open for business.

Pagers are also great tools of the trade for other members of the campaign staff. Schedulers need to be accessible to the candidate 24 hours a day. A good scheduler has a pager so that if the candidate is lost or confused about an appointment, she or he can page the scheduler for additional information.

Sophisticated telephone technology also helps keep the campaign family informed. Specialized phone machines can now be programmed to call hundreds of phone numbers. Consider the possibility of your volunteers receiving an update from you every Monday morning—a list of dates and times of important meetings, announcements of new endorsers, contribution totals and other good news—or even an inoculation against negative hits expected in the next week. These phone machines allow you to press one button and off the message goes. Since most folks aren't home on Monday mornings, it sounds like the candidate called personally and left the message. You can also program the machine so that it recites the recorded message only if it gets an answering machine. If it gets a real voice, then the machine transfers the call back to the headquarters where a staff member can take the call.

Other phone technology has been tried that allows a campaign to record an election-eve message to voters that can be transmitted to hundreds of GOTV-recorded supporters. Though this technology has existed for awhile, it isn't uniformly accepted, as it furthers the impersonal nature of political campaigning. Candidates are reluctant to force-feed a prerecorded message to an already cynical public.

Toll-free numbers and special 900 numbers are also fashionable these days. With 800 numbers, anyone can call the campaign from anywhere and get his concerns answered, information forwarded or volunteer help offered—without it costing the caller anything. With 900 numbers, supporters call the campaign and pledge money for it, with the pledge being added to the contributor's phone bill. This has been tried in many states, especially for initiative campaigns. However, it requires a large advertising budget to make people aware of the special number, and the money collected often pales in comparison to what it cost to advertise the phone number all over the state.

## Broadcast Technology

Satellite uplinks now allow a campaign to offer TV coverage to stations that can't afford to send a reporter to cover each event. A simple computer program allows the same capabilities with audio, allowing radio talk-show hosts throughout the district to get your missives in a timely manner and in the medium they can use—and make themselves look good. The market is growing, making broadcast voter pamphlets much more appealing than their written counterparts.

If there was one beauty of Ross Perot's infomercials, it was the ability to use cable TV in a way that was affordable, acceptable and targeted to specific audiences. Now, as broadcast cable markets hustle their ability to reach swing voters, look for campaigns to use the ever-increasing, ever-cost-effective technology to narrowcast messages to voters.

In recent California campaigns, state legislative candidates with three or more cable markets in their district were able to personalize the first 20 seconds of a two-minute political spot, and then combine it with a message produced for everyone to see. The results: the local markets had a tailor-made spot for them and everyone saw the greater message in the more elaborate portion of the spot. And all for a fraction of what it would cost to have a professionally-done spot that the campaign could never afford to put on commercial TV.

Technology looms larger than life in cyberpolitics. Exploit the technology, using anything new with the free press, which is always ready to latch onto a new way of possible future campaigning. Even though much of the technology is still new and more newsworthy than effective in reaching targeted voters, politics will never go back.

Remember that although its potential is not its actual impact today, it will be in the not-so-distant future. Start slow. Start sure of what you can do. But start now.

Smart campaigns will not win without technology. In times when money is tight, or even between well-funded candidates, technology is likely to decide who wins and who is left in the microchip dust.

# SCHEDULING THE CANDIDATE

## TIME MANAGEMENT

**M**oney you can always raise. Volunteers you can always recruit. More yard signs you can always put up. But time—when it's gone, you're either the winner or the loser. Nothing can get you another hour to campaign—except better time management.

Candidates are constantly concerned about how they spend their time. As you go through your first campaign, time will be the most valuable commodity that you will waste. You will attempt to design your own brochure. You will refuse to delegate the filling out of your questionnaires. You will constantly leave phone messages for people who won't get back in touch with you. And you will insist on doing trivial campaign tasks, rationalizing that it will take you less time to do the chore than it would to explain how to do it to others.

Time is a campaign's most precious resource. It is why one full-time scheduler is recommended. It is also why a candidate time-management formula— agreed to by the candidate, the manager and the scheduler—is advised.

Getting a handle on your schedule will be more of a problem if you are currently in complete charge of your time and the planning for it. Those who have had the luxury of having an assistant to handle their schedule know what a relief it can be, and how many fewer mistakes are made, when someone who's trained and responsible for the details can replace you and let you worry about the big picture, the perfect speech delivery, and make the high-donor phone calls.

A good schedule is a balance: it's an ever-changing compendium of scheduled appointments, speaking engagements, disciplined phone time, key meetings with staff and consultants, and traveling to all the above. Candidates often hold tightly to their right to control their own time (a natural tendency for everyone), and are eased out of that grip only after the campaign team can prove it is worthy of the responsibility.

# The Scheduler

The best person to help wrest that control from the candidate is the scheduler: that patient, calm, cool, and collected saint who has volunteered to be in charge of details that will undoubtedly get confused, relayed wrong, and simply not received in time. After all, the scheduler is not only responsible for the occasional mistakes she or he will make, but the scheduler is also the one who will be blamed for every luncheon organizer's mistake that gives the wrong time or format for an engagement.

The scheduler should be among the first campaign workers aboard. In fact, many candidates think of a scheduler as a luxury they can afford only after the manager, the fundraiser and the press person are aboard, and money is coming in to pay them all. In many cases, the scheduler will be a volunteer. The best schedulers are often people who have that same responsibility in a professional office, and follow their boss into the campaign.

You will need a scheduler who is well organized. (If his desk looks like your teenage son's bedroom, then he's probably not your best prospect for a scheduler). The scheduler should handle files, tiny pieces of paper with telephone numbers on them, and the schedule book with the same penchant for perfection. This person should have a thick skin and not be easily demoralized by an occasional harsh word from either you, the manager, or a treasured supporter who has to be told you can't attend her fiftieth wedding anniversary party.

Characteristics important for your scheduler include: being trustworthy, dependable, conscientious and self-starting. This person not only has to handle thousands of details, but she must do so tactfully. She must know how to set priorities, and how to convince the candidate every day that those time-management priorities are worth keeping. Good schedulers assume that anything could go wrong, so they constantly check and recheck schedule details.

If you are hired, appointed or delegated to be the campaign scheduler, there is much to consider. The following ideas are for you.

## Duties

Schedulers have many duties. The first is to let the candidate know what's on her schedule each day. Most schedulers have a computer program that will print daily, weekly, monthly and multi-month calendars for the candidate, the manager and others who need to help plan the candidate's time. The scheduler explains the details of each day to the candidate, usually the night before a complicated day. She also confirms and reconfirms the directions, details and formats of the engagements on that schedule. The scheduler's goal each day is to convince the candidate that her time has been managed at its highest and best use, and that she doesn't have to worry about her schedule.

The scheduler receives all invitations for speaking engagements and visibility opportunities. She organizes them according to the day, the target audiences they may reach, and their potential for press opportunities. The scheduler also declines events, makes apologies for cancellations and comes up with better appointments than attending someone else's fundraiser. She determines what the candidate needs to know to do well at any engagement; she advises on proper attire; she arranges for transportation and any necessary advance work; and she makes recommendations to the manager as to who should accompany the candidate.

The best schedulers don't just rely on the incoming mail to fill the candidate's schedule. If the target population the campaign has to move includes senior women in the northern part of the district, then the scheduler needs to know every venue for those seniors, and she gets her candidate appointments with them.

Her job also includes being the best source for information about community events, parades, county fairs, street festivals, and anything else going on in the district. She knows to ask for rules and regulations for placing signs; she will figure out how to get the best booth positions; and she'll get all the event details, even if she has to ask ten different people. A scheduler on the ball can also talk people out of any information that will make the candidate's life easier.

More than any specific detail, task or trait, the scheduler has to be the person who keeps the candidate on track. The scheduler listens patiently to the candidate's complaints about overscheduling with no time for herself, and then sends her off to the next speaking engagement. She must be filled with compassion for the candidate's family, who never sees her; and she must never lose site of the goal: to keep the candidate phoning, to keep her in front of her targeted voters and the press, and to keep her away from the details as much as possible.

## Different Schedules for Different Needs

The master schedule book is the anchor of the campaign and candidate. And although there are many good computer programs that are slowly replacing the handwritten appointment book, the master schedule book is still the best place to centralize the candidate's time management. There should only be one schedule book—and the candidate should never handle it. She may look at it; she may make additions or adjustments to it; but she should not do her own scheduling.

All writing in the schedule book should be done in pencil so that changes can be made easily and often.

There are many different schedules within the campaign schedule, which is why you will need to enter all the pencil scribbles from the master schedule book into a computer. A good scheduling program will allow you to print out different schedules for different people.

Who is to get special calendars and how often they get them becomes the responsibility of the scheduler. In the early days of the campaign, it's important to get the calendar-producing process figured out so that everyone will have the information they need in a timely, accurate, usable format that is easy for the scheduler to produce.

## Candidate Schedule

The candidate should have a daily print-out of her current and next day's schedule. Attached to each day's schedule should be directions—and perhaps a map—to each event, agendas and programs, and any information the candidate needs to know about the event, such as what is expected of her.

## Driver Schedule

If the campaign is fortunate enough to have someone to drive the candidate, then the candidate need not get the travel details and maps. The driver would receive this information each day, along with the weekly schedule so that she can make plans for other days' needs. The driver must also know all event details and contact telephone numbers so that if anything goes wrong she can take care of the problem without worrying the candidate. A driver's schedule must allot some time for the candidate to eat or to freshen up before arriving at an event. Drivers must plan ahead so that the candidate isn't late for key media or other speaking events. She also should always carry extra campaign materials (yard signs, issue papers, brochures, buttons, etc.) so that the candidate need not plan for them.

## Press Schedule

The press should get weekly schedules filled with the candidate's public speaking engagements, fundraisers, key meetings, and VIP appointments. Obviously, the press schedules don't include private meetings that you might not want the press to know about, such as interviews where you are not certain about the outcome or endorsement. If you are meeting with the top labor leaders to convince them of your viability as a candidate, and you emerge without their support, you don't want a reporter standing outside the door waiting to interview the key leaders as to why they aren't endorsing you.

**Print different schedules for:**

➤ Candidate
➤ Driver
➤ Press
➤ Campaign team
➤ Advance team
➤ Family

### Campaign Team Schedule

The campaign staff and volunteers might well have much more on their schedule than appears on the candidate's. For example, critical filing deadlines, phone bank times, key radio talk-show schedules, mailing parties and staff meetings, as well as those events where the candidate will need some show of support (at fundraisers, parades, speaking engagements, etc.)—all of these should be listed on a central campaign calendar that anyone can see or copy.

### Advance Team Schedule

If you have a trusty band of supporters who routinely will attend public events, they will need their own special schedule. This schedule has the upcoming events where campaign hoopla must be presented. Yard signs, balloons, special-event flyers, and brochures should be adorning the place before the candidate ever walks in.

### Candidate's Family Schedule

A scheduler knows in advance that a candidate's family cannot be left out in the cold. Once a week the scheduler should stop by the family home to deliver (or have a member of the family stop by the campaign to get) the candidate's schedule. The most recent schedule should be dated, or color-coded, and placed and replaced on the family refrigerator for easy referral.

Family members need to be advised of those events where they should be on hand. At large fundraisers, the spouse is important to have on hand. For parades, young children are good to involve. For festivals, doorbelling, or other populist events, teenagers in the family may be interested in helping.

The key is to find what members of the family want to do, and then include those activities in the schedule. It's important to limit the number of campaign people who are dealing with the family so that wires don't get crossed, which is why the scheduler usually becomes the designated person to communicate with the family.

# Candidate Time Management

To get control of the candidate's time, it's always best to start at the beginning. What are the highest and best uses of the candidate's time?

- Phoning for money.
- Walking door-to-door or being visible to targeted voters.
- Meeting with or responding to the press.
- Conferring with key campaign staffers.

- Delivering the message.
- Convincing potential endorsers and PACs that she's the best person for the job.

In addition, the candidate needs to travel to the events and appointments that allow her to accomplish all the above. And, she needs time for herself. If a candidate cannot relax, spend time with friends and family, or just escape the campaign every once in a while, she will wear that exhaustion on her face. It's best to plan for time to rejuvenate the candidate—or pay the consequences. A candidate with little sleep who loses her sense of humor or snaps at volunteers is a bummer for everyone, particularly herself.

One way to get control of a schedule and assure that the candidate is accomplishing the tasks that only she can do, is to agree on a time management formula. Typically, this includes apportioning the candidate's waking hours for a week at a time.

Start with the 168 hours in a week.

Plan for a mythical eight hours of sleep each night, with an hour to unwind before going to bed and an hour to get up and prepare to face the day. That's 10 hours a day times seven days: 70 hours, leaving 98 hours a week for possible campaigning.

If the candidate works at a full-time job, there's another 40 hours off the top, leaving only 58 hours a week for campaigning.

Regardless of whether her job is full-time, part-time or no-time, you need to apportion the candidate's time so that whatever time is dedicated to campaigning is used wisely.

# Time Management Formula

A productive candidate's campaign tasks are:

*Fundraising:* Calling people on the phone; meeting with key prospective donors; PAC representatives and committees; her own fundraiser or finance committee; attending fundraisers or meet-and-greets; reviewing a low-donor letter.

*Voter contact:* Going door-to-door in targeted neighborhoods to targeted voters; speaking with important constituencies; visiting senior centers, neighborhood businesses and community events; attending public meetings.

*Campaign tasks:* Answering and returning important phone calls; touching base with volunteers and supporters; reviewing or giving instruction to those filling out questionnaires; refining speeches; greeting people who stop by the campaign office.

**Campaign strategy:** Keeping in touch with the manager, consultant, scheduler, and steering committee; understanding what's going on; reviewing the cash-flow situation; being advised of changes to the strategy and tactics employed in the campaign.

**Press opportunities:** Initiating conversations with reporters; stopping by the news rooms of local newspapers and broadcast media; responding to questions from the press; securing appointments for, and then attending radio talk shows; fine-tuning op-ed pieces for the newspapers; going to locations where radio microphones or TV cameras might be around.

Remember that if a candidate does not make plans for increasing his press exposure, nor working the press, he will be subjected to only responding to them—which in most cases will be too little press or the wrong kind of press.

**Personal/family time:** A candidate on a campaign treadmill still needs time to be real. This means more than just Sunday mornings should be dedicated to personal time. Reading the newspaper, getting your hair cut, getting a massage, running, relaxing with friends, even going to see a play or movie—all count in keeping the candidate grounded.

Campaign volunteers can take care of errands that the candidate need not do in person. They can help with carpooling, child care, taking clothes to the cleaners, washing the candidate's car (or taking it for repairs), grocery shopping, and miscellaneous errands. Some campaign volunteers or longtime friends of the candidate even offer to clean the candidate's house, mow the lawn, do the laundry and pay bills. The only thing volunteers cannot do is be a surrogate parent to the candidate's children when it comes to attending birthday parties and other important events.

**Transportation:** Planes, boats, trains, buses and whatever else gets the candidate to her targeted voters take time. Schedulers who don't allow for rush-hour traffic, construction, or complicated directions to an event, end up with candidates who are needlessly stressed out.

Regardless of whether a candidate campaigns one hour or 100 hours per week, a good time management formula is:

- Fundraising—30% of campaign time
- Voter contact—25% of campaign time
- Campaign tasks—15% of campaign time
- Campaign strategy—10% of campaign time
- Press opportunities—10% of campaign time
- Personal and family—5% of campaign time
- Transportation—5% of campaign time

> **A candidate needs time for:**
>
> ➤ Fundraising
> ➤ Voter contact
> ➤ Campaign tasks
> ➤ Campaign strategy
> ➤ Press opportunities
> ➤ Personal/family time
> ➤ Transportation

# Time Management Formula

## A Candidate's Time Each Day

**30%**

# Candidate Fundraising:

Making personal phone calls, going to appointments with prospects, attending home fundraisers and other events.

**25%**

# Voter Contact:

Meeting with organizations, doorbelling, getting endorsements, giving presentations.

**15%**

## Campaign Tasks:

Reviewing questionnaires, returning phone calls, preparing speeches.

**10%**

### Campaign Strategy:

Meeting with campaign staff, steering committee, determining schedules, briefings.

**10%**

### Press Opportunities:

Interviews, news conferences, editorial boards, writing letters to the editor.

**5%**

**Personal and Family Time:**
Thinking time, family time, personal grooming, time off, time for fun.

**5%**

**Transportation:**
Traveling time around town, to and from office, being stuck in traffic.

**100%**  **VICTORY!**

*FORM 20: TIME MANAGEMENT FORMULA*

The goal is for the scheduler, campaign manager and the candidate to agree in advance on a formula that will work for the campaign to be successful. Candidates usually want to reduce the amount of time required for fundraising; however, anything less than 30 percent is unreasonable.

The first goal is to secure adequate blocks of time for fundraising. Usually the scheduler sets aside certain times each week for the candidate to call prospective donors. Many find it helpful to block each day off into thirds (mornings, afternoons, and evenings). A morning might be blocked off for fundraising, an afternoon for going door-to-door, and evening for meetings.

As a scheduler, you should also know which targeted voters are critical for the campaign to reach, so that if there are events in those areas, they receive priorities. In addition, you can also solicit more events and speaking engagements among those voters.

After agreeing on the formula, you can begin to monitor, and hopefully control, the time management each week. Good schedulers take a careful look each week, and the manager takes a closer look each month, to ensure the candidate's schedule reflects those time-management formula goals. Needed adjustments can be made when necessary, usually increasing the amount of time for fundraising.

# Handling Invitations: Deciding Where to Go and Not to Go

Handling invitations is always a tricky subject. First, it's important to enter all of the invitations into one notebook or computer scheduling program, so that you can easily note any potential conflicts. Then, before you determine if you will accept any invitation, ask yourself the key questions that should drive the candidate's time:

- Will the candidate be among her targeted swing voters?
- Will her opponent be there?
- Will there be an opportunity for free press?
- Will there be a chance to ask for money or meet prospective donors?
- Are there higher priority things for the candidate to do with her time?
- Is there a chance the candidate could be set up for negative exposure?
- Who else will be there, and what will people be talking about?
- If time is tight, could we get in, make a short statement, and be excused?

- Is there another chance to talk with this same audience?
- Will people be angry if the candidate does not attend?
- How long would be proper to stay?
- How long will the candidate be able to speak?

Whenever a request comes into the campaign for the candidate's time, the information should be recorded on a scheduling request form. In many campaigns, only the scheduler is allowed to fill out the form. The campaign simply takes a message from anyone requesting a candidate appearance and forwards it to the scheduler. In other campaigns, the form can be filled out by specified key campaign volunteers and staffers.

All scheduling requests are considered in context with others. You should not promise to confirm an event (unless it is something major such as a televised debate or major campaign fundraiser) any earlier than three weeks prior to the event. Although candidates frequently make great luncheon speakers, the job of the scheduler is not to make every organization's request come true, but to use the candidate's time wisely. Treat everyone who calls with respect and courtesy, but this doesn't mean you have to say yes. Most schedulers find that if they simply explain the schedule conflicts or acknowledge that there are other priorities (even if these don't include another event), most requesters are at least thankful for the honesty.

When someone calls to request time on the candidate's schedule, be sure to get all key information. Your scheduling request form should include:

1. The specifics: date, time, location, and instructions on how to get to the location.
2. The kind of event, and the role of the candidate in relationship to the rest of the event.
3. The sponsoring organization.
4. The name and phone numbers of the person who calls.
5. Whether there will be time for questions and answers.
6. The people expected to attend—who and how many.
7. Other candidates or speakers attending.
8. Whether the press is expected to be there.
9. Whether the campaign can send an alternate speaker.
10. Whether campaign literature can be handed out.

Get all the facts during the initial conversation. If possible, ask the requester to follow up the telephone request with a written confirmation, so that confusion and inaccuracies are reduced. Also, be sure to ask about program details and exactly what is expected of the candidate. Candidates are far more secure on the stump when there is some predictability in the program. If a candidate is expecting a three-minute opening speech, a short question-and-answer period, and then a one-minute closing, she can prepare accordingly. However, if she arrives at an event only to learn she's expected to give

# Scheduling Request Form

**Event** _____ **Date/time** _____

Location and directions _____
_____

Who will accompany candidate? _____

Type of event _____ Sponsoring organization _____

Contact name _____ Phone _____

Address _____

Who will meet candidate? _____ When? _____

Where? _____

Speech details _____

_____ How long to talk _____ Q&A? _____

Questions that might be asked _____

Who is expected to attend? _____ How many? _____

What other candidates will attend? _____

Other information _____
_____

Press? _____ Send surrogate? _____ Distribute literature? _____

Date of request _____ Written? _____ By phone? _____

Accept/reject date _____ Written? _____ By phone? _____

Reason for rejection _____

Followup _____

Notes _____
_____
_____

*FORM 21: SCHEDULING REQUEST FORM*

a five-minute speech to be followed by questions the candidates will ask each other, even the best campaigners can be thrown for a loop.

## Steps in Handling a Schedule Request

1. Keep all schedule requests in one location.
2. Log the event in the campaign calendar.
3. Check to see if there are any conflicts.
4. Determine if this fits into the "highest and best uses" of the candidate's time.
5. Either reject or tentatively accept the invitation by phone.
6. If accepted, add the event to the candidate's schedule.
7. Inform the advance team, press secretary, and/or issues committee of any needs the event might present.
8. Reconfirm the day before the event.
9. Make notes of any special attire or transportation needs.
10. Check to ensure the directions are clear with the driver or the candidate.
11. After the event, debrief the candidate, asking if there is any followup necessary.
12. If the event was particularly helpful or the sponsors are important, send followup thank-you letters or call to express the candidate's appreciation.

## Canceling an Invitation

The dreaded cancellation of an event to someone expecting the candidate is a tough job—but one that someone other than the candidate should do. This is where schedulers get their purple hearts. There are many situations that could necessitate a cancellation:

- A last-minute media opportunity.
- Evidence that the event is a setup to show the candidate in a bad light.
- Dual obligations inadvertently scheduled at the same time.
- Candidate exhaustion.
- A family emergency.
- The event itself being seen as a problem (behind picket lines, few people expected to attend, etc.).
- Too many events scheduled on the same day.
- Last-minute campaign deadlines, such as film crews on location that haven't completed filming the candidate.

In these cases, you should determine if the cancellation is warranted, and as soon as the decision is made—usually along with the candidate and/or the manager—inform the person or organization. The best way to handle a cancellation is promptly, professionally, accurately, and with an outlook toward making good on the obligation. If the cancellation is prompted by a conflict in schedules or something more important coming up at the last minute, then be honest in explaining the details. Apologize for any inconveniences. Most people will be disappointed, but they usually understand the obvious chaos that comes with every campaign cycle.

Good schedulers can inoculate themselves against cancellation blues by simply placing a disclaimer on any scheduled item they confirm. You might say, "I'm confirming this 99 percent, with that 1 percent hold-out that is my advance apology in the event we have to cancel due to a conflict that I can't predict now." Another good line to use is, "This looks like a go, and I'm confirming it with you, but since it's less than three weeks before the election, let me remind you that there could be conflicts that will bump this from our schedule. I'll do my best to see that this doesn't happen, but it might."

There are occasions when you might want to create a conflict. If you find at the last minute that an event is being set up for the opponent's supporters to embarrass your candidate, or ask negative questions in front of the press, you should always have a few important appointments you can create to give the candidate a plausible excuse for not attending a previously confirmed event.

| Cancellations may be necessary due to: |
| --- |
| ➤ Media opportunity |
| ➤ Event may be a setup |
| ➤ Schedule conflict |
| ➤ Family emergency |
| ➤ Problem event |
| ➤ Too many events |
| ➤ Campaign crisis |

# Getting There on Time

Candidates are never on time. All one can do is try to minimize the candidate's tardiness. Anyone who has ever waited for her candidate to show up in a room full of anxious people knows the importance of being on time. Ordinary people may have three or four places, at most, to go in the course of a day. A candidate usually has a dozen. It stands to reason that promptness will be a problem for candidates as long as there are campaigns.

With cellular telephones, there is little reason to leave an entire room clueless about when you will arrive. The candidate's daily schedule should list what time each event starts, what time the candidate is expected, and at least one telephone number she can call if she is running late. The cellular phone numbers of any campaign workers who will be at an event, or of an event's sponsor should also be included.

Candidates are often late because of difficulty in finding parking, confusing directions on how to get to a location, stopping for a quick bite to eat, overstaying their allotted time at a previous event, or just not considering promptness a virtue. To some extent, the scheduler can control some of these items by including carefully detailed directions, arranging for a parking space (or a driver) in advance and providing a brown-bag lunches in the car.

Some schedulers, anticipating the candidate will run late, list arrival times on the schedule that are fifteen minutes early. But candidates soon become aware of this and then revert back to their old ways of being late, despite the time listed on the schedule.

For the record, it's probably acceptable to be 10 minutes late. It is almost expected. However, for a candidate to be consistently more than 20 minutes late becomes more than an irritant. It becomes a clue to others that the campaign is not as well organized as a winning one should be.

# Candidate Visibility: How to Be Seen

Pro-active scheduling is the mark of a great scheduler. Pro-active scheduling includes talking to important leaders and getting them to include your candidate on the podium at important events, as well as persuading event organizers to let your candidate go first so she can get in and out of an event quickly. Badges of courage go to the scheduler who can effectively convince a luncheon organizer to seat her candidate next to the featured speaker and give her candidate a topnotch introduction, while barely noticing the opponent.

Events you can place on the schedule that put a candidate in closer contact with her targeted public might include:

**Candidate visibility:**

➤ Business tours
➤ Shift changes
➤ Meet-and-greets
➤ Shopping malls
➤ Libraries
➤ Grocery stores
➤ Government classes
➤ Police beat
➤ Apartment complexes
➤ Going door-to-door

- Business tours, where a candidate walks downtown or neighborhood business districts to talk with the workers, owners and customers.

- Meeting voters at morning or evening shift changes at plant gates or federal and state office complexes.

- Lunchrooms or conference rooms of large law firms where a partner has offered to introduce the candidate to her colleagues.

- Walking through shopping malls in key neighborhoods where GOTV is important.

- Greeting voters at libraries, department stores, grocery stores, daycare centers, bus stops, etc.

- Speaking to high-school government classes about the importance of good government in areas where parents' swing votes are critical to your efforts.

- Taking a driving tour of a police precinct with police on patrol, or walking the beat with a neighborhood officer.

- Getting into apartment complexes with an agreeable resident who will help you meet voters on Saturday mornings or get permission to take you door-to-door.

- Going door-to-door to meet voters in targeted precincts.

Some of the most ambitious pro-active scheduling involves a campaign marathon: a 24-hour non-stop period of candidate campaigning. The candidate begins one morning and goes throughout the night, going to diners, police and taxi dispatch centers, hospitals, bakeries, and anyplace else where people are awake. All-night radio talk shows love this, as do late-night dance clubs (not the seedy ones, please). This 24-hour blitz shows the candidate ready to be where the people are, no matter the time or location. It also shows the energy, endurance and vitality of the candidate. Usually reporters love to accompany the candidate, just to make sure she or he isn't cheating by sneaking a snooze here and there.

Whatever the location, gimmick, or event, a good scheduler becomes a master negotiator at getting her candidate to the voters who matter most—those who are likely to vote who haven't yet made up their minds. Pro-active scheduling gets your candidate far closer to the winner's circle than all the invitations that may come your way.

# Scheduling Tips

*Never make a permanent commitment.* There are always pressures on the candidate to confirm today for an event next month. Campaign dynamics change rapidly, and what seems like a good event now may not be later on. Unless you're absolutely sure, it's best to wait. Remember: it's easier to get invited to an event at the last minute than it is to get out of an event.

*At the beginning of the campaign, discuss* time commitments the candidate already has. Events like children's birthdays, recitals, anniversaries, etc., should be scheduled from the start, as well as some time each week for the candidate to be with her family. If the candidate is reaching burnout, don't be afraid to give her time off. It's always better to have a happy, healthy candidate in the final weeks than a burned-out, stressed-out one.

*Always consider what an event will do for the campaign.* Toward the end of the campaign, the most important criteria should be raising money, getting an opportunity to meet with key contributors or phoning for support. If an event doesn't meet these requirements, don't schedule it—unless, of course, the candidate's absence is likely to anger targeted voters. Lastly, remember that a candidate can never spend too much time fundraising.

# Staffing the Candidate

Whenever possible, a campaign supporter should travel with the candidate and handle what is called "the advance work."

The three golden rules of good advance are important to remember, particularly in the final days of the campaign when everyone is stressed and there is so much for the candidate to do.

- Plan carefully, anticipating problems.
- Don't panic!
- Never assume anything.

These three rules become the basic rules to live by in any aspect of scheduling or doing "advance" work.

It's the job of the advance team to find out as much about a particular event as possible. They are also responsible for banners, turning out other supporters to be there, handing out flyers and generally making sure that all bases are covered. These are the people who will find directions to the location, secure a parking spot and know where the restrooms are. All this information is communicated to the scheduler for inclusion in the schedule.

# The Time Wasters: Campaign Killers

Campaigns are notorious for wasting time. First, learning how to campaign takes enormous amounts of time. And, there are constant interruptions. People call or drop by to speak to the candidate and upset all the great plans to make important calls for fundraising. Chores that you thought would take minutes will take days, and chores that the candidate likes to do least will be easily disrupted by anything that can distract her.

What are the big time wasters in a campaign? Just knowing what they are will help you recognize them and get the candidate back on track.

Despite having an excellent scheduler to manage your time, as a candidate, you must be ever vigilant about spending that limited time efficiently and not fall into common traps that waste time.

Key campaign time wasters for candidates:

1. *Spending time on the phone trying to reach important people.* How can you improve this?
2. *Designing your own campaign pieces.* How can you delegate this to others?
3. *Being a perfectionist.* Instead of organizing all the campaign files, or doing your own data entry, or arranging the office to your suiting, delegate.

4. *Talking to people who walk in without an appointment* or talking to people who are friends but not important to the campaign. How can you find other time to talk with them?

5. *Explaining to volunteers* in minute detail how to get a particular project done. How can you get past your penchant for doing everything yourself?

6. *Getting caught up in the campaign plan* and constantly reworking the strategy. How can you settle on a plan and stick to it rather than constantly reinventing it?

If you structure your time-management formula correctly, you can control about half of the unplanned-for time. But, to take control, you must make a realistic assessment of the time you have to campaign as well as a commitment to stick to the formula. Remember, if you want this election, you have to be disciplined enough to stick to the program.

# A Candidate's Day

| | The Winner | The Loser |
|---|---|---|
| **6:00 a.m.** | Awakens, goes for a brisk 30-minute walk, then listens to the morning news while preparing for the day. | |
| **7:30 a.m.** | Arrives at a breakfast meeting. Schmoozes and picks up business cards of potential contacts. Asks five people for donations and makes note of five other potential donors. | Misses a breakfast meeting to stay home and design her own brochure. |
| **9:00 a.m.** | Arrives at campaign headquarters, meets with campaign manager about scheduling special events and prospective donors. | |
| **10:00 a.m.** | Spends the next two hours dialing for dollars, receives five contributions, two promises of future help, and leaves messages for eight other potential donors. | Arrives at campaign headquarters and calls a staff meeting. Everyone discusses schedule requests and gives a daily report to the candidate. |
| **12:00 p.m.** | Meets with a potential high donor and two business leaders who contribute to her campaign. | Calls printer to discuss brochure printing options.<br><br>Stops by the local mall to register voters. |
| **1:30 p.m.** | Returns to headquarters and spends two more hours making calls for contributions. | Returns to headquarters to write a four-page fundraising letter to be mailed to all registered voters. |

| | | |
|---|---|---|
| **4:00 p.m.** | Meets with campaign press person to go over questionnaires and an upcoming editorial board meeting. | Meets with volunteers to discuss who will work at the county fair. Briefs volunteers on answering questions about specific issues. |
| **5:30 p.m.** | Attends fundraiser for another candidate. Eats only healthy fruit and vegetables for energy to get through the evening. | Arrives at fundraiser for another candidate. Stays for two hours talking with the other candidate's supporters. |
| **6:30 p.m.** | Arrives at a home fundraiser. Spends a half hour meeting guests, and a half hour in a question-and-answer session. | |
| **8:00 p.m.** | Arrives at local Democratic district meeting. Stays long enough to be seen and to speak with key people. | Arrives at local Democratic district meeting. Waits two hours for the opportunity to say a few words to the group. |
| **9:00 p.m.** | Arrives home. Has a light, healthy dinner and returns phone calls. | |
| **10:00 p.m.** | Spends a quiet hour going over issue papers prepared by campaign staff and selected experts. | Returns home to write a campaign issue paper. |
| **11:00 p.m.** | Watches the news while preparing notes for the next day. | |
| **11:30 p.m.** | Lights out! | |
| **1:00 a.m.** | | Retires for the night. |

*FORM 22: A CANDIDATE'S DAY*

# GOING
# NEGATIVE

## TACTICS THAT MOVE VOTERS—FOR BETTER OR WORSE

Today's campaigns are known for their brutal negatives and their propensity to get right to the dirt. Issue debates quickly give way to the politics of "gotcha." Often campaigns revolve around who survives the negative blasts best—or who makes the next-to-last mistake.

Campaigns usually begin with positive issues, lots of upbeat speeches about accomplishments and high visions, and, of course, the promise not to go negative. However, as the end of the campaign nears, and the race is too close to call, early campaign season wishful thinking may go by the wayside. In fact, more than half the campaigns in this country "go negative." They may be homespun—those campaigns known for their individual energy and positive adherence to the issues. However, the mere fact that we think of all campaigns as negative is an indication that negatives are effective.

Negatives are much more interesting than positives. We are far more apt to remember the negative story of a candidate's drunk driving than his five-point platform for economic reform. It is human nature to remember less-than-positive news. Negatives are also more human. And, they are based on a simple political premise: before a voter will hire you to represent her, she needs to be convinced that you are better than the next candidate. In the world of politics, particularly politics that involves the re-election of almost all incumbents, you need to give voters a reason to hire you and fire the other candidate.

Campaigns that take on a negative air from the start are more obvious today because there is more money being spent to get those messages to us. While aggressive campaigns within one's primary were once seldom waged, they are now commonplace—giving the entire election cycle a sense of unending negative attacks. But, actually, negative campaigns are as old as campaigns themselves.

In the 19th century, U.S. presidents were accused of having slaves as mistresses. Several presidents were charged with fathering illegitimate children, while still others were purported to be drug addicts.

All is fair in love and war—and now politics. If it can end up in print or broadcast on radio and TV, it's fair game. While it's true that the pendulum has moved significantly to the extremes in what the public will tolerate in the realm of today's negatives, an "accountability" curve is developing. While the common response has been for more candidates to resort to aggressive counter-attacks, other responses are coming of age. The community as a whole has taken up some quick fixes. Fair Campaign Acts, complete with their own logos, are now commonplace. Newspaper and TV reporters are doing "truth squad" examinations of negative charges. And candidates themselves are resorting to new techniques. In the past several years there have been dozens of court suits filed by candidates seeking restitution for distortions and lies that appeared about them in the context of a campaign.

With reliance on negatives an almost certain part of one's campaign strategy, there is much to be done to prepare for whatever attack you might have to sustain.

And, in fact, if you are given less than half a chance of winning, you will almost undoubtedly have to consider launching the first volley of negative campaign material yourself.

> *The entire world of "spin"—the ability to define a situation in its best possible terms and conditions— developed as a result of the onslaught of negatives.*

## *No One Volunteers to Go Negative*

In the political climate of today, negative campaigning is hardly the way to win friends, donors and volunteers. It is certainly a practice held in ill repute. However, that doesn't mean you should back away from an aggressive stance. Voters love highly competitive campaigns and strong contenders. Never sign anything which will ultimately tie your hands in the campaign to follow. There isn't a candidate around who hasn't said, "I refuse to go negative." Yet, those who sign innocent-looking pledges not to be aggressive and negative, could easily be signing their own political obituary. The game of politics requires a heads-up approach at all times.

## *Going Negative*

You will have to consider going negative if it appears that it is the only way to jolt the voters into thinking they should hire you over your opponent. There are clues:

- If you are likely to be outspent; to get the voters' attention and interest, you will need to ensure that they know the down side of voting for your opponent.

- If you're running against an incumbent; you must convince voters that he should be fired and you should be hired.

- If your opponent has a background of unscrupulous activity, yet it is generally not known; you will have to make your case.

- If you have little name recognition and your opponent has substantial favorable recognition; you will have to increase your visibility.

- If you get into the race late and the agenda is already controlled by your opponent; you will have to catch up.

- If you are given little chance of winning and thus get no serious consideration by political insiders; you will have to do something dramatic.

# Factors to Consider

Few people are interested in how a campaign gets moving. It is only when the campaign begins to actually contrast the candidates that people start to pay attention. More and more that happens when the campaign becomes aggressive and the negatives start to fly. In reviewing the nature of negatives, there are four things to consider:

1. *Do your opposition research.* Most candidates wrongly state that there is no reason to do opposition research on themselves, as they have been forthcoming about their background and already know the worst that can be said about them. However, what a candidate recalls versus what the public records hold can be two very different things.

2. *Watch for clues as to the nature* and style of the campaign. Your opponent will often reveal critical clues as to what will come next in the course of his campaign strategy. He might be too eager to ask you certain questions. He might be baiting you on a point, trying to get you to deny something he will be saving for an end attack.

3. *See who is helping your opponent.* Often there are detractors from your past who end up actively supporting your opponent. They might remember confrontations from the past differently than you. What's the worst they can say—and how will it be used by your opponent?

4. *Know what is important to the voters.* Minor indiscretions in your past might not be as important as inconsistencies about issues you have discussed. The public is much more tolerant of negative attacks than it is forgiving of your insincere or dishonest reactions. More is usually lost in the reaction to negatives than in the negatives themselves.

**Factors to consider in going negative:**

➤ Opposition research
➤ The nature of the campaign
➤ Who is helping your opponent
➤ What is important to voters
➤ Timing is everything
➤ The next step

5. *Understand that timing can be everything.* A negative attack launched months from election day might not be a big deal. On the other hand, if the campaign is tight, and the days are quickly waning, then it is likely that your attacks or responses will have added emphasis.

6. *Consider the next step.* If you go negative, expect that you will be hit back within hours. Understand that the response could be fair, accurate and on the same point that you attacked your opponent; however it could also be unfair, inaccurate and on an entirely different subject.

There are also a number of people to consider when it comes to negative campaigning. Be clear about how the negatives are likely to effect the people important to your campaign before you launch or respond to an attack.

*Insiders:* How will important people in the insider community react: your party leaders, the community leaders, your endorsers?

*Voters:* How will your targeted voters accept information about you that is negative—and how will they react to the nature of what you attack in your opponent?

*Funders:* One of the most costly consequences of a negative attack on you might be that it dries up all your money. Your reaction to the attack will be critical.

*Volunteers:* Don't forget your volunteers. They need to be informed before the dirt hits the fan, as they are directly influenced by negative attacks—either when you launch them or when you respond to them.

*Opponent:* If your opponent launches a strong slam at you, look to see what prompted the attack. When an opponent goes negative, the nature of the attack and the reaction to your response may tell you much about his ability to campaign.

*His funders:* Don't forget your opponent's funders. Sometimes a candidate who goes negative first gets an added boost with his funders and more money comes in (something you might want to point out). In other cases the effect can be negative.

*The press:* Have supporters watching every move the press makes when you begin or respond to a negative. The truth squads, the analysis of your attacks, and your general appearance during these attack periods may be the subject of individual stories in themselves. And, in some coveted cases, the press may actually take over and begin its own investigation.

All of the above can become entities of their own. Each and every part can become a strong reaction prompting other preparedness you should have anticipated. The goal of understanding your own weaknesses and those of your opponents is to be ready for anything. To go negative or to respond to

---

**People to consider:**

➤ *Insiders*
➤ *Targeted voters*
➤ *Funders*
➤ *Volunteers*
➤ *Opponent*
➤ *Opponent's funders*
➤ *The press*

---

it requires far more work in advance of the attack than after it happens. Forewarned is forearmed.

## The Reaction When You Go Negative

Opponents never take attacks quietly. Even if you have proved your point, don't expect your opponent to respond logically. You probably wouldn't in the same situation. Opponents you attack are likely to:

- Pay an opposition research company, or even a private investigator, to get the rest of the story on you. Remember that even your family becomes fair game at this point, so warn the whole team that times might be tough for awhile.

- Raise a lot of money, using a message that lots of money will be necessary to defeat you, especially since you have gone negative.

- Run to the press with any and all inconsistencies about you your background, platform and record.

- Hit the airwaves to respond to the information. This may have the effect of making your opponent expend funds earlier than anticipated.

## Dangers of Going Negative

Particularly in the case of women candidates, there are many reactions from friends and foes alike to your going negative.

- They may think you are too shrill or harsh.
- They might begin a logical or illogical attack on you.
- You risk credibility with the voters, the press or your funders.
- You could be the one blamed for negative campaigning.
- The attack may hurt you with senior voters.
- You might lose some volunteers over the attack.
- Your issues may get lost in the attack/counter attack.
- You may tune out some of your own targeted voters.
- It may give voters a reason to question your integrity.

> **Dangers of going negative:**
>
> ➤ Appear harsh
> ➤ Invite attack
> ➤ Risk credibility
> ➤ Get the blame
> ➤ Lose senior voters
> ➤ Lose issues
> ➤ Lose targeted voters
> ➤ Question integrity

## Advantages of Going Negative

Lest we seem much too critical of the form of campaigning which seems to work best, let's look at the positive side of going negative:

- It can make you look like a real leader. People love a good fight—and they particularly like candidates aggressive enough to take up the battle and fight for victory. They oftentimes consider this proof that the candidate will stand up for them once elected.

> **Advantages of going negative:**
>
> ➤ *Look like a leader*
> ➤ *Reverse your numbers*
> ➤ *Put opponent off guard*
> ➤ *Generate interest*
> ➤ *Bring in money*
> ➤ *Engage the press*
> ➤ *Spotlight your campaign*

- It can reverse your declining numbers overnight and give you needed momentum to attract press, funding, and volunteers.

- You can put your opponent off guard and make him do something contrary to his prescribed plan.

- It signals your targeted voters that your campaign is far from over—it is just starting to get interesting and exciting.

- It can bring in real money and lots of it. Whether you are under attack or the one going negative, funders usually respond by giving you more money.

- Negatives engage the press. Many members of the press feel they should be doing more critical coverage of elections anyway, and this gives them a reason to take up the charge.

- If you are not the top of the ticket, a negative attack can bring some spotlight to your campaign in and among much higher-profile campaigns.

## How Negatives Are Launched

There's a growing list of the ways in which negatives are leaking out these days. Most campaigns would much prefer that negative attacks on their opponent come from an entity other than the campaign. It's best to keep negative attacks at arm's length from the campaign. However, if you can't get your favorite reporter to bite, and no other special interest groups are hanging around to do the honors, then you might need to take up the challenge with your own resources.

## Kinds of Negatives

Negatives come in all shapes, sizes, intensities and formats. In reviewing more than 500 campaigns in the past few years, every one of them thought there was some form of negative strategy focused upon them from their opponent's camp. The most common negatives were as follows:

1.  *Attacks based upon one incident* in a candidate's life that showed him to be a hypocrite—not as he was positioning himself to voters: moral indiscretions, bankruptcies, wasting money, etc.

2.  *Examples of public arrogance.* These include junkets to Hawaii while important public services were being cut; exorbitant cellular phone bills; using government staffers and other resources to get re-elected.

3. *Taking a vote out of context.* If an incumbent voted for a budget that included cuts for a senior program—among many others—an attack might be, "He stabbed your grandmother in the back."

4. *Absenteeism in office.* Missing a critical vote, or having a poor attendance record, is a popular hit on incumbents.

Other popular negatives used in various campaigns include:

*Personal goofs:* That seemingly minor indiscretion when young and foolish, committed in the company of someone who remembers it—and relates all the colorful details to the opposition. Smoking marijuana, being in the presence of drug use, getting caught in a hot tub with no clothes on, causing a disturbance at a party, drunken driving, and a host of other examples.

*The public record:* Not paying attention to life's important details—a messy divorce, income tax problems, personal credit problems, a poor academic record or a lack of a diploma are all examples.

*Criminal problems:* In these days of easy access to computer files, it's essential to inspect police records. Drunk driving, sexual harassment, domestic violence, restraining orders, child support enforcement violations, and even parking tickets (if there are enough of them) can be attacks easy to document.

*Professional dilemmas:* If a candidate has been fired for cause, had controversial clients, or exhibited questionable ethical behavior on the job, these things could be used against him.

*Civics basics:* A candidate running for office who hasn't voted until recently is a popular attack, even though the most civic minded candidates seldom vote in all elections (such as special elections for local bonds and levies).

*Guilt by association:* Any organization a candidate may have contributed to, been a member of, or simply attended the events of may be an example of an affiliation that the public may find questionable. The NRA, gay organizations, militant women's groups, right-wing religious groups, and racist organizations are examples.

*The exaggeration:* Everyone has a resumé that glamorizes his past. Putting the best face on an accomplishment, job or situation can prove to be a candidate's undoing. Those details when repeated, exaggerated and then revealed by an objective investigator can prove devastating.

*Background checks:* These are easy to do, and they can prove damaging if a candidate who tries to look like the all-American kid has had a dishonorable discharge from the military, couldn't keep a job, or has been divorced several times. Chronic or serious health problems have also been used to taint a candidate image.

***A style problem:*** If a candidate has been accused of being a womanizer, a dirty old man if male or being "loose," anti-man, or an airhead if female, then negatives could be around the corner at the next debate. Being out of touch or even "just plain weird," have and will be used against candidates who don't appear friendly and inclusive.

From judicial campaigns to the top of the ticket, expect to see new and more creative uses of negatives.

The most devastating negatives a candidate can launch are invariably those for which the candidate and the campaign team are not prepared. The most frequent include:

- A voting record that is inconsistent with the candidate's own statements.
- Perception of being owned by a special interest.
- Public arrogance, such as stating that the public's opinion doesn't matter.
- Campaigning at the taxpayers' expense, from mailings to photocopies.
- Financial wheeling and dealing, such as giving campaign contributors special consideration.
- Missing critical votes while in office; high absenteeism.
- Being accused of sexual harassment or domestic violence.
- Not paying child support.
- Lying on a resumé.
- Flip-flopping on critical issues.
- A misstatement that was never corrected and remains in the public record.
- Not voting in every election.
- Family members who have gotten into trouble.
- Being a member of a controversial organization.

> **The most devastating negatives:**
>
> ➤ *Voting inconsistencies*
> ➤ *Perception of special interest*
> ➤ *Public arrogance*
> ➤ *Campaigning on public money*
> ➤ *Wheeling and dealing*
> ➤ *Missing critical votes*
> ➤ *Sexual harassment*
> ➤ *Domestic violence*
> ➤ *Not paying child support*
> ➤ *Lying on a resumé*
> ➤ *Flip-flopping on issues*
> ➤ *Misstatements not corrected*
> ➤ *Not voting*
> ➤ *Family members in trouble*
> ➤ *Controversial associations*

# Tools for Launching an Attack

You have credible concerns about your opponent—and the backup information to make it stick. What will you do with it? Before you launch any attack on your opponent, make sure it won't turn on you. Consider:

1. *Do you have documents* to back up your charges?
2. *Do you have independent sources* that will back you up?

3. *Can you prove* you got the information legally and fairly?

4. *Are you sure you are not guilty* of the same actions?

5. *Will this charge start a full-scale negative campaign,* and if so, is it strong enough and relevant enough to warrant it?

6. *Will the press,* the public and other interested parties consider it fair?

7. *Is this the right time* to launch an attack? Four months before the primary a story might well fall off the news pages. However, a story within days of the election might not be believed.

8. *Is it new?* Rehashing old negatives won't rally voters to your side. Campaigns frequently try rerunning old negatives against an incumbent—mostly to their own demise. Fresh material, please.

9. *Is the charge reasonably easy to understand?* Volumes of information might be good for responding to attacks, but not so effective in trying to launch one.

10. *Can you draw logical conclusions* that could predict your opponent's future actions in office? A minor indiscretion, such as getting caught drinking beer in a park is not necessarily evidence of a serious character flaw.

11. *Can you paint your opponent as a hypocrite,* as someone who's just not like "us," or somehow outside the value boundaries of most of the population?

12. *Would your targeted voters paint your opponent* in the same light, given the same information? You risk your credibility with the public by overdramatizing a situation.

13. *Can you attack your opponent* and still get back to your message? Campaigns that lose sight of their own message as they attack often find that they lose their way as well.

These questions, if answered properly, can save you much grief and embarrassment. As much time and energy should go into preparing an attack as goes into finding the information. You risk ending up further behind if you can't strategize an attack to be effective. Often campaigns get negative information about their opponent, call a reporter and try to "leak" it. The disasters befalling a campaign after leaking negatives are more numerous than are the successes in just releasing an attack.

## Tools of the Attack Trade

The most common and most desired tool of a negative attack is the press. Of course, they do not consider themselves to be anyone's tool—and the perception that they might be used as a tool of either side is usually enough to stop a reporter from even considering negative research and attacks.

If your negative information meets the tests listed above, then perhaps—and only perhaps—the press will cover it. However, be prepared with other options in the event they won't touch it.

**The press:** Make sure you have backup information. Have documentation, non-campaign supporters, and make sure that your challenges are reasonable. Some candidates will do better pre-releasing the information to only one reporter, as good coverage from one is more assured than coverage from many when they all get the information at the same time.

**Third parties:** Independent committees are famous for forming under the guise of objectivity when their mission is usually a single issue: destroy one candidate or one party's best candidates. When they work well, third parties take the direct heat for going negative, leaving the campaign intact. Few voters, however, believe that third parties are truly independent.

**Direct mail:** Mailing the information directly to voters allows you to put the documentable evidence in a brochure. It also allows you to target exactly those voters you wish to move with the information. Direct mail can also help an attack grow. One brochure may have the accusations, the next might have the evidence and more of the story, and still a third piece may have people talking about certain aspects of the charge.

**Opponent's camp:** In a move to slow down contributions and efforts from endorsing organizations, you may want to mail key information—with backup—to your opponent's supporters and contributors. Release information selectively. And, if you can find people who formerly supported your opponent, have them sign the letter. This "thought you should know" letter, can work amazingly well and usually ends up being discovered by the press as well.

**TV and radio:** As election day approaches, you may well find the best use of negative data is to put it in front of the voters yourself through the hot media of radio and TV. If your opponent is launching an attack in one medium, you might try the other.

**Phone banks:** You can use phone banks to ask your opponent's supporters questions such as, "If you knew that candidate cheated on his income taxes, would you still be inclined to vote for him?" These "push" polls are increasingly more prevalent—and effective. This strategy is quick to implement and quite efficient in getting the information to your target.

**Whisper campaigns:** If you have information that doesn't meet all the standards of fair campaigning, you may resort to what some call whisper campaigns. This much-despised strategy involves spreading off-the-record rumors with some small fabric of truth using statements such as, "Have you heard that Sandy's campaign is out of money? Seems she finally had to start paying child support."

**Letters to the editor:** With a simple, willing signatory, lots of negative information can be spread in a few simple paragraphs, usually ending with some pointed question to the readers. Though some newspapers refuse to print such attacks, most will take the letters if they also receive letters from your opponent with his own charges against you.

**Questions in public:** Either candidates or their supporters can ask questions of the opponent at joint speaking engagements. Asking an embarrassing question is usually translated by the crowd as self-serving, and it can backfire. However, if the question is fair, it might attract the press and begin a longer, unraveling attack.

**Early confrontation:** If you are concerned about damaging personal information coming out about you—and you have the goods on your opponent—there is a campaign school of thought that offers the meeting approach as a strategy. However, letting your opponent know what you have on him is like giving him an invitation to preempt you with it. And dealing with each other and cutting deals behind closed doors is likely to be discovered—or even leaked by your opponent—with voters getting the short end of the stick.

# The Worst that Could Happen

Suppose you have some earthshaking information about your opponent. Suppose you have the documentation, the facts, the eye-witnesses, the "spin," and the courage to go with the attack. What could go wrong?

The most traditional problem is no one picks up the news. The press ignores it. Your supporters want you to back off and not go negative. You don't have the money to get the message out yourself. And worse yet, you start thinking that it's no use and back off.

You might decide to "leak" the material to a reporter, only to find that once printed, no one believes it's true—even though you've bored them all with documentation. The negative attack can come out so late that voters just dismiss it as political rhetoric in the heat of the campaign. You begin to sound insincere and insecure whenever the subject is brought up—and your opponent has a pat answer that makes *you* sound like the bad guy.

All of this, and yet you know you're right. You might also know that unless you convince the public that your opponent has a serious flaw, you will lose the campaign.

There are no guarantees about going negative. There are only war stories about the ones that succeeded and those that fell flat. The effective ones are usually those released to one reporter who can help do the research that uncovers the problem. Candidates who leak a little of the problem out, and then continue to intensify the information as the campaign proceeds have also reported success. Still others report that they had to persist in talking with reporters for weeks before the story finally took hold.

One good piece of advice from those whose research fell short—know the opposition research that moves the most voters by polling all the possible attacks you might launch. If the voters think you have a serious charge, then it's likely the press and everyone else will also. Unfortunately, opposition research that reveals the juiciest information usually comes to the campaign late, after all the polling has been done.

> *The best advice is to be prepared.*

Consider having your most critical information—about you and your opponent—on that first poll. Know what you will go to bat for and insist gets out, versus other information that might be nice to get out, but will not have the same impact.

## Conclusion

Negatives may not be new, but they're not diminishing in scope, intensity nor creativity. They are, however, changing. The best advice is to be prepared and ready—whatever it takes to ensure you are not ambushed by material you didn't expect.

Although negatives are thought to disenchant voters from voting at all, the facts refute such notions. Negative campaigns and charges that require you to defend yourself may reveal your depth of character—and perhaps be the best evidence voters will ever have that you are ready, willing and able to fight for them. If you can fight for your turf and survive in today's aggressive political system, you may prove yourself worthy of all those votes you seek.

## SURVIVING THE CAMPAIGN LONG ENOUGH TO WIN

D amage control. It's the very nature of campaigns. What do you do when you have no more money? When your volunteers aren't showing up? When your computer has crashed? When your opponent has just dropped a bombshell about your past that you hoped would never get out? Meanwhile, your patience is shot and your spouse wants more quality time with you.

Ah, yes—the day-to-day beauty of a campaign.

Campaigns, especially in the last 30 days, are a series of crises, a pile of confusion, and interminable chaos. Sometimes it's all you can do to hang on until the end of the day. Yet, it is precisely those campaigns that can operate under these stresses and crises that win. It is also the exhilaration that people remember when it comes time to work on another campaign. Your job is to handle what you can, delegate what you must, ignore what are small irritants, and cope with the crises you can't fix.

## Coping with Crises

Campaigns have institutional memory. Most campaign crises that require real damage control have similar characteristics. Crises are those things which you didn't expect, but should have. They usually:

- Require resources (usually money) you don't have.
- Involve people you can't control—the press, your opponent or well-intended but misguided volunteers.
- Take place in the last three weeks before the election.
- Happen when you are already stressed and exhausted.
- Revolve around personality conflicts that get worse as time and resources are stretched.
- Usually start as a small problem that wasn't addressed when it should have been.

There are some crises you can predict, and hopefully contain, because you can plan for them. These include:

***Running out of money:*** When you're in the last three weeks of the campaign, and you can't make media time buys or send out critical mailings, action must be taken. Campaigns in this situation must focus all their resources on hitting the phones. The candidate is grounded for all but mandatory public events and makes phone calls to previous donors. Finance committees schedule entire evenings or Sundays to make one final direct pitch. Even the phone banks can be diverted to contacting earlier identified supporters for donations.

Money must be directed at voter contact projects at the expense of everything else, including staff salaries, headquarters rent, and everything but the phone bill and lights. The manager or candidate should contact major creditors to see what leeway there may be in putting off bills until the critical payments for voter contact are made.

***Too few people:*** This is one of the most prevalent complaints that leads to short tempers and office stress. Instead of scaling back campaign plans, most campaigns try and "gut out" their work with a smaller-than-needed volunteer squad. Some campaigns can handle this; few do. You risk a major breakdown in overall campaign effectiveness by working what volunteers you do have into the ground. Volunteers who break the day before the election may just sleep through election day when you need them most. Plan for a GOTV you can handle.

***Not enough time:*** Time is finite—the most finite resource of a campaign. To maximize what you can, plan more and plan better. Plan for the problems and the time they take. Plan for interruptions and walk-ins. Plan for candidate disfunction and mandatory think time. The most secret time you can add is always morning time. Planning to add another hour late at night seldom does anything but wreak havoc the next day. Getting up earlier might mean you have to take a "power" catnap later in the afternoon, but that is far better than stretching your life into hours after midnight. During times of crises, try swearing off the junk food for more, smaller healthier meals. Take more vitamins and try to make your campaign schedule one which includes physical activity.

***Shortage of supplies:*** There's no money for more yard signs, brochures or even lapel stickers for the campaigners—and no printer that could turn the project around before election day anyway. So what's a person to do? The best managers and candidates secretly stash a stack of each item that comes off the press into a locked cabinet or car trunk. Supplies are always scarce in those last few days before the end of a campaign. Plan for it now.

***Never enough good press:*** The press always seems to get the wrong story just as the final days of the campaign are upon you. You need to keep in touch with the press—calling them rather than waiting for them to call you. In the last weeks of the campaign you want to be "in their faces" or on their phones before they start formulating story concepts that might be inaccurate or unfavorable to you.

Also, this is a good time to review the state of your campaign and what you know about your opponent's campaign before you call the press. Remember that journalists will be looking for the biggest contrasts between you and your opponent, particularly as election day approaches. Be prepared. Stay in contact. Tell the truth. Don't lose your cool.

**Information and task overload:** Expect to be overwhelmed with work. The line outside your door will stretch longer each day as volunteers, community leaders and staffers want direction, analysis of campaign moves, and hand-holding in a variety of ways. Organize your day before you get to the office. You might never have another opportunity once you get there. Once you have your to-do list completed, go through it and mark the one or two things you must do in order to keep some semblance of control or campaign momentum. Then delegate as much as possible to others.

As work that must be done increases, consider asking a steering committee member or a former campaign manager to assist you. You'd be surprised at the number of high-powered people who will take a two-week leave right before the campaign if you ask them to do so.

**Computer problems:** Once you commit to technology in your campaign, you must regularly back up your computer files or risk campaign shutdown. More than one campaign has been lost because all the names tallied from phone banks were lost in the final days. Computer gurus who are the only ones on the campaign who understand the computer hardware and software are just as important to back up as the files.

**Power struggles:** Never have so many tried so hard to control so much. Campaign volunteers who have been working well in the trenches may well get to the home stretch and feel they can run things better than the manager. Since day one, the steering committee has thought it could run things better, and now, in the last weeks, is telling the manager to check every detail with them. The perennial struggle for control and power over the most mundane projects and pennies remaining in the budget are all signs of a campaign running on empty.

Good ideas, new ideas and reviews of decisions are always welcome in a living campaign. However, the process should be guarded. If you want the most efficient, tested campaign process, then keep all decision-makers informed of what's going on—and don't change the rules in the last quarter.

***Yard sign sabotage:*** Campaigns always scream when the candidate's yard signs disappear. Usually they have been removed by young people, irritated neighbors or property owners who don't like any signs, much less campaign signs. However, yard sign destruction is no crisis; it's just another cost, another project and another opportunity to rile your own forces with reports of untimely vandalism.

In the last days of the campaign every yard sign is likely to be leveled. Have your team ready to replace the signs, and ask them not to escalate the yard sign wars by removing your opponents' signs. No one really wins yard sign wars.

***Other sabotage:*** Phony letters-to-the-editor, allegedly signed by your campaign supporters; questionnaires that never find their way to the right office by the deadline; volunteers who receive notices of campaign events for the wrong day or place; and the list goes on.

Most campaign screw-ups are a matter of details that get dropped, rather than sabotage; however, should you be hit by a stealth activity, be prepared to correct it without whining. The rule is to confront your opponent (campaign manager to campaign manager) and request the guerrilla actions stop, and not to respond in kind.

***Negative attacks:*** The most prevalent and damaging situation that can level your campaign is the dreaded negative attack. How can you prepare for it? What do you do when it hits? How do you return to your agenda? These are the questions you need to answer before you even venture into the world of candidate politics. To prepare for whatever awaits you on the stump, prepare yourself for the attacks. To do so is to directly increase your chances of winning—and surviving the game of politics to spin again yourself.

# *Preparing for Negative Attacks*

**Preparing for an attack:**

➤ *Establish a process*
➤ *Practice the process*
➤ *Manage the candidate*
➤ *Know how much money you can spend*
➤ *Gauge the reaction*
➤ *Watch your back*
➤ *Get back to your agenda*

The first rule in dealing with negatives is to be prepared. A campaign with no surprises beats one that's full of them. Knowing what to expect, as well as being ready for anything, gives you a decided leg up on your opponent. There's no doubt that more campaigns lose because of their own reaction or inaction to a negative than because of the negative information itself.

To prepare for a negative attack:

1. *Establish a process* for handling anything that comes up. A clear process is critical, because you want the best minds—the most objective ones and the most creative ones—around when the going gets tough.

2. *Practice the process* on small problems and get into the habit of working out difficult situations before you have a big one to handle.

3. *Manage your appearance* and stress. Sometimes just staying away from the camera is the answer. Other times, appearing in front of the camera—and looking very much under control—is right.

4. *Know how much money you can spare* to respond to the negative. Can you raise extra money to cover the problem? Usually the answer is yes, particularly if contributors know why you need it.

5. *Gauge the reaction* of others. Determine objective ways to measure the impact of the attack. Focus groups, polling, even talk radio shows—all may be clues to your success.

6. *Watch your back*. When a negative drops, it could be the beginning of a downward slide of your momentum. Don't be obsessed with one negative; watch for others to be launched from other fronts.

7. *Get back to your own agenda*—and insist upon it. The election is won by the campaign and the candidate who can set the agenda for the critical days leading up to the election.

# What to Do When the Attack Hits

Each attack has its own characteristics, timeline and impact. There are, however, some standard options you might consider when you're under attack.

- Admit what you have done and get on with the campaign.
- Restate the negative in your own terms—and with more positive points than cast by your opponent.
- Release the "rest of the story," handing out the facts and anything else that will affect the story.
- Admit the problem and ask for voter forgiveness.
- Admit the problem, stating that it happened a long time ago and hasn't happened since.
- Admit it and prove that it will never happen again.
- Plead stupidity. Voters accept the fact that candidates are human— no one can be all-knowing all of the time.
- Inoculate yourself by releasing the information yourself. Then you can at least determine the time, the place and the people to whom it is released.
- Respond with lots of information and baffle critics with the details. Instead of holding a press conference, explain any negative stories to your staff in the campaign headquarters and invite the public and your supporters.

- Have others stand up for you—at least three character witnesses. Choices might be your third-grade teacher, a retired judge, the former head of the League of Women Voters, a much-loved former elected official, your spouse or child.

- Attack the attack. Call for an end to all negative campaigning and a return to debating the real issues that will make a difference in people's lives.

- If the charge is more untrue than true, then deny it, but be careful. Voters tend to think there is at least an element of truth to every negative hit.

- Demand proof. If the situation warrants, demand that your opponent stand toe-to-toe with you and make the charge again. Tell him that you'll bring the facts, and ask him to do the same.

- Plead the statute of limitations. If the event occurred years ago, question the relevance to the race today. The "that was then—this is now," approach may work the quickest.

- Bait and switch. If the negative is sticking, you might need to dig out your opposition research and counter with an attack of your own against your opponent.

- Ignore the charge and refuse to dignify it with a response. But remember that voters are always suspicious of charges that go unanswered.

- Respond with humor. A powerful antidote, humor is still a great response that usually pleases the press, the voters, the supporters and the candidate. The problem is knowing when and how much to use. Don't trivialize a serious charge.

- Take responsibility for whatever the problem—even if the actual atrocities weren't yours. Voters appreciate someone who's not passing the buck.

# *What Not to Do When the Attack Hits*

Just as you have options of what course of action you might take when all hell breaks loose, you also are well-advised not to fall into some common traps. Candidates who have been left to their own devices report what not to do:

- Don't be caught out of action and unavailable for comment.
- Don't be seen sequestered behind closed doors with political advisors and consultants.
- Don't wimp out or make the facts fuzzy beyond reasonable explanation.

- Don't stonewall or stubbornly insist you were right when the facts clearly give a different impression to most observers.

- Don't justify yourself by throwing excuses at the public in search of one that will actually catch on; it's likely to look as if you are trying to convince yourself as well as the public.

- Don't get caught in a snowball that could end up as an avalanche. One negative not addressed can easily turn into a campaign disaster, as details leak out daily so that you never get back to your agenda.

- Don't blame others. Even if you weren't responsible for the problem, take responsibility. Voters appreciate candidates who take the bad with the good.

# The Candidate's Presence

**You will be judged by your:**

➤ Ability to keep control
➤ Look of confidence
➤ Willingness to accept responsibility
➤ Ability to resume a normal schedule
➤ Calm and considerate demeanor

Even if you're going crazy and the worst lies imaginable are being said about you, you must remain the picture of Hemingway's definition of courage: grace under pressure. You will be judged by the public and press based upon:

- Your ability to keep control of your campaign.

- Your look of confidence.

- Your willingness to accept.

- Your ability to resume a normal campaign schedule.

- Your calm and considerate demeanor.

# Controlling the Backdrop

Be camera-ready and camera-tested. Get that video camera team up and running. See yourself in front of the lights as you discuss the worst possible twists and turns that a negative could take.

Watch for backdrops that compliment or contradict you. Have supporters, family members or community leaders surrounding you if the situation warrants it. If you are worried about the senior population or women voters deserting you based upon the attack, then have a crowd of that same target population surrounding you. Some of them might even speak at a press conference or headquarters "truth" session.

Remember your target. Remember your earlier polling. Remember your message. The three most important ingredients of any campaign strategy are usually the last things on your mind as the negative attacks begin. However, it is precisely at this time when these three aspects of your campaign matter most and should be foremost on your mind.

Be brief when you are dealing with attacks. Campaign folklore is filled with well-intended candidates who kept talking and talking at the press conference that was supposed to have answered all the critical questions. Instead, the candidate's long-winded answers and monologue ended up provoking more questions.

Allow the public to see you being human, but not victimized, nor weak nor defeated. You will be judged on your ability to pick yourself up and get back on track.

# *Humor*

A funny thing happened on the way to the ballot box. A candidate who was smeared with all kinds of nasty details (some true, some not), decided to respond with humor. Humor had always been a tool in getting out of tough situations in the past—and now when all that she had worked for seemed lost, she found her sense of humor.

She called a press conference at a well-known mudhole—and then, wading in waist deep, she countered her attacks one at a time, picking up a hand of mud and flinging it at a life-sized picture of herself.

Many candidates have produced refreshingly funny TV or radio spots that recaptured the public's interest and support just when all seemed too bleak to pull off a victory. Others have produced a great series of newspaper ads that poked fun at themselves and politics—and some have developed the perfect quips or jokes that have made the nightly news and dispelled the heavy negatives against them.

Humor in campaigns is not new, but to the vast majority of voters, it is seen as different, fun and unusually clever in a field of deadly serious, or even boring, messages. Although professional political pundits report that making someone laugh does not necessarily mean you win their vote, more candidates are turning to humor as their favorite tool. Finding the right form of humor, however, is frequently easier said than done.

You need to be careful that the humor doesn't trivialize nor ridicule the truth caught in the midst of that negative. Information that's negative about you can be acknowledged, and then humorously cast—if the negative doesn't involve a value judgment that voters think is important. Don't joke about sexual harassment, or not paying child-support. You can joke about parking tickets, or getting caught drinking beer in a public park.

Humor is best used as an indicator of your own good humor and balance. The public enjoys a leader who's a witty person—though the perennial joke teller is not necessarily someone that audiences warm to when the hour is late.

If the race is tight, and little separates you and your opponent, humor can be an especially valuable tool. Of course, there is risk in using humor. If you try to make people laugh and fall flat, you can turn a receptive audience into a strained one whose voters remember you as someone who's not funny. Your timing and nervousness might not be able to pull off humor that someone else writes for you. And the mood of the audience could be wrong. The reason professional comedians have someone else warm up a crowd is that they want the audience conducive to laughter before they begin.

Humor can also offend. Humor often involves pushing the bounds of exaggeration with metaphors and colorful stories. But you need to guard against looking foolish or full of gimmicks with little substance.

Despite all the disclaimers about humor, however, take it with you on the campaign stump. The best lines are seldom written or rehearsed; they are discovered and then repeated where appropriate. Humor has proven increasingly successful, not just in combating negatives, but in provoking keen voter interest in the candidate as well.

# Keeping the Big Four under Control

As the campaign manager, the "big four" areas of potential crisis that are your responsibility as the campaign moves into high gear are the staff, supplies, money and, of course, your candidate.

## Staff

Resume those staff meetings that you promised months ago but gave up somewhere along the way. A once-a-week staff meeting allows the key people to know what everyone is doing and plan for coordination. Add a few fun events to the campaign calendar, such as a Friday-at-5:00 soda-and-beer session—with or without the candidate. Let everyone participate, and reinstitute the fun with the heavy campaign workload to come.

Encourage your key volunteers and staffers to bring in their friends. Make sure everyone takes a little time off, or has some time with the candidate (it might even be good for the candidate). Go over the chain of command so everyone knows who to turn to when the campaign action requires decentralized action. Your staff and key volunteers need a quick refresher as to what's going to happen; don't assume they know everything all the time. Keep them informed and happy.

# Supplies

Yes, you have stashed supplies, brochures, bumper stickers and buttons away for that last week of campaigning. Despite your diligent efforts to be prepared, you will still need some last minute supplies. Find out early who can print the critical materials in the waning hours. Make sure you have a radio and TV production studio you can call upon to make any last-minute spots. And, of course, know where your consultants are and where they can be found in that last week of the campaign.

# Money

Campaigns that don't have money crises are very few and very far between. Remember that money comes in commensurate with how much time you spend raising it. Don't stop raising it, keep your candidate focused on raising it, and empower everyone in the campaign to help.

# Candidate

Watch for listlessness in the leader of the team. While it's true that adrenaline should be taking over and giving the candidate an added boost when those 20-hour days run back-to-back, it's important to watch for signs of the candidate becoming detached, too tired or run down. Candidates with a cold or the flu are not the exception; they are the rule in the last days of a campaign. Make sure the candidate gets at least some sleep, decent food, at least a little exercise, and some time with family.

Check out the candidate's family. Are they seething about being left out of the campaign "loop"? Do they seem resentful of everyone in the campaign? Are they driving everyone, including the candidate, crazy with advice that seems to be way off track? Whatever the problem, a candidate's family is a smoking gun if unattended and unhappy. Either the manager, a trusted friend or a member of the steering committee should stay in touch with members of the candidate's family. Needless to say, campaign horror stories abound with incidents involving decisions made by the candidate when the family "gangs up" on her to suggest things be done differently.

Check out how you or the campaign can make the candidate's life easier. It may mean different scheduling, a few hours off in the middle of the afternoon, a power nap once or twice a week, or just a chance for her to talk with an old friend when she has to spend the next four hours on the phone raising money.

*The best advice is to think through your actions, saving yourself for the big crises, and delegating the little ones to others.*

# Conclusion

For the candidate in times of crisis: keep your eyes on the horizon. No matter what emergency befalls the campaign, keep to the plan, with a sense of full speed ahead. Your campaign depends on getting the right message out to your target, particularly as the days before the election are dwindling. Never, never stop raising money. Watch your opponent and the strategy he may be employing as you try to cope with any problems that have moved past the radar and onto the front pages. To reduce stress, limit surprises by knowing what both the right hand and the left hand are doing. The best advice is to think through your actions, saving yourself for the big crises, and delegating the little ones to others.

And, when all seems muddled and beyond hope, revive that good old sense of humor. It may just be your best quality—and your route to putting things back into perspective.